INTRODUCTION

TO THE STUDY OF

INTERNATIONAL LAW,

DESIGNED

AS AN AID IN TEACHING, AND IN HISTORICAL STUDIES.

BY

THEODORE D. WOOLSEY,

PRESIDENT OF YALE COLLEGE.

SECOND EDITION, REVISED AND ENLARGED.

NEW YORK:
CHARLES SCRIBNER, 124 GRAND STREET.
1864.

JOHN F. TROW,
PRINTER, STEREOTYPER, AND ELECTROTYPER,
50 Greene street, New York.

TO

FRANCIS LIEBER,

AS A TOKEN OF RESPECT FOR HIS SERVICES IN THE FIELD

OF POLITICAL SCIENCE, THIS WORK IS INSCRIBED

BY HIS FRIEND

THE AUTHOR.

PREFACE TO THE SECOND EDITION.

THIS brief exposition of the law of nations was written for the purpose of supplying a practical want, which the author felt for a number of years, while engaged in teaching that science. The want was that of a compendious treatise, intended not for lawyers, nor for those who have the profession of law in view, but for young men, who are cultivating themselves by the study of historical and political science. The plan of the work shaped itself through its relations to those for whose use it was designed. While the state of the law of nations as it is was regarded as the chief point to be secured, it seemed almost equally important to compare the actual law with the standard of justice, and, by exhibiting the progress of the science in a historical way, to bring it into connection with the advances of humanity and of civilization. The success of the work, of which the first edition, issued early in the summer of 1860, has been for some time exhausted, shows that a want has been met by it, if not satisfied.

In this second edition the author has done what he could, amid many labors, to purge the work from errors, to improve the arrangement, and to supply what was deficient. Meanwhile a war, as just and necessary as it is vast in its proportions, has burst upon the country, and has given rise to new questions touching neutral and belligerent rights, in discussing which, this nation, so tenacious, formerly, of the neutral ground, has seemed inclined to go over to the other position. Naturally, some of these points are looked at in the present edition of this work, with the feeling, it is hoped, that the law of nations must be represented as it is, and that no temporary bias can be permitted to exert any influence in the statement of any doctrine. May the war end speedily,—if possible, before these words shall appear in print,—but not without the destruction of slavery, the union of the States on a basis of justice, and the observance of the rules of international law in the intercourse between all other nations and our republic!

YALE COLLEGE, *Jan.* 1, 1864.

CONTENTS.

INTRODUCTORY CHAPTER.

DEFINITION, GROWTH, JURAL AND MORAL GROUNDS, SOURCES OF INTERNATIONAL LAW.

PART I.

THE ESSENTIAL POWERS OF STATES, AND THEIR RIGHTS AND OBLIGATIONS, ESPECIALLY IN A STATE OF PEACE.

CHAPTER I.

RIGHTS OF STATES AS INDEPENDENT SOVEREIGNTIES. RULE OF NON-INTERFERENCE AND ITS EXCEPTIONS.

CHAPTER II.

TERRITORIAL RIGHTS OF STATES AND RIGHTS OF PROPERTY. STRICT RIGHT RENOUNCED IN THE USE OF NAVIGABLE WATERS.

CHAPTER III.

RIGHTS OF INTERCOURSE. RELATIONS OF FOREIGNERS WITHIN A TERRITORY OF THE STATE.

CHAPTER IV.

THE FORMS AND AGENTS OF INTERNATIONAL INTERCOURSE.

SECTION I.—*The Forms of Intercourse, or International Courtesy.*

SECTION II.—*The Agents in the Intercourse of Nations; or Ambassadors and Consuls.*

CHAPTER V.

OF THE RIGHT OF CONTRACT, OR OF TREATIES BETWEEN STATES.

PART II.

INTERNATIONAL LAW AND USAGE IN A STATE OF WAR.

CHAPTER I.

OF A NATION'S RIGHT OF SELF-DEFENCE AND REDRESS OF INJURIES, OR OF WAR, CAPTURE, AND TREATIES OF PEACE.

SECTION I.—*Of War.*

SECTION II.—*Laws and Usages of War, especially on Land.*

SECTION III.—*Of Civil Wars, Wars with Savages, Piracy, and the Slave-trade.*

SECTION IV.—*Of Capture and Recapture, Occupation and Recovery of Territory.*

SECTION V.—*Of the Suspension and Close of War, especially of Truce and Peace.*

CHAPTER II.

OF THE RELATIONS BETWEEN BELLIGERENTS AND NEUTRALS.

SECTION I.—*Of the Obligations and Rights of Neutral States.*

SECTION II.—*Of the Rights and Liabilities of Neutral Commerce.*

CONCLUSION.

DEFECTS, SANCTIONS, PROGRESS, AND PROSPECTS OF INTERNATIONAL LAW.

INTERNATIONAL LAW.

INTRODUCTORY CHAPTER.

DEFINITION, GROWTH, JURAL AND MORAL GROUNDS, SOURCES OF INTERNATIONAL LAW.

§ 1.

In order to protect the individual members of human society from one another, and to make just society possible, the Creator of man has implanted in his nature certain conceptions which we call rights, to which in every case obligations correspond. These are the foundation of the system of justice, and the ultimate standard with which laws are compared, to ascertain whether they are just or unjust. They involve, amid all the inequalities of condition, a substantial equality of the members of society before the tribunal of law and justice, because the physical, intellectual, and moral natures of all imply the same capacity and destination, and because to the capacity and destination of man his rights or powers of free action must correspond. On this basis within the state, and often without any direct co-operation of its members, a system of law grows up, which, while it may be imperfect, approaches with the progress of the society in knowledge and moral cultivation to the standard of perfect justice.

And even the moral progress of society, the ability of its members to acknowledge their reciprocal claims, and discharge their duties to each other—to fulfil their part in that moral sphere which lies in great measure quite beyond the reach of positive law—this also is dependent to a great degree upon their correct estimate of rights and obligations.

§ 2.

Nations or organized communities of men differ from the individual men of a state, in that they are self-governed, that no law is imposed on them by any external human power, but they retain the moral accountable nature, which must govern the members of a single society. They cannot have intercourse with one another without feeling that each party has rights and obligations. They have, as states, a common nature and destination, whence an equality of rights arises. And hence proceeds the possibility of *a law between nations* which is just, as expressing reciprocal rights and obligations, or just as expressing a free waiver of the rights which are by all acknowledged, and which may also embody by mutual agreement rules defining their more obvious claims and duties, or aiming to secure their common convenience and welfare. (Comp. § 27.)

This law of intercourse between nations has been united with *political* law, or the doctrine concerning the constitution of the state and the relations of the government to the people, under the head of *public* law, as opposed to *private*, or to the system of laws within the state, by which the relations of its individual members are defined and protected.* And yet there is a branch of this law which has both a private and a public character,—private as relating to persons, and public as agreed upon between nations. This law is now extensively called *international* law.

§ 3.

International law in the widest sense.

International law, *in a wide and abstract sense*, would embrace those rules of intercourse between nations, which are deduced from their rights and moral claims; or in other words, it is the expression of the jural and moral relations of states to one another.

* Comp. for example, Klüber, §2, and for the next remark Hurd's Law of Freedom and Bondage, § 25. The Germans excel us in the neatness of their divisions of jural science. *e. g.* Öffentliches recht is divided into Staatsrecht and Völkerrecht.

According to this definition, if we could once find out what are the rights and obligations, the moral claims and duties of nations as such, by mere deduction, the principles of this science would be settled. But such an abstract form of the science, commanding general assent, neither has appeared, nor is likely to appear. The advantage of separating international law in its theoretical form from the positive existing Code, depends not on the possibility of constructing a perfect code according to a true theory, but on the fact, that right views of justice may serve as a touchstone of actual usages and regulations; for in all jural science it is most important to distinguish between the law as it is, and as it ought to be. This same distinction is made by those* who discriminate between international *law*,—the positive admitted law,—and international *morality*. But the latter term must be objectionable to those at least who make a distinction between morals and *jus*. The law of nations, both as it is and as it ought to be, does not confine itself within the jural sphere.

§ 4.

Intern. law in a more limited sense.

In a more limited sense international law would be the system of positive rules, by which the nations of the world regulate their intercourse with one another. But in strictness of truth this definition is too broad, for there is no such law recognized as yet through all nations. Neither have the more civilized states of the East agreed with those of Europe, nor the states of antiquity with those of modern times, unless it be in a few provisions, which together would constitute an exceedingly meagre code.

§ 5.

Actual positive intern. law

Coming within narrower limits, we define international law to be the aggregate of the rules, which Christian states acknowledge, as obligatory in their relations to each other, and to each other's subjects. The rules

* Comp. an article attributed to Mr. Senior in Edinburgh Review, No. 156, for April, 1843.

also which they unite to impose on their subjects, respectively, for the treatment of one another, are included here, as being in the end rules of action for the states themselves. Here notice,

extending beyond Christendom,

1. That as Christian states are now controllers of opinion among men, their views of law are beginning to spread beyond the bounds of Christendom, as into Turkey and China.

but not observed towards savages.

2. That the definition cannot justly be widened to include the law which governs Christian states in their intercourse with savage or half-civilized tribes; or even with nations on a higher level, but lying outside of their forms of civilization. In general, towards such nations, they have acted on the principle that there is no common bond of obligation between them and the other party, observing so much of international law as suited their policy or sense of right at the time. Especially towards savage tribes they have often acted with flagrant selfishness, as if they feared no retribution from a weaker party, or were beyond the reach of public opinion. (Comp. § 136, and § 204.)

3. The rules of action agreed upon by two or more Christian states, but not by all, or the most of them, form no part of international law; although they often illustrate it, and often pave the way for the admission of new modifications of it.

4. Nations, it is conceded by all, have obligations towards foreigners, who are not constituent parts of any nation; or, at least, of a nation by which the law of nations is acknowledged. The consideration of the rights, or moral claims of such persons, belongs to international law, not as the system of rules observed between nations, but as involving obligations which all nations, or all Christian nations, acknowledge.

§ 6.

Genesis of intern. law. Its voluntary nature.

The way in which positive international law becomes such, shows that it must be progressive and somewhat uncertain. Right, as Heffter remarks,* is either *guaranteed*, under the protection and force of a competent

* Völkerrecht, § 2.

power, (as we see it in the state,) or *free*, that is, the individual power or person must protect and preserve it for himself. The law of nations is of this latter kind. First of all, the single state sets up for itself its views of right against other states. If it gives up its isolation, it freely forms in intercourse with other states a common right or law, from which now it can no longer set itself free, without offering up, or at least endangering, its peaceful relations, and even its existence.

Thus a law of nations can grow up only by the consent of the parties to it. It is, therefore, more a product of human freedom than the municipal law of a particular state. Its natural progress is to start from those provisions which are necessary in conducting political and commercial intercourse, while it leaves untouched, for a time, many usages which are contrary to humanity and morality; until, with the advance of civilization, the sway of moral ideas becomes stronger. It grows into a system of tolerable justice and humanity after, perhaps long after, municipal legislation has worked itself clear of many faults and errors. For although both branches of law have the same foundation of justice, and although a state, like Rome, for example, with an advanced system of internal laws, ought to have its views of international obligations purified; yet, as states have diverse interests and opinions, it takes time before a seeming interest can be given up, even after right is acknowledged to be on the other side; and it takes time to bring the views of nations to a common standard.*

Of later growth than state law.

* A state in the lower grade of civilization, like a savage, becomes conscious of its separate existence in the act of resistance, or of defending that existence. Such self-preservation on the part of the individual arouses, it may be, no better feeling than that of independence and self-reliance; in the state it helps the members to feel their unity and dependence, and the priceless value of the state itself. Hence war is a moral teacher: opposition to external force is an aid to the highest civic virtues. But if this were all there could be no recognition of obligations towards foreigners, no community of nations, in short, no world. These conceptions grow up in man, from the necessity of recognizing rules of intercourse, and intercourse is itself a natural necessity from the physical ordinances of God. Self-protection and

§ 7.

Why this law arose in Christian states.

The same causes which have enabled Christian states to reach a higher point of civilization than any other, have made them the first to elaborate a system of international law. These causes have been principally, (1.) the high moral standard of the religion which they in common professed,—a religion which cultivates alike the sentiments of justice and humanity; (2.) the inheritance which came to them of philosophy and legal science from the classical states of antiquity, and especially the system of Roman law; and (3.) a close historical connection since the times of the Roman empire, favoring the spread of common ideas. Thus the same religious and jural views, and a similar historical development, give rise to a community of nations, where it is comparatively easy for common usages to grow up. No such common feeling, but quite the opposite, existed between them and their Mohammedan neighbors; and hence the latter were long shut out from the pale of their international law.

§ 8.

Intern. law elsewhere quite imperfect.

Greece and Rome.

In other parts and ages of the world laws have grown up, in groups of nations, for the regulation of their conduct to each other. But these have all been partial, and were never constructed into a science. The classic states of antiquity had, at the best, a very simple and imperfect body of such rules and usages. Ambassadors and heralds had a sacred character; truces and treaties were acknowledged to be obligatory; war was usually begun with an open declaration, and, perhaps, with solemn formalities; but when once begun, it was waged with little rule or check. The Greeks were favorably situated for the development of a Hellenic international law; for, like the Christian states of modern times, they formed a circle of communities, standing at nearly the same

Greece.

intercourse are thus the two sources of international law; they make it necessary, and the conception in man of justice, of rights and obligations, must follow, because he has a moral nature.

level of civilization, and in religion, as well as historical traditions, connected with one another. And, in fact, the rudiments of such a law appear in the course of Greek history. They generally gave quarter, allowed the ransom of prisoners, respected trophies, and consented to truces for the burial of the dead. They acted on the principle of the balance of power against a dangerous and ambitious state belonging to their circle; they had a usage bearing some resemblance to the modern consular system; and they sometimes by treaties or perpetual leagues, as the Amphictyonic, secured the existence of the parties concerned, or even softened the severities of war.* But towards barbarians they acted almost without rule, and among themselves permitted the most flagrant acts of inhumanity.

Rome.

The Romans had less of international law than the Greeks, and were less scrupulous, if we except their observance, in their earlier days, of the fecial rules, which accorded so well with the formality of their religious character. The reason of this appears to be that, after they became masters of Italy, many of the nations they encountered were of another type than their own, and for the most part in decay, or half civilized; not in any respect their equals. Towards such enemies they could act as their convenience dictated.

No reason for saying that they had no intern. law.

It has been said, that the Greeks had no international law at all; and the same arguments would deny the existence of such a law among the Romans, in their earliest times.† There seems to be no sufficient ground for this opinion. Neither nation may have reached an accurate notion of an international law, but they had usages corresponding to those which nations under such a law now ob-

* Thus the old Amphictyonic league contemplated an armed intervention for the security of any member threatened with utter ruin by another; and no state belonging to the league was to be deprived in war of the use of its fountain water. Æschines de fals. leg. § 115, Bekk.

† A controversy was carried on in regard to the Greeks between Wachsmuth and Heffter, the former affirming the existence of a law of nations among them, the latter denying it. Comp. Osenbrüggen de jure belli et pacis (Lips. 1836), p. 4, seq.

serve; and if these usages were placed under the sanction of religion, to secure for them a more thorough observance, that religious character no more takes them out of the category of laws regulating conduct towards other states, than the same religious sanction given to the duty of hospitality took this duty out of the list of moral precepts. All morality and *jus* are sanctioned by religion, and sometimes the forms of religion grow on to them so as to give them a religious aspect. The fecial law in Rome's earlier days must have been the common property of all the Latin cities, a living law under the protection of the higher powers, introduced to prevent or to initiate a state of war. (Comp. § 115.)

Intern. law in the Middle Ages.

But in mediæval Europe, also, the law of nations was of slow growth, and for a time it scarcely rose above the level which it reached in Greece and Rome. Especially was this the case during the period of dissolution and reconstruction, and so long afterwards as national existence was kept down by the spirit of feudalism. The principal causes which modified it were, together with this of feudalism, the spirit of chivalry, the influence of Christianity, and the centralized government of the Christian church. Feudalism, by breaking up society into portions slightly united together, made the progress of better usages, and the triumph of right over will an uphill work; it increased the tendency to private war, and sanctioned the right of resistance to the central government; and it involved the presence on the soil of a large mass of men who had almost no rights. But the spirit of chivalry, by encouraging high sentiments of honor and fidelity, gave a moral sanction to the observance of treaties, and rendered fraud and unfair advantages over a rival unworthy of the true knight; it threw a lustre over the defence of the weak and unprotected; and it cultivated human feelings towards each other among the rulers of society. The spirit of Christianity, also,—which, indeed, was at work in the origination of chivalry itself—did much to facilitate intercourse among men of a common faith; it stopped, as far as it could, private wars; it opposed the barbarity of selling Christians as slaves, and introduced a somewhat milder treatment of captives taken in war; and it lent its sanction to all moral obligations. But it was neither pure nor strong enough to introduce a kind treatment of infidels, nor did it prevent various kinds of inhumanity, in peace as well as war, between Christians.

The government of the church by a monarch, who gradually gained great political, by means of religious, power, was the source of the most striking peculiarities of the public law of the mediæval period. The presence in Europe of an ultimate interpreter in religious and moral questions, doubtless did great good as well as harm. Every important question of politics had a bearing on religion, which could bring it up for examination and settlement before the Pope; and perhaps the very vagueness of the theory of papal interference aided its success on favorable occasions. In a gloss to the canon law (c. 2, Can. xv., qu. 6), it is said of the dispensing power of the Roman See, that "contra jus naturale Papa potest dispensare, dum tamen non contra Evangelium;" and the great Pope Innocent III., said: "Nos secundum plenitudinem potestatis de jure possumus supra jus dispensare." (C. 4, x. de concessione præbendæ.) This dispensing power extended to oaths. The oath of fealty was the moral cement of society, the last cord which bound the vassal to the suzerain. But the Popes asserted the right of releasing vassals from their oaths of allegiance, on the plea that the suzerain, who was disobedient or hostile to the church, might be proceeded against even to excommunication, and an outlaw as to church rights ought not to rule over Christians. In the disputes of kings, the weaker party often appealed to the Pope, and thus gave him an opportunity to arbitrate or command. Treaties confirmed by word of honor and solemn oath were open to the papal revision. Word might be broken with heretics, as the enemies of Christ. In the noted case of Huss, who had received a safe conduct, the Council of Constance resolved that it was lawful for a competent ecclesiastical judge to proceed against and punish obstinate heretics, "etiamsi de salvo conductu confisi ad locum venerint judicii, alias non venturi." *

* Gieseler, Kirchengesch. II., part 4, 418.

The neighborhood of dreaded enemies of the Christian religion,—of encroaching Mohammedan powers,—brought up the question whether compacts could be made with infidels. This could not be avoided, if the two religions should have any intercourse, as in Spain; but the lawfulness of treaties, especially of alliances with them was denied. Fulk, Archbishop of Rheims, told Charles the Simple, that there was no difference between becoming the ally of Pagans and abandoning God for the worship of idols. (Grotius II. 11, § 3.) And this feeling, that whilst leagues of peaceful intercourse could be entered into with infidels, alliances with them were forbidden by Christian law, long remained; and was strengthened, no doubt, by the apprehension that thus the scandal would arise of Christians leagued with unbelievers against fellow Christians.*

Many cruelties handed down from barbarous times held their ground through the mediæval period. Thus strangers were capriciously treated, and had scarcely any rights. (Comp. § 63.) After this period was over, Cardinal Richelieu showed its influence, by avowing the right of arresting all strangers who came into the kingdom without safe conducts; and a number of examples occur in those times of illustrious strangers, like Cœur de Lion in 1192, who when thrown by some accident on Christian shores were kept in captivity until they were ransomed. Cruelties in war, of which we speak below in §§ 128, 129, although often prevented by the genius of Christianity, were still common enough. Captives were held for a ransom, or even sold. The serf felt the full severity of war.†

§ 9.

Names given to this science.

Our science was called first by Zouch, (professor at Oxford,) in his jus feciale, 1650, *jus inter gentes*. Its common English appellation formerly was, *the law of nations*. Since Bentham led the way, it has been called *inter-*

* Sir E. Coke condemns alliances with infidels in a passage of his 4th institute cited by Ward, and his contemporary Grotius (ubi supra) does not like them.

† See Ward's Hist. *passim*.

national law. A distinction of no great value has been set up between these two terms, according to which the former relates to the historical character or origin of the law, and the latter to its jurisdiction or application.* They will be used by us as equivalents.

The law of nations, *jus inter gentes*, is not to be confounded with the *jus gentium* of the Romans. This term denoted the principles and usages of law common to all nations, that is, practically, to all nations known to the Romans, as contrasted with what was peculiar to the *jus civile*, the law of Rome itself. Gaius says, (Inst. i. § 1,) "quod naturalis ratio inter omnes homines constituit, id apud omnes populos peræque custoditur, vocaturque jus gentium, quasi quo omnes gentes utuntur." Ulpian says, (frag. i. 1, § 4) "jus gentium est quo gentes humanæ utuntur." These common usages of nations may run through all the fields of law, and so will include some rules of the international code. But the two evidently cover different ground, and the civil law never distinctly contemplates a law of nations in the modern sense.

Not the same as jus gentium.

§ 10.

It is important, again, not to confound international law with *natural law*,—or, as it has been variously called, *jus naturale*, lex naturalis, and lex naturæ. Jus naturale is the product of natural reason, and ought, since men are alike in their sense of justice, to be everywhere substantially the same. According to Gaius and most other Roman lawyers, it is not different from jus gentium, as already defined. But Ulpian and others make a distinction between the two, which has passed into the institutes of Justinian, without, however, influencing Roman law. To them jus naturale is that in which men and animals agree,—the law stamped on free animate beings. Savigny thus explains their views: † "there was a time, we may conceive, when men acknowledged only those relations which are common to man and beast, when

Different from jus naturale or lex naturæ.

* Reddie, quoted by Hurd, Law of Freedom and Bondage, i. 46.

† System des heut. röm. Rechts, i. 415.

they followed natural affections and impulses in all freedom. This was the reign of *jus naturale.* To this succeeded an age of founding states, when slavery, private property, and obligations were introduced, and introduced everywhere alike. This was the *jus gentium.* At last *jus* was developed in each state in its own peculiar way by modifying old institutions, or setting up new ones."

§ 11.

Definition of jus naturale by Grotius.

Modern writers have retained the term in an altered signification. Grotius (I. 1, § 10) defines it to be "dictatum rectæ rationis, indicans actui alicui, ex ejus convenientia aut disconvenientia cum ipsa natura rationali ac sociali, inesse moralem turpitudinem aut necessitatem moralem,* ac consequenter ab auctore naturæ Deo aut vetari aut præcipi."

Grotius thus uses the term to include morality and jus, as the foundation of *jus voluntarium*, that is, as the standard to which law civil or international ought to be conformed. But existing law may differ widely from it.

§ 12.

Puffendorf confounds jus naturale and intern. law.

Puffendorf's work on the law of nature and nations differs, to his disadvantage, from that of Grotius, in making little account of usage and voluntary *jus.* According to Grotius, the law of nations is jus illud, quod inter populos plures aut populorum rectores intercedit, moribus et pacto tacito introductum. Puffendorf, as Mr. Wildman says,† "entirely denies the authority of general usage; and

* *I. e.* a morally binding force. Hartenstein, in his valuable essay on the work of Grotius, (Abhandl. der Leipz. Geselsch. i. 504, 509) reduces the uses made by Grotius of the term jus naturale to these three heads: (1.) To the general obligation to satisfy moral claims, especially the more definite claims of jus and equity. (2.) To the claims or rights which grow out of the nature of man, and would be acknowledged in an incorrupt society, were there no organized state. (3.) To certain effects and results of acts of human will. Thus, Grotius would say, man's will originated property, but when once property was introduced, jus naturale indicated that it is wrong for one to take what is another's without his consent.

† Institutes of International Law, I. 28.

his doctrine, putting aside the mass of words with which he has encumbered it, amounts to this; that the rules of abstract propriety, resting merely on unauthorized speculations, and applied to international transactions, constitute international law, and acquire no additional authority, when by the usage of nations they have been generally received and approved of. So that the law of nations, according to Puffendorf, ends, where according to Grotius it begins."

Thus Puffendorf commits the faults of failing to distinguish sufficiently between natural justice and the law of nations; of spinning the web of a system out of his own brain, as if he were the legislator for the world; and of neglecting to inform us what the world actually holds to be the law by which nations regulate their intercourse. Probably he was led into this by not discriminating clearly between the *jus gentium* of the Romans and the *jus inter gentes* of modern publicists.

§ 13.

Positive method in intern. law. Its deficiencies.

An opposite course to this is to exhibit international law in its *positive form*, as it lies in the practice and understanding of a certain group of nations, either without reference to any jural or moral standard, or with recourse to moral considerations only now and then in disputed cases. This is a safe method, but narrow; and almost takes away scientific character from the subject-matter to which it is applied. What would municipal law be worth, if it did not point back to eternal right, and if by tracing it to its source it might not be made purer and more righteous? If international law were not made up of rules for which reasons could be given, satisfactory to man's intellectual and moral nature; if it were not built on principles of right; it would be even less of a science than is the code which governs the actions of polite society.

§ 14.

Intern. law not resolvable into contract obligation.

A very narrow foundation is laid for this science by those who would build it on the obligation to keep express or tacit contracts. In every contract it may be asked whether the parties have a right to act at all, and if so, whether they can lawfully enter into the specific relations which the contract contemplates. Can two nations agree lawfully to destroy the political life of a peaceful neighbor, and divide its territories between them? We look beyond a contract for its moral grounds. It is true, indeed, that a law controlling independent sovereigns can only become such by their free consent; it must, as we have seen, be voluntary. But this code of voluntary rules cannot for that reason be arbitrary, irrational, or inconsistent with justice.

§ 15.

The two aspects of intern. law.

There are, then, always two questions to be asked; *the first*, and most important, What is the actual understanding and practice of nations? otherwise we have a structure that floats in the air, subjective speculation, without authority; and *the second*, On what rational and moral grounds can this practice be explained and defended? otherwise it is divorced from *truth* and *right*, mere *fact* only being left behind.

Jural grounds of intern. law.

But what are the rational and moral grounds of international law? The same in general with those on which the rights and obligations of individuals, in the state, and of the single state towards the individuals of which it consists, repose. If we define natural *jus* to be the science, which from the nature and destination of man determines his external relations in society, both the question, What ought to be the rights and obligations of the individual in the state? and the question, What those of a state among states ought to be? fall within this branch of science. That there are such rights and obligations of *states* will hardly be doubted by those, who admit that these relations of natural justice exist in any case. There is the same reason why they should be applied in regulating the intercourse of states, as in regulating that of individuals. There is a natural destination of states, and a divine purpose in their existence, which make it necessary that they should have certain functions and powers of acting within a certain sphere, which external force may not invade. It would be strange if the state, that power which defines rights and makes them real, which creates *moral persons* or associations with rights and obligations, should have no such relations of its own,—should be a physical and not a moral entity. In fact, to take the opposite ground would be to maintain that there is no right and wrong in the intercourse of states, and to leave their conduct to the sway of mere convenience. (§ 2.)

§ 16.

Moral grounds of intern law.

But there are moral relations, also, which are not relations of justice, and which give rise to international *morality*. It may be, to say the least, that nations have duties and moral claims, as well as rights and obligations. In matter of fact, some of these are generally acknowledged by nations, and have entered into the law of their intercourse, as, for example, the duty of comity and that of humanity. These relations were called by the older writers imperfect rights and obligations, not because the moral ground for them is incomplete, but because the right in particular cases cannot be ascertained, and therefore ought not to be enforced, nor the violation of right regarded as an *injury*. Several recent writers give to them the name of duties and moral claims, an example which we shall follow in this work.*

§ 17.

Among the *jural* principles or foundations of international law, we name

Particular rights and obligations of nations.

1. The obligation lying on the state to protect the individuals who compose it,† not only from domestic, but also from foreign aggression. This obligation

* Mr. Wildman observes, that "the phrase 'moral claim' at once conveys the idea which Puffendorf and Vattel have employed countless pages to confuse." (I. 4.) Dr. Whewell uses this term in his Elements of Morality and Polity. He also uses the terms *jus* and *jural*, which were first employed by Dr. Lieber.

† The English language wants a term besides *citizen* and *subject*, more general than either, and without the idea contained in the latter, of being under the control of an individual. In this work I use *subject*, for want of a better word, to denote

emanates immediately from the prime function and end of a state, and is limited by the rightfulness of the subject's conduct in his intercourse with the stranger.

2. Those qualities or rights which are involved in the existence of the state. These may be called rights of sovereignty simply, or may be ramified into rights of sovereignty, independence, and equality. The exercise of these rights and the right of self-protection may, together, be embraced under the head of rights of self-preservation. (§ 37.)

3. Those rights which the state has in common with individuals or with artificial persons, as the right of property, that of contract, and that of reputation.

4. The right which arises when the free exercise of the state's powers above mentioned is impeded, that is, the right of redress, near to which lie the questionable rights of punishment and of conquest.

Obligations and rights correlative.

Inasmuch as rights and obligations are correlative, there is an obligation lying on every state to respect the rights of every other, to abstain from all injury and wrong towards it, as well as well as towards its subjects. These obligations are expressed in international law.

§ 18.

Observations on certain rights.

Most of the above enumerated powers of states are plain, but one or two need a little explanation.

1. Right of Reputation?

1. The right of reputation. This right when viewed in relation to individuals, seems to consist of two parts, the one objective,—the right to a good name, the other subjective,—the right of exemption from insult and causeless wounding of the feelings. Corresponding to these rights are the obligations to respect a man's reputation, and to refrain from wounding his feelings by aspersions on his character. These rights are generally blended, but may exist apart; for instance, a man may insult another, or make false charges against him, when no one else knows of it. These rights, but

all who are under the law; and *sovereign*, that in which the sovereign power resides, whether an individual or a nation.

principally the objective one, form the ground of the prosecutions for slander and libel; and a large part of *private* feuds arise from their violation. The honor or reputation of a *state* is equally its right; and the injury done by violations of this right will seem very great, when we consider the multitudes who suffer in their feelings from a national insult, and the influence of the loss of a good name upon intercourse with other states, as well as upon that self-respect which is an important element in national character. Regard for national reputation, too, increases with refinement and with closeness of communication. The Fejees or the Hottentots care little how the world regards them, but the opinion of civilized nations is highly valued by all those states which are now foremost in human affairs. Without such a value set on reputation, fear of censure could not exist, which is one of the ultimate bulwarks of international law.

§ 19.

2. Right of redress.

2. The right of redress exists in the case of individuals, although it would seem that a person cannot with justice be his own judge and redress himself. Hence the need of courts and arbitrations in society, which, by their impartiality, knowledge of law and evidence, and habits of judging, approach, as nearly as finite beings can, to the decisions of absolute truth. Societies or states must have not only the right of *redress*, but of *redressing themselves;* the former, as being just and necessary for the protection of all rights; the latter, because they have no natural superior,—because in fact they are vicars of God within a certain sphere. It may be said that thus they become judges in their own causes. This is true, although not in the same sense, nor with the same violation of justice, as when private persons redress themselves; for the proceedings of states are more deliberate, and for the most part the same body within the state is not at once the injured and the redressing party. It may be said also that an impartial court selected from other nations would be more just, and ought to decide in international disputes. This might be

desirable, but it does not appear that nations are for that reason bound to abstain from redressing wrongs. The private person has a natural superior in the state to which he is bound to submit; but God has established no such natural superior over nations.

Redress what? Redress consists in compensation for injury inflicted, and for its consequences. The right therefore ceases when the injured party is placed in as good a situation as before. Mingled up in the same concrete with the act of redress, there may be an act of self-protection against future injury. Goes along with self-protection. A nation may have shown such a disposition to do wrong, that another may demand security as well as indemnity; and this security may proceed, for any thing that appears, even to the length of destroying the wrong-doing state's existence.

§ 20, *a*.

3. Has a state the right of punishing other states? 3. Grotius held that a state has the right to punish injuries, committed not only against itself and its subjects, but also against others over whom it has no guardianship. "Sciendum quoque est," he says (II. 20, § 40) "reges et qui par regibus jus obtinent, jus habere pœnas poscendi non tantum ob injurias in se aut subditos suos commissas, sed et ob eas quæ ipsos peculiariter non tangunt, sed in quibusvis personis jus naturæ aut gentium immaniter violant." This right he derives from a similar right of individuals in a state of nature, which they gave up to society. He adds, that it is more praiseworthy to punish injuries done to others than to ourselves, inasmuch as we are then less likely to be partial.

Few, if any, we suppose, would now undertake to defend the explanation here given by Grotius, of the state's right to punish; and the extent which he gives to the right seems equally objectionable. There must be a certain sphere for each state, certain bounds within which its functions are intended to act, for otherwise the territorial divisions of the earth would have no meaning. In regard to the right of *punishing in any case* outside of the bounds of the state there may be rational doubts. Admitting, as we are very ready to do, that this is one of the powers of the state over its subjects, we can by no means infer that the state may punish those who are not its subjects, but its equals. And yet, practically, it is impossible to separate that moral indignation which expresses itself in punishment from the spirit of self-redress for wrongs. As for a state's having the vocation to go forth, beating down wickedness, like Hercules, all over the world, it is enough to say, that such a principle, if carried out, would destroy the independence of states, justify the nations in taking sides in regard to all national acts, and lead to universal war. And yet extreme cases of outrage may be conceived of, where a burning desire to help the weak abroad, or to punish the oppressor, ought hardly to be disobeyed.

§ 20, *b*.

Relations of a state to general justice.

The inquiry whether a state has a right to punish beyond its own limits, leads us to the more general and practically important inquiry, whether a state is bound to aid other states in the maintenance of general justice, that is, of what it considers to be justice. The prevalent view seems to be that, outside of its own territory, including its ships on the high seas, and beyond its own relations with other states, a state has nothing to do with the interests of justice in the world. Thus laws of extradition and private international law are thought to originate merely in comity. (§§ 69, 79.) Thus, too, crimes committed by its own citizens abroad, it is not bound to notice after their return home. Thus, again, contraband trade is held not to begin within the neutral's borders, and outside of them, as on the high seas, concerns the belligerent alone. (§ 178, note.) And again, when a nation commits a gross crime against another, third parties are not generally held to be bound to interfere. This is the most received, and may be called the narrow and selfish view. On the other hand, the broad view, that a state must aid in getting justice done everywhere, if its aid be invoked, and even without that preliminary, would occasion more violence than could thus be prevented. Such a proceeding, too, would be unjust, as overruling the judgments of the lawful authority.

But there is a middle ground on which the theory of international obligation can be rationally placed. (1.) As already said in § 20 *a*, the interests of justice require that the state, like every moral person, shall have its special sphere of action, within which it may not be invaded, except in extreme and outrageous cases,—which cases are contemplated by the actual law of nations. (§§ 42, 50, 112, *end.*) (2.) Every moral being, much more the state which is a member of a community of nations, is interested in the prevalence of justice everywhere, and is the only asylum of it when attacked,—is bound to aid in maintaining justice even outside of its own sphere, if this aid can be so rendered as to violate no higher and more permanent rules of justice. (3.) In those cases where another state either invokes or does not object to its aid, a state, if its own judgment is clear on the right of the case, may lend its assistance. (4.) When this aid to foreign justice can be rendered within its own territory the obligation is clear, and thus the extradition of criminals, contrary to what is usually taught, and to the opinion expressed in the first edition of this work, cannot, with propriety, be refused in certain cases. (§ 79.) (5.) Private international law must have its origin in justice and not in comity, so that nations, if they can only find out what the principles of justice here are, ought to adopt them. (6.) Some questions, as whether a state is bound to aid foreign custom-house laws by preventing smuggling, and how far a neutral ought to prevent contraband trade of its subjects and from its ports, are beset with special difficulties. Of the latter we shall speak, § 178, note. Of the former, we may say that a tariff may be unreasonable and deleterious to the interests of other states and thus unjust: it cannot be expected that aid can be given in such a case. But where a tariff is admitted to be reasonable, since it is a necessity and is rightfully imposed, to break such laws by smuggling is immoral, and a nation ought to restrain its people from so doing. In such cases the neglect of justice avenges itself by the lawlessness of those who are trained up in the flagitious trade.*

* Comp. R. v. Mohl in a monograph in his Staatr, Völkerr. u. Politik, vol. 1.

§ 21.

4. Natural justice knows nothing of a right of conquest in the broad sense of that term, that is, of mere superior force, carrying with it the license to appropriate territory, or destroy national life. Yet, in fact, nations accept, if they do not justify, such a right of conquest. The reasons for this are, in general, derived from the rule, that it is officious and impossible for nations to sit as judges over each other's conduct, or, in other words, from the independence of nations. (§ 37, § 111.) But more particularly (1.) in the exercise of the right of redress it may be necessary to strip a wrong-doer of a portion of his territory; or in the exercise of the right of self-protection, and, possibly, of punishment, it may be lawful to deprive him of the means of doing evil. (2.) The spirit of conquest generally urges one of these pleas in its defence, over the validity of which, as we have said, nations may not sit in judgment. (3.) Treaties generally perfect the title which possession or conquest begins. (4.) When a settled state of things follows a conquest, it is usually acquiesced in, because, as has been seen, if nations repaired each other's wrongs, the way would be open for perpetual war. Thus international law acknowledges the fact of conquest after it has become a permanent fact in the world's history, and in some degree, the right also.

4. Is there any right of conquest?

Yet the mere fact of having occupied territory or subjugated its inhabitants, can be no sufficient ground in justice, even in a just war, for the exercise of the right of conquest. Redress and punishment ought not to exceed due limits, nor ought self-protection to demand an exorbitant amount of security. In accordance with this the spirit of conquest is regarded by the nations as the spirit of robbery, and as hostility to the human race. This is shown by their combinations to resist it, as in the wars against Louis XIV and Napoleon; by their protests against acquisitions regarded as unjust, and against alliances formed for the injury of weak states; by the pretexts with which aggressors seek to shield themselves from the condemnation of the world; and by the occasional consent of victorious nations to give a price for territory acquired in war, as when the United States paid a sum of money to Mexico for lands ceded at the peace of 1848.*

§ 22.

Moral relations of states, or duties and moral claims.

Moral claims and duties being to a great extent determined by the special circumstances of the case, cannot be so easily defined and enforced as rights and obligations; and opinions in regard to them vary with the varying moral feelings of individuals, of countries and of ages. Hence, with the increase of culture, and the greater sway of pure religion, the influence of moral ideas over nations enlarges. No cause has had greater efficacy in producing changes in international law than this, of which the improvements in the laws of war, and in the treatment of individuals out of their own country, are good illustrations. The rules drawn from this source are less capable of being reduced to a theory than those deducible from jural relations.

§ 23.

Particular duties. 1. Humanity.

One or two recognized branches of duty between nations deserve a brief notice.

1. The duty of humanity, including hospitality. This duty spends itself chiefly in the treatment of individuals, although suffering nations or parts of nations may also call for its exercise. The awakened sentiment of

* The Abbé de Mably, on this subject, uses the following language: "A prince is doubtless in the right in conquering a province which belongs to him, and of which the restitution is refused. He can, even, to punish his enemy for his injustice and to recompense himself for the expenses of war which he has been forced to make, extend his conquests beyond the country which he claims as his own. But arms, of themselves, give no title; they suppose an anterior one, and it is to try this contested right that the war is waged. Were it otherwise, a prince despoiled by his enemy, would no longer have any right to the countries which have been taken from him, and hence it would be ridiculous for the victor to demand a cession from him in treaties of peace. We may add here a very simple argument; if conquests by their nature form a legitimate right of possession to the conqueror, it is indifferent whether the war be undertaken on just or unjust grounds." Droit public, vol. I. part 2, 109, ed. of Amsterdam of 1777.

humanity in modern times is manifested in a variety of ways, as by efforts to suppress the slave trade, by greater care for captives, by protection of the inhabitants of a country from invading armies, by the facility of removing into a new country, by the greater security of strangers. Formerly, the individual was treated as a part of the nation on whom its wrongs might be wreaked. Now this spirit of war against private individuals is passing away. In general, any decided want of humanity arouses the indignation even of third parties, excites remonstrances, and may call for interposition. (Comp. § 21, § 50.) But cruelty may also reach beyond the sphere of humanity; it may violate right, and justify self-protection and resistance.

§ 24.

2. Comity.

Comity is another duty of nations. To this source may be referred in part the privileges conceded to ambassadors, and the preference given in certain cases to foreign over domestic law by the courts of Christendom. Comity, as generally understood, is national politeness and kindness. But the term seems to embrace not only that kindness which emanates from friendly feeling, but also those tokens of respect which are *due* between nations on the ground of right.

A much wider sense is given to the term comity by those who embrace in it all those praiseworthy acts of one nation towards another, which are not *stricti juris*, that is, all that, the refusal or withholding of which, although dictated by malevolence, is not an injury, and so not a ground for war. But usages originating in comity may become rights by lapse of time. (Comp. Phillimore, I. 161, and §§ 26, 28, infra.)

§ 25.

3. Intercourse.

Some have contended that there is a positive obligation on nations to enter into relations at least of commerce, so that the refusal thus to act would be an injury, and possibly a cause of war. It might be said that differences of climate, soil, productions, and acquired skill, enable all parts of the world to aid one another, and that this clearly points out a divine destination and intention that they shall so act. But the better opinion is, that, except in extreme cases, —as when one nation cannot do without the productions of another, or must cross its borders to get at the rest of the world —this is only a duty, an exercise of a spirit of goodwill, to be judged of by each state according to the light which it possesses. In all intercourse the two parties concerned must settle the terms; how then can one force the other into a treaty of commerce, any more than one man force another into a contract.

But although writers are believed to agree substantially in this, there is a disposition on the part of nations to act as if they had a right to require others to exchange products with them. This has been seen in the dealings of later years with certain Oriental and other states. But might not one Christian state with greater reason force another to give up its protective tariff?

It thus appears that intercourse, which is a preliminary to all international law, and the condition, without which rights and obligations would be mere abstract conceptions, is itself referable to the class of duties, and that the refusal to allow it is no injury. There is nothing more strange in this than in the voluntariness of all private contracts, as of the marriage union, which must be presupposed before any family rights can exist. All that rights serve for is, when intercourse is given, to make it jural. Thus we see again the *voluntary* quality of international law.

§ 26.

Vattel's divisions of intern. law.

Vattel divides the law of nations into the natural or *necessary*, so called because nations are absolutely obliged to observe it; and the *positive*, proceeding from the volition of nations. This latter, again, is subdivided into voluntary, conventional, and customary law, which are respectively derived from presumed, expressed, and tacit consent. Of voluntary law Vattel says, that it embraces the rules drawn from the principle that nations, being equal and independent, are obliged to suffer each other to do many blamable things, presuming or acting as if they were right. Thus capture in war is valid, whether made by the aggressor or the injured. But there seems to be no reason for setting off this as a distinct branch, and it is by no means clearly defined. Such cases as Vattel contemplates are to be referred to the obligation under which nations lie of not interfering with each other's sovereignty, and thus run back to the *necessary* law of nations.

Dr. Wheaton, justly discarding this subordinate division of voluntary law, makes natural law one genus, and voluntary, another, under which latter conventional and customary are included. The division of international law into primitive and secondary law, is altogether similar to this, primitive being the law of nature and secondary that of treaty and usage. But these divisions, although avoiding Vattel's error, are of no great value. For, (1.) A requirement of natural law may be confirmed by voluntary, as by a treaty: to which, then, of the two does it belong? (2.) Conventional law hitherto includes no treaties between all the Christian states of the world, and thus is rather to be taken as *evidence* of what international law is, than as *a part* of it. Nay, treaties are often made to except the parties from the operation of a real or supposed international rule. (3.) In reality all international law is voluntary, not in the sense that it derives its sole obligation from the will of the parties, but in the sense that all nations in a certain circle agree to abide by it. (4.) And again, all voluntary law is natural, being built on the foundation of the sacredness of agreements.

Wheaton's.

§ 27.

Perhaps a division like the following may have something to commend it, which separates the rights and obligations known to this science into, (1.) those which are deducible from natural *jus*, which no action of a sovereignty began or can terminate; (2.) those deducible from the idea of a state; (3.) those which are begun and can be

Other divisions.

ended by compact, express or tacit. Another division still, which we have made already (§ 2), follows the division of the three grounds or reasons for international rules, namely, *jus*, morality, and convenience. The first class comprehends natural rights and obligations, which can be defined and enforced; the second, duties and moral claims which cannot be easily defined, and need compact to establish them; and the third, arrangements of a purely voluntary nature. A very considerable part of international law is included under the second and third of these heads; a fact which serves to show the highly positive or voluntary nature of much of the science. Thus exterritoriality, private international law, the rules of respect, some, at least, of the regulations touching ambassadors, the laws of war to a great extent, and, indeed, much else is of this description. These parts of the science cannot be deduced from a theory, nor could they have arisen prior to a long experience.

§ 28.

Custom and free consent alike sources of law.

Whether the free assent of nations take the form of express agreement or of usage, it places them alike under the obligation of contract. Customs within each country existed before statutes, and so observances come in imperceptibly and control the conduct of a circle of nations. A nation which grants privileges to another by tacit consent, and then revokes them without cause, may commit an injury just as if it had broken a treaty. For example, intercourse may become a right by becoming a fact, and to end it would be a proof of a hostile mind.

It is to be remarked, also, that not only obligations of natural justice are recognized in this tacit way, but duties become obligations, and claims or conveniences, allowed, become rights, just as by formal contract. A nation may grant the privilege of transit to the troops of another by treaty; it has now become a right. The same thing may come about by custom or tacit consent. It might seem as if nations could alter their conduct at pleasure, within the spheres of moral claims and convenience. But if they have sanctioned a usage by long permission without protest, they have laid an obligation on themselves, and cannot alter it. It may, however, be difficult to say when such obligations begin, when transit, for instance, silently suffered, becomes a kind of servitude on the soil. There is a difference, also, in usages. Mere forms of intercourse may have little binding force, but principles admitted in common in a silent way, and giving birth to common habits, and mutual privileges conceded without treaty, appeal to the moral sense of nations.

§ 29.

Intern. law adopted by municipal.

As soon as a nation has assumed the obligations of international law, they become a portion of the law of the land to govern the decisions of courts, the conduct of the rulers and that of the people. A nation is bound to protect this part of law by statute and penalty as much as that part which controls the jural relations or in other ways affects the actions of individuals. Otherwise it is a dead letter; there is a want of faith towards foreign powers, and there is danger of quarrel ending in war. All Christian states have, it is believed, in this way sanctioned international law, so far as it seemed to them necessary. It is, says Blackstone, "adopted in its full extent by the laws of England; and whenever any question arises which is properly subject to its jurisdiction, it is held to be a part of the law of the land." "As being a part of the common law of England, the law of nations is adopted by our own law also, for it is well settled, that the common law of England, so far as it may be consistent with the Constitution of this country, and remains unaltered by statute, is an essential part of American jurisprudence." * Parts of it, moreover, have received an express sanction from the Constitution and Statutes of the United States.

§ 30.

Aids for knowing what intern. law is.

The helps in ascertaining what international law is, or has been, may be derived principally from the following documents:—

* 1 Kent, Lect. 1.

1. The sea laws of various ports or districts, which had a commercial importance in mediæval Europe.

2. The treaties in which a large number of important nations have had a part, as the treaty of Westphalia, the Congress of Vienna, and the recent treaty of Paris, in 1856. Other political treaties are evidences of an opinion entertained by the parties in regard to certain provisions of the law of nations; and that, whether they sanction these provisions or suspend their operation. Much the same thing may be said of treaties of commerce, which often touch on mooted questions of maritime law. A brief statement of the leading features of the principal political treaties since the reformation constitutes the second appendix to this volume.

3. Judicial decisions, which often set forth in the clearest manner the state of the law as it is understood by the ablest legal authorities of a particular country, and which, although not always followed, command respect in other countries. The decisions of the English courts, especially of the Admiralty under Sir William Scott (Lord Stowell), although taking a view of neutral rights on the sea which is now becoming obsolete, are distinguished for their ability, and have had a great influence on opinion in this country. Many decisions of the Supreme Court of the United States involve points of international law,—a court, before which, originally, "all cases touching ambassadors, other public ministers and consuls," and, ultimately, various questions affecting treaties and relations with foreign countries may be brought.

4. State papers on controverted points, such as those written in our own country by Jefferson, Hamilton, Webster, and Marcy.

5. Treatises on this branch of science, or on some title of it, some of which with reason, or by accident, have acquired a standing above others. A list of the most eminent text-writers may be found in the first appendix to this work.

§ 31.

In tracing the progress of international law, that is of views or theories concerning it, we may notice several stages, more or less clearly defined, through which it has passed. 1. Among the ancients we have a recognition of right and wrong in the intercourse of states together with some rules regulating intercourse and some rules of humanity in war—placed chiefly under the sanction of religion—but no separation of this branch of law from the rest, as a distinct department. (§ 8.) This period continued until after the revival of learning. In the middle age the science was still undeveloped, but religious institutions and antipathies modified the practice of Christian states. (§ 8.) During the revival of learning, a spirit arose in Italy, which made light of all obligations between states, and almost deified successful wickedness. Soon after this, we perceive that the forerunners of Grotius, as Suarez, Ayala, and above all, Albericus Gentilis, are aware that a system of international law ought to be evolved, and are working out particular titles of it. (Append. I.)

2. With Grotius a new era begins. (§ 11, Append. I.) His great aim was practical, not scientific,—it was to bring the practice of nations, especially in war, into conformity with justice. He held firmly to a system of natural justice between states, without, however, very accurately defining it. To positive law, also, originated by states, he conceded an obligatory force, unless it contravened this justice of nature. In setting forth his views, he adduces in rich abundance the opinions of the ancients, and illustrations from Greek and Roman history. The nobleness of his aim, and his claim to respect as the father of the science, have given to the treatise *de Jure Belli et Pacis* an enduring influence.

3. After Grotius there appear two tendencies. One is to disregard all that is positive and actual in the arrangements between nations, and to construct a system on the principles of natural law; in which way a law for states, differing from ethics and natural justice, is in fact denied. This tendency is represented by Puffendorf. (§ 12.) The other tendency was a reaction against this writer, and satisfied itself with representing the actual state of international law, as it exists by usage and treaty, without setting up or recognizing a standard

of natural justice by its side. Bynkershoek and Moser (see Append. I), with Martens and others in more recent times, are examples here. Many writers however, treading in the steps of Grotius, regard natural justice as a source of right, with which the practice of states must be compared and brought into conformity, and which may not be neglected in a scientific system.

§ 32.

There has been a general progress in the views of text-writers since the age of Grotius, and a substantial agreement between those of all nationalities at the same era. And yet minor differences are very observable. Some of the most striking of these are the differences between the English and the Continental doctrine, arising from the insular position of Great Britain, from her commercial interests, and her power on the sea. Thus we find her behind the Continent in respecting the sanctity of ambassadors until into the eighteenth century. (§ 92, e.) Thus also while her practice in land wars has been humane, her sea-rules and the decisions of her courts have in several ways borne hardly upon neutrals. It is worthy of notice that our courts have followed English precedents, while our Government, as that of a nation generally neutral, has for the most part leaned in its doctrines and treaties towards Continental views.

§ 33.

Hitherto, as may be gathered from what has just been said, there is something of that same uncertainty and want of authority to be discovered in international law, which attends on other political and jural sciences. This is due to causes already noticed; (1.) to the changes in the science growing out of changes in the intellectual and moral culture of successive generations, and (2.) to the fact that states, according to their temporary or their permanent interests, have set up or followed different rules of action.

Whether anything can be done, by means of an international code, to bring more certainty and precision into the science will be considered in the sequel. (§ 203.)

§ 34.

History of intern. law; its importance.

In every branch of knowledge, the history of the branch is an important auxiliary to its scientific treatment. From the changes and improvements in the law of nations, it is evident that the history of this science—both the history of opinion and of practice,—is deserving of especial attention. It is a leading chapter in the history of civilization. It furnishes valuable hints for the future. Notwithstanding its dark passages, it is calculated to animate the friends of justice and humanity. It explains the present state of the science and indicates the obstacles which have retarded its advance. Hence the value of such works as Laurent's "Histoire du Droit des Gens," which in three volumes embraces the East and the classical nations of antiquity; Ward's "Enquiry," embracing the period from the time of the Greeks and Romans to the age of Grotius; and Wheaton's history, which in a sense continues Ward's work down to the peace of Washington in 1842, is surpassed by that of few systematic treatises. Histories of treaties also are of great importance, as aids in understanding the treaties themselves, which are a principal source of international law.

It will be one of our primary aims in this work, as far as our narrow limits permit, to append historical illustrations to the leading titles, in the hope of exhibiting the progressive character of the science, and of conferring a benefit on the student of history. It ought however to be remarked that historical precedents must be used with caution. History tells of crimes against the law of nations, as well as of its construction and its observance, of old usages or principles given up and new ones adopted. There is no value in the mere historical facts, apart from the reasons or pretexts for them, and from their bearings on the spread of justice and the sense of human brotherhood in the world.

§ 35.

Method pursued in this work.

A method which aims to be practically useful in international law, must take notice of the great importance which questions pertaining to a state of war have in that science. In both peace and war the essential qualities of states,—their sovereignty and the like—must be exercised; but war suspends the operations of certain rights, and calls into activity certain others. Then again, in peace every state sustains a similar relation towards every other; but in war a belligerent state has one relation to its enemy, and another to all states besides; or, in other words, the rights and obligations of non-belligerents or neutrals now begin to exist. We have, then, the general faculties or powers of states, their relations of peace, and their relations in or owing to war. In the method here pursued, these general faculties or essential powers of states, instead of forming a distinct division by themselves, constitute together with the rights and moral claims, the obligations and duties, which have their operation especially in a state of peace, the first part of the science. Then follows the second part, having to do with a state of war. Our first part consists of the following chapters: the first treating of the rights and obligations of states as independent sovereignties; the second, of the right of property, and rights over territory belonging to states; the third, of the rights and duties of intercourse between nations, with the relations of foreigners within the territory to the state; the fourth, of the forms and agents of intercourse between the states themselves; the fifth, of the right of contract, or of treaties. The second part, treating of the relations in a state of war, consists of two principal chapters, in the first of which the state of war, as affecting the belligerents themselves is considered; and in the second, the state of war as bearing on the rights and obligations of neutrals.

PART I.

THE ESSENTIAL POWERS OF STATES, AND THEIR RIGHTS AND OBLIGATIONS ESPECIALLY IN A STATE OF PEACE.

CHAPTER I.

RIGHTS OF STATES AS INDEPENDENT SOVEREIGNTIES.—CORRESPONDING OBLIGATION OF NON-INTERFERENCE AND EXCEPTIONS TO IT CLAIMED OR ADMITTED IN THE PRACTICE OF NATIONS.

§ 36.

A STATE is a community of persons living within certain limits of territory, under a permanent organization, which aims to secure the prevalence of justice by self-imposed law. The organ of the state by which its relations with other states are managed is the government.

A state what?

A body of pirates may be organized under law, but is no state, being associated for temporary purposes, and designing to act unjustly by its very existence. A state might arise out of a nest of pirates, but would not begin to be a state until it laid aside its piratical character. Thus it has been doubted whether the Barbary powers were anything more than associations of pirates. But having grown in the course of time more just and civilized, they are now taken into the community of nations.* Those pirates of Cilicia and Isauria, on the other hand, whose powerful confederacy Pompey broke up, clearly formed no state, their settlements being strongholds contrived to secure their families and their plunder.

Pirates no state.

* Comp. Bynkershoek Quæst. juris publici, I. § 17.

§ 37.

Essential attributes or rights of a state.

From the nature and destination of a state, it must in a sense be as truly separate from the rest of the world, as if it were the only state in existence. It must have an exclusive right to impose laws within its own territory, the sole regulation in general of its subjects, the sole determining power in regard to the forms of its organization. No reason can be assigned why in a group of states one should have a right to interfere in the legislation or administration of the rest, which would not give each of them the same right in turn. Nor can any reason be found why one state ought to have more rights or different rights than any other. We find it necessary for the conception of states, and for their occupying the sphere which the Author of society has marked out for them, to predicate of them *sovereignty*, *independence*, and the *equality* of each with the rest. And these its attributes or rights each has a right to preserve; in other words, to maintain its state existence. These three attributes cannot exist apart, and perhaps the single conception of sovereignty, or of self-protection, may include them all. (§ 17.)

By sovereignty we intend the uncontrolled exclusive exercise of the powers of the state; that is, both of the power of entering into relations with other states, and of the power of governing its own subjects. This power is supreme within a certain territory, and supreme over its own subjects wherever no other sovereignty has jurisdiction.

By independence we intend to set forth the negative side of sovereignty, that is, to deny that any other state has any right to interfere with the exercise of a state's rights and sovereign powers. Thus a state may make treaties, political or commercial, or may make war, or change its laws, executive officers, or form of government, or by a just policy add to its resources, so as to become richer and stronger than other states, or plant colonies or acquire territory, or become consolidated with other states, while no other state shall have any just cause to impede or interfere with its unfettered action.

By equality is not meant equality of honor or respect, or

equality of rank according to the etiquette of courts, or the right to have the same commercial or political privileges which have been granted to other states, but simply equality of *state rights*, that is, an equal degree of sovereignty and the possession of all the same rights which other states exercise. This is, perhaps, simply the exhibition of the quality of state sovereignty in a different light. States which are truly sovereign are necessarily equal in rights, since the quality of full sovereignty has no degrees, and the state, as such, has certain rights from its very existence.

It is scarcely necessary to add, that difference of size or of power neither adds to or subtracts from the sovereignty of a state, nor affects its rights in any particular.

These attributes may be laid aside in whole or in part by confederated,

A state, however, may, by its free act, surrender a part of these rights, or it may give up its existence and become merged in another organization. The partial surrender occurs sometimes in confederations. The states composing such confederation may come together on a variety of conditions, most of which imply a surrender of sovereignty and independence in some degree, and therefore the discontinuance of their existence as states, in the highest sense of the word. Some leagues take away from their members the right of separate peace and war, and perhaps add to this a central board for the adjustment of disputes. Others aim at a closer bond between their members, and confer all power, in foreign relations, as well as various other prerogatives, upon a central legislature and administration created by the league. Others, again, aim to secure a very loose kind of union,—one which allows its members to make political leagues with foreign states, and to make war and peace separately, but has a common head and a court for the settlement of certain disputed claims. On types like these respectively the Achæan League, our Union, and the German Confederation in its more modern form, have been constructed.

or by protected states.

A state which is under the protection of another may be sovereign in some respects, but not absolutely sovereign. Such was the republic of Cracow, while it lasted; such have been the Ionian islands, under English protection; Moldavia and Wallachia under that of Turkey, with the guaranty of the great European powers; Servia and Egypt under Turkey, with a different dependence; Monaco under Sardinia.*

Sovereignty in intern. law what?

For the purposes of international law that state only can be regarded as sovereign, which has retained its power to enter into all relations with foreign states, whatever limitations it may impose on itself in other respects. Thus the states of this Union in the view of our science are not sovereign, for they cannot exercise the treaty-making power, nor that of making war and peace, nor that of sending ambassadors to foreign courts. They can only exercise towards foreign nations those private rights which may pertain to any individual or association. It is to be observed, however, that between states of qualified sovereignty the law of nations has application, so far forth as it is not shut out by restrictions upon their power.

In a state which is formed by a union of states, there is no doubt that the central government is responsible for the acts of bodies which have no existence in the view of international law. There is a weak point in our Constitution in this respect, for the responsibility must be borne by the central government, but the evil cannot always be abated. Comp. Phillimore, 1, 143.

§ 38.

A state's obligations not destroyed by a change of government.

A state is a moral person, capable of obligations as well as rights. These relations continue after it has passed through a change of constitution, for notwithstanding the change the state may still preserve its attributes and functions. No act of its own can annihilate an obligation to another state; and its rights still continue, unless its former constitution of government was the condition on which the obligations of other states towards it were founded. The general rule then, as all admit, is, that

* Comp, Wheaton, El. I. 2, pp. 70, 71.

rights and obligations survive a change of government or a revolution. So when a nation separates into parts, or unites with another state to form a new whole, it cannot even by such a process, which destroys or modifies its existence, divest itself of its obligations. Thus debts due to foreigners outlast all such mutations, and not to provide for their payment would be a violation of right. When at the formation of the Federal Constitution the States' debts were assumed, and when at the separation of Norway from Denmark the old debt of the united countries was equitably divided, these were acts of simple justice and good faith. It may happen, however, that a union or division of states renders a past obligation of treaty impossible, or inconsistent with present relations. Thus suppose that Scotland before its union with England had engaged to furnish France with a contingent of troops. This engagement would hardly be thought binding after the union; much less would one be binding, which contemplated an alliance against the very country with which a union now subsisted. It may be said, indeed, that the prior engagement forbade the forming of a new engagement inconsistent with it. This is, indeed, a rule of right, but not a rule which is valid against important state necessity. There is another extreme case, again, where a change of government may dissolve prior obligations. It is where a despotical or usurping government has contracted debts or made treaties against a nation attempting to recover its liberties. The government is *de facto* in possession of authority, and thus its acts are lawful; nevertheless obligations entered into to subjugate the people must be regarded in this extreme case as pertaining to the government alone, and not as resting on the people. (Comp. § 145.)*

* There is a distinction between the sovereignty of a state and that of a prince. The latter is only representative,—a mode of exercising the power of the former. If now the prince is only in form, and not really, the representative of the state, his acts in extreme cases can be repudiated.

§ 39.

All forms of governments legitimate in the eye of intern. law.

A state may sustain relations to other states, and perform its offices generally under any form of government. The law of nations preserves an entire indifference to constitutions, so long as they do not prevent fulfilment of obligations. Every state is in its eye legitimate. And in matter of fact the countries which profess to be bound by the Christian or European law of nations, differ exceedingly from one another in their constitutions, which contain specimens of absolute and constitutional hereditary monarchy, of confederated democracies, and of an elective ecclesiastical principality.

§ 40.

Intern. law knows only governments de facto.

Hence it follows that if a state has altered its form of government, or by some revolution, peaceable or violent, has suffered a disruption, or has become united with another, all these things are beyond the province of international law, whose only inquiry is, whether a certain community or organization is in matter of fact a separate independent existence, discharging the functions of a state, and able to take upon itself state responsibilities. The question of a state's right to exist is an *internal* one, to be decided by those within its borders who belong to its organization. To bring the question before external powers, not only destroys sovereignty, but must either produce perpetual war, or bring on the despotism of some one strong nation or strong confederacy of nations, requiring all others to conform their constitutions to the will of these tyrants. Moreover, it is a question outside of the law of nations, which presupposes the fact that nations exist and have rights, and therefore cannot first inquire into their right to exist. On the other hand, the fact of the existence of a state is in general an open one, easy to be judged of, one which involves no decision in regard to the advantages of one form of government over another, and the only fact which nations need to know, in order that they may enter into and fulfil reciprocal obligations.

With these principles the practice of nations on the whole, and in the long run, agrees. All in the end acknowledge the government *de facto*. Of course, nations which dread revolution will be more slow to allow the title of a revolutionary government, or of one where a family of princes of the same blood, or who have been long allies, are driven from the throne; but they must submit at last to the inexorable facts of divine Providence and history. And if this rule could be overthrown, if a nation or set of nations should act on the plan of withholding their sanction from new nations with certain constitutions, such a plan would justify others who thought differently in refusing to regard the former any longer as legitimate states.

All history is full of examples of such recognitions. Holland and Switzerland, long after their independence was acknowledged in the diplomacy of most European states, were formally admitted into the brotherhood of nations at the era of the peace of Westphalia. The United States, the Spanish states of South America, the two French empires, the kingdom of Greece, all arose from revolutions, and have been acknowledged to possess the full functions of states. Such, too, has been the case in regard to states which have changed the succession, as England in 1688, Sweden in 1818, and also where a disruption has taken place, as that between Holland and Belgium in 1830; nay, such iniquities as the partitions of Poland have become facts of history, into which the law of nations claims no right to look.

It is almost needless to say that this rule cannot have its application, as long as there is evident doubt whether a government is a *fact*. If the question is still one of armed strife, as between a colony and a mother country, or between a state and a revolted portion of it, to take the part of the colony or of the revolted territory by recognition is an injury and may be a ground of war; but every nation must decide for itself whether an independent state be really established, and needs not to wait until the party opposing the revolutionary effort has accepted the new order of things. It is a safe rule in contests involving the violent separation of a state into parts, that when the mother country, in the case of a colony, or the leading portion of the state, in the case of disruption, gives up active efforts to restore the old order of things by war, other states may regard the revolution as perfected, and a new state as having come into the world.

§ 41.

Assistance to provinces, etc. in revolt.

No state is authorized to render assistance to provinces or colonies which are in revolt against the established government. For if the existence and sovereignty of a state is once acknowledged, nothing can be done to impair them; and if the right of interference,—in favor of liberty, for instance,—be once admitted, the door is open for taking a part in every quarrel.

On the other hand, there is nothing in the law of nations which forbids one nation to render assistance to the established government in such case of revolt, if its assistance is invoked. This aid is no interference, and is given to keep up the present order of things, which international law takes under its protection. It may be said that this rule, together with the unlawfulness of taking the side of a revolutionary party in another state, must prevent wholesome reforms, that the partizans of despotism may thus use their power against free institutions, while the partizans of the latter may not oppose despotism. That this effect may follow is quite possible; still the rule is an impartial one, as it applies to any existing state, whether free or absolute, to attempts against existing liberty as well as against existing tyranny. The only other conceivable rules of action for states are, that in internal quarrels every foreign state may take which side it pleases, or that no state may assist either party. The former course of action will find no advocates; the other, which the law of nations cannot be expected,—for the present, at least,—to recognize, must indeed prevent some revolutions from being undertaken, but cannot prevent a change of government when demanded by a nation's united voice.

§ 42.

The rule of non-interference in the affairs of other states is then an established principle. But the exceptions to it which are admitted, or which are claimed to exist, are of great importance, and there is considerable difficulty in determining what is lawful interference and what is unlawful. For, first, there may be interference without a show or pretence of justice. In the second place, a nation which has or pretends to have causes of war with another, aids its revolted provinces in the exercise of the war-right of crippling its enemy. In the third place, there are instances of interference which can be explained neither on the ground of injustice, nor of a state of war, and which the usage of Christian or of many Christian states tolerates.

Exceptions to rule of non-interference.

Whatever be the interference, it can be justified only as an extreme measure, and on one of the two following grounds. (1.) That it is demanded by self-preservation; (2.) That some extraordinary state of things is brought about by the crime of a government against its subjects. And upon these grounds we must judge, not only of the lawfulness of interference at any time *pro re natâ*, but also of the lawfulness of treaties contemplating such interference in the future.* From the nature of these grounds it appears that they are more or less vague and under the influence of subjective opinion. The danger to a state's existence from the designs of another, or of others, evidently cannot be measured. While on the one hand mere suspicion, or calculation of remote probabilities, can be no justifying cause of action; on the other, it is hard to say, just as in cases of individual morality, how much evidence is sufficient to sanction that procedure, which in ordinary times is unlawful. Thus much may be laid down, that a danger resulting from the healthy and prudent growth of

Interference when justified.

* If the principles of intervention cannot stand, treaties of guaranty, which contemplate such intervention, must be condemned also; for they have in view a resistance, at some future time, to the endeavors of third parties to conquer or in some way control the guaranteed states in question. An agreement, if it involve an unlawful act, or the prevention of lawful acts on the part of others, is plainly unlawful.

another state is no reason for interference whatever, and that good evidence of unjust designs, drawn from conduct, ought to be obtained before any measures may be taken to prevent them.

The extreme case of extraordinary crimes, committed by a government against its subjects, is still less capable of exact definition. Here, however, the danger of erring is less than in the other instance, because interference here is more disinterested; and the evil results of a mistake are less, because such cases are comparatively rare.

§ 43.

Having premised thus much in regard to justifying pretexts for interference, let us look now at the actual cases in which international law gives, or is claimed to give to it a sanction We shall consider first the balance of power.

1. Interference for the balance of power.

To prevent acquisitions.

The meaning of the balance of power is this: that any European state may be restrained from pursuing plans of acquisition, or making preparations looking towards future acquisitions, which are judged to be hazardous to the independence and national existence of its neighbors. In further explanation of the system we may say, (1.) That it matters not whether the actual ratio of power between states is in danger of being disturbed by unjust or by just means, provided only the means are political, not economical and strictly internal. If, for instance, the sovereign of a powerful state should in a just way seat one of his family on the throne of a neighboring state, the justice of the transaction would not be a sufficient protection against the interference of other powers. (2.) That acquisitions outside of Europe have not hitherto been drawn into this policy. England has by degrees become a predominant power in several quarters of the world without provoking the interference of the Continent. The reason is, that foreign acquisitions affect the political balance only in an indirect way. (3.) The system has been applied to power on the land, and not much to power on the sea. England has acquired, undisturbed, a great predominance on the sea, while the balance of power has been in full exercise. The reason is obvious. Power on the sea cannot directly control the political relations of Europe, nor destroy the independence of states. (4.) The system has not yet been carried out beyond the borders of the European states, Turkey included. The reason is, that the transatlantic states have not only come at a recent period into the European international system, but can, as yet, have no appreciable influence in European affairs.

The balance of power is a maxim of self-preservation, which must naturally arise among states which are so contiguous to one another as to be liable to sudden invasions. Suppose a confederacy of states, having free power of war and peace, and that the terms of union guaranteed to each state an independent existence. In such a league, if one strong member threatened the existence of weaker ones, it would be the duty of all to interfere. Europe resembles such a confederacy, and the balance of power is the guaranty of national existence against the designs of states of the first rank. Let the members of such a loose union be removed many thousand miles from one another by tracts of ocean. The self-preserving principle now apprehends no danger, and a system of balances is useless.

§ 44.

Historical illustrations.

The maintenance of a certain balance of power, as a fact, if not as a right, characterized the politics of Greece. The Peloponnesian war was really owing, says Thucydides (I. 23), to the alarm which the growth of Athens excited in the confederates, at the head of whom was Sparta. When at the end of that war Athens was subdued, Thebes and Corinth desired its destruction; but the Spartans justly regarded its existence as necessary in the politics of Greece. Subsequently, Athens, when Thebes was beginning to be too powerful, went over to the side of Sparta, her old enemy.

In the middle ages a system of equipoise in Italy was put into motion by the Popes, as soon as the German emperors became strong in the Peninsula. The Pope's policy was to have two Italian interests which could be set against one another, at the pleasure of the Roman See, which thus secured its own safety and influence. But a nearer approach to the modern balance of power is seen in the Italian affairs consequent upon the claims of the French kings, Charles VIII. and Louis XII. to Naples and Milan, from 1494 onward. The dangers from the French invasion under Charles, led Spain, the Pope and Venice to combine against him. Then, in 1508, the league of Cambray united all the powers involved in the Italian quarrels against Venice for her destruction. Then, in 1510, the Pope fearing that the ruin of Venice would leave Italy exposed to France, formed the Holy League to drive this latter power out of the Peninsula. It must be confessed, however, that the league of Cambray against Venice was dictated by motives much more unworthy than those of self-preservation, and had less to do with maintaining the integrity of Italy than with rapacity and revenge.

Not long after this the Austrian family, in two lines, held Spain and the German Empire with other important territorial possessions, and the great resources of these allied houses seemed to be dangerous to the European system. France now was the weight in the opposite scale. The unaccomplished schemes of king Henry IV. were carried out by Richelieu, when he aided the German protestants and Sweden against Austria; and the peace of Westphalia in 1648, prevented, thenceforward, this state, holding as it did the office of Emperor in its hands, from becoming formidable either to Europe or to Germany.

It was now the turn of France to feel the force of the balance of power. The ambition of Louis XIV. was thought to endanger the existence of other European states, and a universal monarchy seemed to be at hand. The coalitions of nearly all Europe, which resisted and finally humbled the Grand Monarch, are among the most righteous examples of measures for preserving the balance of power which history records. Some of the measures, however, which were adopted for the preservation of the balance at this time, were of doubtful justice and policy. It was right to set bounds to the ambition of Louis XIV.; it was right, when his intrigues procured the nomination of his grandson to a throne which had been solemnly renounced for his posterity, to endeavor to prevent, by force of arms, this accumulation of power in the Bourbon line; but what justice was there in the two partition treaties of 1698 and 1700, which disposed of territories appertaining to the Spanish Crown, without asking leave of the king or nation; and was not this high-handed measure a failure in policy, as calculated to offend the pride of Spain? Since the time when the balance of power played such a part in the days of Louis and William of Orange, it has been repeatedly acted on, and may be said to be an established part of the international law of Europe. The most memorable instances of its application in recent times, have been the interposition of the four powers in 1840, which forced Mehemet Ali to renounce the provinces of the Turkish empire, of which he held possession, and that of France and England in 1854, to preserve the integrity of the same empire against the designs of Russia.

§ 45.

2. Interference to prevent revolutions.

We have already seen that where one nation's aid is invoked by the government of another for the purpose of putting down a revolt, such assistance is not opposed by the law of nations. Should it be given in the spirit of hostility to free institutions, the motive lies beyond the ordinary sphere of this science. But a part of the European powers have attempted to establish a right of interference to put down revolutionary principles in that continent, whether their aid be called for or not. This principle has been avowed, if we mistake not, only since the French revolution; for only since then has absolutism become conscious of its dangers, and of the hatred felt towards it by multitudes of persons scattered through the nations. The plea is, as in the case of the balance of power, one of self-preservation. The stability of all governments, it is alleged, and of all institutions sustained by governments, is threatened by the propagandists of liberty, and even the dread of revolution so greatly paralyzes the energies of states, that everything must be done to make it as remote as possible. It is admitted that no interference undertaken for the direct purpose of spreading absolute principles, or absolutism itself, or even for that of crushing free principles, or of overturning settled governments or constitutions set up in an illegitimate way, is to be justified; but it is claimed that revolutions in modern times have been sources of incredible evils, and that the so called right of a people to alter its government by force, is calculated to bring upon Europe eternal commotion and insecurity.

§ 46.

Instances of interference for or against revolutions.

While the French revolution was in progress * some of the leading powers of Europe had shown a disposition to interfere in the affairs of France, partly on the ground that former treaties had been violated, and partly because the king and royal family of France were restrained of their liberty and treated with dishonor. A circular of the emperor of Germany, of July 6, 1791, invited the principal powers of Europe to declare to the French nation, among other things, that the sovereigns "would unite to avenge any further offences against the liberty, the honor and safety of the king and his family; that they would consider as constitutional laws only those to which the king should have given his free assent; and that they would employ every means of terminating the scandal of a usurpation founded on rebellion, and of which the example was dangerous to every government." On the 27th of August, in the same year, the same sovereign, with the king of Prussia, signed a declaration to the same effect, in which they invited the monarchs of Europe to unite with them in using "the most efficacious means to put the king of France in a state to enable him with perfect freedom to lay the foundation of a monarchical government,

* Comp. Wheaton's Hist. p. 347, et seq., and his El. II. 1, 102–109, which I have freely used.

equally consistent with the rights of sovereigns and the welfare of the French nation; in which case they were resolved to act promptly and with necessary forces to obtain the proposed common object. In the meantime they would give the necessary orders to hold their troops in readiness to take the field." *

Louis having accepted the new constitution on the 13th of September, 1791, and announced to foreign powers his intention of supporting it, there was no pretext of a restraint upon the king's liberty for an armed intervention in the affairs of France. But unsettled questions in dispute continued, and at length, on the 7th of April, 1792, the Austrian ultimatum demanded, together with the restoration of the Venaissin to the Pope, and of their possessions and privileges in Alsace to the princes of the Empire, the re-establishment of the French monarchy on the basis of the French king's declaration of the 23d of June, 1789. This necessarily led to the decree in the national assembly that France was in a state of war with Austria. The king of Prussia, on the 26th of June of the same year, 1792, announced to the world the reasons which induced him, in conjunction with Austria, to take up arms against France. Among them we mention "the propagation of principles subversive of social order, which had thrown France into a state of confusion;" and "the encouragement and even official publication of writings the most offensive against the sacred persons and lawful authority of sovereigns. To suppress anarchy in France; to re-establish for this purpose a lawful power on the essential basis of a monarchical form; and by these means to secure other governments against the criminal and incendiary efforts of madmen,—such the king declared to be the great objects of himself and his ally."

The declaration of Austria drew forth at once a counter-statement from the national assembly drawn up by Condorcet, which, among other things, claimed for every nation the exclusive right of making and changing its laws; denied that France had threatened the general tranquillity, seeing she had re-

* Wheaton's Hist. p. 346, seq. The passages in quotations are borrowed from that work through this paragraph.

nounced all designs of conquest; declared that the avowal of the doctrine of the sovereignty of the people, which the nation had made, could not be regarded as disturbing the peace of other states; and rebutted the charge that Frenchmen had excited other nations to insurrection; whilst, on the other hand, emigrants from France had received aid and encouragement from those who brought these complaints, and attempts had been made to excite civil war in France. Such complaints were unreasonable "unless it were lawful to extend servitude and unlawful to propagate liberty; unless everything be permitted against the people, and kings alone have rights."

England could not, in consistency with the historical development of its own institutions by means of a revolution, adopt the principles on which the continental powers declared war against France. An attitude, however, far from friendly, was observed towards that country, and, among the causes of complaint, one was the encouragement given to revolt in other countries, not only by emissaries sent to England, but by a decree of the convention, which was said to express the design of extending French principles and of promoting revolutions in all countries, even those which were neutral. At length, on the death of Louis, in the beginning of 1793, the French ambassador was ordered to leave the kingdom. A state of war ensued, during which Mr. Pitt declared that there had been no intention, if the country had not been attacked, to interfere in the internal affairs of France. But, no doubt, the atrocities in the summer of 1793, and the closing tragedy of the king's execution, were motives, if not pretexts of hostility. Nor can there be much doubt that the interference of the European powers, above spoken of, produced, or at least intensified, those atrocities, by arousing the national feeling of the French, by exciting distrust of the king's good faith, and by making it apparent that no terms could be kept with the sovereigns.

Holy Alliance, Sept. 26, 1815.

The revolution had its course. The interference was avenged, and the parties to it were humbled. But at length France, which destroyed the independence of half of Europe, lost its own, the empire fell, and the old Bourbon dynasty was restored. During the occupation of Paris, consequent on the battle of Waterloo, the three rulers of Russia, Austria, and Prussia, joined afterwards by the French king, formed the Holy Alliance, which has been regarded as a league of absolutism against the rights and the freedom of the nations. This famous league, however, at its inception, appears to have had no definite object in view. It was a measure into which the other sovereigns entered, in order to gratify the emperor Alexander, whose romantic mind, then under the influence of Madame Krudener, contemplated a golden age, in which the intercourse of nations should be controlled by Christian principles. The parties to the Holy Alliance bound themselves, appealing to the Holy Trinity, to exercise their power according to the principles of religion, justice, and humanity; to afford one another on all occasions aid and help; to treat their subjects and soldiers with paternal feeling, and to regard their people as members of a great Christian family, whose guidance was entrusted to them by God.*

Congress of Aix-la-Chapelle, Sept. 29, 1818.

The congress of Aix-la-Chapelle, at which the five great powers were represented, and which removed the army of occupation from the French fortresses, effected an alliance almost as vague as the Holy Alliance, which, according to some of the parties to it, was intended to exercise a supervisory power over European affairs, interfering to prevent all dangerous revolutions, especially when they should proceed from popular movements. They declared, however, their intention to observe scrupulously the law of nations. "The sovereigns have regarded," say they, "as the fundamental basis, their invariable resolution never to depart either among themselves or in their relations with other states, from the strictest observance of the law of nations,—principles, which, in their application to a state of permanent peace, are alone able to give an effectual guaranty to the independence of each government, and to the stability of their general association."

* The whole compact is given by Mr. Manning in an English version, pp. 82–84.

The unmeaning nature of such declarations was shown not long afterwards by acts of interference, undertaken against the consent of one European power, and certainly not accordant with a rigorous view of the law of nations. A feeling of discontent with the anti-liberal movements of most of the continental powers had been growing in intensity in many parts of Europe, when, in 1820 and 1821, revolutions broke out in rapid succession in Spain, Naples, and Sardinia, and the constitution of Cadiz, of the year 1812, was proclaimed in all the three kingdoms. The alarm excited by the revolutionary spirit was the occasion of convoking a congress at Troppau in Silesia, in October, 1820, which was removed near the end of the same year to Laybach in Styria, and at which not only the five great powers were represented by their sovereigns or by ambassadors, but the king of Naples and deputations from small powers appeared. Against the proposed intervention in the affairs of Italy the British government protested in strong terms, although the existing ministry were not averse to the suppression of revolutionary liberalism; while, on the other hand, the French government approved openly of the intervention, in order to gratify the ultra-royalist party at home, but secretly dreaded the Austrian influence which such a measure would increase. Austria, thus supported, sent an army into the Peninsula, overthrew the revolution almost without a blow in the spring of 1821, and brought back the old absolutism in all its rigor.

Congress of Troppau — Laybach, Oct. 28, 1820, and onwards.

The circular despatch of the sovereigns of Austria, Russia, and Prussia, justified these measures by alleging "that there existed a vast conspiracy against all established power, and against all the rights consecrated by that social order under which Europe had enjoyed so many centuries of glory and happiness; that they regarded as disavowed by the principles which constitute the public right of Europe all pretended reform operated by revolt and open hostility;" that they opposed a "fanaticism for innovation, which would spread the horror of universal anarchy over the civilized world; that they were far from wishing to prolong this interference beyond the limits of strict necessity, and would ever prescribe to themselves the preservation of the independence and of the rights of each state." On the other hand, the British government, while it acknowledged the right to interfere, where the "immediate security or essential interests" of one state are seriously endangered by another, denied that "this right could receive a general and indiscriminate application to all revolutionary governments." Such interference was an exception, and "could not, without the utmost danger, be incorporated into the ordinary diplomacy of states, or into the institutes of the law of nations." *

Soon after this, in the middle of 1821, a royalist insurrection occurred in northern Spain, to which France so far extended aid as to allow the insurgents to gather along the borders, to retreat in case of need across the line, and to make open preparation of arms and money on French soil. A congress had been arranged to meet at Verona when that of Laybach broke up. The principal measure here agitated was armed interference in the affairs of Spain, which, if undertaken, would naturally be the work of France. The British envoy, the Duke of Wellington, not only declared the refusal of his government to participate in any such proceeding, but also that England would not even attempt to persuade Spain to conform to the views of the congress. The French envoys, Montmorency and Chateaubriand, against express instruction of their court, urged forward the intervention, which was supported by the other powers, and energetically by Russia, which power at Laybach had hung back from decisive movements by force of arms. The envoys acted herein in the interest of the ultra-royalist party, which was thus able to carry its measures through. For a French army occupied Spain, penetrated as far as Cadiz, overthrew the constitution of Cadiz to which the king had given his assent, and left him "free," but the country enslaved. No stretch of interference had gone so far as this, for Spain would have had a settled constitutional

Congress of Verona, Oct. 1822.

* Circular despatch of the sovereigns, etc., Laybach, May, 1821, and Lord Castlereagh's circular despatch of January 19th, 1821.

government, and probably settled peace, unless the agitators had looked for aid to foreign power.

§ 47.

3. Monroe doctrine.

The proceedings at Verona indirectly gave rise to what has been called the Monroe doctrine,* which met the reigning principle of interference in Europe by a similar principle in the opposite direction. The history of this doctrine is, in brief, the following. At Verona the subject was agitated of attempting, in conformity with the known wishes of the absolutists in Spain, to bring back the Spanish colonies into subjection to the mother country. This fact having been communicated to our government by that of Great Britain in 1823, and the importance of some public protest on our part being insisted upon, President Monroe, in his annual message, used the following language: "That we should consider any attempt on the part (of the allied powers,) to extend their system to any portion of this hemisphere as dangerous to our peace and safety," and again, "that we could not view any interposition for the purpose of oppressing (governments on this side of the Atlantic whose independence we had acknowledged,) or controlling in any manner their destiny by any European power, in any other light than as a manifestation of an unfriendly disposition towards the United States." Soon afterwards a resolution was moved in Congress, embodying the same principle, but was never called up. But the mere declaration of the President, meeting with the full sympathy of England, put an end to the designs to which the message refers.

In another place of the same message, while alluding to the question of boundary on the Pacific between the United States and Russia, the President speaks thus: "The occasion has been judged proper for asserting as a principle, in which the rights and interests of the United States are involved, that the American continents, by the free and independent condition

* Comp. especially the North American Review for April, 1856, and Mr. Calhoun's speech in the Senate on the proposed occupation of Yucatan, May 15, 1848.

which they have assumed and maintain, are henceforth not to be considered as subjects for future colonization by any European power." Was it intended by this to preclude the South American republics, without their will, from receiving such colonies within their borders—of surrendering their territory for that purpose? Such a thing, probably, was not thought of. Mr. Adams, when President in 1825, thus refers to Mr. Monroe's principle, while speaking in a special message of a congress at Panama. "An agreement between all the parties represented at the meeting, that each will guard *by its own means* against the establishment of any future European colony within its borders, may be found desirable. This was more than two years since announced by my predecessor to the world, as a principle resulting from the emancipation of both the American continents." Mr. Adams, when Secretary of State under Mr. Monroe, originated the "principle," and must have known what he meant. But the principle, even in this tame form, was repudiated by the house of representatives, in a resolution declaring that the United States "ought not to become parties" with any of the South American republics "to any joint declaration for the purpose of preventing the interference of any of the European powers with their independence or form of government; or to any compact for the purpose of preventing colonization upon the continent of America."

On the whole then, (1.) the doctrine is not a national one. The house of representatives, indeed, had no right to settle questions of policy or of international law. But the Cabinet has as little. The opinion of one part of the government neutralized that of another. (2.) The principle first mentioned of resisting attempts to overthrow the liberties of the Spanish republics, was one of most righteous self-defence, and of vital importance. And such it will probably always be regarded, if a similar juncture should arise. But the other principle of prohibiting European colonization was vague, and if intended to prevent Russia from stretching her borders on the Pacific further to the south, went far beyond any limit of interference that has hitherto been set up. What right had the United

States to control Russia in gaining territory on the Pacific, or planting colonies there, when she had neither territory nor colony to be endangered, within thousands of miles?

The Monroe doctrine came up again in another shape in 1848. President Polk having announced that the government of Yucatan had offered the dominion over that country to Great Britain, Spain, and the United States, urges on Congress such measures as may prevent it from becoming a colony and a part of the dominions of any European power, which would be, he says, in contravention of the declaration of Mr. Monroe, and which must by no means be allowed. Mr. Calhoun, in his speech on this subject, shows that the case is very different from that contemplated by Mr. Monroe, that the declarations of the latter could not be regarded as expressing the settled policy of this country, and that they were mere declarations without threat of resistance. The "colonization" contemplated by the Monroe doctrine could not apply to Yucatan, and the possibility of England (which was especially intended) acquiring power there was remote. The principle, he adds, "which lies at the bottom of the (President's) recommendation is, that when any power on this continent becomes involved in internal warfare, and the weaker side chooses to make application to us for support, we are bound to give them support, for fear the offer of the sovereignty of the country may be made to some other power and accepted. It goes infinitely and dangerously beyond Mr. Monroe's declaration. It puts it in the power of other countries on this continent to make us a party to all their wars."

To lay down the principle that the acquisition of territory on this continent, by any European power, cannot be allowed by the United States, would go far beyond any measures dictated by the system of the balance of power, for the rule of self-preservation is not applicable in our case: we fear no neighbors. To lay down the principle that no political systems unlike our own, no change from republican forms to those of monarchy, can be endured in the Americas, would be a step in advance of the congresses at Laybach and Verona, for they apprehended destruction to their political fabrics, and we do not. But to resist attempts of European powers to alter the constitutions of states on this side of the water, is a wise and just opposition to interference. Anything beyond this justifies the system which absolute governments have initiated for the suppression of revolutions by main force.

§ 48.

Results of attempt to set up a law of interference in the internal affairs of states.

The attempts to introduce into the European law of nations a right of interference in the internal affairs of other states, have come to the following results: (1.) England has constantly protested against such a principle, and has been scrupulous in placing her interventions on other grounds. When, in 1826, the government of that country, in accordance with ancient treaties, and on application, sent troops to Portugal to sustain the regency there against the pretensions of Don Miguel, it was declared that nothing would be done to enforce the establishment of the constitution, but that others would be resisted in their attempts to overturn it. At that time it was said by Mr. Canning, in the house of Commons, that France had given to Great Britain cause of war by her violation, in 1823, of the independence of Spain. (2.) The principle has been applied only in the case of weaker nations; while the two French revolutions of 1830 and 1848 were allowed to take their course, and the revolutionary governments were soon acknowledged. (3.) France cannot, without gross inconsistency, accede to this principle. (4.) The principle, carried out, must bring Christian states into conflict; for the right of interfering in favor of liberty can be urged even on the ground of self-preservation, as well as that of interfering to put down popular movements; and all free and despotical institutions are dangerous to one another's existence. If the powers of Europe had been equally divided between constitutionalism and despotism, such a principle would not have been avowed, for it might work both ways. Its avowal, therefore, can be ascribed only to the consciousness of superior might. (5.) The interference, as it cannot prevent the moral and intellectual causes of revolution, only by delay embitters and fanaticizes its spirit. It leaves the payment of a debt at compound interest to posterity.

§ 49.

4. Interference in the Belgic revolution of 1830.

The interference of the five great powers in the affairs of the Netherlands has some peculiar characteristics of its own. First, the kingdom had been constituted at the Congress of Vienna, out of Holland, Belgium, and certain neighboring duchies, as a kind of barrier between France and Germany. Fifteen years afterwards, on the outbreak of the July revolution in France, Belgium separated violently from the rest of the Netherlands, and it became evident that two such heterogeneous parts could not be welded together. The king of the Netherlands invoked the mediation of the five powers, who first procured an armistice between the parties, then in the character of unauthorized arbitrators laid down the terms of separation, and finally forced a compliance. The views that governed in the long negotiations, which finally lent the sanction of Europe to this divorce, are given at length by Dr. Wheaton in his History of the Law of Nations, and are a most instructive chapter. Belgium acquired its independence with the rights and obligations of perpetual neutrality; a French prince was prevented from occupying its throne; the Scheldt, with other streams and canals common to Belgium and Holland, was to remain free; Antwerp, as by the terms of the peace of Paris in 1814, was to be a port without fortifications, and the territory of the new kingdom was confined within narrow bounds, because it was born in a revolution. Thus there was "a compromise in this case between the two principles which had so long menaced, by their apprehended collision, the established order and the general peace of Europe." Doubtless, if France itself had not just before asserted the right of revolution, the interference here would have been directed to the point of healing the schism in the Netherlands by main force.

§ 50.

Interference on the score of humanity or of religion can be justified only by the extreme circumstances of the case. In the age which succeeded the reformation, both self-preservation and religious sympathies induced the Protestant states to aid one another against the superior might of the Catholic, and to aid the votaries of their faith within Catholic countries, in order to secure for them freedom of worship. Elizabeth of England sent aid to the revolted Hollanders on religious grounds, and Cromwell's threats slackened the persecution of the Waldenses by the Duke of Savoy. In modern times, the interference of Great Britain, France, and Russia, on behalf of the Greeks, in 1827, was avowedly dictated by motives of humanity. The Greeks, after a bloody contest, had so far achieved their independence, that the Sultan could not reduce them. Accordingly his vassal, Mehemed Ali, of Egypt, was allured to send an army of subjugation into the Morea, and the atrocious scenes of fanatical war were renewed. The Greeks applied to France and England for help or mediation. At length, in consequence of the battle of Navarino, Oct. 20th, 1827, and the French occupation of the Morea, the Peninsula was evacuated by Mohammedan troops, and finally the independence of Greece was acknowledged. Dr. Wheaton says of these events* that the Christian powers were eminently justified in their interference "to rescue a whole nation not merely from religious persecution, but from the cruel alternative of being transported from their native land into Egyptian bondage, or exterminated by their merciless oppressors. The rights of human nature—wantonly outraged by this cruel warfare—were but tardily and imperfectly vindicated by this measure, but its principle was fully justified by the great paramount law of self-preservation. 'Whatever a nation may lawfully defend for itself, it may defend for another if called on to interpose.' The interference of the Christian powers to put an end to this bloody contest,

5. Interference on the score of religion and of humanity.

* Elements, Part II., Chapter 1, § 10.

might therefore have been safely rested on this ground alone, without appealing to the interests of commerce and of the repose of Europe, which, as well as the interests of humanity, are alluded to in the treaty, (for the pacification of Greece, July 6th, 1827,) as the determining motives of the high contracting parties."

EQUALITY OF SOVEREIGN STATES.

§ 51.

Equality.

We have already explained equality to denote equality of rights. All sovereign states stand on the same level in this respect,—the old and the new, large and small, monarchies and republics,—for the conception of a state to be applied to all is the same, and their sovereignty is the same. This, however, is not incompatible with special privileges of a commercial nature granted to one nation before another, or to superior rank in the ceremonial of courts.

Rank of nations.

Formerly the most punctilious rules of etiquette were observed at most of the courts of Europe. Gustavus Adolphus, who said that all crowned heads were equal, was one of the first to despise pretensions of superiority. Rules are necessary to prevent ambassadors and their wives from contending for precedence, or feeling that an insult has been offered to them or their country. But with all the nicety of court etiquette, such quarrels have frequently taken place. Among the most noted of these disputes, was one of long continuance between the ambassadors of France and Spain.* The place of France, until the sixteenth century, according to the ceremonial of the Romish See, had been next to that of the German emperor, but, as Charles V. was both emperor and king of Spain, his successor on the Spanish throne claimed precedence of other kings, and thus brought on a collision. At the Council of Trent the dispute rose to such a point

* See Ward's Hist., II. 272, seq. (Dublin Ed.)

that the French declared that they would renounce obedience to the Pope, if deprived of their place, and it was only settled by allowing the Frenchman to continue in his seat next to the Legate who presided, and the Spaniard to occupy a seat of eminence opposite to him. The most serious outbreak, however, of this rivalry occurred at London in 1661, when, according to the usage of the time, the ambassadors went in procession to meet a newly arrived ambassador from Sweden. The ministers of both nations appeared with an armed retinue. As the Frenchman attempted to put his carriage next to that of the English king, the Spaniards raised a shout, scared the horses, and occupied the place. The French then fired upon them, and received back their fire, so that eight were killed and forty wounded in the encounter; but the Spaniards, having during the melée cut the hamstrings of the French horses, were able to secure the coveted precedence. Louis XIV. threatened war for this outrage, and thus forced the Spaniards into a declaration that their ambassador should never be present at ceremonies where a contest for rank could arise between them and the French.

According to the old rules of Europe, the Pope (whom Protestant nations and Russia regard as only an Italian sovereign) ranked highest in dignity, the German emperor next, monarchies before republics, sovereigns before half-sovereigns, and princes of inferior name closed the list. The following order of rank emanated from the Roman court in 1504: the Roman emperor, king of Rome, king of France, of Spain, Arragon, Portugal, England, Sicily, Scotland, Hungary, Navarre, Cyprus, Bohemia, Poland, Denmark (with which Sweden and Norway were then united), the Venetian republic, the duke of Brittany, Burgundy, Electors of Bavaria, Saxony, Brandenburg, archduke of Austria, duke of Savoy, grand duke of Florence, dukes of Milan, Bavaria, Lorraine, etc.*

Existing rules of rank.

The rules now acted upon in regard to the rank of different states and of their sovereigns are, according to Heffter, the following:

* Heffter, § 28, p. 49. Comp. Suppl. to Dumont V. 202.

1. States to which, for themselves or for their sovereigns, royal honors pertain, have an external rank before those to which these honors do not belong. Such honors are the right of sending ambassadors of the first class, the use of the royal title, crown and corresponding arms, and certain other ceremonial usages. To this rank belong emperors, kings, grand dukes, the elector of Hesse, the Swiss republic, the United States of America, the German confederation.

2. Among states of the same class entire equality of rights obtains, but the rule of precedence, in regard to rank, is settled by treaty and usage. Kings and emperors have a general equality, as is indicated by the fact that the former frequently connect the latter title with that which they are especially known by. A precedence is given to kings and emperors before sovereigns who have inferior titles, and before republics, "whose special relation of rank to other states with royal honors is not definitely fixed." * There is a certain order of the German states in relation to affairs of the confederation, and to this alone. Half-sovereign and protected states rank after those on which they depend. Treaties by which one state concedes the precedence to another over a third, without its consent, are of no obligation upon the latter, and may contain a violation of the respect which is its due.

The rank which a state has once obtained is usually not lost by a change of constitution.

These distinctions fading out.

The tendency of things is, as far as possible, towards entire equality of states. Thus commercial privileges are fast disappearing, and new treaties to a great extent concede the advantages given to the most favored nations. The precedence of ambassadors of the same rank is determined simply by length of residence at the court. And special tokens of respect to one nation more than to another, like those claimed by England in certain narrow seas, have nearly gone out of use.

* Heffter, § 28, p. 50.

CHAPTER II.

TERRITORIAL RIGHTS OF STATES AND RIGHTS OF PROPERTY.—STRICT RIGHT RENOUNCED, ESPECIALLY AS TO THE USE OF NAVIGABLE WATERS.

§ 52.

A NATION is an organized community within *a certain territory;* or in other words, there must be a place where its sole sovereignty is exercised. It may, also, and will have property of its own, like individuals and associations: it may even hold such property within the borders of other states, may be the creditor of foreign states or individuals, or, unless the law of a state prohibit, may possess land there on the tenure of private ownership. Upon the property of its subjects, again, it has a certain lien, as appears from the power to lay taxes and the power to use private property for public purposes. But the right of *eminent domain* with which such power over private property is connected, does not imply that such property is absolutely under the control of the state, or that the state was the prior owner, and conveyed it to the individual under conditions; but the right is rather to be considered as one of necessity, without which, at times, public affairs could not move on, nor the rights of many individuals be protected. Now, although the relations of the state to its territory, to its property and to the property of individuals are different, yet as far as other nations are concerned, they may all be included under the term property. "Such property of states," as Heffter well remarks, "has *only in relation to other states* the same character which property has, namely, the character of exclusiveness and free disposal," that is, of pertaining to the state to the exclusion of all other states, and of being disposed of without restraint on their part upon its will.

Property of states in intern. law, what?

A state's territorial right gives no power to the ruler to alienate a part of the territory in the way of barter or sale, as was done in feudal times. In other words the right is a public or political and not a personal one. Nor in justice can the state itself alienate a portion of its territory, without the consent of the inhabitants residing upon the same, and if, in treaties of cession, this is done after conquest, it is only the acknowledgment of an unavoidable fact. (Comp. § 153, and Grotius 11. 6. § 4.)

Property of a foreign state or sovereign within the bounds of a state involves no restriction of territorial sovereignty. Territorial servitudes, as right of free harbor, of transit, etc., may exist, but are *stricti juris*, the presumption being always in favor of sovereignty. (Comp. Bluntschli, Staatsr. 1. 189.)

§ 53.

Modes of acquiring territory.

The territory of a nation, or that portion of the earth over which it exercises the rights of sovereignty, may have begun to pertain to it in a variety of ways. It may have derived its title 1, from immemorial occupation of land which was before vacant.

2. From occupation by colonies, or other incorporation of land before occupied.

3. From conquest accepted as a fact and at length ending in prescriptive right.

4. From purchase or from gift.

Other claims more doubtful or less generally acknowledged, have been, (1.) that of Portugal, derived from a bull of pope Nicholas V. giving in 1454 to Alfonso V. the empire of Guinea, and the exclusive use of the African seas; as also the more noted bulls of Alexander VI. issued in 1493 soon after the return of Columbus from his first voyage,—the first granting to Spain all lands west of a north and south line drawn a hundred leagues west of the Azores, and the other dividing the occupation of the seas between Spain and Portugal. Such a claim of course would be good only against those who admitted the Pope's right thus to dispose of the world, which few or no Catholic states would now admit. (2.) The claim on the ground of discovery. This was both exceedingly vague,—for how much extent of coast or breadth of interior went with the discovery?—and was good only against those who acknowledged such right of discovery, but not against the natives. Of the natives, however, very little account was made. Being heathen, they were not, in the age succeeding the discovery of America, regarded as having rights, but might be subdued and stript of sovereignty over their country without compunction. And yet when the right to territory in the new world was in dispute, a title derived from them, it might be, to soil far beyond their haunts, would perhaps be pleaded against prior occupation. The English colonies, however, which settled in this country, took, to a considerable extent, the more just course of paying for the soil on which they established themselves, and the United States have acted steadily on the principle of extinguishing the Indian title by treaty and the payment of a price.

§ 54.

1. The territory of a state includes all that portion of terra firma which lies within the boundaries of the state, as well as the waters, that is, the interior seas, lakes and rivers *wholly* contained within the same lines. Thus the sea of Azof, the Volga, Lake Michigan, the Ohio, and the Sea of Marmora are exclusively in the territory respectively of Russia, the United States, and Turkey. It may happen that the boundaries of a state are not continuous, or that one part of it is separated from another, as the Rhine-provinces of Prussia are cut off by Hesse, etc., from the rest of the kingdom. Or it may happen that one sovereignty, or a portion of it, is included within the limits of another. This is the case more or less in Germany, and was formerly true of Avignon and the Venaissin, which were Papal territory enclosed (*enclaves* hence called) in France.

What is territory?

2. The mouths of rivers, bays, and estuaries, furnishing access to the land.

3. The sea-coast to the distance of a marine league. This is a regulation dictated by the necessities of self-protection, as is expressed in the maxim of Bynkershoek, "terræ potestas finitur, ubi finitur armorum vis." For the police of commerce the distance is extended to four leagues, that is, according to the usage prevailing in Great Britain and the United States, foreign goods cannot be transshipped within that distance without the payment of duties. The extent of sea-coast included within national territory has been variously defined. Bynkershoek, and others after him, limit it by the reach of cannon shot;—"quousque tormenta exploduntur." (De domin. mar. cap. 2, from which place the maxim above cited is taken.) Rayneval limits it by the horizon, a very vague and absurd suggestion; Valin, by the depth of the sea: territory should reach out (he would propose) to where there is no bottom. Modern writers, whether limiting it by a marine league, or by cannon shot, agree substantially in making it an incident to territorial sovereignty on the land. Comp. Ortolan, Diplom. de la mer. Vol. I, chap. 8. As the range of cannon is increasing, and their aim becoming more perfect, it might be thought that the sea line of territory ought to widen. But the point is not likely to become one of any great importance.

4. Vessels belonging to the citizens of the nation on the high seas, and public vessels, wherever found, have some of the attributes of territory.

In regard, however, to the territorial character of vessels it is necessary to be more definite, for if they have this property in some respects but not in all, only false and illogical deductions can be drawn from an unqualified statement. Is it true, then, that they are identical in their properties with territory? If a ship is confiscated on account of piracy or of violation of custom-house laws in a foreign port, or is there attached by the owner's creditor and becomes his property, we never think that territory has been taken away. For a crime committed in port a vessel may be chased into the high seas and there arrested, without a suspicion that territorial rights have been violated, while to chase a criminal across the borders and seize him on foreign soil is a gross offence against sovereignty. Again, a private vessel when it arrives in a foreign port, ceases to be regarded as territory, unless treaty provides otherwise, and then becomes merely the property of aliens. If injury is done to it, it is an injury which indirectly affects the sovereign of the alien, whereas injuries to territory, properly so called, affect the public power in an immediate manner. It is unsafe, then, to argue on the assumption that ships are altogether territory, as will appear, perhaps, when we come to consider the laws of maritime warfare. On the other hand, private ships have certain qualities resembling those of territory: (1.) As against their crews on the high seas; for the territorial or municipal law accompanies them as long as they are beyond the reach of other law, or until they come within the bounds of some other jurisdiction. (2.) As against foreigners, who are excluded on the high seas from any act of sovereignty over them, just as if they were a part of the soil of their country. Public vessels stand on higher ground: they are not only public property, built or bought by the government, but they are, as it were, floating barracks, a part of the public organism, and represent the national dignity, and on these accounts, even in foreign ports, are exempt from the local jurisdiction. In both cases, however, it is on account of the crew, rather than of the ship itself, that they have any territorial quality. Take the crew away, let the abandoned hulk be met at sea: it now becomes property, and nothing more.

§ 55.

Freedom of the high seas and of fishing there.

The high sea is free and open to all nations. It cannot be the property or the empire of a particular state. It cannot become *property*, for it cannot be possessed, or have any personal action exercised upon it, which must prevent a similar action of another. It cannot be mixed up with labor, or enclosed, or, like wild land, be waiting for any such future action. It can, as little, become the *empire* of any particular state. Otherwise one state might exclude others from it, and from that intercourse for which it is the pathway, which would be inconsistent with the equality and sovereignty of nations. Such empire could begin only in the consent of the whole world expressed by treaty, which was never given, or in prior discovery and use. But this last is no ground at all, and if it were, would work against the so-called discoverer in favor of the natives of newly found coasts. In fine, the destination of the sea is clearly for the common benefit of mankind; it is a common pathway, separating and yet binding, intended alike for all.

The liberty of the sea and of navigation is now admitted on all hands. But formerly the ocean, or portions of it, were claimed as a monopoly. Thus the Portuguese prohibited other nations from sailing in the seas of Guinea and to the East Indies. No native born Portuguese or alien, says one of the ancient royal ordinances, shall traverse the lands or seas of Guinea and the Indies, or any other territory conquered by us, without license, on pain of death and the loss of all his goods. The Spanish nation formerly claimed the right of excluding all others from the Pacific. Against such claims, especially of the Portuguese, Grotius wrote his *Mare Liberum* in 1609, in which he lays down the general principle of the free right of navigation, and that the sea cannot be made property, and refutes the claims of the Portuguese to the discovery of countries which the ancients have left us an account of, as well as their claims through the donation of Pope Alexander VI. And yet the countrymen of Grotius, who had been defenders of the liberty of the seas, sought to prevent the Spaniards, going to the Philippines, from taking the route of the Cape of Good Hope. The English, in the 17th century, claimed property in the seas surrounding Great Britain, as far as to the coasts of the neighboring countries, and in the 18th only softened down the claim of property into one of sovereignty. Selden, who in 1635 published his *Mare Clausum*, while he contends against the monopolizing pretensions of Spain and Portugal, contends zealously on the ground of certain weak ancient precedents for this claim of his country. The shores and ports of the neighboring states, says he, are the limits of the British sea-empire, but in the wide ocean, to the north and west the limits are yet to be constituted.* Russia, finally, at a more recent date, based an exclusive claim to the Pacific, north of the 51st degree, upon the ground that this part of the ocean was a passage to shores lying exclusively within her jurisdiction. But this claim was resisted by our government, and withdrawn in the temporary convention of 1824. A treaty of the same empire with Great Britain in 1825 contained similar concessions.

The rights of all nations to the use of the high sea being the same, their right to fish upon the high seas, or on banks and shoal places in them are equal. The right to fish in bays and mouths of rivers depends on the will of the sovereign.

Fishery question between the U. States and Great Britain.

Thus the right to fish on the banks of Newfoundland is open to all, but there is no right to dry and cure fish, even on the unsettled coasts belonging to any sovereign, without permission of the same. And here a brief sketch of the fishery question between the United States and Great Britain may not be out of place.

Treaty of 1783.

By the treaty of 1783, which admitted the independence of the United States, Great Britain conceded to them the right of fishing on the Banks of Newfoundland along such coasts of the same island as were used by British seamen, in the Gulf of St. Lawrence, and on the coasts, bays, and creeks of all other British dominions in America; as well as the right of drying and curing fish in any of the unsettled bays, harbors and creeks of Nova Scotia, the Magdalen islands and Labrador, so long as they should continue unsettled; but not the right of drying or curing on the island of Newfoundland.

Treaty of Ghent, 1814.

At and after the treaty of Ghent, which contained no provisions respecting the fisheries, it was contended by American negotiators, but without good reason, that the article of the peace of 1783, relating to the fisheries, was in its nature perpetual, and thus not annulled by the war of 1812. By a convention of 1818 the privilege was again, and in perpetuity, opened to cit-

Convention of 1818.

* Comp. Ortolan, u. s., Chap. 7.

izens of the United States. They might now fish, as well as cure and dry fish on the greater part of the coast of Newfoundland and Labrador, and on the Magdalen islands, so long as the same should continue unsettled; while the United States on their part renounced forever any liberty "to take or cure fish, on, or within three marine miles of any of the coasts, bays, creeks, or harbors of his Britannic Majesty's dominions in America not included within the above-mentioned limits.*

Treaty of 1854.

Finally, by the treaty of 1854, commonly called the reciprocity treaty, leave was given to fishermen from the United States, to take fish, excepting shell fish, on the coasts and in the bays, harbors, and creeks of Canada, New Brunswick, Nova Scotia, Prince Edward's Island and the islands adjacent, without limit as to distance from the shore, with permission to land upon the places named and upon the Magdalen Islands for the purpose of drying their nets and curing their fish; provided, that in so doing, they do not interfere with the rights of private property, or with British fishermen who should have pre-occupied parts of the said coasts for the same purpose. The same rights, with the same limitations, are given to British subjects on the coasts of the United States from the 36th degree northwards. In both cases the treaty does not include salmon and shad fisheries, nor the fisheries in rivers and the mouths of rivers.†

§ 56.

Claims of exclusive control over certain waters.

The claims of exclusive control over certain portions of water are, in a great part, either doubtful or to be rejected. These are broad arms or recesses of the sea; narrow seas not shut up within the territory of a single state; narrow passages, especially such as lead to interior seas; such interior seas themselves; and rivers furnishing the only or most convenient outlet for an inland state, which rise in one country and have their mouths in another.

Bays,

1. Bays of the sea,—called in England the king's chambers,—are within the jurisdiction of the states to whose territory the promontories embracing them be-

* See Wheaton's El. II. 4, § 8, and III. 2, § 9. † Murhard Nouv. Rec. 16. 1. 498.

long. Thus the Delaware Bay was declared in 1793 to belong exclusively to the United States. When, however, the headlands are very remote, there is more doubt in regard to the claim of exclusive control over them; and, for the most part, such claim has not been made. Chancellor Kent (I. 30) inclines to claim for the United States the dominion over a very wide extent of the adjacent ocean. "Considering," says he, "the great extent of the line of the American coasts, we have a right to claim, for fiscal and defensive regulations, a liberal extension of maritime jurisdiction; and it would not be unreasonable, as I apprehend, to assume for domestic purposes connected with our safety and welfare the control of waters on our coasts, though included within lines stretching from quite distant headlands,—as, for instance, from Cape Ann to Cape Cod, and from Nantucket to Montauk Point, and from that point to the Capes of the Delaware, and from the south Cape of Florida to the Mississippi. In 1793 our government thought they were entitled, in reason, to as broad a margin of protected navigation as any nation whatever, though at that time they did not positively insist beyond the distance of a marine league from the sea-shores; and, in 1806, our government thought it would not be unreasonable, considering the extent of the United States, the shoalness of their coast, and the natural indication furnished by the well-defined path of the Gulf Stream, to expect an immunity from belligerent warfare for the space between that limit and the American shore." But such broad claims have not, it is believed, been much urged, and they are out of character for a nation that has ever asserted the freedom of doubtful waters, as well as contrary to the spirit of the more recent times.

and Gulfs.

2. Great Britain has long claimed supremacy in the narrow seas adjoining that island. But the claim, although cheaply satisfied by paying certain honors to the British flag, has not been uniformly acquiesced in, and may be said to be falling into desuetude.* And if it had been urged and admitted in

* Comp. Vattel, I. 23, § 289; Wheaton's Hist. Part I. § 18; Wheaton's Elements, II. 4, § 9; Heffter, § 73. See also § 86.

former times, the force of the prescription would be broken by the plea that the views of the world, in regard to the freedom of commerce, have become much more enlarged. What Grotius contended for in his Mare Liberum against the exclusive claim of Portugal to the possession of oriental commerce, "jure gentium quibusvis ad quosvis liberam esse navigationem," is now for the most part admitted, and the pathways of commerce can no longer be obstructed.

§ 57.

Straits and inland seas.

3. The straits which have figured most largely in international history are those leading into the Baltic and the Black Seas.

The Danish straits.

A. The claims of Denmark to exclusive control over Elsineur sound and the Belts, are now matters of history, but a brief sketch of the past usage may not be without its use. Danish jurists rested these claims rather on immemorial prescription than on the cost of providing for the security of commerce by lighthouses, or by removing obstacles to navigation. In 1319 a charter regulated the duties to be paid by the Dutch. In 1544 the Emperor Charles V. stipulated the payment of the Sound dues by the merchants of the Low Countries. Subsequently, Denmark raised the tariff, which brought on a war with the Dutch and other nations. In 1645 Sweden obtained exemption from tolls, and, at the same time, by the treaty of Christianople, the amount of duties to be paid by the Dutch was again adjusted. France and England, in the seventeenth century, agreed to pay the same tariff with the Dutch.

Things continued thus for two centuries. In 1840, attention having been drawn in England to the Sound dues by the delays and vexations of commerce, negotiations were had which removed part of the complaints.

In 1826 a commercial convention for ten years with Denmark placed the United States on the footing of the most favored nations, which caused a reduction of the duties we had been paying hitherto. In 1843 the justice of the demand began to be more especially drawn into question, and the Secretary of State expressed himself against it. Amid the difficulties of Denmark, in 1848, the Chargé from the United States proposed, as a commutation for the claim, the sum of two hundred and fifty thousand dollars. Five years afterwards the diplomatic agent of the United States was instructed by Mr. Marcy to take the ground with Denmark, that his country could recognize no immemorial usage not coinciding with natural justice and international law. In the next year the President advised that the convention of 1826 should be regarded as at an end; and, after a vote of the Senate to this effect, notice was given to Denmark that it would be broken off in a year from that time. Denmark now, in October 1855, proposed to our government to enter into a plan of capitalizing the dues according to an equitable adjustment, but the government declined being a party to such an arrangement. Meanwhile, as difficulties with the United States seemed to be impending, and as other nations were interested in putting an end to this annoyance, a congress met at Copenhagen to consider this question, and fixed on the sum of thirty-five million rixdollars (at fifty cents of our money to the dollar) as the sum for which Denmark ought to give up the Sound dues for ever. This payment was divided among the nations interested in proportion to the value of their commerce passing through the Danish straits; and an arrangement for extinguishing the claim has since been accepted by them all. In March, 1857, our government agreed to pay, as its portion of the capitalized stock, three hundred ninety-three thousand and eleven dollars.*

B. The entrance into the Black Sea and that sea itself. Until Russia acquired territory on the Black Sea, that sea, with the straits leading to it, and the sea of Marmora lay entirely within Turkish territory. But the existence of another power on the Black Sea modified the rights of Turkey. By the treaty of Adrianople, in 1829, entrance through the straits into the Black Sea, and its naviga-

The Black Sea and the passage into it.

* Comp. especially an article in the North American Review for January, 1857, vol. 84, from which we have drawn freely.

tion, were admitted to belong to Russia and to powers at amity with Russia. The ancient practice, however, had been to prohibit all *foreign vessels of war* from entering the Bosphorus and the Dardanelles; and by the treaty of London, in 1841, between the five powers and Turkey this usage was sanctioned. Finally, by the treaty of Paris, March 30, 1856, "the Black Sea is made neutral. Open to the mercantile marine of all nations, its waters and ports are formally, and in perpetuity, interdicted to flags of war, whether belonging to the bordering powers, or to any other power." The treaty, however, proceeds to grant to Russia and Turkey the liberty of making a convention in regard to a small force, to be kept up within the sea for coast service. By this convention the two powers allow one another to maintain six steam vessels of not over eight hundred tons, and four light steamers, or sailing vessels, of not over two hundred tons burthen each.

§ 58.

Rights over river navigation.

4. Where a navigable river forms the boundary between two states, both are presumed to have free use of it, and the dividing line will run in the middle of the channel, unless the contrary is shown by long occupancy or agreement of the parties. If a river changes its bed, the line through the old channel continues, but the equitable right to the free use of the stream seems to belong, as before, to the state whose territory the river has forsaken.

When a river rises within the bounds of one state and empties into the sea in another, international law allows to the inhabitants of the upper waters only a moral claim or imperfect right to its navigation. We see in this a decision based on strict views of territorial right, which does not take into account the necessities of mankind and their destination to hold intercourse with one another. When a river affords to an inland state *the only*, or *the only convenient* means of access to the ocean and to the rest of mankind, its right becomes so strong, that according to natural justice possession of territory ought to be regarded as a far inferior ground of right. Is such a nation to be crippled in its resources, and shut out from mankind, or should it depend on another's caprice for a great part of what makes nations fulfil their vocation in the world, merely because it lies remote from the sea which is free to all? Transit, then, when necessary, may be demanded as a right: an interior nation has a servitude along nature's pathway, through the property of its neighbor, to reach the great highway of nations. It must, indeed, give all due security that trespasses shall not be committed on the passage, and pay all equitable charges for improvements of navigation and the like; but, this done, its travellers should be free to come and go on that water-road which is intended for them. An owner of the lower stories of a house could hardly shut out persons living in the upper, of which there was another proprietor, from the use of the stairs.—A river is one. As those who live on the upper waters would have no right to divert the stream, so those on the lower cannot rightfully exclude them from its use.

The law of nations has not acknowledged such a right, but has at length come to the same result by opening, in succession, the navigation of nearly all the streams flowing through the territory of Christian nations to those who dwell upon their upper waters, or even to mankind. We annex a sketch of the progress of this freedom of intercourse by means of rivers.

Congress of Vienna. The Rhine, etc.

An Act of the Congress of Vienna, in 1815, declared that the use of streams separating or traversing the territory of different powers, should be entirely free, and not be denied for the purposes of commerce to any one, being subject only to police rules, which should be uniform for all, and as favorable as might be for the traffic of all nations. Other articles require uniform tolls for the whole length of a stream, and nearly uniform,—not exceeding the actual rate,—for the various kinds of goods, rights of haulage, etc.* By this act the Rhine became free; but a controversy having arisen as to what was to be understood by the Rhine, near the sea, it was decided by the nations having sovereignty over its banks, that navigation should be open through the mouths called the Waal and the Leck, and through the artificial canal of Voorne.

* Articles 108–117 in the Appendix to Wheaton's El.

The same act opened the Scheldt, which had been closed by the peace of Westphalia to the Spanish Netherlands in favor of the Dutch, and opened by the French on their occupation of Belgium in 1792. On the divulsion of Belgium from Holland, in 1831, the treaty of separation again provided for the free navigation of this river.*

The Scheldt.

All the other navigable streams of Europe were open to the inhabitants on their banks, either before the treaty of Vienna, or by its general rule above mentioned, with the exception of the Danube. By the treaty of Bucharest, in 1812, and that of Adrianople, in 1829, the commercial use of this stream was to pertain in common to the subjects of Turkey and of Russia. By the recent treaty of Paris, in 1856, the Danube also came within the application of the rule of the treaty of Vienna, to which Turkey was not an original party. This was the last European stream, the freedom of which was to be gained for commerce. †

The Danube.

While Spain, after the independence of the United States, was mistress of the lower waters of the Mississippi, she was disposed to claim exclusive control over the navigation near the gulf. But by the treaty of San

Mississippi.

* Comp. Wheaton's Hist. 282–284, 552; Wheaton's El. II. 4, § 15.

† Five articles of the treaty are concerned with the navigation of the Danube, articles 15–19. Art. 15 declares the freedom of the stream, according to the Vienna act, as a part of the public law of Europe for ever, and prohibits tolls on vessels, and duty on goods, levied on the simple account of the navigation. Art. 16 appoints a commission of delegates from the five great powers with Sardinia and Turkey, to clear out the mouths of the Danube; and, in order to defray the expenses of such improvements, fixed duties, equal in amount for all nations, may be levied. This commission, by article 18, is to finish its work in two years, and then shall be pronounced to be dissolved. Meanwhile, a permanent commission, by article 17, is to be appointed, consisting of delegates of Austria, Bavaria, Turkey and Wurtemberg, to which a commission from the three Danubian principalities is to be joined, who shall draw up rules of navigation and fluvial police, remove remaining obstacles, cause works necessary for the navigation to be executed along the whole course of the river, and when the first mentioned commission shall be dissolved, shall see that the mouths of the river are kept in good order. Art. 19 allows each of the contracting powers at all times to station two light vessels at the mouth of the Danube, for the purpose of assuring the execution of regulations settled by common consent. For the act of navigation of the Danube, growing out of Art. 17, above mentioned, see Murhard Nouv. Rec. xvi. 2, 75.

Lorenzo el Real, in 1795, the use of the stream and liberty to deposit goods at and export them from New Orleans was granted to citizens of the United States. Before this the question of the rights of the parties had been agitated between them. The United States had contended that there is a natural right belonging to the inhabitants on the upper waters of a stream, under whatever political society they might be found, to descend by it to the ocean. It was acknowledged, on the part of the United States, that this was, at the most, an imperfect right, and yet the right was claimed to be as real as any other, however well-defined, so that its refusal would constitute an injury, for which satisfaction might be demanded. There seems to be a weakness in this argument, for by admitting the right to be an imperfect one, the claim of injury for not complying with it was cut off. In 1803, Louisiana, which had been ceded by Spain to France in 1800, was purchased of the latter by the United States, which thus had the territorial jurisdiction over all the course of the river.*

St. Lawrence.

The St. Lawrence, after separating for a great distance the British possessions from those of the American Union, traverses British territory to the sea. The government of Great Britain, for a long time, steadily refused to concede the right of using the lower stream for the purposes of navigation, and the same diplomatic controversy was carried on, as in the case of the Mississippi, between the right according to the strict law of nations, and the claim on the principles of natural justice. Meanwhile, canals and railroads having bound the western part of the Union to the Atlantic seaboard, and New York having become a financial centre even for the Canadas, the importance of the question was greatly lessened. By the reciprocity treaty of June 5, 1854, the navigation of the river, as well as of the canals in Canada, was at length thrown open to the United States, on the same conditions which are imposed on the subjects of Great Britain. This privilege may be revoked by the latter party upon due notice.* On their part the United States granted to British subjects the free navigation of Lake Michigan.

* Comp. Wheaton's Hist. p. 506–511.

La Plata system of rivers.

The vast system of streams which find their way to the sea by means of the La Plata is open for navigation, not only to the inhabitants of the banks, but also in a degree to strangers. The Argentine confederation and Buenos Ayres opened their waters in 1853. In the same year Bolivia, whose territory is on the head waters, made a number of places on the banks of its rivers free ports. Brazil had done the same, and several years ago bound Paraguay by a treaty to the same policy; but the government of this latter country closed navigation above the capital, Assuncion, to foreigners, —allowing the use of the waters only to Brazil and the Argentine republic,—and below, by police regulations, sought to throw the trade principally into the hands of one nation.

Such have been the advances in the freedom of navigation during the last forty years. There is now scarcely a river in the Christian portions of the world, the dwellers on whose upper waters have not the right of free communication, by God's channels, with the rest of mankind. Whether the motive which brought this about has been self-interest or sense of justice, an end approved alike by justice and benevolence has been reached, and the world cannot fail to be the gainer.

CHAPTER III.

RIGHT OR CLAIM OF INTERCOURSE.—RELATIONS OF FOREIGNERS WITHIN A TERRITORY OF A STATE.

§ 59.

Intercourse of states, how far a right.

We have already come to the conclusion that sovereignty in the strictest sense authorizes a nation to decide upon what terms it will have intercourse with foreigners, and even to shut out all mankind from its borders. (§ 25.) If a protective tariff, or the prohibition of certain articles is no violation of rights, it is hard to say how far one state may not go in refusing to have commerce with another. If foreigners may be placed under surveillance, or may have various rights of citizens refused to them, why may they not be excluded from the territory? If it be said that the destination of separate states, as of separate families, is to be helpful to one another, that entire isolation is impossible, still the amount of intercourse must be left to the judgment of the party interested; and if a state, judging incorrectly, strives to live within itself as much as possible, is it to be forced to change its policy, any more than to modify its protective tariff?

And yet some kind of intercourse of neighboring states is so natural, that it must have been coeval with their foundation, and with the origin of law; it is so necessary, that to decline it, involves often extreme inhumanity; it is so essential to the progress of mankind, that unjust wars have been blessings when they opened nations to one another. There could, of course, be no international law without it. The following maxims relating to the so-called right, are, in substance, laid down by Heffter. (§ 33.)

1. Entire non-intercourse shuts a nation out from being a partner in international law.—[This, however, is not true, if international law is taken in its broadest sense, for to treat a nation, or its subjects, when these latter are fallen in with, as having no rights, because they have no intercourse with us, is not only inhuman but unjust.]

What a state may not do as it respects intercourse.

2. No nation can, without hostility, cut off another from the use of necessaries not to be obtained elsewhere. [But necessaries must not be confounded with articles highly desirable.]

3. No state has a right to cut another off from the innocent use of its usual ways of communication with a third state. "The older writers called this the *jus transitus*, or *jus passagii innoxii*, but disputed whether it is a perfect or imperfect right. Only necessary wants create a definite right. The refusal of something merely useful to one party, to grant which does the other no harm, is at most an unfriendly procedure. Many, as Grotius (II. 2, § 13), and Vattel (II. § 123, 132–134), decide, that there is a right in this case, but naturally have to reserve for the owner, the decision whether he will be harmed or not by parting with his commodities."

4. No state can, without violation of right, exclude another from intercourse with a third state against the will of the latter.

5. In its intercourse with others every state is bound to truth and honesty, [without which intercourse must be broken up].

6. No state can exclude the properly documented subjects of another friendly state, or send them away after they have been once admitted without definite reasons, which must be submitted to the foreign government concerned.

To these we may add that

No state can withdraw from intercourse with others without a violation of a right gained by usage.

No state can treat with cruelty, or deprive of their property the subjects of another, whom some calamity, such as the distress or stranding of a vessel, throws within its borders, without wrong and just claim of redress.

§ 60.

Within these limits, intercourse, whether through travellers or merchants, is regulated by the free sovereign act of each state. Whether it will have a passport system, a protective tariff, special supervision of strangers; whether it will give superior commercial privileges to one nation over another; in short, whether it will be fair and liberal, or selfish and monopolizing, it must decide, like any private tradesman or master of a family, for itself. The law of nations does not interfere at this point with the will of the individual state.*

What a state may do.

It deserves to be remarked, however, that non-intercourse and restriction are fast disappearing from the commercial arrangements of the world, and that jealousy of foreigners is vanishing from the minds of all the more civilized nations, in the East as well as in the West. The feeling that there is a

* There is a difficulty in the theory of international law, arising from the weakness of the claim which one state has to intercourse with another, compared with the immense and fundamental importance of intercourse itself. There can be no law of nations, no civilization, no *world*, without it, but only separate atoms; and yet we cannot punish, it is held, the refusal of intercourse, as a wrong done to us, by force of arms, but can only retaliate by similar conduct. I have, in § 25, endeavored to meet this by a parallel case,—marriage is all important, yet for commencing it entire consent of the parties is necessary. And yet, to put intercourse on the ground of comity or even of duty, fails to satisfy me. Practically, we may say that nations will have intercourse by trade and otherwise, whenever they find it to be for their interest; but the case of half-civilized or long secluded nations, like Japan, which satisfy their own wants, and rather avoid than desire foreign articles, shows that long ages may elapse before views suggested by self-interest or suspicion are abandoned. Shall we then force them into intercourse? Perhaps we may, if we get a just occasion of war with them; but not because they take a position which, though disastrous for the interests of mankind, is yet an exercise of sovereignty.

But apart from this theoretical view, there are many duties, duties of mutual help, incumbent on nations who hold intercourse with one another, which serve to facilitate such intercourse. Such are, aid to travellers, use of courts, and the like, which ought to be regarded as the necessary means of promoting admitted intercourse, and therefore as obligatory, when intercourse is once allowed.

certain right for lawful commerce to go everywhere is in advance of the doctrine of strict right which the law of nations lays down. The Christian states, having tolerably free intercourse with one another, and perceiving the vast benefits which flow from it, as well as being persuaded that in the divine arrangements of the world, intercourse is the normal condition of mankind, have of late, sometimes under pretext of wrongs committed by states less advanced in civilization, forced them into the adoption of the same rules of intercourse, as though this were a right which could not be withheld. Recent treaties with China and Japan have opened these formerly secluded countries to commercial enterprise, and even to travel; and the novel sight of an ambassadar from Japan visiting our country will not be so strange as the concessions of trade which this shy people has already granted.* It is conceded, moreover, that the great roads of transit shall be open to all nations, not monopolized by one; and the newer commercial provisions quite generally place the parties to them on the footing of the most favored nations. This freedom and spread of intercourse is, in fact, one of the most hopeful signs in the present history of the world.

§ 61.

Individual aliens entitled to protection.

There could be no intercourse between nations if aliens and their property were not safe from violence, and even if they could not demand the protection of the state where they reside. This protection, be it observed, is territorial in its character, that is, it is due to them only within the territory of a state, on its vessels and when they are with its ambassadors, while the protection of citizens or subjects, as being parts or members of the state, ceases at no time and in no place. The obligation to treat foreigners with humanity, and to protect them when once admitted into a country, depends not on their belonging to a certain political community which has a function to defend its members, nor wholly on treaty, but on the essential rights of human nature. Hence

* Since this was written, in 1859, a Japanese delegation has become a matter of fact. 2d ed.

1. It has been claimed with apparent justice, that aliens have a right of asylum. To refuse to distressed foreigners, as shipwrecked crews, a temporary home, or to treat them with cruelty, is a crime. As for the exile who has no country, international law cannot ensure his protection, but most nations, in ancient and modern times, that have passed beyond the inferior stages of civilization, have opened the door to such unfortunate persons, and to shut them out, when national safety does not require it, has been generally esteemed a flagitious and even an irreligious act. The case of aliens who have fled from their native country on account of crime, will be considered in the sequel.

2. The right of innocent passage has already been considered. It may be claimed on stronger grounds than the right of entering and settling in a country, for the refusal may not only injure the aliens desirous of transit, but also the country into which they propose to go. The right of transit of armies, and of entrance of armed ships into harbors, will be considered by themselves. As their presence may be dangerous, to refuse transit or admission in these cases rests on grounds of its own.

3. The right of emigration. Formerly it was doubted whether an individual had a right to quit his country and settle elsewhere, without leave from his government, and in some countries he who did go had to sacrifice a part of his property.* At present such a right is very generally conceded, under certain limitations. "The right of emigration," says Heffter, "is inalienable: only self-imposed or unfulfilled obligations can restrict it." The relation of the subject to the sovereign is a voluntary one, to be terminated by emigration. But a state is not bound to allow the departure of its subjects, until all preexisting lawful obligations to the state have been satisfied. Notice, therefore, may be required of an intent to emigrate, and security be demanded for the satisfaction of back-standing

* By the *jus detractûs*, *droit de detraction*, property to which strangers out of the country succeeded was taxed. By an analogous tax, as the *gabelle d'emigration*, those who left a country were amerced in part of their goods, immovable or movable. Such odious rights, says De Martens (I. § 90), although existing still, are very generally abolished.

obligations, before the person in question is allowed to leave the country.* De Martens writes to this effect.† "It belongs to universal and positive public law to determine how far the state is authorized to restrict or prevent the emigration of the natives of a country. Although the bond which attaches a subject to the state of his birth or his adoption be not indissoluble, every state has a right to be informed beforehand of the design of one of its subjects to expatriate himself, and to examine whether by reason of crime or debt, or engagements not yet fulfilled towards the state, it is authorized to retain him longer. These cases excepted, it is no more justified in prohibiting him from emigrating, than it would be in prohibiting foreign sojourners from doing the same. These principles have always been followed in Germany. They have been sanctioned even by the federal pact of the German confederation, as far as relates to emigration from the territory of one member of the confederation to that of another."

§ 62.

Relation of aliens to the laws, and their condition.

Foreigners admitted into a country are subject to its laws, unless the laws themselves give them, in a greater or less degree, exemption. This is rarely done, and the general practice of all Christian states treats foreigners—except some especial classes of them—as transient subjects of the state where they reside, or on whose ships they sail over the high sea. They are held to obedience to its laws and punished for disobeying them, nor is it usual to mitigate their punishment on account of their ignorance of the law of the land. They are, again, as we have seen, entitled to protection, and failure to secure this, or any act of oppression may be a ground of complaint, of retorsion, or even of war, on the part of their native country. On the other hand, the law of the land may without injustice place them in an inferior position to the native-born subject. Thus they may be obliged to pay a residence tax, may be restricted as to the power of holding land, may have no political rights, may be obliged to give

* Heffter, § 15, § 33.

† Precis, etc. Paris ed. of 1858, § 91.

security in suits where the native is not, may be forbidden to enter into certain callings, may be subjected to special police regulations, without any ground for complaint that they are oppressed. But most restrictions upon foreigners have disappeared with the advance of humane feeling, and the increasing frequency of intercourse between nations, until they are in almost all Christian countries, in all rights excepting political, nearly on a level with native-born persons. In fact, if foreigners are admitted to establish themselves in a country, it is but justice that all private rights should be accorded to them. Thus the courts of their domicil ought to be as open to them, as to the native-born citizen, for collecting debts and redressing injuries.

§ 63.

Progress of humanity and of comity towards aliens, illustrated.

The progress of humanity in the treatment of foreigners, may be shown by the following brief sketch, including only Greece and Rome, and the Christian states. In Greece different policies prevailed. Aristocratic and agricultural states were in general jealous of strangers, democratic and commercial ones viewed them with favor. Sparta was called ἐχθρόξενος, as excluding them and watching them while in the territory. At Athens, where the policy was humane and liberal, domiciled strangers,—metoeci,—were subject to a small stranger's tax, had heavier pecuniary burdens than the native citizen, were required to serve in the army and navy, and needed a patron for the transaction of legal business. Their great numbers, equal to one half of the citizens, show that they prospered under this policy, which was extended to barbarians as well as to Greeks. Sometimes they attained, by vote of the community, to full citizenship. A special but smaller class of foreigners—the ἰσοτελεῖς,—had a status more nearly like that of the citizen than the ordinary metoeci. In many states of Greece, individual aliens, or whole communities, received by vote some of the most important civic rights, as those of intermarriage, of holding real estate within the territory, and of immunity from taxation. (ἐπιγαμία, ἔγκτησις and ἀτέλεια.)

In Rome, foreigners enjoyed those rights which belonged to the *jus gentium*; they could acquire and dispose of property, could sue in the courts, and had an especial magistrate to attend to their cases at law, but could make no testament, nor had they the *connubium* and *commercium* of Roman citizens.

In the Germanic states, after the fall of the Roman empire, foreigners at first were without rights, and a prey to violence, as having no share in political bodies. Hence they needed and fell under the protection of the seigneur, or of his bailiff. In France, especially, the seigneur, as the price of his protection, levied a poll tax on the stranger, and arrogated the right to inherit his goods, when he had no natural heirs within the district. Even the capacity of making a testament was taken away from him, and sometimes even inland heirs were excluded from the succession. Some lords forbade strangers to leave the district after a certain length of residence, and to marry out of it. And sometimes these rights were exercised over Frenchmen from other juristic territories (chatellenies), under the same suzerains. The name by which this right or aggregate of rights went, is *jus albinagii*, *droit d'aubaine*, which M. Dietz, the highest authority in Romanic philology, derives not from *Albanus*, a Scotchman, nor from *alibi natus*, but from *alibi* simply, formed from the adverb, after the analogy of *prochain*, *lointain*.

At length the droit d'aubaine fell to the king alone, and now consisted first in an extraordinary tax levied upon strangers on certain occasions, and secondly in the king's becoming the heir of strangers who had left no heirs of their body within the kingdom. Many private persons were exempted from the operation of this right by special privilege, and whole nations, as the United States in 1778, by treaty. Abolished by the constituent assembly in 1790, and re-established by the Code Napoleon on the principle of reciprocity, it again disappeared anew from French legislation in 1819, when a law gave to foreigners the right of succession in France to the same extent with native born Frenchmen.*

* See especially Warnkönig, Französ. Rechtsgesch. II. 180–188, 471, and de Martens, I. § 90.

§ 64.

Certain classes of aliens are, by the comity of nations, exempted in a greater or less degree from the control of the laws, in the land of their temporary sojourn. They are conceived of as bringing their native laws with them out of their native territory, and the name given to the fiction of law,—for it seems there must be a fiction of law to explain a very simple fact,—is *exterritoriality.* This privilege is conceded especially (1.) to sovereigns travelling abroad with their trains; (2.) to ambassadors, their suite, family, and servants; and (3.) to the officers and crews of public armed vessels in foreign ports, and to armies in their permitted transit through foreign territory.

Exterritoriality.

This privilege is not constant, nor unlimited. The right of entrance into foreign territory, on which the privilege is founded, is one dependent on a comity which circumstances may abridge. Thus, for reasons of state, a sovereign may have the permission refused to him to set foot on a foreign soil, and much more is the like true of ships and armies. When a sovereign is abroad, his person is inviolate and exempt from the laws of the land, but he may not exercise acts of sovereignty, not accorded to him by his native laws, as, for instance, that of punishing persons in his suite capitally,—as Queen Christina of Sweden put to death one of her household in France,—nor acts hazardous to the safety or the sovereignty of the state where he is sojourning, nor, perhaps, acts which the sovereign of the country himself cannot exercise. Neither then nor at any time will this right apply, so as to exempt real or other property, which he may have in the foreign country, from its local laws, with the exception of such effects as he may have brought with him. For the same right as conceded to ambassadors, we refer to the chapter relating to those functionaries. Ships of war, and vessels chartered to convey a sovereign or his representative, are peculiar in this respect, that the vessel is regarded in a certain sense to be part of alien territory moved into the harbors of another

Limits of exterritoriality.

As to sovereigns,

Ships of war,

state. (§ 54.) The crews on board the public vessels are under their native laws, but on shore, if guilty of acts of aggression or hostility, can be opposed by force and arrested. So also the vessel itself must pay respect to the port and health laws.* Crimes committed on shore expose persons belonging to such vessels not only to complaint before their own sovereign, but also to arrest and trial. Of armies in transit, when such a right is conceded, Vattel says (III. 8, § 130) that "the grant of passage includes that of every particular thing connected with the passage of troops, and of things without which it would not be practicable; such as the liberty of carrying whatever may be necessary to an army; that of exercising military discipline on the officers and soldiers; and that of buying at a reasonable rate anything an army may want, unless a fear of scarcity renders an exception necessary, when the army must carry with them their provisions." If we are not deceived, crimes committed along the line of march, away from the body of the army, as pilfering and marauding, authorize arrest by the magistrates of the country, and a demand at least, that the commanding officers shall bring such crimes to a speedy trial. When the transit of troops is allowed, it is apt to be specially guarded by treaties.

Armies in transit,

The crews of commercial vessels in foreign ports have in general no such exemption from the law of the place. By the law of France, however, crimes committed on board of foreign vessels in French ports, where none but the crew are concerned, are not considered as pertaining to the jurisdiction of the courts of France, while offences committed on the shore and against others than the vessels' crews, come before the tribunals of the kingdom. This is a compromise between territorial sovereignty and the principle or fiction that the ship is a part of the domain of its own nation, wherever found.

Crews of commercial vessels in French ports.

Vessels driven into foreign harbors out of their course.

Vessels, driven into foreign waters against the will of the master, are exempted from or-

* Ortolan, I. 218.

dinary charges and jurisdiction, and allowed to depart unhindered.*

§ 65.

Exemptions to foreigners in certain Eastern countries.

Exemption from local jurisdiction has been granted to foreigners from Christian lands, resident in certain oriental countries; the reasons for which lie in the fact, that the laws and usages there prevailing are quite unlike those of Christendom, and in the natural suspicion of Christian states, that justice will not be administered by the native courts, which leads them to obtain special privileges for their subjects. The arrangements for this purpose are contained in treaties which have a general resemblance to one another. In Turkey, and some other Mohammedan countries, foreigners form communities under their consuls, who exercise over them a jurisdiction, both in civil and criminal matters, which excludes that of the territorial courts. In civil cases an appeal lies to the courts at home, and in criminal, beyond the imposition of fines, the consul has power only to prepare a case for trial before the same tribunals.† But the extent of power given to its functionaries each nation determines for itself.

The same system in general has been followed in the treaties of Christian states with China, of which that made by the United States in 1844, and spoken of below under the title of consuls, may serve as an example. Quite recently the same exterritorial jurisdiction has been granted by the government of Japan to functionaries of the United States resident in that country.‡

* Comp. Heffter, § 79, and Webster's Letter to Ashburton respecting the Creole, Works, VI. 303–313.

† Wheaton, El. II. 2, § 11.

‡ An Act was passed by Congress, in 1860, to carry into effect certain stipulations in the treaties between the United States and China, Japan, Siam, Turkey, Persia, Tripoli, Tunis, Morocco, and Muscat, and by which our laws in criminal and civil matters are extended over American citizens in those countries; also the common law, including equity and admiralty. Ministers and consuls have full judicial powers, and can punish according to the magnitude of the offence. The President is authorized to appoint seven Marshals to execute processes, one in Japan, four in China, one in Siam, and one in Turkey. Murder and insurrection, or rebellion

§ 66.

Aliens losing in part or entirely the character of aliens.

Foreign residents in most Christian countries can sustain, in the course of time, a closer or more distant connection with the body politic within whose borders they live. They can acquire nationality, or in other words become naturalized, or they may remain in the territory as domiciliated strangers.

Naturalization.

Naturalization implies the renunciation of a former nationality, and the fact of entrance into a similar relation towards a new body politic. It is possible for a person, without renouncing his country, or expatriating himself, to have the *privileges* of citizenship in a second country, although he cannot sustain the same *obligations* to both. Is it also possible for him to renounce his country, and become a citizen of another, so far as even to be bound, like his fellow citizens, to take up arms against the land of his birth? Most nations hold that this transfer of allegiance is possible, and embody the conditions of it in their naturalization laws. Even England, which retains the doctrine of indelible allegiance, admits strangers to citizenship by special act or grant. (§ 66 infra.) But inasmuch as the conditions of naturalization vary, there may arise here a conflict of laws, and two nations may at once claim the same man as sustaining to them the obligations of a citizen. International law has not undertaken to decide in such conflicts, and the question is scarcely one of practical importance, except when the naturalized person returns to his native country, and when he is caught fighting against her. There is no doubt that a state, having undertaken to adopt a stranger, is bound to protect him like any other citizen. Should he return to his native soil, and be ap-

against the government of either of said countries, with intent to subvert the same, are made capital offences, punishable with death. Our consuls or commercial agents on islands not inhabited by any civilized people, or whom we have not recognized by treaty, are also empowered to exercise judicial functions over American citizens. By the treaty with Japan, signed at Yedo, July 29, 1858, offences shall be tried in the offenders' court, when the American is the offending party, and the courts of each nation, that is, the consular and the Japanese, are open to creditors belonging to the other nationality.

prehended for the non-fulfilment of civic duties which devolved on him before his emigration, there would be no ground of complaint on that score. Should he be required anew to enter into the status of a citizen, this force must be regarded by his adopted country, on her theory of civic rights, as a wrong calling for redress. Should he be subjected to ill-treatment when a captive in war, on the ground of fighting against his native country, here, too, there would be reason for retaliation. In short, the nation which has naturalized, and thus bound itself to protect a person, cannot abandon its obligation, on account of views of civic obligations which another nation may entertain.

Whether anything short of completed naturalization can sunder the tie to the place of origin, may be a question. It is held that a domiciled stranger may not with impunity be found in arms against his native country.* For the effects of incipient naturalization, compare the case of Koszta in the appendix to this chapter. The English practice in the earlier part of this century, of impressing seamen from neutral vessels, on the ground that they owed allegiance to their native sovereign, was objectionable, whether this doctrine of inalienable allegiance stands or falls; for to seize sailors on foreign vessels is to act the sovereign out of one's own territory; it is to execute one's own laws where the laws of another sovereign are supreme. (Comp. § 202.)

We add here the regulations of some of the more important countries in regard to naturalization.†

Rules of several nations as to naturalization.

In England it was formerly granted only by act of parliament; but by a statute of 1844, one of the principal secretaries of state can, on petition from an alien desirous of being naturalized, grant him all the capacities and rights of a natural-born British subject, except the capacity of being a member of the privy council or a member of either house of Parliament. The Secretary may except other rights also. (Phillimore I. § 354.)

In France a stranger becomes a citizen, when after reach-

* Kent, I. 76, Lect. IV.

† Fœlix (droit intern. privé, 3d ed.) I. 81–100.

ing the age of twenty-one, obtaining liberty of domicil, and declaring his intention to remain in France, he resides there for ten consecutive years. His naturalization must also be pronounced to be in force by the head of the state. In addition to this the child of foreign parents, born on French soil, may claim the quality of a Frenchman in the year succeeding his majority. Naturalization in a foreign country involves the loss of French citizenship.*

In Prussia an appointment to a public function brings the right of citizenship with it, and the same is the case in Austria, and perhaps elsewhere. In Prussia the higher administrative authorities have the right to naturalize strangers of good character who possess the means of subsistence, excepting Jews, subjects of other members of the Germanic confederacy, and persons incapable of taking care of themselves.

In Austria leave to exercise a profession, ten years of residence, and the consent of the authorities, are pre-requisites to naturalization.

In both of the last named states nationality is shaken off by emigration, for which permission has been obtained from the government.

In Russia an oath of allegiance to the emperor naturalizes, but naturalized strangers can at any time renounce their character, and return to their own country.

In the United States, the person wishing to be naturalized must make a declaration on oath, before certain judicial persons, of an intent to become a citizen and to renounce his former nationality, two years at least after which, and after five years of residence, he may become a citizen in full of the United States, although not necessarily a citizen of any state in the Union.

In many countries, a woman on her marriage to a native acquires nationality, and loses it on her marriage to a foreigner. In the laws of some countries, wives and minor children follow,

* Demangeat on Fœlix, I. 88, gives the latest legislation on this subject. The term of ten years can be reduced to one in favor of inventors and others who confer important services on France.

as a thing of course, the status of the head of the family, and the son of a foreign resident born and brought up on the soil, has peculiar facilities of naturalization.

§ 67.

Domicil, what?

Domicil being more a legal than a political term, has had nearly the same, although a somewhat vague definition, always and everywhere. A definition of Roman law is expressed in these terms: "In eo loco singulos habere domicilium non ambigitur, ubi quis larem rerumque ac fortunarum suarum summam constituit, unde rursus non sit discessurus si nihil avocat, unde quum profectus est peregrinari videtur, quo si rediit peregrinari jam destitit." * According to Savigny † "it is the place which a man has freely chosen for his durable abode, and thereby also as the centre of his jural relations and of his business." But in the case of a minor, who can exercise no jural choice in the matter, his domicil is held to be that of his father. ‡ The domicil, says Vattel, "is the habitation fixed in any place, with the intention of always staying there. A man then does not establish his domicil in any place unless he makes sufficiently known his intention of fixing himself there, either tacitly or by an express declaration. However, this declaration is no reason why, if he afterward changes his mind, he may not remove his domicil elsewhere. In this sense, he who stops, even for a long time, in a place, for the management of his affairs, has only a simple habitation there, but no domicil." (I. § 218.) With the first part of this definition Story justly finds fault: few foreigners have the intention of *always* staying abroad; few, therefore, could have any domicil. "It would be more correct to say that that place is properly the domicil of a person in which his habitation is fixed without any present intention of removing therefrom." § "Two things must concur," says the same eminent jurist, "to constitute domicil,—first, *residence*, and secondly, *intention* of making it the home of the party," and

* C. J. C. 10. 39. I [illegible] de incolis.

† System d. h. röm. Rechts, VIII. 58.

‡ Fœlix I. 54.

§ Conflict of Laws, Chap. III, § 43.

when once domicil is acquired it is not shaken off by occasional absences for the sake of business or of pleasure, or even by visits to a former domicil or to one's native country.

It is often a matter of difficulty to decide where a person has his domicil. Story has laid down a number of practical rules for determining this point, some of the more important of which are the following: (1.) A person who is under the power of another is considered to have the domicil of the principal party, as a child of the father, a wife of the husband. (2.) There is a presumption in favor of the native country, when the question lies between that and another domicil, and in favor of the place where one lives or has his family, rather than in favor of his place of business. (3.) Free choice is necessary; hence constrained residence is no domicil, and in case of change a new domicil begins, as soon as choice begins to take effect. (4.) A floating purpose to leave the soil at some future period does not prevent domicil from being acquired, for such a purpose does not amount to a full and fixed intention.

According to some authorities a man can have more than one domicil,—for example if he have establishments of equal importance in two places between which he divides his time, —or he may have no domicil at all.* This latter position is denied by others, † on the ground that a former domicil must remain until a new one is acquired.

Whether long residence with a fixed purpose to return at the end of a certain time is enough for the acquisition of domicil may be a question. The Roman law denies this character to students who remain even ten years away from home for the purpose of study, ‡ on the ground, no doubt, that they never intended to establish themselves in the place of their sojourn.

The subject of domicil becomes of great importance when we ask who is an enemy, and who is a neutral. This bearing

* Savigny, System VIII. § 359.

† As by Story, § 47.

‡ C. J. C. 10, 39. L. 2, de incolis. "Nisi decem annis transactis eo loci sedes sibi constituerint."

will be considered when we reach the subject of the effects of war upon neutrals. It is of importance also in another department of international law, to which, in the order of topics, we are now brought.

§ 68.

Conflict of laws as to a particular person.

A man may change his domicil from one country to another, and may hold property in both: he may in a third execute a contract to be fulfilled in a fourth: he may inherit from relatives in another, and have heirs in another still: in short, with the increase of commerce and of emigration, in modern times, private jural relations stretch far beyond the bounds of any one territory, where an individual has his domicil. But the laws of these countries and their judicial procedures may differ widely from one another. What law then shall rule in each special case, where diverse laws come into conflict?

A simple rule would be to apply the law of the place of the court (*lex loci fori*, or *lex fori* alone) to all jural relations coming before it. A nation insisting rigidly on its own sovereignty would follow such a rule. But, as Savigny remarks, modern legislation and court-practice aim not to keep up local sovereignty and jurisdiction, but to decide without respect to territorial limits, according to the inner nature and needs of each jural relation.

§ 69.

Private international law.

It is the province of *private international law* to decide which of two conflicting laws of different territories is to be applied in the decision of cases; and for this reason this branch is sometimes called the *conflict of laws*. It is called *private*, because it is concerned with the private rights and relations of individuals. It differs from territorial or municipal law, in that it may allow the law of another territory to be the rule of judgment in preference to the law of that where the case is tried. It is *international*, because, with a certain degree of harmony, Christian states have come to adopt the same principles in judicial decisions, where different municipal laws clash.

It is called *law*, just as public international law is so called; not as imposed by a superior, but as a rule of action freely adopted by the sovereign power of a country, either in consideration of its being so adopted by other countries, or of its essential justice. And this adoption may have taken place through express law giving direction to courts, or through power lodged in courts themselves.

The foundation of this department, as of all privileges granted to strangers, is not generally regarded as being *justice* in the strict sense, but the humanity and *comity* of nations, or, in other words, the recognition of the brotherhood of men, and the mutual duties thence arising. Justice may close the avenues of commerce, and insist that the most rigid notion of sovereignty be carried out in practice, but goodwill grants concessions to aliens, and meanwhile enlightened self-interest discovers that the interests of all are alike promoted. But comp. § 20*b*.

Growth of private international law.

This branch of the law of nations, almost unknown to the Romans and to mediæval jurisprudence, has been slowly growing, in the hands especially of the jurists of Holland, France, and Germany, since the middle of the seventeenth century; but, although it has made great advances within the last age, it is still incomplete. "In this doctrine," says Savigny, writing in 1849, "and especially in the first half of it, [which treats of collisions in place, as the second part, according to the division of this eminent jurist, treats of collisions in *time*], hitherto the opinions of writers and the decisions of courts run confusedly across one another; the Germans, French, English, and Americans often stand on entirely opposite sides. All, however, unite in a common lively interest in the questions which here arise,—in the endeavor after approximation, removal of differences, and agreement,—more than in any other part of the science of law. One can say that this branch of science has already become a common property of civilized nations, not through possession already gained of fixed, universally acknowledged principles, but through a community in scientific inquiries which reaches after such possession. A vivid picture of this unripe but hopeful condition is furnished by the excellent work of Story, which is also in a high degree useful to every investigator, as a rich collection of materials." *

Its leading rules and principles.

The details of private international law belong to the lawyers and the courts. We shall confine ourselves to a brief sketch of the leading principles, in regard to which the legal authorities of Christian countries are tolerably harmonious; and in so doing shall principally follow the eminent Prussian jurist already named, the eighth volume of whose "System of Roman Law of the Present Day" is devoted to this subject. And we should have left out of our introduction to the science of international law all notice of this branch, as many have done, were it not that it puts in a striking light the tendency towards a common acceptance of the same principles of justice,—towards a brotherhood of nations under the same rules of right.

§ 70.

Personal capacity.

I A principle of private international law in which there is a general agreement is, that the jural capacity of a person is determined by the law of his domicil. Questions such as those of citizenship, minority, legitimacy, lunacy, the validity of marriage, the legal capacity of a married woman, belong here. Thus a person having, according to the laws of his domicil, reached his majority, can make contracts which are binding in a foreign country, although persons of the same age domiciled there would be minors. So also a woman belonging to a country where a married woman can perform legal acts of herself, can do this in a country where such power is denied to married women, and *vice versâ.*

And according to this rule, if a person changes his domicil, he acquires a new jural capacity, by which, in foreign parts, his

* For a classification of the schools or theories of writers on private international law, see Von Mohl, Gesch. d. Staatsw. I. 441.

actions are to be measured. This is true universally, but in many cases the courts of the earlier domicil, especially if it were the person's native country, have shown a leaning, not to be justified, towards holding him under their territorial law.

The reasons which justify this principle are, (1.) that otherwise extreme inconvenience would "result to all nations from a perpetual fluctuation of capacity, state and condition, upon every accidental change of place of the person or of his movable property." * (2.) That the person subjects himself and his condition, of free choice, to the law of the place where he resides, by moving there or continuing there.

Exceptions to the rule above given.

But there are several very important exceptions to the rule, that the *lex domicilii* is to determine in regard to personal status and jural capacity. These exceptions arise from the natural unwillingness of nations to allow laws to have force in their courts, which are opposed to their political systems, or to their principles of morality, or their doctrine of human rights.

1. One of these is, that if a person suffers in his status at home by being a heretic, a country, which regards such disabilities for such a reason as immoral, and perhaps is of the same religion with the heretic, cannot permit his *lex domicilii* in this point to have any effect in its courts, but applies its own law.

2. Where the laws forbid or limit the acquisition of property in mortmain, or by religious houses, ecclesiastical foundations in another land are affected by such limitations. On the contrary, in a state which has no such laws, religious corporations, which at home lie under restrictive legislation, are exempt from it.

3. A man passing from a country where polygamy has a jural sanction into a state under Christian law, can obtain no protection for his plurality of wives: the law not of his domicil but of the place where the judge lives must govern.

4. "So in a state where negro-slavery is not tolerated, a negro slave sojourning there cannot be treated as his master's

* Story, Chap. IV. § 67.

property,—as destitute of jural capacity." And this for two reasons: "Slavery as a legal institution is foreign to our polity, is not recognized by it; and at the same time from our point of view it is something utterly immoral to regard a man as a thing." So Savigny.* To the same purport Fœlix says: "On ne reconnait pas aux étrangers le droit d'amener des esclaves, et de les traiter comme tels." And to the same effect Heffter. "No moral state can endure slavery. In no case is a state bound to allow the slavery which subsists in other, although friendly, lands, to have validity within its borders." †

This principle is received into the practice of the leading nations. The maxim that the "air makes free," has long been acted upon in France; it prevails in Great Britain, and with slight modifications in Prussia. So if a cargo of slaves is stranded on the soil of a state, which does not recognize the status of slavery in its institutions and laws, there is no process under international law, excepting treaty made for that express purpose, by which they can be prevented from availing themselves of their freedom, or by which the owner can recover them as his property. There is a close analogy between the condition of such slaves on a foreign soil and that of prisoners of war in a neutral port, escaping on shore from the vessel where they are confined, who cannot be recaptured, since they enjoy the benefit of the right of postliminy. (§ [illegible].) So also when a master freely brings his slaves into a jurisdiction where slavery is unknown, he can neither legally act the master there, nor force them away with him to his own domicil. They may acquire a domicil like any other person in the territory where they are thus sheltered, and should they revisit the country of their enthralment, the *lex domicilii* would now determine their status to be that of freemen.‡

* VIII. §§ 349, 365. Comp. Story, § 96.

† Fœlix, u. s. I. 30, § 15; Heffter, § 14. Comp. § 138 infra.

‡ Comp. the Louisiana Reports, vol. 13, p. 441, where it is held, that "where a slave was taken from Louisiana, with the consent of the owner, to France, although afterwards sent back here, she was thereby entitled to her freedom, from the fact of having been taken to a country where slavery is not tolerated, and where the slave becomes free by landing on the French soil." Priscilla Smith *v.* Smith. So in the

8

The case of the Creole presents an extreme example of this refusal on the part of nations to recognize the law of the domicil where it sanctions slavery. This vessel, containing slaves in transportation from one port of the United States to another, was by their act forced to put into a port of the Bahama islands in the winter of 1841–2. The slaves having secured for themselves a refuge on shore, the colonial authorities, and afterwards the British government, refused to give them up, as being free persons. If the slaves had merely fled to British territory, it was conceded that they could not be demanded back. But it was contended by Mr. Webster, that the law of nations exempts from interference property on vessels driven into foreign ports by disasters of the sea, or carried there by unlawful force.* This exemption from territorial law is undoubtedly made by the law of nations. (Comp. § 64.) But the question is, whether such a rule of comity and humanity should override a greater act of humanity and compel the territorial authorities to use force in order to prevent the slaves from retaining their liberty. By what process could this be done in a land where slavery is unknown, and how could a passenger be required to return on board a certain vessel which he had left?

Case of the Creole.

It is to be observed, however, in regard to applications of foreign law, which the moral sense or political principles of a nation reject, that questions growing out of a status which cannot be recognized by the courts, if they do not affect the personal capacity itself, may be decided according to the foreign law. Thus a contract relating to the sale and purchase of slaves might be held legal, if legal in the domicil of the contracting parties. And it is probable that the children of a polygamist Turk,† by a second or third wife, would not be treated as bastards in all respects by Christian courts.

case of Eliz. Thomas *v.* Generis *et al.* (vol. 16, p. 483, of the same Reports), it is held, that a slave taken to the State of Illinois, with express or implied consent of her master, became free, and being once free, could not again be made a slave by removing her to a slave State.

* Webster's Letter to Ashburton. Works, VI. pp. 303–313.

† Comp. Demangeat on Fœlix, I. 29.

§ 71.

II. The general leaning has been toward the rule that *movable* property follows the law of the owner's domicil, while *immovable* follows the law of the place where it lies (the *lex loci rei sitæ*, or, briefly, *lex rei sitæ*). But Savigny and others, especially German lawyers, contend that in *all* cases the *lex rei sitæ* should be followed. A comparatively modern maxim, that *mobilia ossibus inhærent*, or that a man's movables should be conceived of as passing with him wherever he dwells, expresses the former view, which is followed in our country. Against this, however, there are serious objections.

Rights of property.

1. The proper seat of the right to a thing is the place where it is. "He who wishes to gain, have, or exercise a right to a thing betakes himself for this end to its place, and subjects himself voluntarily to the local law which rules where the thing is situated." * There is the same reason for voluntary submission to law in this case as there is why the *lex domicilii* should govern in respect to personal capacity.

2. It is often difficult to say whose domicil is to condition the law,—*i. e.* what person is meant. If we say the proprietor's, it is doubtful in transfers of property whether the old or the new owner is intended; and so in suits concerning property, which of the two litigant claimants ought to have the law of his domicil followed.

3. There are two extremes of movable property,—the one nearly as fixed in place as real,—of which kind are furniture, libraries, museums, etc.,—and the other so changeable in place that no particular *lex loci* can be applied to them. Such are travellers' luggage, and merchants' wares sent abroad. In the former case, no reason can be given why law should treat the things in question otherwise than it treats real estate. In the latter, the *lex loci* must be determined, by enquiring what is the spot where the owner wishes that they should rest and change place no longer. If this is his domicil, the *lex domicilii* and

* Savigny, u. s., § 366, page 169, seq.

lex rei sitæ coincide. If not, he shows an intention of submitting to a certain other *lex rei sitæ.*

The capacity of a person to acquire or to part with property is to be decided according to the law of the domicil, since this is a capacity which follows the rule already laid down touching personal capacity.

The capacity of a thing to become private property follows the *lex rei sitæ.* And the same is to be said in regard to the power of acquiring and the restrictions on acquiring by occupation.

As to the forms of free transfer of property, there is great diversity of practice. Savigny contends that the same principle of the *lex rei sitæ* should be followed, without respect to the domicil, or the place where the contract was concluded.

As regards prescriptive right to real property, all agree that to this the *lex rei sitæ* must be applied. Opinions, however, differ as to the law which ought to regulate the title to movables so acquired, as much as the laws of different nations vary from one another. "Roman law demands possession for three years before a title can vest; Prussian for ten; French, in the case of things stolen or lost, for three; and, in other cases, shuts off the prior owner's right of suit as proprietor at the commencement of the possession."* Now, as the title here depends on possession, which is a *mere fact*, it is plainly reasonable that the law where the fact occurs should be applied in questions of usucapion or prescription, which is right grow-out of a *continued fact.*

The prosecution of claims to property is regulated by the laws of the place where the suit is brought, (the *lex fori*,) which may be, however, either the *locus rei sitæ*, or the defendant's domicil.

Jura in re, or rights inhering in things without ownership, as servitudes on land, right of cultivating or building on the land of others, (*emphyteusis* and *superficies*,) etc., follow the same rule, *i. e.* are determined by the *lex loci.*

* Savigny, u. s., p. 186, § 367. The French law is (Code civile, art. 2279,) "en fait de meubles la possession vaut titre."

§ 72.

III. In cases of obligation it is of importance to decide what is the proper court before which the obligation ought to be brought, (the *forum contractûs*,) and what is the law there to be applied. (*a*.) To determine the court it is necessary to ask what is the seat or place of an obligation, with what spot of earth this incorporeal act is most closely connected. There are two seats which can be thought of,—that where the obligation is begun, and that where it receives its fulfilment. The place where an obligation is assumed, however, is in itself accidental, unessential, and without influence on the subsequent steps in the completion of the contract. Unless, therefore, some definite expectation of the parties connects their transaction by an important link with this place, it must be decided that the place of the fulfilment of the obligation, which gives the act body and substance, ought to determine the court where he who complains of the non-fulfilment of it should bring his suit.

Right of obligation.

But what is the place of fulfilment? It is to be known from the express or tacit will of the parties. (1.) When that will is made known, or when, though not expressed, it can refer only to a definite place,—as in contracts for the repair of a house, or the rent of a house or grounds, or in guardianship, and in general and special agencies,—there is no difficulty in regard to place. (2.) Where a debtor changes his domicil before paying the debt, the court is that of his former domicil, because the expectation of the parties had fastened on this, as the place where the obligation would be discharged. (3.) If a person away from his domicil assumes an obligation, it may be that the circumstances create an expectation that the place of the origin of the obligation will be the place of fulfilment, or it may not be. Here the general rule holds. Thus a man, during a sojourn at mineral springs, may incur a debt for his board and lodging, and may make contracts of business at the same place. It is clear that this is the place of fulfilment in the first case, and need not be in the last. (4.) In cases where no definite place of fulfilment can be derived from the terms of the obligation, the *forum contractûs* must be the domicil of the debtor.

(*b*.) The same rules which apply to the court apply to the law which is to be used in its decisions. Thus, (1.) If the contract mentions, or necessarily implies a particular place of fulfilment, *the law of that place* is to rule. (2.) If the obligation grows out of a continuous course of business of the obligated person, the law of the place where the business is carried on must be applied. (3.) If the obligation has arisen out of a single act of the obligated person in his domicil, the law there must prevail, although he change his domicil afterward. (4.) If the obligation arise from a single act of a person away from his domicil, and under circumstances implying the fulfilment in that place of temporary sojourn, the law of that place must govern in judicial decisions. (5.) If none of these suppositions are true, a suit must be regulated by the law of the obligated person's domicil, since there is a presumption, where no other place or local law can be assigned to the fulfilment, that it was expected to come to pass there.

It is to be observed, however, that the complainant may bring his suit likewise before the court of the domicil of the defendant, *i. e.* he may choose between two forums; but, in either case, the law must be applied as has been just laid down, that is, the law of the place of fulfilment of the obligation, or, in default of any fixed place, the place whose law is naturally to be presumed or the domicil of the debtor.

If, again, the application of the above-mentioned rules would subject a contract to laws which would make it invalid, while, by the law of the domicil, it would be binding, it is certainly to be presumed that it was not the intention of the parties to subject themselves to laws which would render their own purpose nugatory.

Capacity to incur obligations is determined by the law governing the person concerned, that is, the law of his domicil.

The interpretation of contracts is controlled, according to the prevailing opinion, by the law and custom of the place of performance.* But Savigny remarks that the problem here is not to find out a rule of law, but to find out the true intention of the parties, according to rules of interpretation which are of a universal nature.

The validity of an obligation depends partly on the form, partly on the substance. For the former, compare what is said below in § 75. The substantial validity generally depends on the law of the place which controls the obligation. Whenever a law of a strictly positive nature opposes the matter of the contract, the *lex fori contractûs* must be applied. Thus if a suit for interest due on money be brought in a place where the usury laws would render such a transaction void, the judge must follow his own law.†

In cases of bankruptcy, where great differences of legislation exist, a simple rule would be that the courts of the insolvent's domicil should settle claims and distribute assets, whether domestic or foreign. But here there is a complication of difficulties. The creditors are of various kinds,—some privileged, some unprivileged, some having a simple claim of debt, others with a lien also on the insolvent's property, etc. And this property may be immovable property in a foreign land. Moreover, the foreign sovereign and courts often refuse to act in harmony with the court of the bankrupt's domicil. In these circumstances, some authors hold that the bankrupt's court ought to throw out of view foreign property, and that the creditors ought to sue in every jurisdiction where the debtor's property lies. The English courts, in distributing a bankrupt's assets, include foreign movable property only; most of those of the United States, neither movable nor immovable. Savigny contends that it is feasible for the *forum domicilii* to act alone in cases of bankruptcy, these questions of difficulty as to foreign property notwithstanding.

§ 73.

IV. The appropriate seat of the right of succession, inasmuch as it adheres to the person deceased, is his place of abode; and therefore the law of the domi-

Right of succession.

* Comp. Story, u. s., § 272, § 280.

† Savigny, u. s., § 374, page 277. But comp. Story, §§ 303–305.

cil, that is, of the domicil which the testator had at his death, ought to control in suits growing out of this right. No other law can claim to compete with, or prevail over it, unless it be the *lex rei sitæ*, the law of the place where the inheritance lies. But the estate, as a whole, or the inheritance, is something ideal, consisting of things in various places and of various rights in things, claims, etc. No place, therefore, can be found, saving the domicil of the deceased man.

And yet there has been in practice no general observance of this rule. In former times the practice was to apply the principle of territoriality to every piece of property, of which the right of *aubaine*, as explained above (§ 63), was an extreme instance. In more recent times, English, French, and our own courts apply the law of the domicil in cases of succession to all movable property wherever situate, and the law of the situation (*lex loci*) to immovable property. In Germany, since the beginning of the present century, this distinction between the two kinds of property is less and less observed, and the law of the domicil is applied to the whole of an estate.

The court to which testaments and intestate estates belong, is that of the last domicil of the deceased proprietor.

The capacity of a testator to make a will so far as it depends on his jural condition or state, may be under the territorial law of two places,—that of his domicil at the time of making the will, and that of his domicil at the time of his decease. If invalid according to either of these laws, the will is defective. Thus, a will would be invalid, if, by the law of either of these places, the power of making testaments is not vested in private persons, and succession is regulated by intestate laws alone. The capacity in respect to physical qualities, as age, etc., depends on the law of the domicil where the will was made. The same law, for the most part, regulates the substance of wills and their interpretation.

The personal capacity of persons to whom property is devised, heirs or legatees, is judged of by the laws of the domicil which they had at the time of the testator's death. But when laws in their domicil, contrary to the moral or political ideas prevailing where the testator lived, would cut them off, the law of the court which examines the will, *i. e.* commonly of the testator's domicil, must have application.

§ 74.

Family rights.

V. Family rights. (*a.*) Marriage. There is no doubt that the proper seat of matrimonial relations is the habitation of the husband as the head of the family. The law of his domicil must be followed, and the law of the place where the marriage was performed, so far as defining the relations is concerned, is of no importance. In England and the United States the doctrine is held, that the validity of marriage contracts must be tried by the law of the country where the marriage was celebrated.*

The hindrances to marriage depend in part on the personal quality of each of the parties; in part, on their relationship to one another. On general principles we might expect that the condition of the woman, according to the laws of her country, ought here to come into view. But as the laws regulating the possibility of marriage depend on the moral and religious views of each particular country, it must follow that the legal hindrances at the domicil of the man alone are to be regarded, and not those in the home of the bride, or at the place where the marriage ceremony occurred. In the matter of impediments to marriage the practice of nations differs widely.

As to the formalities necessary for the celebration of a marriage, the general doctrine is that the *lex loci contractûs* must decide. Savigny, however, thinks, that where an inhabitant of a state which requires religious ceremonies of marriage, forms a civil marriage in a foreign country according to its laws, this is not enough; on the ground that the laws of his domicil have a moral and religious basis, and hence a coercive character. The marriage ought to be celebrated anew according to the religious forms of the man's own domicil.

It is much disputed what law ought to be followed where

* Comp. Story, § 89; Fœlix, II. 493.

the rights of property of the married pair are called in question. Here, too, the greatest differences exist between the law of different countries. The points especially in debate are, (1.) whether foreign property, as well as domestic, should follow the *lex domicilii* of the husband. Story contends against this, and in favor of following here the *lex rei sitæ;* Savigny and Fœlix would have the law of the domicil control throughout. (2.) What is to be done if the domicil is changed during marriage? Here some maintain that the law of the prior domicil, and others that of the new domicil should be followed. Others still claim that the law of the new domicil should be applied to the property acquired since the change of residence, and the law of the earlier to all held before the change. Savigny holds, that at the time of marriage, there was a tacit subjection of both parties to the law of their habitation, which ought, therefore, to be enforced afterwards. A new law might place the wife in a worse condition than she had expected at the time of marriage.

Intestate succession between a married pair is controlled by the law of the last domicil of the deceased party.

Divorce, on account of its relations to morals and religion, is the subject of strict positive law, which the judge of the place where that law reigns must follow. This law will be that of the present domicil of the husband; for the laws of the earlier domicil can have given neither of the married parties a right, or even a well-grounded expectation of being separated hereafter by the rules there prevailing, since the above-mentioned peculiar character of divorce laws leads to an opposite inference. In regard to divorce, the opinions of writers, and the decrees of courts, vary exceedingly from one another.

(*b.*) Guardianship. The guardian empowered according to the law of the ward's domicil, which will usually be that of the deceased parent, exercises control over the ward's property wherever situated. But in the case of immovable property, the *lex rei sitæ* may prevent such control of a foreigner, and it may be necessary to appoint a special guardian residing within the jurisdiction. In the United States, the power of guardians is considered as strictly local; they can exercise control neither over the person, personal property, nor real property of wards, in other states.*

§ 75.

Forms of legal acts.

VI. Acts having a legal validity are everywhere reduced to certain forms; a certain number of witnesses is required to prove them; a certain magistrate to authenticate them. Now if the law of every state demanded that a document, to be legal, should have the form required within its jurisdiction, there would be endless embarrassment, and sometimes legal acts could not be performed at all. Thus, a Prussian cannot make a will when at home without the intervention of a court, while in France the formalities of wills belong to notaries alone. Hence, if Prussia insisted that her legal forms should be necessary in all wills wherever made, a Prussian stranger in France could not make one, to the great detriment, it might be, of his family. The general rule, therefore, that has been adopted is that *locus regit actum*, or that the law and usage of the place where a legal act is performed, determines its validity, that is, that an act which is authentic in its own place is so everywhere. Any other rule would call in each place for the knowledge of the formalities necessary in every place. It is to be assumed that the laws of all civilized countries, however they may differ from each other, aim to give the due solemnity and certainty to legal acts and documents. This rule has little application within the province of personal status and of rights to things. Its importance consists in its application to obligations, testaments, and marriages.

§ 76.

Use of courts allowed to strangers.

The comity of nations allows to strangers a free use of the courts of each other's country. In France, however, a foreigner bringing a suit is obliged to furnish security that the costs of suit will be satisfied; while the native Frenchman is not obliged to do this. The same rule

* Story, §§ 499, 504.

prevails in some other countries on the continent. But to this rule, there are in France two exceptions apart from exemptions by treaty; one in commercial transactions; the other where the foreign demandant possesses in the realm immovables of sufficient value to pay expenses. The same rule holds in England, where the foreigner himself is not actually in the country.

In most countries, free use of the courts is given to strangers not domiciled, if they have occasion to bring suits *in personam* * against such other strangers. In France, however, this humane provision does not exist except in the case of foreign merchants, and where treaties provide for such protection. The doctrine is that foreigners in such complaints must invoke the aid of their own courts or that of the defendant party.

In suits against foreigners the practice of nations differs.

Suits against foreigners.

In countries under Roman law, the maxim, *actor sequitur forum rei*, generally prevails; that is, the plaintiff must sue in the court of the defendant's domicil. In countries under English law, however, personal actions "may be brought in the domestic forum, whoever may be the parties and wherever the cause of action may originate." "All real and possessory actions must be brought in the place where the property lies.†" The rule embodied in the maxim abovementioned admits of exceptions where it is followed. Thus, in France, a Frenchman may summon a foreigner, even one not resident in France, before the French tribunals for the fulfilment of obligations by him contracted towards the Frenchman, whether within or without the realm.‡

Proofs.

The maxim *locus regit actum* will imply that testimony in writing, and all documents, in the form proper at any place, ought to be received as valid in all other courts. The same law-maxim, perhaps, may be used to answer the enquiry what weight is to be given to parol evidence, in regard to facts occurring abroad, by the courts of countries where such evidence is not usually admissible. As testimony by witnesses is a satisfactory form of proof in the foreign country in regard to a given fact, why should it not be

* Story, §§ 542, 543 † Wheaton, II. 2, § 20. ‡ Fœlix, I. §§ 169–186.

received as such in other countries where the same facts come before the courts? Such, indeed, is the opinion generally adopted.*

Many countries aid one another's judicial proceedings by consenting that their judges may accept rogatory commissions, or act as agents of foreign courts for the purpose of examining witnesses or otherwise ascertaining facts. These are acts of reciprocal comity, which cannot extend to cases where the interrogation would be prejudicial to public or private rights. Such commissions are not in vogue in England and the United States, says Fœlix, where, consequently, if foreign testimony is to be taken, some agent of the court, who has no power to compel witnesses to testify, is deputed to take the evidence in the foreign country.†

Rogatory commissions.

§ 77.

The judgment of a court and the execution of it are acts of sovereignty. Comity alone gives them effect out of the country where they originate. Many writers on international law maintain that a definitive decision by a competent court in a foreign country, under due forms of law, and where opportunity of appeal is allowed, ought to stand and receive its execution in any other country, as much as the decisions of its own tribunals,—provided, however, that such judgment contain nothing contrary to the interests or rights of the foreign country. This principle has passed in a degree into the laws and practice of the European states. Some of them have adopted in this respect the rule of reciprocity. France, on the other hand, takes ground which greatly restricts the effects of foreign judgments within her borders. An ordinance of 1629, still in force, prescribes, that judgments rendered in foreign sovereignties, shall have no execution in France, and that subjects of the French king, against whom they are rendered, may bring their cases up anew for revision before the tribunals of their own country. According to M. Fœlix, this law does not prevent judgments rendered against a

Effect of foreign judgments.

* Fœlix, I. § 233

† Fœlix, I. § 241.

stranger from being executed in France, if judged not inconsistent with the rights and interests of the nation. England again takes a third position. He who has obtained a foreign judgment in his favor, brings before the court a claim to the thing adjudged to him. The foreign judgment is regarded as a decisive proof of the justice of the claim, unless some irregularity can be shown by the opposite party.*

§ 78.

Crimes committed in a foreign country.

Each nation has a right to try and punish according to its own laws crimes committed on its soil, whoever may be the perpetrator. But some nations extend the operation of their laws, so as to reach crimes committed by their subjects upon foreign territory. In this procedure municipal law only is concerned, and not international; and, as might be supposed, laws greatly differ in their provisions. (1.) One group of states, including many of the German states, some of the Swiss cantons, Naples, Portugal, Russia, and Norway, punish all offences of their subjects, committed in foreign parts, whether against themselves, their subjects, or foreigners, and this not in accordance with foreign but with domestic criminal law. (2.) At the opposite extreme stand Great Britain, the United States and France, which, on the principle that criminal law is territorial, refrain from visiting with penalty crimes of their subjects committed abroad. Yet they do not adhere to this rule with absolute rigor. The two former try and punish slave-trading carried on by their subjects in foreign vessels, and crimes perpetrated in foreign countries where exterritorial jurisdiction is conceded to them. Great Britain punishes high treason, murder, homicide, bigamy, illegal acts of British crews, and crimes perpetrated in certain barbarous countries. France notices *no crimes of Frenchmen against foreigners*, nor "délits" of one Frenchman against another on foreign soil; nor "crimes" of Frenchman against Frenchman except on complaint of the injured party; but punishes offences against the safety of France, together

* Fœlix II. § 347–404, esp. § 357. But comp. Story, § 603–607.

with counterfeiting its seal, coins, and paper money. (3.) Certain states, as Belgium, Holland, Sardinia, Darmstadt, punish foreign crimes of their subjects against the state or their fellow-subjects, but only certain crimes of such subjects in foreign parts against foreigners. The two former call to account only for grave crimes, as murder, arson, rape, forgery;—Belgium adopting the same standard which she applies to her treaties relating to the extradition of fugitive foreigners. Sardinia makes punishable all "crimes" of its subjects abroad, but "délits" are subject to the rule of reciprocity. The scale of punishment also is in all cases one degree less than that of the same offences committed at home. (4.) Wurtemberg makes the fact of punishment, (in a milder former than for similar crimes at home,) dependent on the questions whether the given offence has a penalty affixed to it by the laws of the foreign state where it took place, and whether it would be punishable there, if committed against Wurtemberg.

The same difference of practice exists in the case of crimes committed by *foreigners in a foreign* country against a state or one of its subjects, who are afterwards found by the injured state within its borders. England and the United States seem not to refuse the right of asylum, even in such cases. France punishes public crimes only, and such as Frenchmen would be liable for, if committed abroad. (See this § above.) So Belgium and Sardinia, but the latter state also, in the case of wrongs done to the individual Sardinian, first makes an offer of delivering up the offending foreigner to the *forum delicti*, and if this is declined, then gives the case over to its own courts. Many states, again, act on the principle that it is as right to punish a foreigner as a subject for foreign crimes against themselves or their subjects.

Nearly all states consider *foreign crimes*, against *foreign states* or their subjects, as beyond their jurisdiction. A few refuse sojourn on their soil to such foreign wrong doers. A few go so far as to punish even here, in case the party most nearly concerned neglects to take up the matter. Thus Austria, if an offer of extradition is declined by the offending state, punishes and relegates the criminal.*

From this exposition it is evident (1.) that states are far from universally admitting the territoriality of crime; (2.) that those who go farthest in carrying out this principle depart from it in some cases, and are inconsistent with themselves. To this we may add (3.) that the principle is not founded on reason, and (4.) that, as intercourse grows closer in the world, nations will the more readily aid general justice. Comp. § 20 *b*.

§ 79.

Criminals escaping into a foreign country. Extradition.

The considerations which affect the question, What a government ought to do in regard to fugitives from foreign justice, who have escaped into its territory? are chiefly these: *First*, that no nation is held to be *bound* to administer the laws of another, or to aid in administering them; *secondly*, that it is for the interest of general justice that criminals should not avoid punishment by finding a refuge on another soil, not to say that the country harboring them may add thereby to the number of its worthless inhabitants; and, *thirdly*, that the definitions of crime vary so much in different nations, that a consent to deliver up all accused fugitives to the authorities at home for trial, would often violate the feeling of justice or of humanity. Some have contended for an absolute obligation to deliver up fugitives from justice; but (1.) The number of treaties of extradition, shows that no such obligation is generally recognized. Else what need of treaties giving consent to such extradition, and specifying crimes for which the fugitive should be delivered up? (2.) It may be said that the analogy of private international law requires it. If a nation opens its courts for the claim of one foreigner on another, and in so doing applies foreign law to the case, why should it not open them for claims of a foreign government against violators of its laws? But the analogy fails. In *private* claims, the basis of right is admitted

* These facts are drawn from an essay on the doctrine of asylum, by R. v. Mohl, in his Staatsr. Völkerr. u. Politik, vol. I. 644–649.

with a general agreement by the law of all states. In *public* prosecution of criminals, different views of right are taken, as it respect offences, method of trial, and degree of punishment. There is a class of persons, particularly,—political offenders,—whom the world often regards as unfortunate rather than guilty, who may make useful inhabitants of another land, having sinned not against the morality of the universe, but against the absurd laws, it may be, of an antiquated political system. It is chiefly on their account that (3.) nations, the most humane, or the most jealous of their own sovereignty, have felt it to be base and wrong to send back voluntary exiles to their native land.*

We conclude that there is a limited obligation of nations to assist each other's criminal justice, which only special treaties, expressing the views of the parties at the time, can define. Of such treaties there is no lack. The United States and Great Britain entered into one in 1842, providing for extradition in cases of murder, assault with intent to murder, piracy, arson, robbery, forgery, and utterance of forged paper. Another between the United States and France, made in 1843, relates to charges for murder, attempts to murder, rape, forgery, arson, and such embezzlement by *public officers*, as subjects to infamous punishment in France, to which subsequently robbery and burglary were added. Quite recently, in 1859, an additional article includes persons charged as principals, accessories, or accomplices, in forging, or knowingly passing or putting into circulation counterfeit coin or bank notes, or other paper currency as money, with intent to defraud, and also embezzlement by any *salaried persons*, to the detriment of their employers, which subjects to infamous punishment. In both treaties it is required that the evidence of criminality must be such as to justify apprehension and commitment, according to the law of the place of the accused person's refuge.

The case of political refugees has some points peculiar to

* The feeling at Athens is shown in the very instructive oration of Demosthenes against Aristocrates, § 85, Bekker, *κατὰ τὸν κοινὸν ἁπάντων ἀνθρώπων νόμον, ὃς κεῖται τὸν φεύγοντα δέχεσθαι.*

itself. A nation, as we have seen, has a right to harbor such persons, and will do so, unless weakness or political sympathy lead it to the contrary course. But they may not, consistently with the obligations of friendship between states, be allowed to plot against the person of the sovereign, or against the institutions of their native country. Such acts are crimes, for the trial and punishment of which the laws of the land ought to provide, but do not require that the accused be remanded for trial to his native country.

§ 80.

International copy-right, and patent-right.

A peculiar question touching international law is presented by the rights of authors and inventors. Have these such an absolute right of property that the book or machine cannot be reproduced in a foreign land without their consent,—the book not even in a foreign translation, and if so, ought not the patent to be perpetual every where? These are questions which have been considered seriously only in more recent times; about which, therefore, there is no agreement of nations. But many treaties in modern times have provided protection to such persons, and this protection for a limited time is likely to become universal, whereever applied for.*

* For the law of copy-right comp. O. Wächter, das Verlagsrecht, Stuttgart, 1858, esp. pp. 741–832; P. Burke, the law of international copy-right between England and France, Lond. 1852. The leading principles of the laws and treaties thus far made are reciprocity between the states concerned, a limited term of protection, and that the right of translation belongs to the author or his assigns. In this country, no international law or treaty relating to copy-right as yet exists. The foreigner, although by the admission of all jurists having a property to his work, is unprotected.

§ 81.

APPENDIX

A case, remarkable as involving several points of international law, relating to the condition of aliens and the protection due to them, is that of Martin Koszta. This man, who had been engaged in the Hungarian rebellion of 1849, fled into Turkish territory with a number of others, and, at length, after refusal to deliver him up to Austria, was, with the understanding of that government, sent out of Turkey into foreign parts. "It was alleged that he engaged never to return," says Mr. Marcy, "but this is regarded as doubtful."* The man chose the United States as his place of exile, and in 1852 made the usual declaration, preparatory to being naturalized, which our laws require. In 1854 he returned to Turkey, on account, it is said, of private affairs. At Smyrna, being provided with a *tezkereh* or passport from the American consul there, and from the acting chargé at Constantinople, he was seized on land, thrown into the water, taken up by the boat's crew of an Austrian frigate, and put into irons. This was done at the instigation of the Austrian consul-general at Smyrna, and after refusal of the Turkish governor to allow his arrest. Intercessions for his release on the ground of his American nationality, were ineffectual. Finally, when it was reported that a design had been formed of removing the man by stealth into the dominions of Austria, the captain of a public vessel of the United States, then in port, prepared to resort to force, unless he was released. This led to an arrangement, by which he was put under the custody of the French consul-general until the governments, which were at issue, should agree what to do with him. He afterwards went back to the United States.

Case of Koszta.

The following are some of the points which arise to view in the discussion of this case:

1. Granting that the man was an Austrian subject, could he be legally seized in Turkey? His crime had been a political one. The Turks had refused, with the approbation of ambassadors of the most important Christian powers, to deliver up the Hungarian fugitives, on the ground of the political nature of their offence.

It was said that the exterritorial consular jurisdiction mentioned below (§ 96,) authorized his arrest. The reply of Mr. Marcy to this is, that such jurisdiction was intended for a different set of cases, and such is probably the fact. The Austrian officials, then, in seizing him, committed an offence

* Mr. Hülsemann's letter to Mr. Marcy, and his reply in Senate documents, 33d Congr., 1st Session, vol. I.

against the sovereignty of Turkey, and so, an offence against the law of nations.

2. Was he an Austrian subject? Austrian nationality ceases according to what is said in § 66, on the authority of M. Fœlix, when a subject emigrates with the consent of the government. He had more than the consent of his government to his abandonment of his country; he was forced into exile. But to this it might be replied, that he had agreed in writing never to return to Turkey, and that the Austrian claim upon him would revive on his failing to fulfil this condition. It is indeed questioned by Mr. Marcy, whether he engaged never to return; and it might perhaps be said, that, if such an engagement existed, it related only to return for political purposes. But to this Austria might reply, that she could not know what his purposes were, and that the promise must be absolute, in order to prevent his doing political mischief in the neighborhood of Hungary. This, however, is a point on which our diplomatist preserves silence.

3. What were his relations to the United States? Not those of a citizen, but of a domiciled stranger. His oath, declaring his purpose to become a citizen, and his long stay here, put this out of the question, and his temporary absence could not shake this character off. Moreover, he had a passport, certifying to his American nationality. He would therefore be entitled, by the law of nations, to the protection of the Turkish authorities against his Austrian captors. Had he been even a fugitive prisoner of war, he could not lawfully have been seized on shore, unless treaty had so provided. He would equally be entitled to all that protection which officials of the United States were authorized to extend to him within Turkish territory.

4. Would it have been in accordance with international law for the captain of the frigate to use force in protecting him within the port of Smyrna? Active and aggressive force certainly not. As things were, the demonstration of force saved the use of it. But to complain of such force would have fallen to the duty of Turkey, as it would have taken place within her waters. As for force, absolutely considered, for instance on the high seas, Austria could not have complained, if the evils of a sudden wrong on her part were in that way sought to be prevented.

At the bottom this was a case of collision between original and transferred allegiance, the latter in its incipiency, in which the obligation to protect the person, within the limits of the law of nations, clearly lay on the United States. How Austria could have dealt with him within her own limits is another question.

CHAPTER IV.

THE FORMS AND THE AGENTS OF INTERCOURSE BETWEEN NATIONS.

SECTION I.—*The Forms of Intercourse, or International Courtesy.*

§ 82.

General comity between nations.

WE have hitherto considered the duties and usages of nations, so far as relates to the treatment of individual aliens who are within their territory. We now pass on to the conduct which is due from one body politic to another, and to the representatives by whom public intercourse is managed.

The general duties here required are those which are included in the word comity: we call them duties at their origin, as being more or less indefinite, and not of strict obligation; but they become obligatory, if by compact or compliance with usage a nation takes them upon itself in a specific shape. These duties are such as polite treatment of a sovereign or of his ministers in a foreign country, courtesy in diplomatic intercourse, the observance of court-etiquette, and of respect on the sea towards a foreign flag. Besides duties such as these, we place under this head respect for the reputation of a foreign state, which is, as we have seen (§ 18), a thing of strict justice.

The use of formal expressions of courtesy among nations consists in their preventing jealousies and quarrels. At the same time they may themselves be the causes of disputes, for, when once established by usage, to withhold them is a slight; and to pay attentions of different kinds, or in different degrees, to equal and sovereign states, may be more provoking than if both states had been treated with equal want of politeness.

But on the whole, as in the society of individuals who are equals, so among states it is probable that without them there would be a far greater amount of unfriendliness.

§ 83.

Regard for the reputation of another state.

Every nation, as we have seen, has a right of reputation; every other, therefore, is bound to abstain from deeds and words, which are calculated to wound its sense of character, or to injure its good name, or that of its sovereign, before the world. No nation, then, through its public documents, or by its official persons, can with right reflect on the institutions or social characteristics of another, or make invidious comparisons to its disadvantage, or set forth in any way an opinion of its inferiority. So with regard to its functionaries, an intended insult to whom is an insult to the state which they represent. But a state is not bound to repress the free remarks made by the press and private persons upon foreign states and sovereigns, although comity, if not justice, requires that foreign sovereigns should have the power to prosecute for libel or scandal before its courts. Nor again ought regard for the feelings of another government to preclude a state from remonstrating, even in strong terms, against conduct which it judges to be oppressive or flagitious, although that conduct may be confined in its effects to the subjects of the wrong-doing state. (Comp. § 111.)

The Hülsemann affair.

It may be made a question, how far documents, which are not strictly public, may be complained of by foreign states, as embodying insults against themselves. A noted case of such complaints occurred in 1850, after our government had sent a secret agent to ascertain whether Hungary, in its war with Austria, was likely to achieve its independence. So much the government had a right to do, as it interfered in no manner in the struggle. But when the instructions to this agent were published, containing the expression "iron rule," applied to the sway of Austria over Hungary, the Austrian government directed its Chargé d'affaires at Washington, Mr. Hülsemann, to communicate its displeasure at this offensive expression, and at the apparent sympathy with a part of the empire in revolt. It was replied by the United States, that there had been no interference in the quarrel between Austria and Hungary; that a sympathy with a people struggling for its independence was, on our part, unavoidable; and "that a communication from the President to either House of Congress, is regarded as a domestic communication, of which ordinarily no foreign state has cognizance." This is true, because ordinarily the departments of a government do not discuss the affairs of foreign countries, with which one or other of them has nothing immediately to do. But it is evident that communications may be made between the departments of a government, for which a foreign state may demand redress. The degree of publicity, now given to political documents, is such, that they are brought before the eyes of the world, and cannot be regarded as private. If a man allows his private letters, reflecting on individuals, to be published, he may commit a wrong; and so may a nation or a government, if it make or allow to be made public what may fairly be called insults to foreign states.

§ 84.

Treatment of foreign sovereigns, etc.

It may be inexpedient to admit foreign sovereigns into a country, but comity requires that this be ordinarily allowed, and that, besides the exterritoriality which they enjoy (§ 64), such marks of respect should be paid to them, and to the members of sovereign houses, as may be required by the usages of Christian states. So also in their transit through, or passage along the coasts of another country they are to be saluted in a manner becoming the dignity of their stations, as the highest representatives of an independent state.

A more free and indefinite treatment of sovereign houses by one another, consists in friendly announcements of interesting events, as births, deaths, betrothals, and marriages; and in corresponding expressions of congratulation or condolence, amounting in the latter case even to the putting on of mourning. These courtesies of intercourse are called by some text-writers *state-gallantry*.

Ceremonial of courts.

Every court has its own ceremonial and rules of precedence at state festivals and the like. While observing these, which are nearly alike wherever there is a monarch and a court, a state is bound to make no distinctions in external politeness between foreign representatives, so far as such traditional rules do not make it necessary; and foreign representatives are bound to conform to the ceremonial *lex loci*, if consistent with the honor of their country.

Diplomatic correspondence of states.

It is evident that correspondence, between the legate of one state and the minister or sovereign of another, requires both those forms of address which are usual among diplomatists, and an abstinence from all expressions of anger and of contempt. Otherwise, an offence against the self-respect of the nation, with whose functionaries he holds intercourse, is committed, and he may need to atone for his fault by apology or by recall, or else furnish ground of complaint against his nation.

§ 85.

Ceremonial of the sea.

In regard to the forms of international politeness on the sea, a distinction is to be made between what is done within the waters of a nation, and what is done on the high seas, where nations are entirely equal. On the high seas, and, indeed, in the waters of third powers, ships of war are under no imperative obligation from usage or law to salute one another, and yet such marks of respect are not unusual, and are in some degree expected, so that the absence of them, although no insult, might be regarded as discourteous. They ought generally to be returned if offered by one of the parties.* But within its own sea line a sovereign state may

* Bynkersh. Quaest. J. P., 2, § 24. "Quod ad mare exterum, quod in nullius Principis dominio est, nullius quoque est aliis reverentiam imperare, et salutem navibus suis præstandam exigere. Sunt quædam, quæ, tametsi honeste præstentur, inhoneste tamen petuntur. Inter ea refero, si quis minor dignitate majorem, in publico sibi obviam factum, salutet vel non salutet, et siquæ minorum Principum navis, in mari extero, navibus majorum Principum, quaqua etiam dignitate sint, salutem dicat vel neget.

prescribe the ceremonies with which its forts and ships of war are to be approached or passed, but it must require nothing which can be degrading to other states. And in cases, where the claim of a nation over certain waters is not acknowledged, to refuse compliance with a prescribed ceremony is a mode of showing national independence, at which no offence can be justly taken.

Forms of politeness on the sea.

Various forms of international politeness on the sea, are, or have been in vogue, such as furling, inclining or lowering the flag, lowering the topsails, firing salutes with cannon, sometimes accompanied with salvos of musketry, lowering and raising the flag several times in succession, salutations with the voice, and finally, complimentary visits to each other's vessel. To take down the flag, or to lower the topsails, is a token of inferiority, which is now nearly or quite obsolete. "To lower or furl the flag," says Ortolan,* "is not now practised between vessels of war, as a token of respect, and is a sign, rather, of mourning or of danger. But merchant vessels often greet vessels of war by lowering and raising the flag three several times."

The etiquette of the sea requires that a ship of war entering a harbor, or passing by a fort or castle, should pay the first salute, except when the sovereign or his ambassador is on board, in which case the greeting ought to be made first on the shore. So also the earliest salutation should proceed from a ship meeting or joining a fleet, and from an auxiliary squadron on its approach to the main armament. When single vessels encounter one another, an admiral's ship is to receive the first compliment, and so downward, according to rank, the inferior vessel always commencing salutations. Privateers greet ships of war without having a right to expect the return of the compliment. Merchant ships salute foreign ships of war by demonstrations with sail and flag, or with cannon, if they have any, but the ship need not slacken its course for such purposes. A superior vessel, as one commanded by an admiral, may respond to a compliment with a smaller number of shot, but in

* Diplom. de la mer, Vol. I. Book 2, Chap. 15.

general the marks of respect between public vessels must be equal.*

The rules of sea politeness are often embodied in instructions given to commanders of vessels by their respective governments, which directions, through the Christian states of the world, have a general uniformity. They are also sometimes a subject of special treaty. "They are of use," as Ortolan, himself a naval officer, remarks,† "as honors paid to the independence of nations, as a public authorized recognition that the sovereignties of the world are entitled to mutual respect. They help the crews of public vessels, from the commanders down to the marines, to feel that the national honor is in their hands, and thus raise the sense of character of those who are representatives of nations upon the seas."

§ 86.

Disputes in Cent. XVII. concerning ceremonies at sea.

Formerly, above all in century XVII., the tokens of respect which certain nations demanded of others, in seas over which they asserted dominion, gave rise to bitter feelings and to hostilities, or rather served as a pretext for wars which were waged on other grounds. Especially was the English claim to sovereignty in the narrow seas around Great Britain, a fruitful source of animosities from the beginning of the reign of James I. onward. The demand was, that all foreign vessels should first salute English vessels of war by lowering flags and topsails, without any corresponding mark of respect being made obligatory on the other side.‡ This France and Spain forbade their vessels to comply with; and in 1634, by an arrangement between France and England, the

* Comp. Heffter, § 197. † Diplom. de la mer, u. s.

‡ In a communication to the court of France in 1667, the Dutch say that they are willing that France should salute them with two cannon shot less, but cannot consent to lower their flag, unless France shall do the same in return. They add, that although the English in an article of the treaty prescribing tokens of respect are not expressly bound to return the salutation with the flag which the Dutch offer to them, it is with justice presumed to be incumbent on them, and that if the English have failed in such reciprocity, they have failed in their duty, for which reason the Dutch afterwards refused to lower their flag, as by treaty required. See Ortolan, I. 369.

ships of each state, when nearer to the other's territory, should give the first salute. But from Holland, England was led, by commercial jealousy and a feeling of superior strength, to require those humiliating marks of respect with great pertinacity. The war between the two nations, which broke out in 1652, was preceded by an engagement between Blake and Van Tromp, growing out of the demand that the flag of Holland should be lowered; and in the treaties of 1654, 1662, and 1667, the Dutch agreed to pay this compliment within certain seas in future. In 1671 the captain of a king's yacht sailed out of the Meuse through a Dutch fleet, having received orders to test their compliance with this rule: the vice-admiral in command declared his willingness to lower his own flag to the royal flag of England, but refused to allow the whole fleet to join in the act. For this the yacht fired upon him, but its captain was put into the Tower on reaching England, for not continuing his fire although the Dutch had not retaliated. The English ambassador at the Hague claimed that reparation was due for this refusal of the vice-admiral, inasmuch as not only single vessels, but also whole fleets, were obliged to strike the flag to an English vessel of war. The refusal of the States-general to redress this grievance was a leading pretext of the already meditated war of 1672.* At the peace of 1674, it was stipulated that fleets as well as single vessels, belonging to the Dutch republic, should furl the flag, and lower the topsail before any English vessel of war, between Cape Staten in Norway and Cape Finisterre in Northern Spain. Even in 1784,†

* Bynkershoek's critique on this transaction (u. s) is worthy of notice. While he inclines to admit that the treaty of 1654, rightly interpreted, sustained the English claim that a whole fleet of the Dutch should salute a single English ship in the English seas, by lowering flag and topsails, he claims, (1.) that the affair occurred near the shore of Zeeland, and therefore outside of the English dominions; (2.) that a yacht, though with guns on board, is a vessel of pleasure, not of war; and (3.) that the Dutch vessels constituted a fleet, and that fleets can be compared to forts, garrisoned places and harbors, which by common usage are to be saluted first. Moreover a fleet at anchor occupies a part of the sea, which thus passes under the sway and dominion of the occupant, to whom, therefore, being now in his own territory, the first tokens of respect are to be rendered. This last plea is evidently worthless.

† Ortolan, I. 372.

these absurd tokens of inferiority were again confirmed in a treaty.

The French, in the same century, set up similar pretensions against Holland, although without the pretext of dominion over the narrow seas. But their claims were not so galling, or so persevering, as those of England. In an ordonnance of 1689, Louis XIV. went so far as to require that when French vessels of war met those of other nations equal in rank, they should demand the first salute, and use force, if it were withheld. This is mentioned as a grievance by William III. in the declaration of war, which he made at the beginning of his reign.

In the 18th century a number of treaties established equality and reciprocity in the ceremonial of the sea, and the practice of nations has nearly reached this point in all respects.

Section II.—*The Agents in the Intercourse of Nations, or Ambassadors and Consuls.*

§ 87.

Persons appointed to manage the intercourse between nations.

Nations holding intercourse with one another need to have some understanding as to the conditions of the intercourse, and certain functionaries by whom the intercourse between the sovereignties may be carried on, and that between the citizens or subjects may be reduced to rule. Such persons we may call generically ambassadors; but they may have various other denominations, as legates, envoys, chargés d'affaires, foreign ministers, and nuncios, which term, together with others, is appropriated to the Pope's messengers to foreign courts. The word ambassador may denote also a particular class or rank of agents of national intercourse. We may divide ambassadors, again, into ordinary and extraordinary, or resident and temporary, into open and secret, those with limited powers and plenipotentiaries,—although this title is often used in a vague sense below its proper meaning,—those who are sent to do business, and those who represent the state at some ceremony of a foreign court, and the like.

Again the sovereign, or head of a department, or even a military officer, may discharge the functions of an ambassador, or be joined with one in negotiations, without holding the office or having the title. An ambassador differs from a commissary or commissioner to whom some business not of a diplomatic nature is entrusted; from a deputy who is sent by subjects, as by a province, to a sovereign; and from a consul who under a treaty, or by the practice of two nations, protects the private affairs of individuals of the one within the territory of the other, and watches over the commercial interests of the nation which he represents.

The word ambassador comes through the mediæval Latin *ambactia* or *ambaxia*, meaning service or charge, either from the Celtic *ambactus*, *client*, or *retainer*, used once in Cæsar's Gallic war (VI. 15), or from the Gothic *andbahts*, with nearly the same sense.* Both words may be, indeed, of the same origin. The signification will, then, correspond with that of *minister*. The Greek equivalent denotes an *elder* of the people. The Latins used the words *orator*, and more commonly *legatus*, person acting by delegated authority, whence this branch of international law is called *jus legatorum*, and *jus legationum*, the rights of legation.

§ 88.

Origin of the privileges of ambassadors.

Ambassadors always and everywhere have had special immunities, and often something of a sacred character. This sacredness, which they have shared with heralds, and bearers of flags of truce, cannot be accounted for from their being originally ministers of religion, selected before others for their gravity or dignity; but the protection of religion must have been given to them because their functions and duties were of pre-eminent importance. They were the agents in all the intercourse of two tribes or nations, and above all in making peace and preventing war. If not pro-

* Comp. Dietz, Etymol. voce *ambascia*, and Grimm, Wörterb. voce *amt*.

tected, they would not expose themselves to the danger of going among enemies or strangers. They carried with them the dignity of representing their nation. Thus the importance of their work, the necessity that they should be assured of safety, and the dignity of their office caused those religious sanctions to be thrown around them, by which the more important relations and rights were defended in ancient times.

§ 89.

Temporary and resident ambassadors.

Ambassadors in ancient times were *sent on special occasions* by one nation to another. Their *residence* at foreign courts is a practice of modern growth. Some have thought that it was suggested by the Pope's legates, sent to reside, or appointed from among ecclesiastics residing, in different parts of Christendom. By others, according to Mr. Ward (II. 290), it has been attributed "to Ferdinand the Catholic, whose policy led him to entertain [ambassadors] at various courts, as a kind of honorable spies;" but Flassan * makes Louis XI. of France, Ferdinand's earlier contemporary, the introducer of the new usage. "Before him ambassadors had only temporary and limited missions, but this prince judged it best to multiply them, and to prolong their stay abroad, especially at the courts of Burgundy and England. As these courts penetrated into his design, they in turn despatched to him permanent ambassadors, who converted diplomacy into intrigues and trickeries. Louis XI. on sending the Sieurs du Bouchage and de Solliers to the Dukes of Guienne and of Brittany, gave them for their instructions, 'If they lie to you, lie still more to them.'" But the residence of ambassadors at foreign courts did not become the common practice until after the reformation. Henry VII. of England "would not in his time, suffer Lieger ambassadours of any foreign king or prince within his realm, or he with them, but upon occasion used ambassadours." * In the middle of century XVII. it was

* Diplom. Française, I. 247.

† Coke's 4th Inst. 155, cited by Ward, u. s., who says that Lieger is derived from the Dutch. But the true explanation is to be found in the word *Leger* of German origin, used in the trading marts to denote an agent of foreign merchants

said in Poland of a French envoy, that as he did not return home according to the custom of ambassadors, he ought to be considered as a spy. And a century afterwards Bynkershoek (de for. leg. § 1) defines *ordinary* legates as those who "non unius sed omnium rerum, atque adeo et *explorandi* ergo in amicorum aulis habentur." Grotius affirms (Cent. XVII. in the middle) that *legationes assiduæ* may, without infringement of rights, be rejected by nations, being unknown to ancient practice (II. 18. 3). But the usage is now fixed among all nations of European origin: and ambassadors by remaining in foreign countries serve the interests of their own state in various ways, far more than persons could who should be sent abroad on special occasions. In fact, to attempt to break away from the usage might be regarded as indicating a want of comity, if not of friendship. But although the sending of ambassadors and even of resident ambassadors seems almost essential to a participation in the international law of Christendom, there are some few of this circle of nations who hold no such communication with each other. England and some other Protestant states entertain no ministers at the Pope's court, nor does he at theirs. On the other hand, the principal Christian states keep up diplomatic relations with some states out of their pale of civilization and religion, as with Turkey, Persia and China, sending temporary ambassadors to the latter, and ordinary ones to the two former.

§ 90.

Is there any obligation to receive ambassadors.

The question whether a nation is bound to receive the ambassador of another, depends on the question of the right of intercourse which has been already considered. Nor is it impossible that intercourse commercial, if not political, should subsist without such an agent. But if a nation has already entered into diplomatic ties with another, to dissolve them is a breach of friendship, and is often the step immediately preceding war. By treaty

resident in a town where they had a depot of their goods, and transferred to the agent of a prince. See Hüllmann, Städtewesen des Mittelalt. I. 202.

or usage, a right had sprung up, which, together with the duty of comity, the dismissal of an ambassador invaded.

But these are exceptions to the rule that nations cannot suspend their diplomatic intercourse, already established, without offence. (1.) A nation may refuse to receive *any* ambassador when the sovereignty of the party sending him is doubtful. This may happen when a state is convulsed by civil war, both factions in which claim to exercise sovereignty, and when a new government after a revolution is not yet fully established. (2.) A nation or sovereign may refuse to receive a *particular* individual as the representative of a foreign power without giving cause of offence. Thus, it is held that a sovereign is not bound to receive his own subject in this capacity, on the ground that the privileges of his office would place him beyond the reach of the native jurisdiction. So a person who has rendered himself obnoxious, or is of a notoriously bad character, may be rejected. Richelieu told the English ambassador at Paris, that the Duke of Buckingham would not be accepted as ambassador extraordinary; and at an earlier date, Francis I. of France refused Cardinal Pole as the Pope's legate, on the ground of his being a personal enemy of the king's ally, Henry VIII. of England. (3.) A state or sovereign may refuse to receive a minister sent on an errand inconsistent with its dignity or interests. The United Provinces, during their struggle for independence, declined treating with envoys from friendly German powers, bearing proposals of peace incompatible with their honor; and Elizabeth of England rejected the nuncio of Pius IV., sent to invite her to appoint deputies for the Council of Trent, because his mission might have the ulterior object of stirring up disaffection among the English.

§ 91.

Right of sending ambassadors.

The right of sending ambassadors is an attribute of sovereignty, but the power of appointing them may be vested in some representative of the sovereign. Thus, in this country, it is exercised by the President and senate, or during the recess of the senate, by the President alone, subject to their confirmation or rejection; and it has sometimes been intrusted to the commander of an army. Can a deposed sovereign, a monarch without a kingdom, perform this function? In the case mentioned by Mr. Ward (II. 292–295) of Leslie, Bishop of Ross, calling himself ambassador of Mary, Queen of Scots, who was then after dethronement a prisoner in England, the lawyers consulted by the government decided, that "the solicitor of a prince *lawfully* deposed, and another being invested in his place, cannot have the privilege of an ambassador, for that none but princes and such other as have sovereignty may have ambassadors." The word *lawfully* seems to make the opinion futile, for who is to decide. The word *actually* would have better agreed with that safe usage, which is a part of international law, of acknowledging the sovereign *de facto*, and to which the United States have ever adhered. When James II. lived in exile, his ambassadors were received as those of the sovereign *de jure* by a part of the European states. The more common practice we apprehend to be for sovereigns who sympathize with a deposed prince to hold communications with him by persons not openly sustaining the character of envoys. The whole matter may be disposed of in a word: nations and sovereigns, according to their biases, will be quick or slow to recognize a revolutionary government; some will cling to the old as long as they can, others will fall into the current of things sooner or later, but fall into it at length they will. And if an actual sovereign feels himself injured by the acknowledgment of the claims of a deposed one, such conduct will be attributed to hostile feeling, and may provoke war. The acknowledgment of the sovereignty of a new state is sometimes first made by receiving its ambassadors.

A protected or dependent state may employ political and other agents, but generally cannot send ambassadors either to the principal state or to third powers without the consent of the former.* The peace of Kainardsché, in 1774, allowed the

* Bynkershoek disposes of this subject as follows: Quæst. J. P. II., § 3. "I should not be willing to say, as some do, that no one rightfully sends legates saving the sovereign, for thus we should have to do away with legates of provinces and

Hospodars of Moldavia and Wallachia to send each a chargé d'affaires of the Greek religion, and with the privileges conceded by the law of nations, to Constantinople. The members of a confederation may, or may not, exercise this right, according to the nature of the compact: no state of our confederation "shall, without consent of congress, enter into any agreement or compact with a foreign power," or "enter into any treaty, alliance, or confederation;" and the power of appointing ambassadors being vested elsewhere, they are, perhaps, by that provision of the constitution also, cut off from the exercise of a similar function. But the members of the German confederation can severally entertain their representatives at foreign courts.

A messenger sent from a province, or revolted portion of a country to the sovereign, not being an ambassador, has no rights of one. Bad, then, as the act was, when Philip II. of Spain detained two noblemen sent from the Low Countries in 1566, and finally had them put to death, it was no offence against the rights of legation. (Bynkersh. Quæst. J. P. II., § 3.)

An ambassador being the representative of a sovereign, it follows that the power of choice lies with him, and thus, as it respects the country, religion, rank, etc., of the ambassador, no complaint can be made by the foreign state, except so far as a slight or intention to insult may be inferred from the circumstances of the case.* Formerly it was not an unfrequent thing

towns, of whom there has been, and still is, a great abundance. I should rather say, that every one can send legates in the discharge of that business which he has the power of doing, but that according to the dignity of the sendor they have different rights, and are held in different degrees of honor. If a prince in his own right sends them, they have the full rights of legates; if another, the whole thing depends on the will of him to whom they are sent," etc. But thus the question becomes one of words. Have these legates the privileges of ambassadors, and is a prince or state in any way bound to receive them? If not, can they be ranked in the same class?

* Even women have been acknowledged as representatives at foreign courts, but more frequently have been secret emissaries. The wife of Marshal Guebriant acted in this capacity for France, at the court of Ladislas IV., King of Poland, in 1646. The noted Chevalier d'Eon, who, after inferior diplomatic employments, was appointed French ambassador at London, was thought to be a woman, but was not. Comp. Klüber, § 186, note.

for a native of one country to serve as the ambassador from another in the land where he owed allegiance. But, as we have already said, some nations,—as France, under the old regime and the first empire, and the United Provinces from 1727,—refused to receive native-born persons in this capacity. When, however, nationality has been transferred in accordance with the laws of the states concerned, there can be no objection against such ministers, unless it be of a personal nature. In some Catholic countries, again, in Austria, Spain, and France, the usage has prevailed that the sovereign of the land shall nominate the nuncio whom he receives from the Pope; the reason for which usage lies probably in the fear of papal interference, and of unacceptableness with the native clergy.

Sometimes smaller sovereigns have concurred in appointing the same person as their ambassador, and sometimes the same person has held this office for his sovereign at several courts.

When an ambassador is sent abroad, there must be some evidence of his official position. For this purpose he is furnished with credentials certifying his diplomatic character and rank; namely with a letter of credence, (lettre de créance,) sometimes, also, with one of recommendation, and with a *full power*, indicating the subjects on which he is authorized to treat, and the amount of power with which he is invested. According to their rank some agents of foreign governments are directly accredited to a sovereign, and others to his minister of foreign affairs. Until such credentials are presented, a foreign government may reject, or on other evidence receive, the person claiming to be an ambassador, according to its pleasure.

§ 92 *a*.

Privileges of ambassadors.

An ambassador, from the time of his entrance into the foreign country in that character, until the time when, at the expiration of his office, he leaves the country, has in modern days enjoyed very great privileges or immunities, which even the breaking out of war before he can leave the country will not terminate. Even before he has had opportunity to show his credentials to the proper department of government, he cannot be injured or obstructed without a violation of international law, if he announces his official character; and should a government to which he is sent refuse to receive him, he must be free to withdraw without receiving marks of disrespect. If he is recalled, free exit and passports, where they are necessary, must be granted to him; but if he remain in the country after that a sufficient time for removal, denoted in his passports, has elapsed, he takes the jural relation of any traveller from his native land.

The more essential immunities conceded to the ambassador grow out of the consideration that he cannot do the business intrusted to him well, unless his person be safe, and he be independent of the control of the foreign government; and comity adds to these other less important privileges, as marks of respect to the representative of a foreign sovereignty. These immunities have been arranged under the heads of inviolability and exterritoriality. Such for instance, is Klüber's classification. But to this it may be objected that exterritoriality may be taken in a narrower and a more extended sense. The term stands, as we have already explained it, for that legal fiction which regards the agents of a government in a foreign land as being outside of the country where they discharge their functions, or as carrying with them into another territory almost as entire an exemption from its laws as if they were at home.* But there is no such complete exemption, and hence it will be best, if we arrange the rights of ambassadors under these heads, to define what immunities are allowed; otherwise the term, by its vagueness, will lead us astray. De Martens remarks (§ 215), that the "extension of exterritoriality pertains only to the positive law of nations, to treaties or usage, and is susceptible of modifications, which in fact it undergoes; whence it is not enough always to appeal to exterritoriality, in order to enjoy those rights which may be derived from the extended notion given to the word."

* This fiction was known to Grotius, who says (II. 18, § 4, 5) that as legates "fictione quadam habentur pro personis mittentium, ita etiam simili fictione constituuntur quasi extra territorium."

1. When we speak of the inviolability of an ambassador, we mean that neither public authority nor private persons can use any force, or do any violence to him, without offending against the law of nations. It is not, however, intended that he may not be repelled by force, if he attempts to injure other individuals or to violate the laws. The right of self-defence cannot cease on his account, nor can he enter places closed to the public, nor do a great variety of illegal acts without having passive resistance at least used against him. The state within whose bounds he resides, is bound to protect him against aggressions from its subjects, by law and penalty, and by troops or a police force, when necessary. In one case only, apart from the necessities of self-defence, can active force be exerted upon his person, and that is when, after committing some great crime, and being ordered home, he refuses to go, when he may be removed without personal injury.

1. Inviolability of ambassadors.

2. Inviolability of person could not stand alone, without protection to the house, furniture, equipage, and, in fact, the people of the ambassador. We shall arrange these with other immunities under the head of exterritoriality, and shall consider first,

2. Exterritoriality.

A. his immunity from the jurisdiction of the country of his sojourn, both criminal and civil.

If the ambassador were subject to the criminal jurisdiction of the foreign country, his person could not be inviolate, as he would be liable to arrest, imprisonment, and punishment; nor would the nature of the acts inseparable from the processes of criminal laws, be consistent with his freedom as a negotiator. This immunity is therefore conceded to ambassadors by all the nations of Christendom, and, although some of the earlier writers had some scruples in admitting it, or even contended against it, the modern writers are believed to be unanimous in regarding it as a part of international law. For the exceptions to this immunity which have occurred in extreme cases, see § 92 *e*.

(*a*.) As immunity from criminal jurisdiction,

In the case of a native of the country still owing allegiance, but representing a foreign sovereign, it has been questioned whether jurisdiction, civil or criminal, is suspended during the discharge of his functions. The most noted case in which such a person felt the severity of the law, was that of Wicquefort, a native of Amsterdam, who, while he held an office under the States-general, became the Duke of Lüneburg's resident at the Hague, and while in the service of this prince, in 1675, was accused of betraying state secrets to foreigners, was tried, convicted, and sentenced to imprisonment for life with confiscation of goods.* In this case it might with justice be maintained that he held an office of responsibility, and could not be released from penal liabilities as long as it lasted; if he took on him duties to a new sovereign, he was still accountable to the old one. He betrayed secrets to which in his office he had access, and ought therefore to suffer. But if a private citizen of a country is acknowledged by its government as an ambassador from another state, it is fairly to be inferred that all the immunities are conceded to him, which are considered to belong to that class of persons, and without which he could not freely discharge its duties. His sovereign had a right (§ 90) to refuse to recognize him in that relation to another sovereign: in so recognizing him he gives up jurisdiction over him for the time being.†

(b.) and from civil jurisdiction.

Opinions have been divided in regard to an ambassador's exemption from civil jurisdiction. Entire exemption in this respect cannot be argued from the nature of his functions, and yet every where this exemption is allowed, so far as it can be derived from the notion of exterritoriality. At the least, according to Heffter, no step can be taken towards an ambassador which cannot be taken towards an absent stranger. No measures involving force can be used against his person, or the effects which he has with him.

Hence the private person, to whom an ambassador owes money, has no remedy against him except through his sover-

* Comp. Bynkersh. de for. leg. 11, and 18, and Wheaton's Hist., p. 234.

† So substantially Wheaton, El. III. 1, § 15. Heffter says the right of punishing is scarcely taken away from such an ambassador's sovereign. § 214. Bynkersh. u. s., holds the same opinion: "subditos nostros, quamvis alterius Principis legationem acceperint, subditos nostros esse non desinere." So others.

eign, or by suit in the ambassador's native courts after his return home. Such, at least, is the understanding and practice in most countries. Prussia appears to claim somewhat more of jurisdiction.* In a case, the discussion of which is given at great length by Dr. Wheaton, the owner of a house at Berlin, rented to the American ambassador, claimed under the Prussian civil code to detain the minister's goods found there at the expiration of the lease, on the ground that damages were due for injuries done to the house during his occupation of it. The government of Prussia sustained the claimant, but the discussion shows that while a pledge given by an ambassador for the security of a debt could have been detained by the lender, the goods in the house could not be kept from their owner without a violation of international law. The laws of the United States, accordingly, "include distress for rent among other legal remedies which are denied to the creditors of a foreign minister."

An ambassador is bound to observe the police laws in regard to public security and order within and without his hotel, but cannot be called to account for transgression of them, any more than for his pecuniary obligations.

One or two exceptions to this exemption are laid down by the writers beside that derived from the ambassador's acting in a capacity other than his official one, which we shall consider by itself. (§ 92 *e*.)

They are, (1.) when he is the subject of the state where he acts; (2.) when he is in its service; (3.) when he voluntarily recognizes the jurisdiction of the courts by appearing before them as a plaintiff, and thus submitting himself to the defendant's court.†

§ 92 *b*.

B. The immunity from local jurisdiction granted to a foreign minister extends to his hotel and goods. His house is a sanctuary, except in case of gross crime, for himself and his retinue; and that whether it belongs

Immunity of ambassador's hotel and goods.

* Comp. Wheaton, El. III. 1, § 17, 274–287, and Vergé on de Martens, § 216.

† Comp. de Martens, § 216; Wheaton, El. III. 1. § 15; Bynkersh. de for. leg.

to his own government, or is hired, or is given to him for his use by the state to which he is sent.* His goods also, or all that is necessary for the comfort of himself and his family, together with his equipage, enjoy the same exemption. His papers relating to the business of his embassy are inviolate. These exemptions are plainly as essential for the discharge of his duties in his office, as is his personal exemption from foreign jurisdiction.

It is to be observed, however, that if he chance to possess real property in the foreign country, or personal property, aside from that which pertains to him as an ambassador, (§ 92 *e*), it is subject to the local laws.

His hotel no asylum for criminals.

His privileges do not include the right of asylum for persons outside of his household. If the fiction of exterritoriality explained the privileges of ambassadors, the right of asylum would be fairly deducible from it, and a criminal taking refuge in such a sanctuary would be given up, if at all, by a process of extradition. But it so happens that the house of an ambassador has ceased to be an asylum, since the notion of exterritoriality has been most current. The right was attached in the middle ages to many religious places, and was conceded after this analogy, on account of their sacredness, in some countries, to the hotels of ambassadors; but the usage, if we are not deceived, was never general throughout Europe, and even where it obtained, as in Rome and Madrid, was sometimes opposed and violated by the government. Similar to this right, if not an extension of it, was the freedom or privilege (*jus quarteriorum*) of the quarter of the city

16. It does not appear that the ambassador has a right to do this without leave of his own government, for it may prevent the due exercise of his functions.

* Sometimes extraordinary ambassadors have quarters provided for them by the state to which they are sent, their stay being ordinarily short. In 1814, Austria and England purchased houses for their foreign ministers in Paris, and in 1817, Prussia, in Paris and Petersburg. Klüber, § 192, note. Houses for the reception of foreign ambassadors were in use in the empire of Charlemagne. A capitulary of A. D. 850 (Perz, III, 407) speaks of publicæ domus, in singulis civitatibus—antiquitus constructæ, nostris usibus et externarum gentium legationibus satis congruæ. The Romans also sometimes entertained foreign legates in public villas outside of the walls at the public charge.

where the ambassador resided, and which was indicated by the arms of his sovereign. This right (or wrong rather) prevailed in a number of places, as at Venice, Rome, Madrid, and during the meetings for the choice and coronation of an emperor, at Frankfort on the Main. At Rome, in the 16th and 17th centuries, the harboring of criminals, under plea of exercising this right, gave occasion to more than one dispute between the Papal and the French governments.

It is now admitted that if a transgressor, not of the ambassador's train, takes refuge in his premises, he can be demanded by the local authorities, and, if not delivered up, can be searched for and seized within the hotel, for which purpose such force in breaking doors open and the like, may be used, as is necessary for his apprehension. For as Bynkershoek (de for. leg. § 21) asks, "legati, ut latrones recipiant, mittuntur? vel, sine receptione commode legationi vacare non possunt?"

Freedom from imposts, etc.

It is also a freedom commonly allowed to ambassadors, but rather by national comity, than as a fair deduction from theory, that the personal effects of an ambassador are exempt from taxation, and that duties are remitted on articles from abroad which he needs for himself and his family. His importations, however, before they reach his hotel, are liable to the search of custom-house officers, and if he has sent for contraband goods, they may be confiscated. As for the rest, he is obliged to pay taxes (even on his hotel, if it belongs to him or to his government), tolls, and postages, but is exempt from the quartering of troops.*

§ 92 *c*.

Ambassador's liberty of worship.

C. The liberty of worship in a foreign land is now conceded by the law and usage of Christian nations to ambassadors of every rank, even when their religion or sect is not tolerated by the laws of the land. This liberty might be deduced from the rule of exterritoriality, as in the parallel case of a ship of war in a foreign port, or still better, from the consideration that, religion being a prime necessity

* De Martens, §§ 227–229; Wheaton's El. III. 1, § 18.

of man's nature, an earnest nation could have no diplomatic intercourse with another nation, within whose territory its religion was prohibited. But the argument, which would support this liberty of worship by natural justice and the rights of conscience, has here no application, since a great part of the nations of Christendom have always assumed the right of allowing or prohibiting outward worship at their pleasure.

This freedom of worship extends to the household of the ambassador, and sometimes by comity or connivance, if not by treaty, to his countrymen, who may be residing at the same capital. It is not limited by his presence, but when he is on a journey, or during the intervals between two legations, it may still be kept up. But his household, and even his wife, it is held, if of another religion than his own, have no separate right of worship. It is held, also, that if there be religious rites publicly allowed, of the same sect to which the ambassador belongs and where he is residing, he may be forbidden to have a chapel and services of his own, which now are no longer necessary. Thus, when the Emperor Joseph II. granted toleration at Vienna to the adherents of the Augsburg Confession, it was declared that domestic worship at the hotel of Lutheran ambassadors would no more be permitted. But in Constantinople, where the Greek Church is tolerated, the Russian ambassador has a public place of worship, after the observances of that religion, under his protection.

This worship may be such in the fullest sense, that is, there may be a chaplain or chaplains and whatever other persons are necessary for the services of religion, due administration of the sacraments, and the like. But it must be strictly house-worship, in a room fit for the purpose, yet without bell, organ, or other sign, indicating to passengers in the street that a chapel is near by. And it is held, that natives of the country cannot, without leave from the government, partake in the services; nor has the chaplain a right to appear abroad in his canonicals. A French ambassador at Stockholm, Chanut, claimed the right of admitting Swedes to his Catholic chapel, at services not tolerated in the country, which amounted to a claim of power to suspend the laws. When, in 1661, the Dutch imprisoned the French ambassador's chaplain for performing mass, their reason was that the ambassador had left the country. Most preposterous was the claim of Philip II. of Spain that the trains of ambassadors at Madrid should go to mass.

It is held, that the ambassador may not set up worship as his own affair, but by leave of his government. Where freedom of worship, as with us, is unlimited, all these restrictions are inapplicable, unless imposed by way of reciprocity; and the necessity for separate worship in general ceases. Treaty sometimes gives greater liberty than is here laid down.*

§ 92 *d.*

D. The same exemption from local jurisdiction, which the ambassador himself enjoys, is granted by the law of nations to his family and train, as to his chaplain, physician, private secretary, and secretary of legation, and to his domestic servants. Dr. Wheaton remarks, in regard to the latter, that the laws and usages of most countries call upon ambassadors to furnish official lists of their servants, that they may be entitled to their exemption.† The secretaries are peculiarly protected, as being necessary to carry on the business of the embassy; and above all, the secretary of legation, as a responsible person intrusted by the ambassador's government with more or less of his power during his absence or at his death, and by virtue of his appointment a public officer.

Privileges of his family and train.

The reasons for this exemption in the case of servants, especially of natives of the country whom the foreign minister hires, are of little cogency, since others could be speedily found to take their places; but the exemption is well established. Should it, however, appear that a criminal was taken into an ambassador's service in order to protect him, it is doubtful

* Comp. Klüber, § 215; Heffter, § 213; De Martens, §§ 222–226.

† This had become obsolete for a while before Bynkershoek wrote his work De foro legatorum. In chap. 16, he says, "optimo exemplo in quibusdam aulis *olim* receptum fuit, ut legatus teneretur exhibere nomenclaturam comitum suorum, sed pessimo exemplo id *nunc* ubique gentium negligitur."

whether this would be endured,—at least it would be a ground of complaint against the employer;—and if any of his servants while in his employment carries on a traffic in which he incurs debts, such person loses his privileges; he is considered to sustain two characters, one of which will not shield him from the consequences of acts done in the other.* An ambassador may also give up his control over domestics hired within the foreign country, but perhaps cannot do this in regard to those whom he has brought with him.† At several congresses, as at Münster and Nymwegen, the assembled envoys, in order to check the riotous conduct of their herd of domestics, gave the police over them into the hands of the magistrates of the town.

An ambassador's power over his suite.

E. From the rule of exterritoriality strictly carried out, and from the necessity of some government over an ambassador's train, it might be argued that jurisdiction over them, criminal as well as civil, ought to be lodged in him. If, however, such power pertained to him, it could only be by the laws of his own country. But then a foreign government cannot be expected to permit a stranger to perform the highest acts of criminal justice within its territory, unless it be for the purpose of carrying out military law on a vessel of war, or in an army passing through the land. Hence the jurisdiction of ambassadors in modern times over their trains is actually confined to subordinate measures. In criminal cases a follower of his, committing a crime outside of the hotel, is delivered up to him, he gathers and prepares the evidence, and sends the accused home for trial. He exercises *voluntary* jurisdiction, as far as his suite, and, if permitted by the foreign and his own country, as far as his countrymen sojourning near him are concerned, in receiving and legalizing testaments, authenticating contracts, affixing his seal, and the like.‡ "But the right of *contentious* jurisdiction," says Heffter, "is nowhere, within my knowledge, conceded to ambassadors at Christian

* Bynkershoek asks whether those who follow in an ambassador's train, "unice ut lucro suo consulant, institores forte et mercatores," are his *companions*, and decides in the negative. De for. leg. § 15, ad calc.

† Heffter, § 221; Vattel, iv. 9, § 124.

‡ Heffter, § 216.

courts, even for the persons of their suite; but they here simply execute requisitions directed to them, especially in regard to the hearing of witnesses, and all this according to the laws of their own country."

When a crime is committed by a native servant belonging to the foreign minister's household, or when persons attached to the trains of two ambassadors break the public peace by quarrels, the only convenient way of proceeding is to deliver them over to the courts of the country to be tried.

Formerly ambassadors sometimes exercised the power of blood over their retinue. The most noted case of this kind occurred at London in 1603, when Sully, then Marquis of Rosny, was ambassador there. One of his people having killed an Englishman with whom he had a quarrel at a brothel, Sully assembled a council or jury of Frenchmen, condemned the man to death, and delivered him up to the English authorities for execution. He was pardoned by James I., whereupon the French claimed that, as he was judged by his own tribunal, the pardon was unauthorized.*

§ 92 *e*.

Limits of the privileges of an ambassador.

An ambassador can claim exemption only for the property which he holds in the foreign country as an official person. If he has another character, as that of a merchant or a trustee, his property so held is subject to the laws of the land. Formerly it was not uncommon for merchants to represent the minor princes of Europe at the smaller courts. Bynkershoek says that in his time they made great gains by importing goods free of duty, on the pretence that these were necessary for their own use, and then selling them. But the practice of employing merchants as foreign ministers or residents is believed to have become almost obsolete, and this source of gain is cut off by better regulations. (§ 92 *b*.)

Ambassadors committing crimes.

There is now a very general uniformity both of opinion and practice, that ambassadors committing grave crimes whether against the state, or against moral

* Ward, II. 316.

order, must be remanded home to their sovereign for judgment, and that only self-defence will allow the killing of such a functionary. But neither opinion nor practice was so uniform two centuries and more ago, especially in England. The case of Leslie, bishop of Rosse, to which we have already referred, furnishes us with the opinion of English lawyers on the question whether an ambassador, cognizant of and privy to a treason, is punishable by the prince, in whose realm and against whom the treason is committed. The answer was, "We do think that an ambassador, aiding and comforting any traitor in his treason toward the prince with whom he pretendeth to be ambassador in his realm, knowing the same treason, is punishable by the same prince against whom such treason is committed." Leslie stoutly protested against all right of jurisdiction over him, and was not tried, but was detained for some time in prison and then banished the kingdom. A few years afterwards, a contrary opinion was given by men better informed in the law of nations, Albericus Gentilis and Francis Hotman, in the case of Mendoza, the Spanish minister in England, who had plotted to bring in foreign soldiers and dethrone Elizabeth: they decided that an ambassador who had even been concerned in a conspiracy could not be put to death, but must be remanded to his prince for punishment. And a little after in the reign of James I., when the Spanish ambassadors charged the Duke of Buckingham with a conspiracy against the king, which was regarded as false and libellous, Sir Robert Cotton, being consulted whether any proceedings could be instituted against them, maintained that an ambassador as representing the person of a sovereign prince is "exempt from regal trial: that all actions of one so qualified are made the act of his master until he disavow them: and that the injuries of one absolute prince to another are *factum hostilitatis*, not treason." And he proposed "that a formal complaint against the ambassador should be sent to the king of Spain requiring such justice to be done upon him 'as by leagues of amity and the law of nations is usual, which if he refused, it would be a dissolution of amity, and equivalent to a declaration of war."

And yet, at the same time when such doctrine now universally regarded as sound was taught, Coke thinks that "if an ambassador commits a crime which is not merely a *malum prohibitum* by act of parliament, private law, or custom of the realm, but *contra jus gentium*, as treason, felony, adultery, he loses privilege, and may be punished in England like any other alien." This opinion had weight with succeeding lawyers. Foster presents a view somewhat similar to this, namely, that although ambassadors owe no allegiance to the sovereign of the country, they are members of society, and therefore bound by the eternal universal law which keeps all civil societies together; and hence may be brought to justice like other offenders, if they commit those enormous offences, which are against the light of nature and the well-being of all society. And Sir Matthew Hale expresses the opinion, that if the ambassador or his associates commit any capital offence, save treason, as rape, murder, or theft, they may be proceeded against by indictment in the ordinary course of justice, like other aliens.

The case which seems to have led him to this opinion was the noted one of Sa, although it applied only to the companions of ambassadors. Sa, in 1653, during the commonwealth, being the brother of the Portuguese ambassador and one of his train, fell into a quarrel with one Gerrard, and wounded him, but he was saved from death by the interference of another gentleman standing by. Thereupon, with other Portuguese, fifty in number, Sa came on the next night to the same place, and with his associates killed one person and wounded many. The ambassador was required to deliver up the delinquents, and Cromwell resolved that Sa should be tried by the law of the land. The case was referred to a special court of men learned in the law who decided that he could be indicted. He was tried before a jury, found guilty, and suffered death. It seems from a statement of the case, that if he had been an ambassador, his privilege would have protected him, but a distinction was made between the principal and the members of his train.

The law of England afforded no sufficient protection to ambassadors until 1708, when, on the occasion of the arrest for debt and ill usage of the Russian minister, a very severe law was enacted, by which it rested with the chancellor and chief justices, or any two of them, to inflict such punishment as they should think fit on the person whom they should find guilty of bringing a suit against a minister or his servants.

A little after this, in 1717, Gyllenborg, the Swedish ambassador in England, was engaged in a conspiracy to invade the country and dethrone the first George. He was arrested, his dispatches seized, and his cabinet broken open. The case so far was like many acts of violent infraction of international law, and deserves to be mentioned, only because the secretaries of state maintained, by way of apology to the other ministers resident in London, that the measure was necessary for the peace of the kingdom.* Extreme necessity would be a good plea even for killing an ambassador, as Bynkershoek says at the end of his work de foro legatorum, but the question in such cases is, could not simple sending home, forcible expulsion, if necessary, answer every purpose.†

§ 93.

Relations of an ambassador to a third power.

Bynkershoek lays it down "non valere jus legationis nisi inter utrumque Principem, qui mittit legatos, et ad quem missi sunt; cætera [legatos] privatos esse." Grotius had already taught the same thing, and nearly all modern writers concur in this opinion. Vattel, however, (IV. 7, § 84) maintains that innocent transit through a third

* One of the most atrocious violations of international law on record, was the murder of two French ministers, Bonnier and Roberjot, on their way home from the Congress of Rastadt in April, 1797, by Austrian hussars. This seems to have been a piece of villainy on the part of an Austrian minister of State,—carried further by the soldiers than was intended,—for the purpose of getting possession of valuable papers.

† This subsection is principally drawn from Ward's History, II. 292–330. For the law of 7 Anne, c. 12, referred to, see Kent, I., 183, Lect. ix. Coke, 4th Instit. 153, Foster's crown-law, 188, Hale's pleas of the crown, and the passages referred to in the text are cited by Ward. Comp. also Bynkersh. de for. leg. 18, who, after citing the few examples to be found of regular legal punishments of foreign ministers, says, "novi ævi exempla de legatis qui varie deliquerant non punitis tot ubique in annalibus occurrunt, ut ipsa copia laboremus."

country may not be refused to an ambassador, unless suspected of sinister designs on his way; that to insult him is to insult his master and the whole nation to which he belongs; and that to injure him is picking a quarrel with all nations "who are concerned to maintain as sacred the right and means of communicating together and treating of their affairs." There is so much truth in this, that an injury done to an ambassador, on his way through a land where his countrymen enjoy protection, is a far greater crime than one done to a private man, and that all comity and hospitality ought to be shown to him. But his status is not the same as in the land to which he is accredited. The exterritorial immunities avail only there, and inviolability elsewhere is of a qualified kind. Hence (1.) a state may refuse transit to a foreign minister; (2.) he and his goods may be liable to seizure; (3.) if he enters a territory where he is an enemy, or is bound to one which is hostile to that through which he is passing, he may be seized and impeded from pursuing his journey; and all this without offence against international law. And yet it appears to be desirable, both on the ground of the general good and on the score of justice, that ambassadors should everywhere be safe at least from violence and from arrest.

Quite a number of examples might be cited, where the rights of legation have been treated as of no account by third powers and by enemies. The noted case mentioned by Thucydides (II. 67), in which the Athenians caught in Thrace and killed envoys from the Peloponnesians, on their way to Persia, where they hoped to bring the great king into their alliance against Athens, might have been an act of cruelty, but was not against the modern *jus inter gentes.* Similar to this was the case of Rinçon and Fregoze, envoys of Francis I. of France, passing through the duchy of Milan, the one on his way to Venice, the other to the Porte. This was then hostile territory, and they were seized and killed seemingly by the procurement of the governor of Milan, the emperor Charles V. showing indifference to the crime. "Alia quæstio," says Bynkersh. (u. s.), speaking of this affair, "de jure legationis, alia de jure honestatis." Refusals of passports, detentions and expulsions from the country have been not uncommon. Thus in 1572, when all Frenchmen in England found without a passport were ordered to be arrested, du Croc, the French minister to Scotland, on his way thither, shared their fate, at which when the French court complained, Secretary Walsingham averred that he was justly detained for want of a passport. In the same century, a Turkish ambassador was arrested on his way through Venice to France, and when the French resident there claimed his liberation, the republic answered that a sovereign power is not bound to recognize the function of a public minister, unless his credentials are addressed to itself. When, in 1573, the Duke of Anjou, afterwards Henry III. of France, was elected king of Poland, the ambassadors who were on their way to announce his election, were refused a passport in Saxony, and detained by the Elector. In 1744, Marshal Belleisle, while passing through Hanover in the capacity of an ambassador, was seized by the English, then at war with France, and carried as a prisoner to England. And in 1763, Count Wartensleben, minister of the States-general to a part of the German powers, was arrested at Cassel as executor of a will. But there is no right whatever of seizing an enemy's ambassador on neutral soil or a neutral vessel. (Comp. §§ 163, 184.)

§ 94.

Rank of ambassadors.

The rank of an ambassador has nothing to do with the transaction of affairs,—except so far as the capacity to represent their sovereign may be restricted to those of one class,—but only to the ceremonial of courts. Formerly, there was but one class of foreign ministers, or at most two—ambassadors and agents—known to Europe, but since the beginning of the eighteenth century there have been three grades. Moreover, sometimes extraordinary have claimed precedence over ordinary ministers of the same class. The quarrels of ambassadors about rank led to a regulation in the protocol of the plenipotentiaries of the eight principal powers concerned in the congress of Vienna, dated March 19, 1815, which is to the following effect:—

"To prevent the embarrassments which have often occurred and which may yet arise from the claims to precedence between different diplomatic agents, the plenipotentiaries of the powers signing the treaty of Paris have agreed to the following articles; and they feel it their duty to ask those of other crowned heads to adopt the same regulation:

Art. I. Diplomatic employés are divided into three classes;
that of ambassadors, legates, or nuncios;
that of envoys, ministers, or others accredited to sovereigns;
that of chargés d'affaires accredited to ministers charged with foreign affairs.

Art. II. Ambassadors, legates, or nuncios alone have the representative character.

Art. III. Diplomatic employés on an extraordinary mission have not for that reason any superiority of rank.

Art. IV. Diplomatic employés shall take rank among themselves in each class according to the date of the official notification of their arrival.

The present rule shall bring with it no innovation in regard to the representatives of the Pope.

Art. V. There shall be in each state a uniform mode determined upon for the reception of the diplomatic employés of each class.

Art. VI. The ties of relationship or of family alliance between courts give no rank to their diplomatic employés. The same is true of political ties.

Art. VII. In the acts or treaties between several powers which admit of the *alternat*, the lot shall decide between the ministers, as to the order to be followed in signatures." *

In the protocol of the congress of Aix-la-Chapelle, dated November 21, 1818, a new class of ministers was constituted by the plenipotentiaries of the five great powers. They say—

"To avoid the disagreeable discussions which may arise in the future on a point of diplomatic etiquette, which the rule annexed to the *recés* of Vienna, by which questions of rank were regulated, does not seem to have provided for, it is decided between the five courts, that *resident ministers* accre-

* By the *alternat* is intended the practice, sometimes adopted in signing conventions, of alternating in the order of priority of signature, according to some fixed rule, so as to cut off questions of rank. The lot has also been used. Comp. Klüber, §§ 104–106.

dited near them shall form, in respect to their rank, an intermediate class between ministers of the second order and *chargés d'affaires*."

According to these rules, on which the present practice everywhere is based, there are four classes of diplomatic agents. To the first belong ambassadors of temporal powers, together with legates *a* or *de* latere and nuncios of the Pope. * To the second all diplomatic employés accredited to sovereigns, whether called envoys, ministers, ministers plenipotentiary, or internuncios. To the third resident ministers accredited to sovereigns. To the fourth *chargés d'affaires* accredited to ministers of foreign affairs, with whom would be reckoned consuls invested with diplomatic functions.†

In regard to the rank of the minister who shall represent a state at a particular court, the general rule is that one of such rank and title is sent, as has been usually received from the other party; and that the sovereigns having a royal title neither send ministers of the first rank, nor receive them from inferior powers.‡

In regard to diplomatic etiquette Dr. Wheaton observes, that while it is in great part a code of manners, and not of laws, there are certain rules, the breach of which may hinder the performance of more serious duties. Such is the rule requiring a reciprocation of diplomatic visits between ministers resident at the same court.

As for the ceremonial of courts an ambassador is to regard himself the representative of national politeness and goodwill, but to submit to no ceremony abroad which would be account-

* There is no distinction between legates *a* and legates *de* latere. These are cardinals, nuncios are not. Internuncios form an inferior grade of papal diplomats, belonging to the second or third class. From early times the bishop of Rome had vicars, delegates, or legates, in the countries of Europe, who had oversight of religious affairs and some delegated jurisdiction. Legates for some time had a permanent office, which might be attached to a particular bishopric. Only in modern days have these representatives of the Pope become assimilated to the envoys from temporal powers. In France by the concordat of 1801, all intermeddling with the affairs of the Gallican church was prohibited to them, by whatever name they went.

† Comp. Heffter, § 208. ‡ Heffter, § 209.

ed degrading at home; for nothing can be demanded of him inconsistent with the honor of his country. A question somewhat agitated among us, who have no distinct costume for the chief magistrate or for those who wait on him, is, In what costume should our diplomatic agents appear at foreign courts? In none other, it may be answered, than such as is appropriate when we pay our respects to the President of the United States, unless another is expressly prescribed. The rule is to emanate from home, and not from abroad; and no rule, it is to be hoped, will ever be given out, inconsistent with the severe simplicity of a nation without a court.

An ambassador may be recalled, or sent home, or for some urgent reason declare his mission terminated, or it may expire by its own limitation, or by the completion of a certain official work, or by the death of the sovereign sending the ambassador, or of the sovereign to whom he is sent, or yet again by a change in his diplomatic rank. When, for any cause not implying personal or national misunderstanding, his mission is terminated, a letter of recall is generally necessary, which he is to deliver up, and ask for an audience to take leave of the sovereign or chief magistrate of the country where he has been residing. And again, when his rank has been changed without removal from his station, he presents a letter of recall and one of credence, as at first.*

The inviolability of foreign ministers belongs also to heralds, bearers of flags of truce, etc. (Comp. § 134.) Couriers and bearers of despatches are privileged persons, as far as is necessary for their particular service. But agents attending to the private affairs of princes, and secret envoys, when not accredited, are not entitled to the privileges of ambassadors under the law of nations.

* For all the details of an ambassador's duty the Guide Diplomatique of Ch. de Martens (4th edition), Paris, 1851, is probably the best book. The second volume is a kind of complete letter writer, useful, no doubt, to raw hands. But unfortunately the book is in French, and, so far as I know, has not been translated into English. Would it not be a good work to set up a French school at Washington for members of Congress expecting to go on missions?

§ 95.

Consuls.

The commercial agents of a government, residing in foreign parts, and charged with the duty of promoting the commercial interests of the state, and especially of its individual citizens or subjects, are called consuls. These, under the regulations of some countries are of different grades, being either consuls-general, consuls, or vice-consuls, from whom consular agents differ little. The consular office, also, may have a connection with that of diplomatic agents. (§ 94.)

Origin of the consular office.

Nothing exactly like the office of consuls was known to the ancients. The nearest resemblance to it was borne by the *proxeni* of Greece, who, as their name implies, stood in the relation of hospitality to a public body or state, and like other hosts and guests, might hand down the office in their family. Their chief duties were to entertain and honor the ambassadors of the foreign state within the country where they resided, to help in distress its private citizens doing business there, and perhaps to represent them in commercial suits.*

The consuls of the middle ages, so far as they resembled modern consuls, seem to have been of two kinds; first, a college of judges or arbitrators, whose functions were exercised within the city or state which appointed them, and secondly those who were chosen to settle disputes among the merchants of their town who resided in a foreign town or district. As for the first class it was not strange that merchants, who formed guilds by themselves, should have magistrates of their own; and the name given to them, *consuls* of the merchants, or of the sea, was borrowed from one of the prevailing names of the head officers of many Italian cities.† As for the second, it can be traced back to century XII. In 1190, a charta of king Guy, of Jerusalem, grants the privilege to the merchants of Marseilles of appointing consuls of their own at Acco (St. Jean d'Acre), and in 1268, king Jacob of Arragon (Jayme I. 1213–

* Comp. Schömann, Griech. Alterth. II. 22.

† Comp. Hegel, Gesch. d. Städteverfass. von Italien II. 205, et seq.

1276), gives to merchants of Barcelona the same privilege for parts beyond the sea under his sway. A charta of 1328, calls them in the Provençal dialect "regens dels mercadiers que van per mar." * Such consuls were either resident, as those of the large trading cities of the Mediterranean, or temporary during the stay abroad of merchants setting sail in a vessel together. From a statute of Marseilles of 1253–55, in Pardessus (Lois maritimes IV. 256), we learn that the appointment of consuls for foreign parts was there instrusted to the rector of the town with the syndics and guardians of the treasury; that such consuls, under advice of their council, had the power of imposing fines and of banishing;—subject however to the review of the home government on complaint of the aggrieved person,—that if no consuls should have been appointed for any place where ten or more Marseilles merchants were residing, these of themselves might make choice of one, until the office could be filled; that the consul refusing to serve was finable; and that no man enjoying special privileges in the place, and no one but a wholesale dealer, could hold the office. The consul, if parties are willing to submit their differences to him, is directed to call in two assistants. The fines which he may exact from parties whose differences he has settled are to go, half to him and half to the treasury of Marseilles. Important information in regard to this office is also given by the statutes of Ancona of the year 1397.†

§ 96.

Functions and duties of consuls.

The functions of modern consuls are determined by special treaties and by the laws of their own land. Among their usual duties in Christian lands, besides those of general watchfulness over the commercial interests of their nation, and of aid to their countrymen in securing their commercial rights, may be enumerated the duties—

Of legalizing by their seal, for use within their own country, acts of judicial or other functionaries, and of authenticating

* Du Cange voce Consul. Comp. Leonhardi in Ersch u. Gruber's Encyclop. voce Consulat.

† See Pardessus, u. s. V. 108, 116, et seq.

marriages, births, and deaths, among their countrymen, within their consulates;

Of receiving the protests of masters of vessels, of granting passports, and of acting as depositaries of sundry ship's papers;

Of reclaiming deserters from vessels, providing for destitute sailors, and discharging such as have been cruelly treated;

Of acting on behalf of the owners of stranded vessels, and of administering on the personal property left within their consulates by deceased persons, where no legal representative is at hand.

Our laws require masters of vessels, on entering a port for traffic, to lodge with the consul their registers, sea-letters and passports; and make it a consul's duty to send destitute seamen home at the public expense.

Jurisdiction of consuls in and out of Christendom.

In general, throughout Christian lands, the principle of the control of the laws and courts over foreigners with the exemption of certain privileged persons, is fully established. But as Christian states were reluctant to expose their subjects to the operation of outlandish law and judgments, they have secured extensively by treaty to their consuls, in Mohammedan and other non-Christian lands, the function of judging in civil and even in criminal cases, where their own countrymen are concerned. In such cases, according to the laws of France,* the consul is assisted by two French residents. "The Frank quarter of Smyrna is under the jurisdiction of European consuls, and all matters touching the rights of foreign residents fall under the exclusive cognizance of the respective consuls." By our treaty of 1834 with the Sultan of Muscat, our consuls there are exclusive judges of all disputes between American citizens, and by our treaty with China in 1844, American citizens committing crimes in China, are subject to be tried and punished only by the consul, or other public functionary, empowered so to act by our laws. Disputes, also, between citizens of the United States, or between them and other foreign residents, are not to be tried by the laws and courts of China, but in the former case come

* Pardessus, Droit commercial, VI. 294, et seq.

before our authorities, and in the other are to be regulated by treaties with the respective governments to which the other parties at law are subject. Similar arrangements have recently been made with Japan.* (§ 65.)

Privileges and status of consuls.

Consuls on exhibiting proof of their appointment receive an *exequatur*, or permission to discharge their functions within the limits prescribed, which permission can be withdrawn for any misconduct. They have, during their term of office, according to the prevailing opinion, no special privileges beyond other foreigners, and are thus subject to the laws, both civil and criminal, of the country where they reside. They enjoy no inviolability of person, nor any immunity from jurisdiction, unless it be given to them by special treaty. Heffter, however (§ 244), makes the safe statement that they possess "that inviolability of person which renders it possible for them to perform their consular duties without personal hindrance." Vattel (II. 2, § 34) goes still farther. A sovereign, says he, by receiving the consul, "tacitly engages to allow him all the liberty and safety necessary in the proper discharge of his functions." His functions require that he be "independent of the ordinary criminal justice of the place where he resides," and "if he commit any crime, he is, from the respect due to his master, to be sent home." But the best authorities agree that it is at the option of a sovereign, whether the consul shall have the benefit of such comity or not,† and it seems inconsistent with modern ideas of the territorial jurisdiction of the sovereign, that a man who is very generally a merchant should be exempt from the law which applies to people of his class about him. Chancellor Kent cites Warden, as producing authorities to show that in France "a consul cannot be prosecuted without the previous consent of his government;" but Fœlix sets the matter in the following light: ‡ that by a convention of France with Spain in 1769, the consuls of the latter, being Spanish subjects, obtained im-

* Comp. Kent, I. 45, Lect. II.; Wheaton El. II. 2, § 11.

† Comp. among others, Bynkersh. de for. leg. 10, near the end.

‡ Fœlix, I. 406, § 221

munity from arrest, excepting for atrocious crime and for commercial obligations. This covered only "debts and other civil cases not implying crime or almost crime, and not growing out of their mercantile character." Since that time all other nations, with whom France has stipulated that their consuls shall be placed on the footing of the most favored nation, may claim the same immunity, "but with this exception, consuls, being foreign subjects, are to be treated in France like all other members of the same nation."

Although a consul has none of the privileges of an ambassador, yet an insult to his person, or an attack on his place of official business involves more of insult to his country than similar treatment of an ordinary stranger could do. He has in fact something of a representative character, and calls for the protection of his government in the exercise of his functions.

Consuls in the Mohammedan countries, owing, perhaps, to the fact that formerly diplomatic intercourse passed to some extent through their hands, and to their official character of protectors of their countrymen in those lands, have nearly the same rights as ambassadors, including the right of worship, and in a degree that of asylum.

Who may be consuls.

By the practice of some nations, only a native can be employed to attend to the commercial interests of his country in foreign ports. The United States, however, have hitherto freely employed foreigners in that capacity, especially in ports where our own commerce is small.

CHAPTER V.

OF THE RIGHT OF CONTRACT AND ESPECIALLY OF TREATIES.

§ 97.

A CONTRACT is one of the highest acts of human free will: it is the will binding itself in regard to the future, and surrendering its right to change a certain expressed intention, so that it becomes morally and jurally a wrong to act otherwise; it is the act of two parties in which each or one of the two conveys power over himself to the other in consideration of something done or to be done by the other. The binding force of contracts is to be deduced from the freedom and foresight of man, which would have almost no sphere in society, or power of co-operation, unless trust could be excited. Trust lies at the basis of society; society is essential for the development of the individual; the individual could not develop his free forethought, unless an acknowledged obligation made him sure in regard to the actions of others. That nations, as well as individuals, are bound by contract, will not be doubted when we remember that they have the same properties of free will and forecast; that they could have no safe intercourse otherwise, and could scarcely be sure of any settled relations toward one another except a state of war, and that thus a state of society, for which the portions of the world are destined would be impossible. We have already seen, that without this power a positive law of nations could not exist, which needs for its establishment the consent of all who are bound by its provisions. National contracts are even more solemn and sacred than private ones, on account of the great interests involved, of the deliberateness with which the obliga-

Of contract, especially between states.

tions are assumed, of the permanence and generality of the obligations,—measured by the national life, and including thousands of particular cases,—and of each nation's calling, under God, to be a teacher of right to all within and without its borders.

With whom can states make contracts?

Contracts can be made by states with individuals or bodies of individuals, or with other states. Contracts between states may be called conventions or treaties. Among the species of treaties those which put an end to a war and introduce a new state of intercourse, or treaties of peace, will be considered here, only so far as they partake of the general character of treaties: their relations to war will be considered in the chapter devoted to that subject.

§ 98.

Lawful treaties, what?

Treaties, allowed under the law of nations, are unconstrained acts of independent powers, placing them under an obligation to do something which is not wrong, or

1. Treaties can be made only by the constituted authorities of nations, or by persons specially deputed by them for that purpose. An unauthorized agreement, or a *sponsio*, like that of the consul Postumius at the Caudine Forks, does not bind the sovereign,—it is held,—for the engager had no power to convey rights belonging to another.* And yet it may be morally wrong for the sovereign to violate such an engagement of a subordinate; for it might be an act of extreme necessity, to which the usual forms of governmental proceedings would not apply. Again, from the nature of the case a faction, a province, or an integral part of a *close* confederation has no treaty-making power; although a *loose* confederation, like the Germanic, might exist, while conceding such a prerogative to its members. Individuals, or other dependent bodies, can make commercial arrangements with a foreign power, unless their laws forbid; but the arrangements apply to a particular case, and obligate none else; they are like any

* Comp. Vattel, Book II. §§ 208–212.

other private contracts; nor has a government over such a contracting party anything to do in the premises, save to protect, and, if expedient, to procurė it redress against injustice. *Political* engagements, or such as affect a body politic, can be made only by political powers. Only the actual sovereign, or power possessing the attributes of sovereignty at the time, can bind a nation by its engagements.

§ 99.

Treaties made by a sovereign with limited powers.

2. If the power of a sovereign or of a government is limited by a ground-law, written or unwritten, a treaty cannot override that constitution. No one can lawfully exercise power, which does not, of right, belong to him. Thus under constitutional forms, where the treaty-making power is placed in particular hands, no others can exercise it, and where it is limited in extent, it cannot be lawfully exercised beyond that limitation. Where, however, an unlimited power of making treaties is given to a government, or to some department of it, the public domain and property may be alienated, or individual rights may be sacrificed for public purposes.* And yet even the most absolute despot may make treaties, which neither his subjects nor third powers ought to regard as binding. Could the house of Romanoff, for instance, resign the throne of Russia to whom it pleased? The true view here is, that the province of absolutism is not to dispose of the national life, but to maintain it without those checks on the exercise of power which exist elsewhere. No power, however uncontrolled, was given to destroy a nation, or can lawfully do so.

An interesting inquiry here arises, whether the treaty-making power in a federative union, like the United States, can alienate the domain of one of the States without its consent. Our government, when the northeastern boundary was in dispute, declared that it had no power to dispose of territory claimed by the State of Maine. "The better opinion would seem to be," says Chancellor Kent, "that such a power of ces-

* Kent, I. 166, 167.

sion does reside exclusively in the treaty-making power under the Constitution of the United States, although a sound discretion would forbid the exercise of it without the consent" of the interested state. But it might be asked, whether the treaty-making power is not necessarily limited by the existence of states, parties to the confederation, having control for most purposes over their own territory. Could the treaty-making power blot out the existence of a state which helped to create the union, by ceding away all its domain? Such fearful power was never lodged in the general government by the Constitution and could never be lawfully exercised in the ordinary contingencies of the confederation. Only in extreme cases, where the treaty-making power is called upon to accept the *fact* of conquest, or to save the whole body from ruin by surrendering a part, could such an exercise of power be justified. (Comp. §§ 52, 153.)

§ 100.

Treaties obtained by foul means not binding on a nation.

3. A treaty, in which the treaty-making power flagitiously sacrifices the interests of the nation which it represents, has no binding force. In this case the treacherous act of the government cannot be justly regarded as the act of the nation, and the forms ought to give way to the realities of things. Moreover, the other party to the treaty ought not to draw advantage from the iniquity of an agent whom it has itself tempted. What, for example, was the cession worth, which the king of Spain made of his rights to the crown to Bonaparte in 1807, and who could think himself bound by such an act, even if it lay within the competence of the sovereign?

Nor those obtained by false statements or by force.

4. Treaties obtained by false representations, or by force, are not binding. The rule for nations here is the same which in all law holds good for individuals. In the former case, the consideration which led to the making of the treaty did not exist, but a false statement was purposely made in order to bring about the contract. In the latter case, the engagement was not the free act of an independent will.

But this rule will not invalidate a treaty, where one of the parties acts under a wrong judgment, or has a false impression, for which the other is not responsible. For the consideration is not real objective good, but the expectation of good, which may not be realized. Having, under the sway of this expectation, influenced the conduct of the other party, he has brought himself under obligation. Thus, if a garrison capitulates under a mistake as to the force of the besieging army or the probability of relief, and discovers the mistake before the capitulation takes effect, this is still binding. Again, when we speak of force invalidating a treaty, we must intend unjust duress or violence practised on the sovereign or the treaty-making agent. A disadvantageous treaty made to prevent further conquest, or to release the sovereign or others from lawful captivity, is as binding as any other; for a fair advantage of war has been used to obtain terms which otherwise would not have been conceded. Thus when Pope Paschal II. was taken prisoner in 1111, by the Emperor Henry V., or John of France, in 1356, by Edward III. of England at Poitiers, or Francis I. in 1525, at Pavia, by the officers of Charles V., the treaties made to procure their liberty were respectively binding, so far as nothing immoral was involved in their articles, or the persons making the treaties did not transcend their powers. In the case of Paschal, the feeling of the age, or at least of the stricter party in the church, regarded the practice of lay investitures, to which he gave his consent, as something irreligious; and it was claimed that he was under compulsion when he performed the act. But why, if he renounced his engagement as constrained and unlawful, did he not return to his imprisonment? John, with true feudal honor, when a prince of his blood violated his stipulation, put himself again into the hands of the English king; while Francis, unlike his ancestor, and unlike St. Louis, who kept his faith with the Saracens, given almost in fear of death, neither stood to his engagements, nor went back into captivity at Madrid. In the case of Francis, it may be doubted whether the estates of Burgundy could be transferred without their consent to another sovereign: feudal law, not then extinct, would not give such power into the hands of the suzerain without the vassal's concurrence. But why did he make a treaty if not free, and why, if not able to execute it, did he not restore all things, as far as in him lay, to their condition anterior to the treaty? *

§ 101.

Treaties to do an unlawful act not binding.

5. A treaty can never obligate to do an unlawful act, for neither party can give consent to do evil in expectation of a good to be received. Thus a treaty contradicting a prior treaty with another power is void, and if observed, an act of injustice. Thus, too, a combination to commit injustice, for example, to put down liberty or religion, or to conquer and appropriate an independent country, as Poland, is a crime which no formalities of treaty can sanction. This rule, it is true, is not one of much practical application to the concerns of nations, for *beforehand*, most of the iniquities of nations are varnished over by some justifying plea, and the only tribunal in the case is the moral indignation of mankind, while, *after* the crime has triumphed, mankind accept the new order of things, rather than have a state of perpetual war. But the rule is useful, so far as it sanctions the protests of innocent states, and their combinations to resist the power and danger of combined injustice.

§ 102.

Kind of treaties.

Treaties are of various kinds. They may define private relations, like commercial treaties, or political relations. They may be temporary, or of unlimited duration, and among the latter, some, or some provisions which they contain, may be dissolved by war, and others, intended to regulate intercourse during war, may be perpetual. They may secure co-operation merely, as treaties of alliance, or a closer union, as confederations, or the uniting of two or more states into one. All the intercourse of nations may come under the operation of treaties; and they may reach to the explanation or alteration—as far as the parties are concerned—of interna-

* Comp. Flassan, Diplom. Française, I. 323, seq., and Ward's Hist. II. 361.

tional law. Hence the importance of collections of treaties, and of the history of diplomatic intercourse.

Besides these leading divisions, treaties may differ from one another in many ways. They may, for instance, be made by the treaty-making powers in person or by their agents, may be open or secret or with articles of both kinds, may be absolute or conditioned, may contain promises of performance on one or on both sides, may be attended or not with a pecuniary payment, be revocable at the will of either party or irrevocable. They may be principal or accessory, preliminary or definitive. They may be simple, consisting of one engagement, or contain many articles, some leading, others subordinate. They may contain new provisions, or confirm or explain old treaties. Thus some of the more important treaties, as those of Westphalia and Utrecht, have been confirmed many times over.*

§ 103.

Treaties, 1. of alliance.

Treaties of alliance may be defensive or offensive, or both. *Defensive treaties*, as generally understood, are made to secure the parties to them against aggression from other states. They may, also, aim at the maintenance of internal quiet, or of neutrality amid the conflicts of neighboring powers. To attempt to gain any of these objects is not necessarily contrary to the law of nations or to natural justice. Mutual aid, indeed, against the disturbers of internal quiet, may secure an absolute government against popular revolutions in favor of liberty (§ 41), but if a confederation or alliance may secure to its members the enjoyment of free institutions, there is no reason, as far as international law is concerned, why institutions of an opposite kind may not support themselves in the same way. The law of nations, we have seen, shows no preference for any one kind of government, but acknowledges all established governments as having a right to exist. *Treaties of neutrality* are reciprocal engagements to have no part in the conflicts between other powers,—to remain

* Comp. Klüber, §§ 146, 147.

at peace in an apprehended or an actual war. They are suggested by, and prevent the evils of that interference of nations in each other's affairs, for the preservation of the balance of power or the safety of the parties interfering, which is so common in modern history. *Alliances at once offensive and defensive* have one of the usual and more important characteristics of confederations.

Sometimes a treaty-engagement is made to do a certain specific act of limited extent in contemplation of a possible future state of war, as to supply a certain amount of money or number of troops. The party entering into such a stipulation, if the agreement was general, and had no special reference to a particular war with a particular nation, is held not to have taken a belligerent attitude.* Much, however, would depend upon the amount of assistance promised, and it stands open to the party injured by such aid afforded to his rival, to regard it as an act of hostility or not, as he may think best.

A treaty of alliance can bind the parties to no injustice (§ 101), nor justify either of them in being accessory to an act of bad faith on the part of another. Hence a defensive, still more an offensive alliance, can only contemplate, if lawful, the warding off of intended injustice. Where justice is doubtful, the benefit of the doubt, it is held, ought to accrue to the ally. It is held, also, that in cases where compliance is plainly useless, or would be ruinous, an ally is not obliged to aid his friend. With regard to defensive alliances, the question may arise, what constitutes a defensive war, since certain wars have been defensive in spirit, though offensive in form. The best answer seems to be, that clearly menaced injustice may be prevented by an ally;—that he ought not to wait until the formality of striking the blow arrives, but fulfil his obligation by giving aid, as soon as it is needed.† Thus a defensive alliance scarcely differs from a justifiable offensive one.

* Vattel, III. § 97; Wheaton's El. III. 2. § 14.

† Comp. Wheaton, El. u. s. III. 2. § 13.

§ 104.

A confederation is a union, more or less complete, of two or more states which before were independent. It aims to secure a common good, external, as mutual protection against powerful neighbors, or internal, as commerce and community of justice by means of common institutions. If, by the terms of the league, the parts are so far united together as to act through one organ in all external relations, and if this organ has many of the properties of sovereignty in internal affairs, the resulting government is not a league of states (a Staatenbund, as the Germans call it), but a state formed by a league. (Bundesstaat.) But the two have no exact limits to separate them.

2. of confederation.

States have, as far as others are concerned, an entire right to form such leagues, or even to merge their existence in a new state, provided, however, that no obligation toward a third power is thereby evaded, and no blow is aimed at its safety. When so constituted, a union must be respected by other powers, who are henceforth to accommodate their diplomatic and commercial intercourse to the new order of things. If any of the members came into the union with debts on their heads, the obligation to pay them is not cancelled by the transaction; or if in any other way owing to the new state of things foreign states are wronged, compensation is due. In the opposite case, when a league or union is dissolved, the debts still remain, justice requiring not only that they be divided between the members in a certain ratio, but also that each of the members be in some degree holden to make good the deficiencies of the others. Comp. § 38.

§ 105.

Treaties of guaranty* are to be classed among treaties as it respects their form, and as it respects their objects among the means of securing the observance of treaties. They are especially accessory stipulations, sometimes incorporated in the main instrument, and

3. Treaties of guaranty, and guaranties of treaties.

* Comp. Vattel, II. 16, § 235, seq.; Klüber, §§ 157–159; Heffter, § 97; Wheaton's El. III. 2, § 12.

sometimes appended to it, in which a third power promises to give aid to one of the treaty-making powers, in case certain specific rights,—all or a part of those conveyed to him in the instrument,—are violated by the other party. We say certain specific rights, because an engagement to afford assistance against the violation of all rights, would be, as Klüber remarks, a league or treaty of alliance. A guaranty may refer to any rights whatever, for instance to the payment of a sum of money stipulated in a treaty, as when Russia, in 1776, guaranteed a Polish loan of 500,000 ducats; to the secure possession of ceded territory; to the integrity of a state, as the French emperor guaranteed the integrity of the Austrian states in the peace of Vienna, of 1809; to the right of succession, as the famous pragmatic sanction of the Emperor Charles VI. (Append. II. 1735) was guaranteed by Spain, France, the empire, etc., and the succession of the Bourbons in Spain by Austria, in the treaty of Vienna, 1735, (Append. II.); to religious franchises, as in the guaranties of the treaties of Westphalia; to the maintenance of an existing constitution, which might imply help against revolted subjects; to national independence, as when in the Paris peace of 1856, England and France pledged themselves to sustain the national existence and integrity of Turkey,—to any or to all of these. Guaranties often extend to all the provisions of a treaty; and thus approach to the class of defensive alliances.

Guaranties may be given to each other by all the parties to a treaty, where there are more than two, or by certain parties to certain others, or by a third power to secure one of the principals in the transactions. At the peace of Aix-la-Chapelle, in 1748, the eight contracting powers gave mutual guaranties. At the peace of Westphalia, and that of Paris, in 1763, all the powers concerned did the same. Sometimes a treaty renews or confirms previous ones, and the question may arise whether a general guaranty to such a treaty is also a guaranty to all past treaties which it includes. Thus, the treaty of Teschen* (1779, Append. II.), which was guaranteed by Russia, renewed

* Comp. de Martens, § 338.

the treaties of Westphalia. Did then Russia become a guarantee to that peace? Certainly not in the same sense in which France and Sweden became such, when it was made (Append. II, 1648), and at most, only so far as the relations between those powers were concerned who were parties to the principal treaty.

The political importance of general guaranties is none other than that of alliances framed in view of existing affairs. They are a mode of providing beforehand against infractions of rights by securing the pledge of a third party, and a convenient way of intervening in the affairs of other states, and of keeping up the present order of things. Whether they are justifiable in such cases depends not on the form which they take, but on the propriety of intervention. (Comp. § 42, note.)

A guaranty requires the party making it, to give aid when called upon, and so much aid as he had stipulated, and in a case to which, in his judgment, the guaranty relates. If the party, on whose account he became a security, declines his assistance, he has nothing to do with the case further, unless, indeed, grounds of public interest, apart from his obligation, make his intervention of importance. If the parties to a treaty alter it or add to it, he, of course, is not bound by his guaranty in regard to these new portions of the treaty: if the alterations are essential, it may be doubted whether his guaranty, made, perhaps, in view of another state of things, has not ceased to be obligatory. If by the assistance promised, he cannot make good the injury, he is bound to nothing more, much less to compensation. If he guarantees a debt, and the payment is refused, he is not bound to make it good; for in this, according to Vattel,* lies the difference between a *surety* and a *guarantee*, that the former is obliged to perform what the principal party has failed to do, while the latter is only bound to do his best to bring the other to a compliance with his engagement.

Origin of guaranties to treaties.

Treaties of guaranty, when they pledge a stronger power to maintain the independence and integrity of a weaker, do not differ greatly from those treaties

* Vattel, II. 16, § 240. Comp. Wheaton, u. s.

of protection which were not unknown to the middle ages. Of such a description was the treaty between John of England and the king of the Isle of Man in 1205, which Mr. Ward notices in his history (II. 159), and which soon afterward (in 1212) was changed into a treaty, whereby the king of England became the suzerain of the other. Guaranties in their modern form do not seem to have been in use much before the date of the treaties of Westphalia. Before this time persons called conservators were sometimes appointed to watch over the execution of treaties, who might be ministers or governors of provinces with power to adjust difficulties between the parties; and even private persons added their seals to that of their sovereign, and were bound to declare against him, if he broke his word. At the treaty of Senlis, in 1493, between Charles VIII. of France and the Emperor Maximilian, not only individual subjects but a number of towns attached their seals on behalf of their respective sovereigns. The Sieur de Bevres, one of the sealers, declares under his name that, if the Emperor and his son, Archduke Philip the Fair, should not observe their agreement, he would be bound to abandon them, and give favor and assistance to the king of France. First in 1505 the treaty of Blois mentions foreign princes as its conservators. They add their confirmation also to a peace made at Cambray seven years later. From this to modern guaranties the step was an easy one.*

§ 106.

Other modes of confirming the faith of treaties.

Various other ways of securing the parties to a treaty against each other's want of good faith have been taken, some of which are obsolete while others are still in use. One way was to add to the solemnity of the oath which confirmed the treaty, by taking it over the bones of saints, the gospels, the wood of the true cross, the host and the like. Another kind of religious sanction is found in

* See Mably. I. Part II. 129–131, Amsterdam edit. of 1777, and Flassan, Hist. de la Diplom. Française, I. 244, in his remarks on a treaty between Louis XI. and the Emperor in 1482.

the treaty of Cambray (the "paix des dames," Append. II) of Aug. 5, 1529, in which the parties submitted themselves to the jurisdiction and censures of the church, even to the point of suffering the secular arm to be called in to support the ecclesiastical; and appointed procurators to appear at Rome on their behalf and undergo the condemnation and fulmination of such censures,* etc.

Hostages.

Another mode of securing the faith of treaties, formerly much in use but now almost obsolete, was that of giving hostages, one of the last examples of which occurred after the peace of Aix-la-Chapelle in 1748, when two British peers (Lords Sussex and Cathcart) remained on parole at Paris until Cape Breton should be restored to France. The understanding in giving hostages was that their freedom and not their lives secured the treaty: hence, when it was violated, they might be detained in captivity, but not put to death. Escape on their part would be gross treachery. On the fulfilment of the obligation they were of course free. The mode of treating them within the laws of humanity, as whether they should be confined, according to early practice, or be allowed to go about on parole, would depend on the pleasure of the party secured by them. It is asked whether a prince serving as a hostage could be detained, if he should inherit the crown during his captivity. Without doubt he might in the times when hostages were commonly given, because even sovereigns were then so detained. And if the practice prevailed now, it might be doubted whether the principle of exterritoriality would not have to be sacrificed in such a case.†

Pledges.

Treaties are also still confirmed by pledges, which generally consist in territories or fortresses put into the hands of the other party, who more rarely contents himself with simple hypothecation without transfer.‡

* Comp. Mably, u. s. The provision is found in Art. XLVI. of the treaty (Dumont, IV. 2, 15), and is a striking proof of the small trust which the parties put in one another. They show in the same place a dread that the Pope might absolve one or the other (as he had already done in the case of Francis) from his oath and faith, and endeavor to guard against it.

† Comp. Vattel, II. Chap. 16, §§ 245–261, and Ward's Hist. I. 172–175.

‡ Comp. Klüber, § 156.

The occupation of the French fortresses by the allies, according to the terms of the second treaty of Paris, may be regarded as coming under this head, since it secured the payment of the indemnities, (Append. II. 1815,) although it was equally intended to secure the Bourbon dynasty.

§ 107.

At what time do treaties begin to be binding?

Treaties are binding, unless some other time is agreed upon, at the time when they are signed by an authorized agent, and their ratification by their sovereign is retroactive.

If, then, an ambassador, in conformity with a full power received from his sovereign, has negotiated and signed a treaty, is the sovereign justified in withholding his ratification? This question has no significance in regard to states, by whose form of government the engagements made by the executive with foreign powers need some further sanction. In other cases, that is wherever the treaty-making power of the sovereign is final, the older writers held that he was bound by the acts of his agent, if the latter acted within the full power which he had received, even though he had gone contrary to secret instructions. But Bynkershoek defended another opinion which is now the received one among the text-writers, and which Wheaton has advocated at large with great ability.* If the minister has conformed at once to his ostensible powers and to his secret instructions, there is no doubt that in ordinary cases it would be bad faith in the sovereign not to add his ratification. But if the minister disobeys or transcends his instructions, the sovereign may refuse his sanction to the treaty without bad faith or ground of complaint on the other side. But even this violation of secret instructions would be no valid excuse for the sovereign's refusing to accept the treaty, if he should have given public credentials of a minute and specific character to his agent; for the evident intention in so doing would be to convey an impression to the other party, that he

* Wheaton's El. B. III. 2, § 5; Bynkershoek, Quæst. J. P. II. 7; de Martens,

is making a sincere declaration of the terms on which he is willing to treat.

But even when the negotiator has followed his private instructions, there are cases, according to Dr. Wheaton, where the sovereign may refuse his ratification. He may do so when the motive for making the treaty was an error in regard to a matter of fact, or when the treaty would involve an injury to a third party, or when there is a physical impossibility of fulfilling it, or when such a change of circumstances takes place as would make the treaty void after ratification.

All question would be removed, if in the full power of the negotiators or in a clause of the treaty itself, it were declared that the sovereign reserved to himself the power of giving validity to the treaty by ratification. This, if we are not deceived, is now very generally the case.

§ 108.

Violation of treaties.

Treaties, like other contracts, are violated, when one party neglects or refuses to do that which moved the other party to engage in the transaction. It is not every petty failure or delay to fulfil a treaty, which can authorize the other party to regard it as broken,—above all, if the intention to observe it remains. When a treaty is violated by one party, the other can regard it as broken, and demand redress, or can still require its observance.

§ 109.

Interpretation of treaties.

The laws of interpretation in the case of treaties are substantially the same as in the case of other contracts. Some writers, as Grotius and Vattel, go at large into this subject.* The following are among the most important of those laws:

1. The ordinary *usus loquendi* obtains, unless it involves an absurdity. When words of art are used, the special meaning which they have in the given art is to determine their sense.

2. If two meanings are admissible, that is to be preferred which is least for the advantage of the party for whose benefit a clause is inserted. For in securing a benefit he ought to ex-

* Grotius, II. 16; Vattel, II. Chap. 17. Comp. Wildman, Vol. I. 176–185.

press himself clearly. The sense which the accepter of conditions attaches to them ought rather to be followed than that of the offerer.

3. An interpretation is to be rejected, which involves an absurdity, or renders the transaction of no effect, or makes its parts inconsistent.

4. Obscure expressions are explained by others more clear in the same instrument. To discover the meaning, the connection and the reasons for an act must be considered.

5. Odious clauses, such as involve cruelty or hard conditions for one party, are to be understood strictly, so that their operation shall be brought within the narrowest limits; while clauses which favor justice, equity, and humanity, are to be interpreted broadly.

Repugnant clauses and conflicting treaties.

Sometimes clauses in the same treaty, or treaties between the same parties are repugnant. Some of the rules here applicable are

1. That earlier clauses are to be explained by later ones, which were added, it is reasonable to suppose, for the sake of explanation, or which at least express the last mind of the parties. So also later treaties explain or abrogate older ones.

2. Special clauses have the preference over general, and for the most part prohibitory over permissive.

In treaties made with different parties the inquiry in cases of conflict touches the moral obligation as well as the meaning. Here the earlier treaty must evidently stand against the latter, and if possible, must determine its import where the two seem to conflict.

In general, conditional clauses are inoperative, as long as the condition is unfulfilled; and are made null when it becomes impossible. Where things promised in a treaty are incompatible, the promisee may choose which he will demand the performance of, but here and elsewhere an act of expediency ought to give way to an act of justice.*

* For some remarks on the language used in making treaties, which logically belong here, see § 150, in the section relating to treaties of peace.

PART II.

INTERNATIONAL LAW AND USAGE IN A STATE OF WAR.

CHAPTER I.

OF THE RIGHTS OF SELF-DEFENCE AND REDRESS OF INJURIES PERTAINING TO NATIONS, OR OF WAR, CAPTURE, AND TREATIES OF PEACE.

SECTION I.—*Of War.*

§ 110.

Of war in general.

PEACE is the normal state of mankind, just as society and orderly government are natural; and war, like barbarism, must be regarded as a departure from the natural order of things. But as the present state of nature in the individual, being abnormal and unnatural in the higher sense, leads to injuries, trespasses on rights, and attempts at redress, so is it in the society of nations. International law assumes that there must be "wars and fightings" among nations, and endeavors to lay down rules by which they shall be brought within the limits of justice and humanity. In fact, wars and the relations in which nations stand to one another, as belligerent or neutral, form the principal branch of international law,—so much so that in a state of assured and permanent peace there would be little need of this science, whose tendency, therefore, justly estimated, is to bring about a time when it shall itself lose the greater part of its importance.

In the sections of this chapter we shall need to consider war as to its notion and moral ground, the mode of commencing it, and those states of international intercourse which lie between war and peace, the relation into which it brings the belligerent parties, its usages and laws on land and sea especially those which affect property taken on the latter, and lastly its suspension and final termination. Then, in another chapter, the rights and obligations of neutrals will be treated of, as affected by the relations of the belligerents.

§ 111.

War may be defined to be an interruption of a state of peace for the purpose of attempting to procure good or prevent evil by force; and a *just* war is an attempt to obtain justice or prevent injustice by force, or, in other words, to bring back an injuring party to a right state of mind and conduct by the infliction of deserved evil. A just war again, is one that is waged in the last resort, when peaceful means have failed to procure redress, or when self-defence calls for it. We have no right to redress our wrongs in a way expensive and violent, when other methods would be successful.

War and a just war, what?

By justice, however, we intend not justice objective, but as it appears to a party concerned, or, at least, as it is claimed to exist. From the independence of nations it results that each has a right to hold and make good its own view of right in its own affairs. When a quarrel arises between two states, others are not to interfere (Comp. § 20) because their views of the right in the case differ from those of a party concerned; or at least they are not to do this unless the injustice of the war is flagrant and its principle dangerous. If a nation, however, should undertake a war with no pretext of right, other states may not only remonstrate, but use force to put down such wickedness.

Who is to judge?

It may be said that as individuals ought not to judge in their own cause, so nations ought to submit their differences to third parties and abide by the issue. It would doubtless be desirable, if resort were more frequently had to arbitration before the last remedy of wrongs were used, and probably, as the world grows better, this practice will more and more prevail. But in the past a multitude of aggressions have occurred which could not be so prevented, which needed to be repelled by the speediest means;

Are nations bound to submit their differences to arbitrators?

nor have the intelligence and probity of men been such that good arbitrators could always be found. The question, however, relates to duty, and does not affect the justice of a war which a nation should undertake on grounds which approved themselves to its own unaided judgment. (Comp. § 19.)

Ought an ally to judge?

A state bound by treaty to assist another in the event of war, must of course judge whether the *casus fœderis* exists, and is also bound to pass judgment on the nature of the war, since no treaty can sanction injustice.

§ 112.

Rightfulness of war in general.

The rightfulness of war, that is of some wars, will be clear when we consider that to states, by the divine constitution of society, belong the obligations of protecting themselves and their people, as well as the right of redress, and even, perhaps, that of punishment. (§ 20.) To resist injury, to obtain justice, to give wholesome lessons to wrong-doers for the future, are prerogatives deputed by the Divine King of the world to organized society, which, when exercised aright, cultivate the moral faculty, and raise the tone of judging through mankind. War is a dreadful thing when evil suffered or inflicted is considered; and yet war has often been the restorer of national virtue, which had nearly perished under the influence of selfish, luxurious peace.

For what may war be undertaken?

A war may be waged to defend any right which a state is bound to protect, or to redress wrong, or to prevent apprehended injury. And (1.) a state may go to war to defend its sovereignty and independence,—that is, its political life,—or its territory. This reason for war is analogous to the individual's right of self-preservation, and of defending his house when attacked.

(2.) The state being bound to protect the individual inhabitant in all his rights, is his only defender against foreign violence, and may redress his wrongs even by war. But here it is reasonable to consider the extent of the injury, and the greatness of the evil which the remedy may involve. A state may forbear to redress its own public wrongs, much more the smaller ones of individuals.

(3.) A state may engage in war to obtain satisfaction for violations of its honor, as for insults to its flag or its ambassadors, or its good name. We have seen (§ 18), that a state has a right of reputation, that this right is extremely important, and that infractions of it cannot fail to arouse a deep sense of wrong in a high-minded people. Redress, therefore, is here as just and natural, as suits for libel or slander between individuals. It is plain, however, that every small want of comity or petty insult does not warrant hostile measures, though it may call for remonstrance.

(4.) Violations of those rights which nations concede to one another by treaty may call for the redress of war. A contract is broken, and there is no court before which the party doing the injury can be summoned.

(5.) The prevention of intended injury is a ground of war. This indeed is a case of self-defence, only the injury must not be remote or constructive, but fairly inferrible from the preparations and intentions of the other party. The injury, again, which is to be prevented may not be aimed directly against a particular state, but may affect the equilibrium of a system of states. Thus the ambition of a leading state, it is now held, may, by disturbing the balance of power in Europe, provoke the interference of others upon the same continent. (Comp. § 43.)

(6.) In some rare cases a great and flagrant wrong committed by another nation, against religion for instance, or liberty, may justify hostile interference on the part of those who are not immediately affected. (§ 50.) And this, not only because the wrong, if allowed, may threaten all states, but also because the better feelings of nations impel them to help the injured.

§ 113.

Kinds of war, offensive and defensive war.

Wars may be waged against foreign states in the same political system, or nations out of the pale of Christian civilization, against savages, against pirates, or by the parts of a state against each other. Of the most of these, after the first, international law has usually but a word to say. Wars, again, have been divided into defensive and offensive. This distinction is of no very great importance, since, as we have seen, the two may differ less in essence than in form, and, as it respects form, the one runs into the other. A wronged nation, or one fearing sudden wrong, may be the first to attack, and that is perhaps its best defence. Moreover, offensive wars, however apt to be unjust, have usually some pretext of justice to urge in their favor, which nations, except in extreme cases, must respect, unless every nation is to become a judge and a party.

§ 114.

Measures for redress falling short of war.

Nations have sometimes resorted to measures for obtaining redress, which have a hostile character, and yet fall short of actual war. *Embargo*, *retorsion*, and *reprisal*, are of this description.

Embargo.

1. An embargo (from the Spanish and Portuguese, *embargar*, to *hinder* or *detain*, the root of which is the same as that of *bar*, *barricade*), is, in its special sense, a detention of vessels in a port, whether they be national or foreign, whether for the purpose of employing them and their crews in a naval expedition, as was formerly practised, or for political purposes, or by way of reprisals. A *civil embargo* may be laid for the purpose of national welfare or safety, as for the protection of commercial vessels against the rules of belligerent powers which would expose them to capture. Such was the measure adopted by the United States in December, 1807, which detained in port all vessels except those which had a public commission, and those that were already laden or should sail in ballast. The right to adopt such a measure of temporary non-intercourse, is undoubted. Great Britain, although injured by the act, acknowledged that it afforded to foreign nations no ground of complaint. And yet, in the half century since that event, uninterrupted intercourse has come to be regarded almost as an absolute right, and the injuries in-

flicted in such a way on friendly states would cause them to protest with energy or to retaliate.

Hostile embargo.

A *hostile* embargo is a kind of reprisals by one nation upon vessels within its ports belonging to another nation with which a difference exists, for the purpose of forcing it to do justice. If this measure should be followed by war, the vessels are regarded as captured, if by peace, they are restored. "This species of reprisal," says Kent, (I. 61,) "is laid down in the books as a lawful measure according to the usage of nations, but it is often reprobated, and cannot well be distinguished from the practice of seizing property found in the territory upon the declaration of war." Although such a measure might bring an adversary to terms, and prevent war, yet its resemblance to robbery, occurring, as it does, in the midst of peace, and its contrariety to the rules according to which the private property even of enemies is treated, ought to make it disgraceful, and drive it into disuse.

Retorsion.

2. Retorsion (from *retorquere*, French, *retordre*, retort), or retaliation, is to apply the *lex talionis* to another nation,—treating it or its subjects in similar circumstances according to the rule which it has set. Thus, if a nation has failed in comity or politeness, if it has embarrassed intercourse by new taxes on commerce or the like, the same or an analogous course may be taken by the aggrieved power to bring it back to propriety and duty. The sphere of retorsion ought to be confined within the imperfect rights or moral claims of an opposite party. Rights ought not to be violated because another nation has violated them.

Reprisals.

3. Reprisals (from *reprendere*, Latin, *repressaliæ*, in mediæval Latin, *reprisailles*, French), consist properly in recovering what is our own by force, then in seizing an equivalent, or, negatively, in detaining that which belongs to our adversary. Reprisals, says Vattel, "are used between nation and nation to do justice to themselves, when they cannot otherwise obtain it. If a nation has taken possession of what belongs to another; if it refuses to pay a debt, to repair an injury, to make a just satisfaction, the other may

seize what belongs to it, and apply it to its own advantage, till it has obtained what is due for interest and damage, or keep it as a pledge until full satisfaction has been made. In the last case it is rather a stoppage or a seizure than reprisals; but they are frequently confounded in common language." (B. II. § 342.) *Reprisals* differ from *retorsion* in this, that the essence of the former consists in seizing the property of another nation by way of security, until it shall have listened to the just reclamations of the offended party, while *retorsion* includes all kinds of measures which do an injury to another, similar and equivalent to that which we have experienced from him.* Embargo, therefore, is a species of reprisals.

Reprisals may be undertaken on account of any injury, but are chiefly confined to cases of refusal or even obstinate delay of justice. Grotius adds that they are authorized, "si in re minime dubia plane contra jus judicatum sit." (III. 2, § 5, 1.) But this is an unsafe opinion, and to be acted upon only in an extreme case, for the sentence of a regular tribunal will always be supported by some plausible, if not valid reason: there should be the fullest proof of an intention to deny or to overturn justice.

Where the property of a state is seized by way of reprisals, the proceeding needs no defence; on the other hand, to take the goods of private persons as security for the reparation of public wrongs is indefensible except on the ground that a state and its subjects are so far one as to give it a claim on their property for public purposes, and that the injured state takes the place of the injurer, and exercises its power by the only means within its reach. As therefore, when a man's land is taken for a public road, he has a claim for compensation, so, when a man loses his property by the violent process of a foreign state against his own country, not he, but the whole society ought to make his loss good. Still reprisals are inhumane, and like seizure of private effects in land war, will, it is to be hoped, ere long entirely cease.

* Pinheiro-Ferreira in de Martens, Vol. II. § 255.

Greek and Roman usages.

The Romans knew nothing of reprisals,* but with great formality defined and observed the limits between peace and war. The Greeks, however, had usages, similar to this, drawn from their simpler semi-barbarous times. Thus, before war was declared, and after the denial of justice, they gave license to their citizens to take plunder from the offending state on land and sea. There was also a custom prevailing between border states, when a homicide had been committed, and the man-slayer was not given up to the relatives of the deceased, of allowing them to seize and keep in chains three countrymen of the wrong-doer, until satisfaction should be rendered.

Mediæval and

The Greeks here present to us two forms of reprisals, the one where the state gives authority to all, or in a public way attempts to obtain justice by force, which is called *general*, and the other, where power is given to the injured party to right himself by his own means, or *special* reprisals. The latter has now fallen into disuse, and would be regarded as an act of hostility, but with the other was a received method of redress in the middle ages; nor was it strange that a private person, by the leave of his superior, should wage a war of his own, when private wars were a part of the order of things. Mr. Ward (I. 176), and the English historians, mention an instance of reprisals between the English and France in the 13th century, which might seem to pertain to the Dyaks or the Ojibways. In 1292, two sailors, a Norman and an Englishman, having come to blows at Bayonne, the latter stabbed the former, and was not brought before the courts of justice. The Normans applied to Philip the Fair for redress, who answered by bidding them take their own revenge. They put to sea, seized the first English ship they met, and hung up several of the crew at the mast head. The English retaliated without applying to their government, and things arose to such a pitch, that 200 Norman vessels scoured

* Osenbrüggen, de jure etc., p. 35. Schömann, Antiq. juris publici, p. 366, and his Griech. Alterthümer, 2, p. 6. Comp. Bynkershoek, Quæst. J. P. I. 24. The Greeks said, σῦλα διδόναι, ῥύσια καταγγέλλειν κατά τινος.

the English seas, hanging all the sailors they caught, while the English, in greater force, destroyed a large part of the Norman ships, and 15,000 men. It was now that the governments interposed, and came at length into a war which stripped the English of nearly all Aquitaine, until it was restored in 1303.

Every authority in those times, which could make war, could grant letters of reprisals. But when power began to be more centralized, the sovereign gave to magistrates, governors of provinces and courts the right of issuing them, until at length this right was reserved for the central government alone. In France, Charles VIII., at the instance of the states-general held at Tours, in 1484, first confined this power to the king, for, said the estates, "reprisals ought not to be granted without great deliberation and knowledge of the case, nor without the formalities of law in such matters required." The ordinance of Louis XIV., on the marine, published in 1681, prescribes the method in which injured persons, after they had shown the extent of their damages received from a foreigner, and after the king's ambassadors had taken the proper steps at the foreign courts, should receive letters of reprisals permitting them to make prizes at sea of property belonging to the subjects of the state which had denied them justice, and having brought their prizes before the court of admiralty, should, in case everything was lawful, be reimbursed to the extent of their injuries.

modern usage.

Since the end of the 17th century but few examples have occurred of reprisals made in time of peace, and a number of treaties restrict the use of them to the denial or delay of justice.*

§ 115.

War between independent sovereignties is, and ought to be, an *avowed open* way of obtaining justice. For every state has a right to know what its relations are towards those with whom it has been on terms of amity,—whether the amity continues or is at an end. It is necessary,

Commencement of war. Declaration.

* Ortolan, I. 391–401.

therefore, that some act show in a way not to be mistaken that a new state of things, a state of war, has begun.

Greek and Roman practice.

The civilized nations of antiquity generally began war by a declaration of their purpose so to do. Among the Greeks, a herald, whose person was sacred and inviolate, carried the news of such hostile intent to the enemy, or accompanied an ambassador to whom this business was committed. Only in rare cases, when men's passions were up, was war *ἀκήρυκτος*, *i. e.*, such, that no communications by heralds passed between the enemies. Among the Romans, the ceremonies of making known the state of war, were very punctilious. This province belonged to the Fetiales, a college of twenty men, originally patricians, whose first duty was to demand justice, *res repetere*, literally, to demand back property, an expression derived from the times when the plunder of cattle or other property, was the commonest offence committed by a neighboring state. Three or four of the college, one of their number being pater patratus for the time, and so the prolocutor, passed the bounds of the offending state, and in a solemn formula, several times repeated, demanded back what was due to the Roman people. On failure to obtain justice, there was a delay of three and thirty days, when the pater patratus again made a solemn protestation that justice was withheld. Then the king consulted the senate, and if war was decreed, the pater patratus again visited the hostile border, with a bloody lance, which he threw into the territory, while he formally declared the existence of the war. This custom, which seems to have been an international usage of the states of middle and southern Italy, continued into the earlier times of the republic; but when the theatre of war became more distant, the fetialis, consul, or prætor, contented himself with hurling his lance from a pillar near the temple of Bellona in the direction of the hostile territory, while the declaration of war itself was made by the military commander of the province through an ambassador. It was thus always a principle with the Romans, as Cicero (de offic. I. 11) has it, "nullum bellum esse justum, nisi quod aut rebus repetitis geratur, aut denuntiatum ante sit et indictum." But the form satisfied them, and they cared little for the spirit.*

Mediæval practice.

So also in the middle ages, war could not be honorably begun without a declaration; but the spirit which dictated this, seems to have been, as Mr. Ward remarks, rather a knightly abhorrence of everything underhanded and treacherous, than a desire to prevent the effusion of blood by giving the enemy time to repair his fault. Even in the private warfare which characterized that age, as much as in the duel, a challenge or formal notice to the enemy was necessary. The declaration of war was made by heralds or other messengers: that of Charles V. of France against Edward III., was carried to that king by a common servant, the letter containing it bearing the seals of France. Such formal challenges were sanctioned by law. Thus the public peace of the Emperor Barbarossa, in 1187, contains the clause that an injured party might prosecute his own rights by force, provided he gave to his adversary three days' notice that he intended to make good his claims in open war. And the Golden Bull of the Emperor Charles IV. in 1356, forbids invasions of the territory of others on pretext of a challenge unless the same had been given for three natural days to an adversary in person, or publicly made known before witnesses at his usual place of residence; and this, on pain of infamy, just as if no challenge had been offered.†

Modern practice.

The modern practice ran for some time in the same direction, but since the middle of the eighteenth century formal declarations have not been extensively made, and are falling into disuse. Instances of the same may be gathered from still earlier times. Thus no declaration preceded the expedition of the grand Armada in 1588, —before which indeed a state of hostilities existed in fact,— and the war between England and Holland, in 1664, began with an act of the English Council, authorizing general repri-

* For the Greeks, see Schömann, u. s. For the Romans, Osenbrüggen, pp. 27–34, Bekker-Marquardt, Röm. Alterthüm. IV. 380–388.

† Ward, II. 123, seq.

sals, which became a full-blown war without any declaration. Thus also the war of Orleans, so called, was begun by Louis XIV. in 1688, before he issued his manifests; in the war of the succession the battle of Dettingen had been fought before the French declared war against Great Britain and Austria; and in the seven years war hostilities began on this continent between England and France two years before the parties to this important war made their declarations.*

Reasons for the modern usage.

This disuse of declarations does not grow out of an intention to take the enemy at unawares, which would imply an extreme degradation of moral principle, but out of the publicity and circulation of intelligence peculiar to modern times. States have now resident ambassadors within each other's bounds, who are accurately informed in regard to the probabilities of war, and can forewarn their countrymen. War is for the most part the end of a long thread of negotiations, and can be generally foreseen. Intentions, also, can be judged of from the preparations which are on foot, and nations have a right to demand of one another what is the meaning of unusual armaments. It is, also, tolerably certain that nations, if they intend to act insidiously, will not expose their own subjects in every quarter of the globe to the embarrassments of a sudden and unexpected war. And yet the modern practice has its evils, so that one cannot help wishing back the more honorable usage of feudal times.

This rule, be it observed, of declaring war beforehand, so long as it was thought obligatory, only bound the assailant. The invaded or defensive state accepted the state of war as a fact, without the formalities of a declaration.

§ 116.

What notice of a state of war ought to be given?

But if a declaration of war is no longer necessary, a state which enters into war is still bound (1.) to indicate in some way, to the party with whom it has a difficulty, its altered feelings and relations. This is done by sending away its ambassador, by a state of

* Comp. Bynkersh. Quæst. J. P. I. 2, and among modern systematists Phillimore III. 75-102.

non-intercourse, and the like. (2.) It is necessary and usual that its own people should have information of the new state of things, otherwise their persons and property may be exposed to peril. (3.) Neutrals have a right to know that a state of war exists, and that, early enough to adjust their commercial transactions to the altered state of things, otherwise a great wrong may be done them. Such notice is given in manifestos. "These pieces," says Vattel, "never fail to contain the justificative reasons, good or bad, for proceeding to the extremity of taking up arms. The least scrupulous sovereign would be thought just, equitable, and a lover of peace; he is sensible that a contrary reputation might be detrimental to him. The manifesto implying a declaration of war, or the declaration itself, which is published all over the state, contains also the general orders to his subjects relative to their conduct in the war." *

§ 117.

Effects of a state of war.

The old strict theory in regard to a state of war was, that each and every subject of the one belligerent is at war with each and every subject of the other. Now as it was also a received rule that the persons and goods of my enemy belong to me if I can seize them, there was no end to the amount of suffering which might be inflicted on the innocent inhabitants of a country within the regular operations of war. It is needless to say that no Christian state acts on such a theory, nor did the Greeks and Romans generally carry it out in practice to its extreme rigor. In particular there is now a wide line drawn between combatants and non-combatants, the latter of whom, by modern practice, are on land exempted from the injuries and molestations of war, as far as is consistent with the use of such a method of obtaining justice.

Non-intercourse with the enemy.

It follows from the notion of war, as an interruption of peaceful intercourse, that all commerce between the subjects of the belligerents is unlawful, unless expressly licensed, or necessary for the war itself. Hence all partnerships with an enemy's subjects, and all power of prose-

* Vattel, B. III. 4, § 64.

cuting claims through the courts of the enemy are suspended during the war; and all commercial transactions with the subjects or in the territory of the enemy of whatever kind, except ransom contracts (§ 142), whether direct, or indirect, as through an agent or partner who is a neutral, become illegal and void. In the case where the business is conducted by a neutral partner, his share in the concern alone is protected, while that of the belligerent's subject is, if seized, liable in his own country to confiscation. (Comp. § 168.)

License to trade with the enemy.

It is not unusual, however, for a belligerent to grant to its own subjects a license to carry on a certain specified trade with the enemy, which, if the other party allows it, becomes a safe and legitimate traffic. It is common, also, for the subjects of one belligerent to obtain such a license from the other; but, of course, this of itself will not protect them against the laws of their own country. (Comp. § 147.)

§ 118.

Enemy's subjects and enemy's property within a belligerent's country.

From the strict theory of hostile relations laid down above, it would follow, (1.) that an enemy's subjects within the country could be treated as prisoners of war. But such rigor is unknown, unless in measures of retaliation. The most severe treatment of the foreigner allowed by modern usage is to require him to leave the country within a certain time.* (2.) That enemies' property within the country at the breaking out of a war was liable to confiscation. This principle would apply also to debts due to them at that time. And it would be a further application of it, if shares in the public stocks, held by a foreign government, were confiscated. With regard to the two former cases, the Supreme Court of the United States has decided, in accordance with the body of earlier and later text-writers, that by strict

* Bonaparte in 1803, upon the rupture with England after the peace of Amiens, ordered the arrest of all Englishmen in France between sixteen and sixty years of age, that they might serve as hostages for such Frenchmen as might be captured on board of French vessels after the breach of peace and in ignorance of it. The Batavian republic was bidden to issue the same order. (Garden, VIII. 151).

right such property is confiscable, but they add, that such a measure requires the sanction of the national legislature, which, it is to be hoped, will never consent to disgrace the country by an act of that kind.* For the usage is now general, if not fixed, with the single exception of measures of retorsion, to allow the subjects of the enemy to remain within the territory during good behavior, in the enjoyment of their property, or to give them, by public proclamation, reasonable time to remove with their effects from the country. The English and French in the late Crimean war allowed Russian vessels six weeks' time to leave their ports and reach their destination. In many cases treaties have given additional security to the goods, claims and persons of enemies' subjects so situated. The treaty of 1795, between the United States and Great Britain, commonly called Jay's from its negotiator, declared it to be unjust and impolitic to confiscate debts due to the subjects of a nation that has become hostile.† It was also stipulated in this instrument, that the citizens of either power might remain unmolested during war, in the dominions of the other, so long as they should behave peaceably, and commit no offence against the laws; and that, if either government desired their removal, twelve months' notice should be given them to this effect. Of treaties containing similar provisions, "a list lies before me," says Mr Manning, "too long for insertion, but even the Barbary powers have in a great number of instances concluded such agreements." ‡

With regard to the shares held by a government or its subjects in the public funds of another, all modern authorities agree, we believe, that they ought to be safe and inviolate.

* Comp. Kent, I. Lect. 3, p. 59, seq.

† In Article X. it is provided, that "neither debts due from individuals of one nation to individuals of the other, nor shares nor money which they may have in the public funds or in the public or private banks, shall ever, in any event of war or national difference, be sequestered or confiscated; it being unjust and impolitic that debts and engagements, contracted and made by individuals, having confidence in each other and in their respective governments, should ever be destroyed by national authority on account of national differences and discontents."

‡ Comment. p. 126.

To confiscate either principal or interest would be a breach of good faith, would injure the credit of a nation and of its public securities, and would provoke retaliation on the property of its private citizens. "The Emperor Napoleon I. during his stay at Posen, imagining that the cabinet of London had the intention of confiscating stock in the public debt belonging to Frenchmen, ordered his minister of finance to examine whether, in case they should so act, it would not be necessary to have recourse to the same rigor. The matter is a very delicate one, said he; I am not willing to set the example, but if the English do so, I ought to make reprisals. M. Mollien replied that such an act was so contrary to English policy, that he could not believe it, that he wished the cabinet of London would commit such a mistake, but that its results would be the more disastrous for them, if it were not imitated. On this occasion he sent to the Emperor the memoir of Hamilton,* the friend, counsellor, and minister of Washington, on the question whether the political, more even than the moral rule, did not forbid every government, not only to confiscate capital which had been lent to it by the subjects of a power with which it was at war, but even to suspend, as far as they were concerned, the payment of interest. Napoleon did not insist further on the matter." †

We close this subject with referring to some of the opinions which text writers have expressed on the several points considered. As for immovable property in an enemy's country Bynkershoek says, that in strict justice it can be sold and confiscated, "ut in mobilibus obtinet," but he adds that it is a general usage throughout Europe for the rents to go to the public treasury during war, but for the property itself after the war to revert "ex pactis" to the former owner. (Quæst. Jur. Publ. I. 7.) As for other property, except debts, all jurists hold the same doctrine of its liability to confiscation. (Comp.

* Probably the letters of Camillus. See the note at the end of this section.

† From a biography of Count Mollien, contributed by Michel Chevalier to the Revue des deux mondes, in the year 1856, cited by Vergé on de Martens, § 258, ed. of 1858.

Manning, p. 127.) As for debts, even Grotius decided that "hæc non belli jure quæsita sed bello tantum exigi vetita." But Bynkershoek (u. s.), while he mentions that the right to confiscate them had been questioned, adds, "sed videtur esse jus commune ut et actiones publicentur, ex eadem nempe ratione quâ corporalia quælibet. Actiones utique sive credita non minus, jure gentium, sunt in dominio nostro quam alia bona; eccur igitur in his jus belli sequamur, in aliis non sequamur." There must, however, be actual confiscation. "If the sovereign,"—Bynkershoek goes on to say,—"has exacted debts due to enemies from his subjects, they are duly paid, but if not, at peace the creditor's former right revives, because occupation in war consists rather in fact than in jural power. Debts, therefore, if not confiscated, in time of war suffer a temporary suspension, but upon peace return by a sort of postliminy to their old owner." Accordingly, he adds, that treaties often provide for the non-payment to the creditor of confiscated debts. Vattel takes the same ground as to debts, but adds that all the sovereigns of Europe have departed from this rigor, and, as the usage has altered, he who should act contrary to it, would injure the public faith. (B. III. 5, § 77.) Mr. Manning says that "debts due from individuals to the enemy may be confiscated by the rigorous application of the rights of war—but the exercise of this right has been discontinued in modern warfare;—and it may be regarded as established, that though debts cannot be claimed by an enemy during war, yet that the right to claim payment revives on the return of peace." (pp. 129, 130.) Dr. Wheaton says that for nearly a century and a half previous to the French revolution no instance of confiscation of debts had occurred, with the simple exception of the Silesian loan in 1753. And he sums up his view of international law on this point in the words, that property of the enemy found within the territory of the belligerent state, or debts due to his subjects by the government or individuals, at the commencement of hostilities, are not liable to be seized and confiscated as a prize of war. This rule, he adds, is frequently enforced by treaty-stipulations, but unless it be thus enforced, it cannot be considered as an inflexible, though an established rule. (El. IV. I. 345–347.)

Finally, as to public debts due to individual subjects of the enemy, I will cite but the single authority of Mr. Manning: "One description of property is invariably respected during war, namely the sums due from the state to the enemy, such as the property which the latter may possess in the public funds. This is justly regarded as entrusted to the faith of the nation; and during the most bitter animosity of our wars with France no attempt has been made on either side to confiscate such property, which cannot be touched without a violation of public faith." *

§ 119.

Have all in each hostile state a right to carry on war?

If each and all on the one side were enemies to each and all on the other, it would seem that every person had a right, so far as the municipal code did not forbid, to fall upon his enemy wherever he could find him, that, for instance, an invading army had a right to

* In the letters of Camillus, written by Alexander Hamilton just after Jay's treaty in 1795, this subject is considered at length, particularly in letters 18–20. (Works, vol. VII.) In letter 19, he examines the right to confiscate or sequestrate private debts or property on the ground of reason and principle. He admits at the outset the proposition that every individual of the nation with whom we are at war is our enemy, and his property liable to capture. To this there is one admitted exception respecting enemy's property in a neutral state, but this is owing to the right of the neutral nation alone. Reason, he maintains, "suggests another exception. Whenever a government grants permission to foreigners to acquire property within its territories, or to bring and deposit it there, it tacitly promises protection and security."—"The property of a foreigner placed in another country, by permission of its laws, may justly be regarded as a deposit of which the society is a trustee. How can it be reconciled with the idea of a trust, to take the property from its owner when he has personally given no cause for the deprivation?" Goods of enemies found elsewhere differ from those which are in our country, since in the latter case there is a reliance on our hospitality and justice. And the same argument which would confiscate the goods would seize the persons of enemies' subjects. The case of property in the public funds is still stron er than that of private debts.

The result which Hamilton reaches is sound, but if we admit the principle that every individual belonging to the belligerent nation is an enemy, and every enemy's property liable to capture, we must deny the validity of exceptions, unless treaty or usage has established them. The foreigner brought his property here, it can at once be said, knowing the risk he might run in the event of a war. Why should he not seize on all the property and persons within reach, and dispose of them at discretion. But no such unlimited enmity is now known in the usages of nations. It is to be hoped that the theory from which such consequences flow will be abandoned and disappear altogether. The true theory seems to be that the private persons on each side are not fully in hostile relations but in a state of non-intercourse, in a state wherein the rights of intercourse, only secured by treaty and not derived from natural right, are suspended or have ceased; while the political bodies to which they belong are at war with one another, and they only. Of course until these political bodies allow hostile acts to be performed, such acts, save in self-defence, may not be performed; and accordingly the usages of war visit with severity those who fight without a sanction from their governments. The plunder which such persons seize belongs not to themselves but to the public, until public authority gives them a share in it.

§ 120.

Treatment of enemies' property on land and sea.

There has long been a difference between the treatment of enemies' property—including in this term the property of individual subjects of the hostile state—on land and on the sea, or more generally between such as falls within the power of invading armies, and such on the sea and along the coast, as falls within the power of armed vessels. The former, as we shall see when we come anon to consider the laws and usages of warfare, is to a certain extent protected. The latter, owing to the jealous feelings of commercial rivalship, hardened into a system by admiralty courts, has been extensively regarded as lawful prey. We must, however, admit that there is some pretence of reason for this difference of practice upon the two elements. For, *first*,

incur the risk? He should incur it, say the older practice, and the older authorities. He should not, says the modern practice, although international law in its rigor involves him in it. He should not, according to the true principle of justice, because his relation to the state at war is not the same with the relation of his sovereign or government: because, in short, he is not in the full sense an enemy.

an enemy's intercourse with other states by sea more directly increases his capacity to sustain and protract the war. And *secondly*, there is a difference on the score of humanity between land and maritime capture. On the land, interference with private property, by stripping families of their all, is often the source of the deepest misery. It also embitters feeling, and drives non-combatants into guerilla warfare or into the regular service. Invasion always arouses a national spirit; but invasion with plunder rather defeats the end of war than promotes it, until a nation is bowed down to the dust. And at that point of time it disables the conquered from giving the compensation for which the war was set on foot. But capture on the sea is effected for the most part without much fighting; it rather deprives the foe of his comforts and means of exchanging his superfluities than destroys the necessaries of life; and it afflicts more directly the classes which have some influence upon the government, as well as the resources of the government itself, than the day-laborer and the cultivator of the soil, who have special claims to be humanely treated.

§ 121.

Forces employed in war, especially on the sea. Privateers.

On the land, in addition to standing armies, a militia and volunteers, often commanded by regular officers, have been employed in carrying on war, especially in national defence. As the different military corps are frequently united in their operations, and no great harm can be done by the less disciplined, if under proper officers, to employ a militia or volunteers can furnish no just ground for complaint. On the sea the practice of commercial states has long been to make use not only of public but also of private-armed vessels for the purpose of doing injury to the enemy. This usage in Europe runs back to the time when permanent public navies scarcely existed; for during a considerable part of the middle ages, the European states having small fleets or none at all, impressed or hired merchant vessels for the uses of war. Private persons also engaged in naval warfare on their own account, employing their own vessels either at the public expense—called *Kruyssers*, cruizers by the Dutch; or at their own expense—*Kapers*, *Vrybuyters*, captors, free-plunderers,—or hiring a public vessel with a crew and outfit of their own; of which last description an expedition undertaken in the reign of Louis XIV. against the Portuguese at Rio-Janeiro, to get satisfaction for an insult on a French ambassador, was an example.*

A private-armed vessel or privateer is a vessel owned and officered by private persons, but acting under a commission from the state, usually called letters of marque.† It answers to a company on land raised and commanded by private persons, but acting under rules from the supreme authority, rather than to one raised and acting without license, which would resemble a privateer without commission. The commission, on both elements, alone gives a right to the thing captured, and insures good treatment from the enemy. A private vessel levying war without such license, although not engaged in a piratical act, would fare hardly in the enemy's hands.

The right to employ this kind of extraordinary naval force is unquestioned, nor is it at all against the usage of nations in times past to grant commissions even to privateers owned by aliens. The advantages of employing privateers are (1.) that seamen thrown out of work by war can thus gain a livelihood and be of use to their country. (2.) A nation which maintains no great navy is thus enabled to call into activity a temporary force, on brief notice, and at small cost. Thus an inferior state, with a large commercial marine, can approach on the sea nearer to an equality with a larger rival, having a powerful fleet at its disposal. And as aggressions are likely to come from large powers, privateering may be a means, and perhaps the only effectual means, of obtaining justice to which a small commercial state can resort.

* Bynkersh. Quæst. J. P. I. 18; Ortolan, II. 52. Martens: les Armateurs, Chap. I.

† From the signification, *border*, *the marches*, it is said. Letters of license to go across the boundary and make reprisals.

§ 122.

On the other hand, the system of privateering is attended with very great evils. (1.) The motive is plunder. It is nearly impossible that the feeling of honor and regard for professional reputation should act upon the privateersman's mind. And when his occupation on the sea is ended, he returns with something of the spirit of a robber to infest society. (2.) The control over such crews is slight, while they need great control. They are made up of bold, lawless men, and are where no superior authority can watch or direct them. The responsibility at the best can only be remote. The officers will not be apt to be men of the same training with the commanders of public ships, and cannot govern their crews as easily as the masters of commercial vessels can govern theirs. (3.) The evils are heightened when privateers are employed in the execution of belligerent rights against neutrals, where a high degree of character and forbearance in the commanding officer is of especial importance.

Evils of privateering.

Hence many have felt it to be desirable that privateering should be placed under the ban of international law, and the feeling is on the increase, in our age of humanity, that the system ought to come to an end. We cite as expressing this feeling only writers belonging to our own country. Dr. Franklin, in several passages of his correspondence, makes decided protests against it, as well as against the spirit of plunder in which it originates. "The practice of robbing merchants on the high seas, a remnant of the ancient piracy, though it may be accidentally beneficial to particular persons, is far from being profitable to all engaged in it, or to the nation that authorizes it." "There are three employments which I wish the law of nations would protect, so that they should never be molested nor interrupted by enemies even in times of war;—I mean farmers, fishermen, and merchants." In some observations on war, he pursues this subject of the evils of privateering, at great length, and ends thus: "There is then the national loss of all the labor of so many men during the time they have been employed in rob-

Testimony to the evils of privateering.

bing, who, besides, spend what they get in drunkenness and debauchery, lose their habits of industry, are rarely fit for any sober business after a peace, and serve only to increase the number of highwaymen and housebreakers." *

Privateering, says Chancellor Kent, "under all the restrictions which have been adopted, is very liable to abuse. The object is not fame or chivalric warfare, but plunder and profit. The discipline of the crews is not apt to be of the highest order, and privateers are often guilty of enormous excesses, and become the scourges of neutral commerce. Under the best regulations the business tends strongly to blunt the sense of private right, and to nourish a lawless and fierce spirit of rapacity." †

Dr. Wheaton says, that "this practice has been justly arraigned, as liable to gross abuses, as tending to encourage a spirit of lawless depredation, and as being in glaring contradiction to the more mitigated modes of warfare practised by land." ‡

Endeavors to stop privateering by treaty.

Dr. Franklin expressed his feelings in regard to privateering, in the treaty of 1785, between the United States and Prussia, which he drew up. In this treaty it was provided that neither of the contracting parties should grant or issue any commission to any private armed vessels, against the other, empowering them to take or destroy its trading vessels, or to interrupt commerce. On the expiration of the treaty in 1799, this article was not renewed. Another article of the same temporary treaty deserves mention, which engages that all merchant vessels of either party, employed in regular commerce, shall be unmolested by the other. But before this treaty with Prussia, an unfulfilled agreement had been made between Sweden and the United Provinces, as early as 1675, to terminate this practice. Russia, in 1767 and the following years, abstained from giving commissions of this nature, but made use of them again in 1770. In 1792, the French legislative assembly agreed to suppress privateering,

* Franklin's Works, edited by Sparks, IX. 41, 467.

† Kent, I. 97, Lect. 5.

‡ El. IV. 2, § 10.

14

but the revolution soon made this a dead letter.* After the French revolution, although privateering continued to receive the sanction of the nations, some few voices were lifted up against it, and even against all capture of merchant vessels pursuing a lawful trade. Thus the reviewer of a pamphlet, entitled "War in Disguise" (Edinburgh Rev., No. 15, p. 14), says: "We cannot help thinking that the practice of maritime capture is inconsistent with the generous and enlightened notions of public hostility which were brought to maturity in the last century, and that it is a stain upon that lenient and refined system of policy, by which the history of modern Europe is distinguished from that of the rest of the world."

Treaty of Paris in 1856.

The most important step towards the entire abolition of privateering has been very recently taken. The powers which concluded the treaty of 1856, at Paris, united in a declaration, by the first article of which "privateering is and remains abolished." (Comp. § 175.) Other states were invited to adopt the principles of this declaration, but it was agreed that they must be accepted as a whole or not at all.

Attitude of the United States.

The United States, among other states, were invited to become a party to this declaration. The secretary of state, Mr. Marcy, in a letter of July 28, 1856, addressed to M. de Sartiges, minister of France at Washington, declined the proposal, although it secured what this country had so long been wishing for, the greater freedom of neutral vessels. The reluctance to adopt the principles of the declaration, was owing to a cause already suggested,—that the relinquishment of privateering would be a gain to nations, which keep on foot a large naval force, but not to the United States, where a powerful navy is not maintained, on account of its great cost, and its danger to civil liberty. On the breaking out of a war, therefore, with a nation powerful at sea, the United States must rely, to a considerable extent, on merchant vessels converted into vessels of war. The secretary, however, declares that our government will readily agree to an arrange-

* Kent, I. 98; Ortolan, II. 54.

ment, by which the private property of the subjects or citizens of a belligerent power shall be exempted from seizure by public armed vessels of the enemy, except it be contraband of war, and that "with this we will consent to the placing of privateering under the ban of the law of nations." It will be the policy of our government, hereafter, it may be presumed, in all treaties, to couple the abolition of privateering with the entire immunity of merchant ships engaged in a lawful trade.* (Comp. § 175.)

§ 123.

The restrictions on privateering are of three kinds.

Restrictions on privateering to prevent its evils.

1. The laws of some states narrow the range of their operations, and regulate the composition of their crews. They are forbidden to cruise in the rivers or within the sea-line of a hostile state, and the majority of a crew is required to consist of natives.† But these rules have not passed into international law, or general usage.

* The annotator on de Martens, ed. of 1858, M. Vergé, in speaking of this proposition of our government, expresses himself as follows: "In the usages of war on land, the soldiers of belligerent powers have no right, and can, in the way of fact, exercise no control over the private property of the subjects of the hostile power. Why should not the same principles be applicable to maritime war? The additional proposition of the cabinet of Washington, is evidently logical. Vainly has it been contended (in the Journal des Débats of October 22, 1856) that the claim of the United States, that land and sea warfare should be put on the same footing, is not admissible, nor just, nor good even, since the calamities of war afford this advantage, that in acting on the population of countries, they render war shorter and more unfrequent. It seems in all cases difficult to maintain the proposition that the pillage of private property by privateers is just, rational, and legitimate. One cannot admit that private property, which is free even in the enemy's land itself, on the soil invaded by an army victorious, and invested with the right of conquest, can be justly taken and plundered on the sea, on that element free by its nature, which is neither friendly nor hostile territory. Let us hope that the initiative so gloriously adopted by the congress of Paris, will be fruitful for the future, and that diplomacy will one day reach the point of rendering commerce free for belligerents as for neutrals, that private goods and citizens, who are strangers to the profession of arms, will be freed from the disasters of war, and that private property will remain outside of contests exclusively concentrated in armies acting in the name and under the direction of the public power." II. § 289. Comp. the recent resolutions of the chamber of commerce, of Hamburg and Bremen, under § 139.

† Comp. Ortolan, II. 57–59; Heffter, § 137.

2. To give it the character of an honest and lawful pursuit, commissions, as already said, are granted, and bonds are taken from those who receive the letters of marque. These regulations, which vary with the municipal law of each country, subject the owners and officers of privateers to heavy penalties in case of transgression.*

It is only the commission which gives an interest in a prize, since all captures vest originally in the state. This maxim draws its truth from the right notion of war, as we have endeavored to set it forth,—that war is undertaken by the state, for the sake of the state, and against another state.

3. Many treaties provide that the subjects of either of the treaty-making powers, while in a state of peace, shall not take out letters of marque from a third power at war with the other party, and that those who violate this provision may be held by the other party to have committed the crime of piracy. Such treaties of longer or shorter duration have been made, for instance, by the United States, with France, Sweden, Prussia, Great Britain, Spain, Central America, and Colombia. In the absence of such treaties, a neutral may with impunity accept a military commission from a belligerent, for sea or land service. But municipal law often forbids the citizen or subject to take this step. (Comp. § 162, § 165.)

Section II.—*Laws and Usages of War, especially on Land.*

§ 124.

The laws and usages of war

The subject of prize, or the rules of captured property,† especially on the sea, we shall consider by itself in another section. At present we pass on to the

* For the rules of responsibility of owners, commanders, and sureties, Comp. Kent, I. 98, 99, Lect. V. A maritime ordinance of Pedro IV., king of Aragon in 1356, speaks of such security. A sum of money was to be deposited in the hands of certain public officers by the owner of a vessel. Pardessus, Collection, V. 471. And another rule of 1364, passed by the German Hanse towns, to the same effect, is cited by de Martens, § 289, note c.

† Comp. for this section, the instructions for the government of armies of the

important topic of the laws and usages of war. These rules are necessarily somewhat vague and fluctuating, partly because they have less to do with justice than with humanity, where clear lines of definition are wanting; partly because much must be left to the discretion of commanders with varying dispositions and principles; partly because nations sometimes enter with excited passions, sometimes with cool calculation, into war, and their spirit will modify all its movements.

are somewhat vague,

Notwithstanding this vagueness, the rules of war have grown in humanity and mildness in recent times. The principal causes of this amelioration are,

yet are improving.

1. The growth of a feeling of the brotherhood of mankind, fostered by the spirit of Christianity. Thus, for instance, slavery having ceased in nearly all Christian countries under the benign sway of the Gospel, how could the old practice of enslaving captives taken in war fail to go out of use?

Causes of their amelioration.

2. The influence of writers such as Grotius, and the example of great captains, who under the control of humane feelings have followed a better practice.

3. The greatly increased intercourse among Christian countries, the inhabitants of which are no longer strangers to one another, and beyond each other's view; but are connected by various ties, which soften the asperity of a sense of injury.

4. The marked separation of the soldiery as a distinct class from the citizens, and an improved feeling among soldiers themselves, which is due to the substitution of regular for irregular troops, to the spread of professional honor among officers, and to the cooler and more scientific way in which wars are carried on.

5. Add to this that an organized commissariat renders it unnecessary for the soldier to procure his daily food by plunder, while modern systems of finance and credit meet the expenses of armies abroad. "Paid soldiers only," says Col. Napier,

United States in the field, prepared by Dr. Lieber, revised by a board of officers, and approved by the President in 1863.

"can be kept under discipline; soldiers without money become robbers." *

6. The different mode of warfare which the use of gunpowder has introduced. "There is as much difference," says the same authority, "between the modern and the ancient soldier, as between the sportsman and the butcher. The ancient warrior, fighting with the sword and reaping his harvest of death when the enemy was in flight, became habituated to the act of slaying. The modern soldier seldom uses his bayonet, sees not his peculiar victim fall, and exults not over mangled limbs, as proofs of personal prowess."

§ 125.

Fundamental rules of war.

The rules which lie at the basis of a humane system of war are,

1. That peace is the normal state of Christian nations, to which they are bound to seek to return from the temporary and exceptional interruptions of war.

2. That redress of injuries and not conquest or plunder is the lawful motive in war; and that no rule of morality or justice can be sacrificed in the mode of warfare.

3. That war is waged between governments by persons whom they authorize, and is not waged against the passive inhabitants of a country.

4. That the smallest amount of injury, consistent with the sad necessity of war, is to be inflicted. And, finally,

5. That the duties implied in the improved usages of war, so far as they are not of positive obligation, are reciprocal, like very many rules of intercourse between states, so as not to be binding on one belligerent, as long as they are violated by the other. This leads us to retaliation in war.

§ 126.

Retaliation.

That retaliation in war is sometimes admissible all agree: thus if one belligerent treats prisoners of war harshly, the other may do the same; or if one squeezes the expenses of war out of an invaded territory, the

* Penins. War, III. 377 (Amer. ed. of 1842.)

other may follow in his steps. It thus becomes a measure of self-protection, and secures the greatest amount of humanity from unfeeling military officers. But there is a limit to the rule. If one general kills in cold blood some hundreds of prisoners who embarrass his motions, his antagonist may not be justified in staining himself by similar crime, nor may he break his word or oath because the other had done so before. The limits of such retaliation it may be hard to lay down. Yet any act of cruelty to the innocent, any act, especially, by which non-combatants are made to feel the stress of war, is what brave men shrink from, although they may feel obliged to threaten it. (Comp. § 114. and the instructions for the government of our armies, §§ 27, 28.)

§ 127.

Particular rules of war. 1. As to unlawful weapons, and ways of injuring the enemy's person.

The use of poisoned weapons, the poisoning of springs, the employment of hired assassins, have long been condemned, as opposed to the idea of war, which is an open honorable way of seeking redress.* Such practices characterize savage warfare. Grotius (III. 4, § 17) is decided in condemning the practice of poisoning springs, but thinks that it is right to corrupt water so that it cannot be used, which is no worse than to turn the channel of a stream in a direction where the enemy cannot get at it. He says also (§ 18), that whilst hired assassins must never be used, above all when they violate express or implied confidence, an enemy may undertake to kill another in a private and concealed way. This he supports as usual by testimonies from Greek and Roman writers. Modern times would use another language. Bynkershoek, in 1737, falls below the standard of Grotius, and allows of fraud to any

* For the history of the rules of war, comp. Mr. Ward's Hist., Chapters IX., XV., and elsewhere; also an excellent article in the Oxford essays for 1856, by Montague Bernard, Esq., which has been of great use to the present writer, and from which the passages appearing as quotations in the next pages are taken. See also Gen. Halleck's Int. Law and Laws of War, Chap. XVI. This work of the learned military officer would have been of important service to the author of this book, i he could have seen it sooner.

extent in war. "Ego omnem dolum permitto, sola perfidia excepta, non quod contra hostem non quodlibet liceat, sed quod, fide data, quatenus data est, hostis esse desinat,"—(Quæst. J. P. I. 1,)—opinions which it gives us pain to cite from such a writer. The Greeks, Romans, and some other states of antiquity, professed to abhor these methods of fraud in carrying on war.* The Emperor Tiberius, when an offer was made him to put Arminius out of the way by poison, rejected it, although he committed many worse crimes. "Non fraude," Tacitus makes him say, (Annal. II. 88,) "neque occultis, sed palam et armatum populum Romanum hostes suos ulcisci." The spirit of chivalry was still more opposed to fraud and secret stratagem. Enemies often gave notice of an intention to make an attack at a certain time, and the true knight rejected every advantage, save that which his skill and prowess in knightly warfare afforded him.

2. Allowable weapons in modern war.

The laws of war are loose in regard to the instruments of death used against an enemy. Formerly chain-shot and red-hot shot were objected to, but they do not seem to be now. "Now invention racks itself to produce the biggest gun, the deadliest projectile, the most frightful engine of wholesale slaughter, and the shallows of Kertch and Cronstadt are planted thick with infernal machines. It is possible to go too fast and too far in this direction."† What is here quoted from an English essay written a few years since is more true of sea warfare than of land. As Heffter remarks (§ 119), war on that element is the more harsh and destructive. "Its maxims, owing to a want of the proper equipoise between naval powers, have been far from reaching the same level of humanity on which land-warfare stands. It is still half a war of plunder." As for war in general, Klüber (§ 244) lays it down that the customs of war ("Kriegsmanier") condemn not only poisoned weapons, poisoning of wells and of utensils, attempts to spread the plague among the enemy, but also the use

* Comp. Dionys. Hal. antiq. III. 8, *οὐδ' ἐκ τοῦ φανεροῦ ἐπέθεντό ἧμιν, ὡς ὁ κοινὸς, ἀξιοῖ τοῦ πολέμου νόμος, ἀλλ' ὑπὸ σκότους.*

† Montague Bernard, u. s., p. 127.

of chain-shot and bar-shot (*boulets à bras*), shooting bits of iron, brass, nails, etc. (*tirer à la mitraille*). The loading of muskets with two balls, with jagged balls, or with balls mixed with glass or lime, he also holds, somewhat too broadly, to be forbidden. Special treaties have prohibited as between the parties the use of chain, bar, and hot shot, as well as of pitch-rings (*cercles poissés*). An infernal machine invented about the year 1585, which was a kind of fire ship, was disapproved of by some, but went out of use because it did not do its work well.

On the whole, it may be said that weapons whose efficiency consists simply in inflicting a bad wound, and instruments of wholesale slaughter which cannot be foreseen or avoided by flight, are against the customs of most kinds of warfare; but that naval warfare too much, and sieges, of necessity, make use of summary and wholesale means of death. Naval warfare is the storming of one floating fortress by another, but its laws need not be altogether assimilated to the storming of fortified places on the land.

Kind of troops employed.

Hitherto the practice of using barbarians in the wars of Christian nations with one another, has not been absolutely condemned by the law of nations. The French used the American Indians against the English in America, and the Turcos, a force made up of Algerines, Kabyles, and Negroes, in Italy; the English employed savages against their revolted colonies, in spite of the rebukes of Lord Chatham; and the Russians brought Circassians with them into Hungary in the war following 1848. But nothing is clearer than that troops who are accustomed to an inhuman mode of warfare, and belong to a savage race, cannot be trusted to wage war according to the spirit of humanity, and ought not to be employed.

3. Breach of faith: solicitations to crime.

Breach of faith between enemies has always been strongly condemned, and that vindication of it is worthless which maintains that, without an express or tacit promise to our enemy, we are not bound to keep faith with him. But no rule of war forbids a commander to circulate false information, and to use means for deceiving his enemy with regard to his movements. If he abstains from them, he must do so by the force of his own Christian conscience. To lead the officers, counsellors, or troops of an enemy to treachery by bribes, or to seduce his subjects to betray their country, are temptations to commit a plain crime, which no hostile relation will justify.* Yet to accept of the services of a traitor is allowable.†

§ 128.

A combatant is any person directly engaged in carrying on war, or concerned in the belligerent government, or present with its armies and assisting them; although those who are present for purposes of humanity and religion,—as surgeons, nurses, and chaplains—are usually classed among non-combatants, unless special reasons require an opposite treatment of them. The ancient rule was, that a combatant taken in battle became the property of his captor, who could kill, enslave, or sell him. Ransom was a kind of sale to those who were most interested in paying a high price. Among the Greeks the general practice was not to refuse quarter to a Greek who gave himself up on the field of battle, and to allow his friends to redeem him, if they would; the price for which was more or less fixed between contending parties. This usage prevailed also among the Romans, as well as that of exchanging prisoners, but any degree of injury to the enemy was allowed in their *jus belli*. Neither law, nor the feelings of humanity, nor aught save considerations of prudence, restrained them. After the disaster in the Caudine Forks, when they gained their next victory over the Samnites, they slew alike the resisting and the unresisting, armed and unarmed, slaves and free, boys and adults, men and cattle, nor would any living thing have been left alive, unless the consul had given the signal for withdrawing.

4. Treatment of captured persons, esp. of soldiers.

* A qualification is here necessary, that when a nation has been conquered and is under a usurper's sway, and in similar cases, it cannot be wrong for those who are engaged in a war of liberation to lead the people to revolt.

† Vattel, III. 10, §§ 180, 181.

(Livy, IX. 14.) By the rules of both nations leading officers of the hostile army, after being taken, might be put to the sword. Such was the case with the Athenian generals taken at Syracuse, (Thucyd. VII. 86,)—against the will, however, it should be added, of the Spartan general Gylippus,—and many an illustrious warrior, taken captive by the Romans, had his death delayed, only to endure the humiliation of being led in triumph. Similar cruelty was universal in ancient times, as among the Jews, where David's campaigns dealt death in frightful forms upon surrounding nations; and yet, a century and a half after David, a prophet, to the king of Israel's inquiry, "Shall I smite them?" could answer, "Wouldst thou smite those whom thou hast taken captive with thy sword and thy bow?"—showing that a more humane mode of warfare was then in vogue.

War put on all its horrors in the invasions of the empire by the Germans. Then came the times of feudalism and knighthood, when many mitigations of the barbarian practice grew up. Captives, in wars between Christians, were ransomed and sometimes released on parole to raise the money necessary for this purpose. But the common soldier did not receive much benefit from the relaxation of the old severities. During the wars just before the reformation, especially those of the French invasions of Italy, the cruelties of war seemed to revive, and the religious animosities of the century and a half afterwards did not extinguish them. In the thirty years' war Gustavus Adolphus made a convention with the Imperialists to give and receive quarter: only the Croats on one side, and the Pomeranians on the other, were excepted from this act of humanity. In the wars of England between the king and the parliament no quarter was allowed to the Irish, who served in the royal army, and when Prince Rupert retaliated, he was told that there was a great difference between an Irishman and an Englishman. In these wars the exchange of prisoners, practised just before in the wars of Germany, became systematic. Cartels fixing the rate of ransom for prisoners exchanged are said to have been of somewhat later date. For the two centuries past, cruelty to prisoners and non-resisting soldiers has been exceptional. The present practice is to spare the lives of those who yield themselves up, to exchange them with captives taken by the other party, or to give them up on payment of a ransom, and meanwhile "to supply them with the necessary comforts at the expense of the state to which they belong." It were well if such comforts were to be found in a state of captivity, but the prison-hulks of some civilized nations, and the general neglect of the prisoners, seem almost calculated to make them unserviceable when exchanged. Officers and others, whose word can be relied on, are often set free, on their parole not to serve during the war or until ransomed. Persons escaping from captivity, and retaken, or even recaptured in war, are not held to merit punishment, for they only obeyed their love of liberty; but the breach of parole justly subjects such persons to heavy punishment. (Heffter, § 129.) Deserters, if captured, acquire no rights from joining the other belligerent, and may be put to death. The property belonging to combatants, or taken on the field of battle, has been considered to be lawful plunder, and usually goes to the victorious officers and troops (such of it as is not stolen), as a reward of successful bravery.

5. Treatment of irregular soldiers.

The treatment which the milder modern usage prescribes for regular soldiers is extended also to militia called out by public authority. Guerilla parties, however, do not enjoy the full benefit of the laws of war. They are apt to fare worse than either regular troops or an unarmed peasantry. The reasons for this are, that they are annoying and insidious, that they put on and off with ease the character of a soldier, and that they are prone, themselves, to treat their enemies who fall into their hands with great severity.

§ 129.

6. Non-combatants and their property.

It is in regard to non-combatants and their property that the mildness of modern warfare appears in most striking contrast with the severity of ancient. The old rule was to regard every human being pertaining to the enemy's country as a foe, to lay waste territory, kill or take captive those who could serve in the enemy's armies, enslave women and children, and carry off all the property of value which could be transported. Wars to a considerable extent were ravaging forays into a hostile country, and the more harm was done, the sooner, it was thought, redress could be procured. War thus, especially at Rome, fed the public treasury, supplied the market with slaves, and laid the foundation of the wealth of noble families. The *mango* or slave-dealer accompanied the armies, and forwarded the captives, purchased by him at wholesale, to the city market. If a territory was conquered, the former inhabitants were stripped often of a part of their lands, and we find one third confiscated by the Romans on a number of occasions; or they were removed in mass, as was common in the East, into another country. When the Germans conquered the empire, the horrors of war for the inhabitants were not as great as those which the Romans in their best days inflicted on the conquered, for the provinces yielded with slight struggles, and the possessors of the soil were generally allowed to retain a part, from one to two thirds, of their lands.

Usages of the ancients.

In the middle age the treatment which Christians received from Christians during invasions was somewhat better, although between them and Mohammedans the law of the sword prevailed. Still, although women, children, and ecclesiastical persons were mercifully used, every able-bodied peasant was accounted an enemy; armies were quartered on an invaded district; and pillage, as well as devastation, was the rule. In 1346, the English, under Edward III., marched through Normandy, burning and ravaging; but though they collected a vast booty, the army at Crecy was very soon afterwards in severe want. Nearly seventy years after this, when Henry V. invaded France, a truer policy prevailed, the army was accompanied by stores, only bread and wine were exacted from the peasants, even when offering resistance; and orders to the troops forbade injuries to property and insults to women. At the end of this century the invasions of Italy by the French

Of the middle age.

under Charles VIII. and Louis XII. were characterized by a return to greater barbarity. The invaders lived on the resources of the country, and the spirit of plunder was insatiable.

Of the thirty years' war.

The same spirit was seen in that terrible scourge of Germany, the thirty years' war. Count Mansfeld's maxim was that war should support itself, while Christian of Halberstadt, of the Protestant party, like Mansfeld, was no better than a robber and incendiary. On the side of the Imperialists, Wallenstein did not curb the rapacity of his troops, who plundered on every hand for food, and Tilly's armies were worse governed. Nor did the French under Guebriant behave much better. But how could armies be kept from plunder and brutality, which, being unpaid, lived by requisitions, made food and winter-quarters the object of their campaigns, and were a *colluvies* of all nations, without good officers or a sense of professional honor. Gustavus Adolphus paid and disciplined his troops, but the generals of the Swedes after his death allowed greater license to their forces: thus Baner, after the victory of Wistock, laid Saxony and Bohemia waste.

Of the time of Louis XIV.

In the earlier wars of Louis XIV. the treatment of non-combatants and their property was no better,—in some respects was even worse. Turenne laid waste large tracts of country to deprive the enemy of the means of subsistence. The crimes of the armies under Catinat, Feuquieres and Melas, the terrible ravages of the Palatinate, were sanctioned by orders from Paris. But in the war of the succession Marlborough and Villars introduced something like humanity into the conduct of their armies. By an understanding between the commanders, each belligerent levied contributions on the district occupied by his troops, which were not to exceed a certain amount, determined by commissioners of the two hostile parties. If the local authorities thought that too large a sum had been demanded, "they sent in complaints to the head-quarters of the friendly army, which were attended to immediately." Villars declares his satisfaction at having fed an army of two hundred battalions, and of more than three hundred squadrons of cavalry for three months on a space near the Rhine of a hundred square leagues without forcing a peasant to quit his dwelling.

"The Prussians and Austrians in the time of Frederick the Great contented themselves with levying contributions where they moved, and speaking generally, the habit of depending for subsistence on magazines, and on the cumbrous provision-trains which followed armies on their march, is noted by Jomini as a characteristic of the eighteenth century." In the war of our revolution the British government declared it to be right in war (1.) to demand provisions, and raise contributions, which may be enforced, if necessary, by the sword; (2.) to ravage a territory where you have no other way of bringing an enemy to an engagement or to terms; (3.) to treat rebels as enemies. The right to ravage has not been asserted or acted upon since, unless in a few cases, which were pretended to be extreme. In the last war between Great Britain and our country, nothing was taken from private persons without being paid for, and the same may be said, we believe, of our war with Mexico.

Of Frederick the Great.

And of the English in the American war.

The wars of Napoleon were marked by the enormous requisitions which were levied upon invaded countries, producing amounts nearly large enough to save the necessity of increased taxes upon France itself. The rule with Bonaparte was to make the war pay for the war. Thus, after the battle of Jena, in 1806, the requisition upon humbled Prussia was more than a hundred millions of francs: half that sum was imposed on the province of Valencia, after Suchet's conquest of it in 1812, and the conquering army was to have a donative of two hundred millions besides, to be collected chiefly from the same quarter of Spain.

Of Napoleon.

During his Peninsular wars, Wellington was among friends, —where all codes require private property to be respected,— until he entered France in 1813, and there policy, if nothing else, demanded the observance of the same rule. But he seems to have regarded requisitions as iniquitous, and when the ministry at home proposed that he should adopt them, he opposed the system, as needing terror and the bayonet to carry it out, —as one for which the British soldier was unfit, and as likely to injure those who resorted to it.* The right to levy contributions was again enforced by the Prussians in the war of 1848 with Denmark, but it slumbered, we believe, in the recent war of the allies against Russia.

§ 130.

Summing up.

To sum up all that has been said on this topic, we may lay down the following rules of war:

1. Private persons, remaining quiet, and taking no part in the conflict, are to be unmolested, but if the people of an invaded district take an active part in a war, they forfeit their claim to protection. This marked line of separation between the soldier and the non-soldier, is of extreme importance for the interests of humanity.

2. The property, movable as well as immovable, of private persons in an invaded country, is to remain uninjured. But if the wants of the hostile army require, it may be taken by authorized persons at a fair value; but marauding must be checked by discipline and penalties.

3. Contributions or requisitions are still permissible, on the plea, first, that they are a compensation for pillage, or an equitable repartition of what would accrue from this source,—which, if pillage is wrong, is no plea at all;—and again, that they are needed for defraying the expenses of governing a conquered province, which is a valid plea when conquest has been effected, but not before; and thirdly, on the plea that in a just war it is right to make the "enemy's country contribute to the support of the army, and towards defraying all the charges of the war." † But if the true principle is that war is a public contest, waged between the powers or authorities of two countries, the passive individual ought not to suffer more than the necessities of war require. Vattel adds, "that a general who would not sully his reputation, is to moderate his contributions.

* Napier, u. s., IV. 21. † Vattel, III. 9, § 165.

An excess in this point is not without the reproach of cruelty and inhumanity." But many generals will go to the extreme of what they think can be exacted, without regard to their reputation; and cruelty and inhumanity are as unavoidable in such transactions, as they would be if sheriffs and their men were to levy on goods by force of arms, and pay themselves out of the things seized. Moreover, requisitions are demoralizing, and defeat their own ends. They foster the lust of conquest, they arouse the avarice of officers, they leave a sting in the memories of oppressed nations; who, when iniquity is full, league together to destroy the great plunderers of mankind. The only true and humane principle is that already laid down, that war is waged by state against state, by soldier against soldier.* The state resists an effort to obtain justice; the soldier obstructs the way of the armed officer of justice, and must be resisted.

* We cannot forbear inserting, as bearing on this point, an opinion of Portalis, in his speech at the installation of the council of prizes, which we borrow from Heffter, § 119. "The right of war is founded on this, that a people, in the interests of self-conservation, or for the sake of self-defense, will, can, or ought to use force against another people. It is the relation of things, and not of persons, which constitutes war; it is the relation of state to state, and not of individual to individual. Between two or more belligerent nations, the private persons of which these nations consist, are enemies only by accident; they are not such as men, they are not even as citizens, they are such solely as soldiers."

To the same effect are Talleyrand's words in a despatch to Napoleon, of Nov. 20, 1806. "Three centuries of civilization have given to Europe a law of nations, for which, according to the expression of an illustrious writer, human nature cannot be sufficiently grateful. This law is founded on the principle, that nations ought to do to one another in peace, the most good, and in war, the least evil possible.

"According to the maxim that war is not a relation between a man and another, but between state and state, in which private persons are only accidental enemies, not such as men, nor even as members or subjects of the state, but simply as its defenders, the law of nations does not allow that the rights of war, and of conquest thence derived, should be applied to peaceable, unarmed citizens, to private dwellings and properties, to the merchandize of commerce, to the magazines which contain it, to the vehicles which transport it, to unarmed ships which convey it on streams and seas; in one word, to the person and the goods of private individuals.

"This law of war, born of civilization, has favored its progress. It is to this that Europe must ascribe the maintenance and increase of her prosperity, even in the midst of the frequent wars which have divided her."

4. Extraordinary cases, as retaliation (§ 126), and perhaps, in fighting with barbarians or semi-barbarians, who acknowledge no rules of war, the necessity of reading them a severe lesson (comp. § 136), will justify a departure from these principles. But pillage and devastation are seldom politic, even when they are supposed to be just.

§ 131.

7. Public property.

The older practice made little distinction between public and private property, little between public property of different kinds. That which had the least relation to military affairs, as libraries, works of art, public buildings for peaceful purposes, might be plundered or destroyed. For nearly two centuries the Palatine manuscripts, which were taken from Heidelberg in the thirty years' war, remained at Rome, and Napoleon transported pictures to the Louvre from every quarter where his arms penetrated.

The treasures of the Palatine library, or rather a part of them, were restored after the peace in 1815. When the allies entered Paris after the battle of Waterloo, they recovered the works of art which the French emperor had robbed them of. At the same time a requisition was made on Paris of a hundred millions of francs, which was afterwards greatly reduced in amount. Great complaint has been made against these measures by Frenchmen of all political shades; against the latter as extortionate and oppressive, and the other, as a shameful abuse of victory. But the requisition was not beyond the means of the capital, nor unauthorized by the practice of the French themselves, and the recovery of the works of art was an act of simple justice, not precluded by previous treaty.

The rule is now pretty well established, that while all military stores and buildings are lawful plunder, and while every edifice in the way of military movements,—whether, indeed, public or private,—may be destroyed, whatever does not contribute to the uses of war, ought to remain intact. It was a blot to the British character, when they burned the capitol at Washington, and the excuse for it, on the ground of retaliation, although insufficient, showed the necessity for an excuse to the civilized world. Even military hospitals are spared, if not misused for a hostile purpose.

§ 132.

8. Sieges and storms of forts and towns.

Among the ancients, the license of war in successful sieges and storms was unlimited. The butchery of the Platæans, the intended but revoked cruelty of the Athenian people towards Mitylene, their treatment of the Melians, the sack of Thebes by Alexander, and many similar events, show, that on such occasions, rapine, wholesale slaughter, and enslavement, whether of garrisoning troops, or of citizens, were dependent on the conqueror's will. So, too, the sack of Syracuse, although captured without a storm, that of Carthage, that of Corinth, and of other towns by the Romans, repeated the same scenes. The sieges of Europe, down to modern times, were terminated in a manner not less disgraceful to the general and the soldier. Thus Rome suffered as much when taken by the generals of the Emperor Charles V., as in any siege it ever sustained. "When Henry II. of France, entered the Low Countries, every city which did not surrender before he opened fire, was given up to destruction, the garrison hung, the inhabitants put to the sword." The fate of Magdeburg, in the thirty years' war (in 1631), is perhaps the most dreadful act in the gloomy drama, and naturally provoked the retaliation of the Protestants, when Wurtzburg was captured. If Cromwell put the garrisons of Tredah and Wexford to the sword, after the storming of those cities, it was a cruel policy, but was less than the practice of war at that time permitted.

More modern usage in sieges and storms, though in some respects very harsh, shows an advance in humanity. There is a distinction to be made between *forts* and *fortified towns*. Any means of assailing a fort may be used which are likely to be successful, but many generals abstain from bombarding a garrisoned town, and resort to storming in order to save the inhabitants; or if the nature of the place, or anything else, renders bombardment necessary, they give notice to the inhabitants, that they may retire to a place of safety. It was a proceeding worthy only of barbarians, when Suchet drove the people of Lerida, in Catalonia, into the citadel, then threw shells among the unprotected multitude, and compelled the governor to capitulate by such an appeal to his humanity. Formerly, it was regarded somewhat in the light of a crime, if a commander of a fortress held out as long as he could, and instances may be adduced where such officers were put to death for their obstinacy. Now, in ordinary cases, surrendering at discretion only reduces the soldiers to the state of prisoners of war. A commander who should blow up the works of his fortress, and break through a blockading army, would, according to the opinion of some, be doing an act contrary to the laws of war; but this does not appear to be true, although the blockader might be justified in refusing quarter to those, or at least to those officers who should seek thus to deprive them of the fruit of their toils.*

When a fortified town has been stormed, the prevailing usage of modern, as of ancient warfare, is, to let the soldiers have full license. The frightful scenes at the storms of Ciudad Rodrigo, Badajos, and St. Sebastian, under so humane a general as Wellington, show that it is thought impossible at such times to curb the ferocity of soldiers. Wellington himself was of this opinion; but says Napier,† "let the plunder of a town after an assault be expressly made criminal by the laws of war, with a due punishment attached;—let a select, permanent body of men, receiving higher pay, form a part of the army, and be charged to follow storming columns, with power to inflict" even death, if necessary; let money, in proportion to the importance and delay of the services, be paid to the successful troops, and, "with such regulations, the storming of towns would not produce more military disorders than the gaining of battles in the field."

* Comp. Napier, u. s., IV. 252. † Id. IV. 216.

§ 133.

Laws of war on the sea.

The liability of private property to capture on the sea, we have already considered, and the regulations of capture we shall reserve for a separate section. It has, moreover, already appeared, that the usages of naval warfare are more like those relating to attacks on forts, than like those which control ordinary land operations; and that even submarine instruments of death, exceptionable as they are, are not yet discarded. A word remains to be said in regard to the treatment of sea ports and coasts by vessels of the enemy. For a long time it was lawful to descend upon coasts, bombard towns, levy contributions, and burn places which refused to pay them.* Even in 1813, the British admiral, Cochrane, had orders to destroy property on the American coast, but the injury done to Newark, in Canada, by our forces, was given as the reason. More recent operations have shown a milder spirit. Odessa was not attacked in the late war with Russia, as being merely a commercial port. On the whole, there are signs that ravages by forces on both elements and requisitions on the ground of exemptions from them are growing obsolete.

§ 134.

Commercia belli.

Communications between enemies in war have long been carried on by heralds, persons bearing flags of truce, cartels for the exchange of prisoners and other purposes, etc. A belligerent may decline to receive a flag of truce, or to hold any intercourse with the enemy, or may even fire upon those who persist in attempting to open such intercourse after being warned off, but the bitterness of war rarely reaches this point.

Contracts lawful during war, as safeguards and passports, licenses to trade, armistices, ransom contracts, contracts to pay

* The German word *brandschatz*, literally denoting an estimate of the burning, or an equivalent to the burning of a dwelling or town, and applicable to the operations of both military and naval war, contains in itself the history of whole ages of barbarity.

requisitions and the like, will be considered elsewhere, as far as may be necessary. (Comp. § 146, § 147, § 142.)

§ 135.

Spies.

A general rule of war allows the punishment of death to be inflicted upon spies who are found in disguise within the lines of an army. The case of Major André, painful as it was, was strictly within military usage. But military spies in their regimentals, when taken, are treated as ordinary prisoners of war.

SECTION III.—*Of Civil Wars, Wars with Savages, Piracy and the Slave-trade.*

§ 136.

We have thus far contemplated wars between sovereign states; but there may also be intestine or internal wars; wars with hordes of savages, or with nations not governed by our international code; and wars with pirates.

Internal wars.

By internal war we intend movements more serious and lasting than sedition, waged by portions of the people of a country against one another,—including in the term *country* the complex body of a nation and its colonies or other dependencies. In some cases the connexion with dependencies may be so remote that the war may almost be called a foreign one. A civil war is one in which the opposing parties are distributed over the territory; while a war in which they are localized may be called a rebellion, insurrection or revolt. A civil war again does not aim at the destruction of unity, but rather at some change of government, constitution or laws, while the other may aim at sundering parts before united.

With internal wars international law comes into contact so far as the laws of war, that is, of humanity and natural justice, are concerned, and also in the bearings of the war upon the interests and rights of foreign states—a point to be considered in the sequel. (§ 166 *b*.) In every state there are laws against resistance to the authority of the government, defining sedition, treason, and the like, and punishing in person or property or both. When an internal war breaks out, the government must determine whether the municipal or the international code, in whole or in part, shall be adopted. In general the relation of the parties *ought* to be nearly those of ordinary war, which humanity demands, and *will be*, because otherwise the law of retaliation will be applied. Municipal law may be enforced with less evil in the way of pecuniary than of personal penalties; fines or confiscations may be efficacious in strengthening the government and deterring from rebellion. If slaves, as among us, form a part of the property of the rebels, since slavery is local and the law of nations knows of no such thing (§ 70, § 138), the advancing military power of the government may set them free and use or protect them; and indeed, if force overthrows the local laws on which slavery rests, they become free of course.

The same rules of war are required in such a war as in any other—the same ways of fighting, the same treatment of prisoners, of combatants, of non-combatants, and of private property by the army where it passes: so also natural justice demands the same veracity and faithfulness which are binding in the intercourse of all moral beings.

Nations thus treating rebels by no means concede thereby that they form a state, or that they are de facto such. There is a difference between belligerents and belligerent states, which has been too much overlooked.

When a war ends to the disadvantage of the insurgents, municipal law may clench the nail which war has driven, may hang, after legal process, instead of shooting, and confiscate the whole instead of plundering a part. But a wise and civilized nation will exercise only so much of this legal vengeance, as the interests of lasting order imperiously demand.

Wars with savages.

Again, as savage tribes are not governed by the justice which is acknowledged in Christian lands, international law is here likewise inapplicable. But here one of the parties being a subject of a code which he believes to be founded in justice, it would be flagitious for him to depart from the essential principles which he observes towards other Christian states. Thus while summary punishment for robbery and treachery may be expedient, the Christian state is bound by its own character and practice, in warring with savages, to exercise good faith and humanity, to treat prisoners well, to respect treaties and truces, and to regard the civil rights of the savage communities. For though too degraded to understand what their obligations are, they can be raised far above their present level by humane examples; while civilized men, falling down in their dealings with savages to their level, only increase their spirit of suspicion and revenge, and sink them to lower depths of ferocity.

Dealings with civilized nations who do not own our code.

Here let it be added, that the civilized and half-civilized nations of the world, which have not owned our law of nations, deserve a peculiar consideration. The object in their case ought to be not only to act justly and kindly towards them, but also to lead them to adopt our international law. Why should they not, if it is based on the true principles of human nature, presupposes a universal morality, and is thus fitted to be the law of mankind? In all probability a short time will be needed to bring Persia, Siam, China, or Japan, under this law, compared with that during which Christian states have been making and breaking it.

§ 137.

Pirates and their treatment.

With piracy, however, the law of nations has to do, as it is a crime not against any particular state, but against all states and the established order of the world. Piracy is robbery on the sea, or by descent from the sea upon the coast, committed by persons not holding a commission from, or at the time pertaining to, any established state. It is the act (1.) of persons who form an organization for the purposes of plunder, but who, inasmuch as such a body is not constituted for political purposes, cannot be said to be a body politic; (2.) of persons who, having in defiance of law seized possession of a chartered vessel, use it for the purpose of robbery; (3.) of persons taking a commission from two belligerent adversaries. The reason for ranking these latter among pirates is, that the *animus furandi* is shown by acting under two repugnant authorities. It has been held by some that a vessel which takes commissions even from two *allies*, is guilty of piracy,* but others, as Wheaton (El. II. 2, § 15), and Phillimore (I. 394), regard such an act only as illegal and irregular.

On the other hand it is not held to be piracy, if a privateer or other armed vessel, exceeding its commission, prey on commerce admitted by its sovereign to be friendly. Offences of this kind entitle the injured party to compensation, but the jurisdiction belongs to the vessel's sovereign, who is responsi ble for the conduct of his officer.

Piracy being a crime against nations, may be brought before any court, no matter what the nationality of the plaintiff or the origin of the pirate may be. It is a natural although not a necessary consequence of this principle, that an acquittal by any court in Christendom is an effectual bar against another trial for the same offence.

As pirates acquire no title to what they take, on recapture it reverts to the proprietor without application of the rule of postliminy. (Comp. § 143.)

The punishment of piracy depends on the muncipal law of the state where the offence is tried: the established penalty is death.

The law of each state may enlarge the definition of the crime of piracy, but must confine the operation of the new definition to its own citizens and to foreigners on its own vessels. So by treaty two states may agree to regard as piracy a particular crime which is not classed under international piracy. The effect of such a treaty is to give to both states jurisdiction for this crime over the citizens or subjects of both, but its operation has no bearing on other nations.

In the time of Bynkershoek it was made a question whether

* This is taught by Hautefeuille (I. 190 ed. 2) after Massé, de Martens (sur les armateurs, Chap. 2. § 14) and Valin.

the Barbary powers were pirates, as earlier writers on the law of nations had pronounced them to be. He decides that they form states, and may be "justi hostes" in war; and that in fact Europe had acknowledged this by making treaties with them. No one now will question this, especially as in the course of time these states,—those of them which still exist,—have in a measure laid aside their piratical habits.*

§ 138.

Is the slave-trade piracy?

In the progress of humane and Christian principles, and of correct views of human rights, slavery has come to be regarded as an unjust and cruel degradation of man made in the image of God. It is, accordingly, a *status* unprotected by the law of nations, and supported where it exists, only by local law. (§ 70.) Hence persons seized to be sold as slaves in a territory where the importation of slaves is forbidden, commit no crime when they get possession of the vessel, and either slay the crew, or compel them to sail for another country. They are only defending their lawful rights. Thus, when certain blacks who had lately been imported into Cuba from Africa, and were therefore illegally held in bondage, and were by right free according to Spanish law, rose on the crew between Havana and Puerto Principe, killed the captain, and finally came into the waters of the United States, it was held by the Supreme Court that if they had been slaves, our treaties with Spain would have required their restoration, but that they were not slaves, and if not slaves, not pirates.†

With new views of men's rights, and with fuller knowledge of the woes inflicted on Africa by the slave-trade, this traffic, which misguided benevolence at first suggested, became abhor-

* For piracy in general, comp. especially Bynkersh. Quæst. J. P. I. 17, entitled de Piratica, et an Barbari in Africa sint piratæ. Comp. also Kent, Lect. IX., and Wildman, II. 150. The principal passages of the Roman lawyers respecting restoration of things taken by pirates without postliminy, are one from Ulpian (Dig. 49, Tit. 15, 24), "qui a latronibus captus est, servus latronum non est; nec postliminium illi necessarium est," and one from Paulus (u. s. 19, § 2), "a piratis aut latronibus capti liberi permanent."

† United States *v.* The Amistad, 15 Peters, 518–598.

rent to the feelings of Christendom, and has everywhere become unlawful. Denmark, we believe, led the way, in 1792, by prohibiting the slave-trade, and importation into her colonies of slaves from abroad after the year 1802. Under the constitution of the United States, the importation of slaves could not become illegal before 1808, but acts passed in 1794 and 1800, forbade all citizens and residents to carry slaves from this country to a foreign one, or from one foreign country to another. In 1807 the importation of slaves was made to cease after January 1, 1808, and in 1818 a law was passed increasing the penalties of the trade, and applying to all participation of citizens of the United States in it. In 1819 the vessels and effects of citizens found to have been engaged in the trade were made liable to seizure and confiscation. And by the act of March 3, 1820, all persons over whom our jurisdiction extends, that is, all persons in vessels owned within the United States, and all citizens on foreign vessels, concerned in the slave-trade, or in kidnapping negroes or mulattoes, were to be deemed pirates and to suffer death.

In Great Britain, the first act declaring the slave-trade unlawful was passed in 1807, but not until 1824 was it pronounced to be piracy. Nearly all the nations of Europe have subsequently passed laws more or less stringent against the traffic. Its abolition was conceded by Spain in her treaty with Great Britain, in September, 1817. Portugal agreed to prohibit it north of the equator, by treaty with England, of January 22, 1815, and it ought by the same treaty to have come altogether to an end when the independence of Brazil was acknowledged in 1825. It ceased to be legal in Brazil by 1830, and in 1831, a law of that country not only freed all slaves who should be imported afterwards, but also provided for their reconveyance to Africa.

In 1824, the House of Representatives in our Congress, by a very large majority, requested the President to make arrangements, by which the slave-trade should become piracy under international law; but nothing was hereby effected. (§ 198.) Great Britain, both before and after this, in a number of treaties, secured the suppression of the trade, with the mutual right of search, of which we shall speak hereafter. (§ 197.) In her treaty with Brazil, of March 13, 1827, it was stipulated that, after three years, a subject of the Emperor of Brazil, carrying on the trade, should be deemed and treated as a pirate. This must mean that whatever may be done under the laws of nations, for the detection and seizure of pirates, might be done under the treaty towards Brazilian slave-traders, as search, capture, and trial before the captor's courts; but England forbore to take the steps to which the treaty gave her a right.*

However much the slave-trade may deserve to be ranked with piracy, or ranked as a worse crime still, it is not yet such by the law of nations, and would not be, if all the nations in Christendom constituted it piracy by their municipal codes. For the agreement of different states in the definitions and penalties of crimes, by no means gives to any one of them the right to execute the laws of another. That power must be acquired by treaty between separate states, or by consent of all states, in which latter case it would belong to international law. Meanwhile, the fact that the slave-trade has not been placed in this category, adds greatly to the difficulty of suppressing it, as will appear in the sequel. (§ 199.)

SECTION IV.—*Capture and Recapture, Occupation and Recovery of Territory.*

§ 139.

Capture in general, especially from enemies.

Capture of private property has nearly disappeared from land warfare, but is allowed by international war, as well in the case of neutrals as of enemies, at sea. The same humane principles, however, which have put a stop to it on the one element, are at work to abridge its sphere on the other. The rule already adopted by the principal European powers, that free ships engaged in law-

* Wildman, II. 150, seq. For the section in general, Comp. Kent, Lect. IX.

ful trade make free goods, is sure to become universal; and if so, the hostile property exposed to the cruisers of the other belligerent may become so inconsiderable, that the trade of plundering on the sea will be hardly worth carrying on. Meanwhile, the only specious pretexts for marine capture are these two, that the enemy's commerce furnishes him with the means of war, so that it may justly be obstructed, and that the captured vessels are pledges for the reparation of injuries. The former pretext will amount to nothing, if hostile trade can be conducted in such a way as to exempt it from capture. The other pretext will require that ships and goods captured be regarded, until peace settles all questions between nations, as simply detained to be restored, or have an equivalent paid for them if necessary. We must profess, however, that we indulge that "pious chimæra," as it has been called, that all private property on the sea, engaged in a lawful trade to permitted ports, ought to cross the seas in safety; we have the sanction of the authority of Franklin, and of sober propositions made by our own government, for regarding such a rule as both desirable and practicable; we must esteem it nearer to justice, and certainly to humanity, than the present inequality of risk on the two elements; and it will probably be found, owing to the new rule in favor of neutrals, that marine capture will not be worth retaining.*

The fact, meanwhile, is, that on land the property of combatants, when taken in battle, goes to the victors, and that soldiers have generally free license of plunder at the storming of towns. On the sea all private property of the enemy's subjects is lawful plunder, unless secured by a special permit. And on both elements most kinds of public property of the enemy are exposed to hostile depredations. The right is exercised even against such vessels as have had no notice of the commencement of hostilities, and everywhere except in neutral waters.

* In a meeting of the chambers of commerce of Hamburg and Bremen, resolutions have been recently passed to memorialize the congress expected to meet at Paris, in favor of the exemption of private property on the sea from capture. The resolution passed at Bremen, Dec. 2, 1859, is as follows:—"That the inviolability

§ 140.

Property in prizes, how and when begun.

From the principle that states are the belligerent parties, it flows, as we have seen, that an authority derived from the state is necessary, before a prize can be taken. It flows, also, from the same principle, that all private title to prize must be derived from the laws of the state. When does such a title commence? Some have said, at the moment of capture, or of taking possession, as though the vessel taken were a *res nullius;* others, after twenty-four hours' possession; others, when the prize is carried *infra præsidia*, and is thus secure against recapture;* and others, finally, when a court has adjudged it to the captor. "The question," says Kent, "never arises but between the original owner and a neutral purchasing from the captor; and between the original owner and the recaptor. If a captured ship escape from the captor, or is retaken, or the owner ransoms her, his property is thereby revested. But if neither of these events happens, the question as to change of title is open to dispute, and many arbitrary lines have been drawn, partly from policy, to prevent too easy disposition of the property of neutrals, and partly from equity, to extend the *jus postliminii* in favor of the owner." † Thus there is no settled view or principle as to the time when a title from capture begins. Perhaps no definite rule can be laid down any more than in answering the question when occupation ends in ownership, which the laws of different states will determine differently. The state's title begins in the fact of seizure according to the

of person and property in time of war, on the high seas, extended also to the subjects and citizens of belligerent states, except so far as the operations of war *necessarily* restrict the same, is imperatively demanded by the sentiments of justice universally entertained at the present day." They then request the senate of Bremen to support this principle, and to lay the subject before the German confederation or the proposed congress.

* Comp. Bynkersh. Quæst. J. P. I. 4. The twenty-four hours' rule grew up in modern Europe, and is purely arbitrary. The rule that the prize must be carried infra præsidia was a Roman one; "cujus juris non alia ratio est quam quod tunc omnis rei persequendæ et recuperandæ spes decollaverit." Bynkersh. u. s.

† Kent, I. 101, Lect. V.

rights of war—that is, "when the battle is over, and the *spes recuperandi* is gone." (Phillimore 3, 460.) But the title can be contested in certain circumstances by neutral governments, as on the ground that capture was made in their waters; or by private subjects of neutral governments, as in the various cases of seizure of neutral goods and ships; or by subjects of the enemy, as where licenses to trade were not respected by the captor. If, now, a neutral buys the prize immediately after capture, he buys it subject to the claims of injured parties, and has his remedy in the captor's courts, provided the latter conveys that for which he had no good title. If the owner ransoms her, he extinguishes the captor's title, of whatever kind it be, good or bad. The laws of the state determine the steps which the captor, as the state's agent, must take in regard to the property, and especially at what time he is allowed to have an entire or partial interest in the things taken. It is the first duty of the captor, says Mr. Wildman (2, 176,) to bring in his prize for adjudication, but "if this is impossible, his next duty is to destroy the enemy's property: if it be doubtful whether it be the enemy's property, and impossible to bring it in, no such obligation arises, and the safe and proper course is to dismiss." Of course, if this doctrine, based on English decisions, be true, destruction of neutral ships or property by mistake must be made good by the cruiser's government.*

§ 141.

Complete title given by a court.

By modern usage, a complete title to a prize taken at sea, is given to the captor only by the sentence of a competent court. By a competent court is intended one which, by the law of the state, has jurisdiction in matters pertaining to prize, no matter what other jurisdiction it may have, or not have. Such courts in the United States, are the district and circuit courts of the confederation, with appeal up through the circuit to the supreme court of the

* The doctrine is unsafe for neutrals, where the cruiser pertains to a belligerent *de facto*, attempting to become a nation, not to a lawful and acknowledged power.

Union; such were, in France, after 1659, the council of prizes, with appeal to the council of state, and thence to the royal council of finance; and such are, in the British dominions, the vice-admiralty and admiralty courts, with appeal to a committee of members of the privy council, called Lords Commissioners of Prize Causes. And, in general, the court must be one acting under the authority of the captor's sovereign, and holding its session at home or within the territory of an ally. A consul or ambassador, residing abroad, has no jurisdiction, it is held, in prize cases; and when the French government, in 1796, allowed their consuls and vice-consuls, in neutral ports, to decide such questions, Sir W. Scott declared it a thing unheard of. (Manning, p. 381; Heffter, § 138.) Neutrality is too delicate a thing to allow either the courts or territory of neutrals to be used in such cases.* It is not necessary, however, that the prize itself should be conveyed into the ports of the captor's sovereign or of his ally, but if a neutral consents, it may be taken into a convenient port of that description. Such consent the neutral may give or withhold, as he judges best, and it is not generally withheld; but perhaps the strictest notion of what neutrality requires, and the true policy of neutrals, which is to render capture on the high seas as inconvenient as possible, demand of them to close their ports to prizes, unless some urgent cause, as a storm or the vessel's condition, should render temporary sojourn there necessary. It will be the captor's right, if the neutral opens his ports, to carry there prizes taken from the neutral's own subjects as well as those belonging to any other nationality.

§ 142.

Ransom of captured vessels.

It may, for various reasons, be inconvenient to send a prize into a port, and a captor so situated will be apt, if permitted, to let the prize go free again for less than its worth. For these reasons, and in accordance with the

* Sir W. Scott knew of no instance where neutral courts exercised such jurisdiction, but Mr. Manning produces one from a treaty made between Denmark and Genoa in 1789. (P. 381.)

practice of ransom formerly so common on the land, it has been, since about the end of the 17th century, the custom to allow captors to liberate a captured vessel on an engagement to pay a certain ransom. The receipt for the ransom is of the nature of a passport or safe conduct, and contains a permission, good against all cruisers of the belligerent or his ally, to pursue a certain voyage. Only in cases of necessity can the route and time laid down be departed from without violating the contract. The contract insures against molestation from other cruisers, but not against other kinds of hazard, and the ransom would still be binding, if nothing were said to the contrary, in case the vessel perished by the perils of the seas.

Hostages to secure the ransom.

As it is difficult to enforce the payment of ransom during war, the custom has prevailed more or less to deliver over to the captor hostages, who might be detained until the liquidation of the contract, and whose expenses were provided for in the ransom-bill. The hostage being only collateral security, his death or flight cannot release from the contract. If the master or owners refuse to fulfil their stipulation, the hostage's remedy lies in an appeal to the courts of his own country.

If a ransomed vessel is captured out of its course and condemned, the ransom is deducted from the proceeds of the vessel, and only the remainder goes to the second captor. If the captor's vessel is recaptured, with the ransom-contract, or with the hostages, or with both on board, there is held to be a complete end to all claim for payment.* If, on the other hand, the captor's vessel is taken after putting the ransom-bill and hostage in a place of safety, the contract continues unimpaired: nay, it is held so to continue, if the captor's vessel is taken, and the securities for the payment of ransom are concealed so as not to come into the actual possession of the second captor. And, again, when a captor's vessel was captured with the hostage and ransom-bill on board, in which there was an

* So Wildman, II. 273, after Valin. But why, if the first captor had transmitted the bill, retaining the hostage who is only a collateral security, should not his claim be still good?

agreement that payment should be binding notwithstanding such second capture, the English courts decided that the first captor, being an alien, could not by their laws bring a suit for the recovery of a right acquired in actual war. But in this case the hostage might sue, or in case of his death, the captor after the end of the war.*

The master of a vessel being an agent for the owners, they are bound by his act, when not fraudulent nor contrary to usage. But if the ransom should exceed the value of ship and cargo, it is held that the owners by surrendering these may be free from obligation.

A ransom contract is valid under the law of nations, although made in war, since it contemplates a state of war which it seeks to mitigate. Nevertheless no nation is bound to allow its citizens to give or receive ransom-bills. By a French ordinance of 1756, privateers were forbidden to ransom a vessel until they had sent three prizes into port. The power of granting ransom has been taken away by acts of parliament from English cruisers, except in extreme cases to be allowed by the courts of admiralty. The reason alleged for this legislation is, that captors might abuse their power of ransoming vessels and injure neutral trade.

§ 143.

Recapture. Rights of the original owner.

If according to the received right of war a thing taken from the enemy becomes the property of the captor, it ought when retaken to become the property of the second captor. But since the captor's right comes to him from the state, the state may decide how far he shall be rewarded, if at all, for his risks and labor in retaking what had belonged to a fellow-subject. It seemed inequitable that the original owner should wholly lose his right to what had been recently his own, while the recaptor, an inhabitant of the same or of a friendly country, at the end of two acts of violence, came into possession of the same property. And yet policy as well as justice should hold out a prospect of reward for a re-

* Wildman, II. 275.

capture, which the cruiser would otherwise be apt to shrink from, and which brought with it its hazards. We are led then to the questions when and how far the rights of the original owner revert to him, and to the right of salvage or the premium granted for recapture. And as the return of property to its first owner appears in the shape of the Roman doctrine of postliminy, it is necessary to explain briefly what the Roman postliminy was, and how it differs from that which is known to modern international law.

Jus postliminii.

By ancient *jus gentium* all things seized by the enemy became his property, and thus free persons became slaves. The Romans regarded such a person, if a captive from among themselves, as suffering *capitis deminutio*, or losing his status of freedom, precisely as a foreigner would lose his, if taken by Romans. Suppose now such a person to be recaptured, or ransomed, or to have escaped, it would be hard to say what was his status on his return to Rome. To remove all difficulty the *jus postliminii** was devised, as a legal fiction, according to which he was treated as not having been away, or at least as having only been absent from his threshold, and all his lost rights or rights in abeyance were restored to him. The same *jus* was extended so as to cover certain kinds of things captured by the enemy, namely, slaves, ships of war and transport, mules, horses and land, which thus returned on recapture to their original owner. Postliminy had no application to civil war, where the factions were not enemies in a political sense, nor to war with pirates, because they were robbers, incapable of rights; but only to legitimate war between two states. Nor could its advantages be open to a deserter or other betrayer of his post, or to one whom the state itself had given up to the enemy. If a free person, taken in war, was ransomed by another, whose tie of relationship to the captive did not oblige him so to act, his rights seem not immediately to

* Probably from *post* in the sense *behind*, and *limen* the *threshold*. Comp. postscenium, postsignani. As postscenium denotes the space behind the scene, so might postliminium, originally, the space behind the threshold, thence the fact of return behind the threshold or into the house.

have reverted to him by *jus postliminii* on his return to Roman soil, but he continued in the relation to the ransomer not strictly of a slave, but of one whose body could be held until the ransom was paid. By a law of the later Roman empire, five years' service was equivalent to this ransom. If a slave taken by the enemy was thus ransomed, he remained under the ransomer's control until his ransom was paid by his former master. The ransomer within a certain time could not refuse to restore the slave on the offer of the ransom money, and then the *jus postliminii* began.*

It must be regarded as a striking illustration of the sway of Roman law over the European mind, that the lawyers have taken this road to help the first owner to his property after recapture. For the application of the modern postliminy is quite different from that of the Roman. (1.) As to persons, freemen to whose status it applied by Roman law more than to anything else, do not lose their status in modern times by captivity in war. They are absent, like travellers or merchants, and their rights and obligations go on, as far as personal presence is not necessary for their exercise. It is true, indeed, that a prisoner of war escaping from a vessel in a neutral port, is protected against recapture by this right, as he would be among the Romans.† But two nations might, if they pleased, agree to give up such escaped captives; and the not doing so may be best explained on the ground that the laws of one country do not extend into the territory of another, and especially that the laws of a war in which I have no part, ought not to affect my friend or subject within my borders,—the principle in short which makes express conventions of extradition necessary. And,

* I follow especially E. F. Hase, das jus postliminii und die fictio legis Corneliæ. Halle, 1851.

† Paulus, in 19, § 3, Dig. XLIX. 15. "Si in civitatem sociam amicamve, aut ad regem socium vel amicum venerit, statim postliminio redisse videtur; quia ibi primum nomine publico tutus esse incipit."—Here not simply a state or king *allied in war*, but any non-hostile, friendly, or, as we should say, neutral power is included. This is denied by Grotius, III. 9, § 2, and Bynkersh. Quæst. J. P., I. 15, but such a sense given to amicus would restrict the postliminy to times of war, whereas Paulus is speaking generally of its existence in war or peace. Comp. Hase, p. 58.

again, Roman postliminy applied to slaves, but as slavery is not sanctioned by the modern law of nations (comp. § 70,) it can obtain no application in regard to them.

As for the private relations of returned captives, the Roman law held marriage to cease with captivity, which is abhorrent to Christian doctrine. Public personal relations by modern law continue after captivity, but the laws of each state determine how far their advantages, as salary during absence for example, can be claimed on return to one's own country. The Roman law refused to admit such claims.* (2.) As to the limit of time within which the *jus postliminii* takes effect, we are not aware that Roman law contains any definition. Modern usage gives complete possession of booty to the enemy on land, after he has held it for twenty-four hours,† so that the former owner cannot claim it again from the purchaser; the reason for which limit is the difficulty of identifying such articles after a lapse of time. On the other hand, land is restored to its original owner, until peace or destruction of national existence has transferred sovereignty to a conqueror. (3.) By modern law captured ships with the goods on board, carried *infra præsidia* by the enemy and condemned, become absolutely his, so that, if they are afterwards recaptured or repurchased by a neutral, the former owner has nothing to do with them: their connection with him has wholly ceased. It is only in the interval between capture and complete possession that his right of postliminy continues. This was otherwise by Roman law; the right affected all those kinds of things which were under its operation at all, when they came into the power of the enemy, and the more, the more clearly they had passed into his dominium.‡ (4.) As to limit of place modern postliminy takes

* Heffter, § 190.

† The Romans had a practice often mentioned by Livy (as V. 16), of bringing back the booty, allowing former owners to take their property back, and selling the rest. Two, three, or thirty days were allowed for this reclamation.

‡ Bynkersh. Quæst. J. P., I. 5, denies that there is any postliminy when a vessel has not been brought into port. "Qui sciunt quid postliminium sit, sciunt quoque non esse nisi ejus, quod in hostis dominium transierat. Dicendum erat [*i. e.* instead of calling it by this name,] ante deductionem in portum, res non esse factas hostium, sed remansisse prioris domini, recuperatas igitur ei cedere et non recuperatori."

effect only within the territory of the captor or his ally, with the single exception already mentioned of captives escaping ashore in a neutral port. But the Roman, it seems most probable, took effect within the borders of any friendly nation.

A nation may make what laws it pleases in regard to the recapture of the goods of one of its subjects by another, but is bound to follow the *jus postliminii* in cases affecting the property of neutrals.

§ 144.

Rewards for capture and for recapture. Salvage.

The laws of some states hold out special rewards to encourage the capture of vessels, especially of commissioned vessels, of their enemies. Such is the head-money of five pounds, due under a section of the British prize act, to all on board an armed vessel acting under public authority, for every man on board of a similar captured vessel who was living at the beginning of the engagement. Such, too, in a sense, are the advantages given to other vessels which have assisted the capturing one, or even started to render assistance.* But the claim for compensation is far more reasonable when the crew of one vessel have saved another and its goods from pirates, lawful enemies or perils of the seas. This is called salvage, and answers to the claim for the ransom of persons which the laws of various nations have allowed. The legislation of a particular state may withhold salvage from its citizens or subjects, but cannot deprive a neutral or an ally of the exercise of this right.

Amount of salvage.

The laws of different nations vary in the amount of reward which they assign to the rescuer of vessels. In regard to the salvage to be paid to our recaptors or rescuers by the owners of foreign vessels and goods, the law of the United States adopts the principle of reciprocity, measuring the amount by that which is paid by the law of the state to which the vessel belongs. In regard to the amount to be paid by citizens or resident foreigners the law contains various provisions, of from one half to one twelfth of the value; more

* Wildman, II. 321–326.

being granted for the salvage of an armed vessel recaptured, than of an unarmed, and more to a private vessel recapturing than to a public armed vessel. In no case is salvage allowed, if the recapture occurs after condemnation by a competent authority, since the property is regarded as having passed over from the original owner to the captor. The provisions of the law of the most important nations are given at length by Dr. Wheaton. (El. IV. 2, § 12, 419–424.)

§ 145.

Effect of temporary conquests.

"Recte dixit Grotius,"* says Bynkershoek, "postliminium etiam in integris populis locum habere, ut, inquit, qui liberi fuerunt, suam recipiant libertatem, si forte eos vis sociorum eximat hostili imperio." (Quest. J. P., I. 16.) A state, after temporary occupation or after the short-lived government of a conqueror, may be restored to its pristine condition. Such was the case with Holland, part of Germany and Spain in the times of Napoleon. The interruption of former rights and the actions of the conqueror give rise to several perplexing questions in regard to the condition of such a country; and as occupation is separated by no very distinct limits from "*debellation*" or complete conquest, or at least as the occupier sometimes acts the conqueror, hereby, perhaps, the perplexity is increased. We follow Heffter (§ 188) principally, in our brief representation of the rights and obligation of a state restored in this postliminary way.

Such restoration follows, as a matter of course, whenever the conquering occupant by treaty abandons his conquests or is driven out, whether by the inhabitants or by an ally. But if a third party dispossesses the conqueror, the state cannot, according to international justice, recover its independent existence without his consent, although this may be demanded by equity or humanity.

If mere occupation, without the assumption of the attributes of government had taken place, everything goes back to

* III. 9, § 9.

to the old state. The restored regime can claim even from allies and neutrals property which had passed over to them from the occupier, so far as the right of war gave him no power to dispose of them.

If the occupant conqueror set up and carried on a new government, then

1. None of his changes in the earlier constitution, no mode of administration, officer or law, has any claim to permanence.

2. No retroactive exercise of the powers of government, affecting subjects or third persons, rightfully belongs to the restored regime, so far as relations are concerned which pertained to the period of occupation. Thus taxes for the interim cannot properly be collected, on the ground that they would have been due to the old government if the occupation had not taken place. For the rights of sovereignty, so far as they pertained to the old regime, had in fact passed over into the hands of the new.

3. Whatever the government by conquest did in the legitimate exercise of political power is valid. The new government succeeds to it in its acquisitions and obligations, and cannot set aside its doings on the ground that it had no right to exist. Thus what was due to the usurping government in back-standing taxes, what it acquired by treaty or otherwise, belongs to its successor. On the other hand, if that government disposed of state property, or contracted state debts, its proceedings here also are valid, inasmuch as it represented the state. This has been denied, but not with justice, except in those extreme cases, where the temporary government had alienated property or borrowed money not in the exercise of political authority nor for public purposes, but with the spirit of a plunderer. (Comp. § 38, § 99.)

Section V.—*Of the Suspension and the Termination of War, especially of Truce and of Peace.*

§ 146.

Intercourse in war. 1. for the purposes of war.

The possibility of intercourse in war depends on the confidence which the belligerents repose in each other's good faith, and this confidence, on the unchangeable sacredness of truth. Even Bynkershoek who allows every kind of violence and every kind of craft has to say, in words already cited, "ego quidem omnem dolum permitto, sola perfidia excepta." (Quæst. J. P., I. 1.) That faith should be kept with heretics has been denied, but no one has maintained that it is not to be kept with enemies.*

Such being the undoubted principle of obligation in war as well as in peace, war is enabled to put on a milder form for that reason, and to interrupt its violence for a time either towards particular persons or entirely. Among these intermissions of war are to be enumerated:

1. The *commercia belli*, to which we have already referred (§ 134), and of one of which, ransom-contracts, we have spoken at large (§ 142). Some conventions in war have a lasting operation, as determining how the war shall be carried on, what kinds of arms shall be accounted unlawful, how prisoners shall be treated and the like, or as placing certain persons or places in a relation of neutrality to both parties. Others are transitory and special, as contracts relating to requisitions, to ransom, to exchange of prisoners, and to capitulations. Prisoners are generally exchanged within the same rank man for man, and a sum of money or other equivalent is paid for an excess of them on one side. Capitulations formerly were often made on the condition of not being relieved by a certain day. They are usually formal agreements in writing between the officers in command on both sides, who have, unless the power is taken from them with the knowledge of the other party, power to make all such arrangements.

* Comp. Heffter, § 141.

§ 147.

2. Licenses to trade. Safe conducts.

2. Next to these may be classed permissions given to individuals which suspend the operations of war, as far as their persons are concerned, for the purpose of enabling them to perform a work of peace. These modes of plighting faith are not necessary for the conduct of the war.

One of these is licenses to trade with the enemy. A license to trade with the enemy being an exception to the ordinary rules of war is to be strictly interpreted, and yet, where there has been evident good faith in following it, slight deviations will not be noticed. If the person, the port or town, the kind and quality of the goods, the limits of time, are prescribed in the license, departures from its terms, with the exception of unavoidable delay, will make it void. Thus it has been decided that a license to neutral vessels becomes void when hostile vessels or those of the country giving the license are substituted for them; that a license to import will not cover re-exportation; that one prescribing a certain course of navigation is avoided by voluntary departure from such course; that a license to sail in ballast is forfeited by carrying part of a cargo, or to import certain articles will not protect other articles, not named, although destined for a neutral port, or again to proceed to a certain port is vitiated by calling at an interdicted port for orders. A general license to sail to any port will not include a blockaded one, which is shut by higher laws of war. A license although it has expired will protect in case of unavoidable hindrances. No consul and no admiral, according to English doctrine, can give a license, which is a high act of sovereignty, without authority of the government.* A license protects against all cruisers of the enemy, but not against any action of the country to which the licensed person or vessel pertains. (Comp. § 117.)

Safeguard and passports.

Passports and safeguards, or safe conducts, are letters of protection, with or without an escort, by which the person of an enemy is rendered inviolable.

* These and many more particular cases touching the interpretation of licenses by the English courts may be found in Wildman, II. 245–269.

These may be given in order to carry on the peculiar commerce of war, or for reasons which have no relation to it, which terminate in the person himself. As, like licenses, they are exceptions to the non-intercourse of war, they are *stricti juris*, as far as relates to the person, the time of his sojourn, his route and residence, and in a degree to his effects and attendants. If he remain beyond the prescribed time with no inevitable necessity from illness or other cause, he can be treated as a captive. If he is discovered in intrigues his passport is vitiated. If he acts as a spy, of course he forfeits the right of protection; for he is thus committing an act of hostility, whether the officer who gave him the passport is privy to his designs or not. Arnold's pass could be of no avail to André, when once his true character was brought to light.

§ 148.

Truce or armistice.

3. A temporary suspension of the operations of war at one or more places is called a truce or armistice.* A truce may be *special* referring to operations before a fortress or in a district, or between certain detachments of armies, or *general*, implying a suspension of hostilities in all places. A general truce can be made only by the sovereign power or its agents, specially empowered for this purpose. A special or partial truce may be concluded according to the usage of nations by a military officer, even by a subordinate one within his district. This usage rests on the consideration that both policy and humanity require that such a discretionary power should be lodged in those who, being on the spot, can best understand the exigencies of the case. If an officer should be restricted in the use of this power contrary to usage, and yet should exercise it, his agreement, at least if not corruptly made, would be binding on his sovereign, provided that the other party knew nothing of the restriction. For that

* Truce, in mediæval Latin treuga, in Ital. tregua, properly denotes, according to Dietz, *security*, *pledge*, and is the same with Gothic triggva, old German triuwa, French treve. In old French true, in Anglo-Norman trewe, has this sense. Can *truce* be the plural of *true* or trewe—*induciæ*? Armistice, not used in Latin, but formed analogically, is, we believe, quite a modern word.

party had a right to infer from prevalent usage and the nature of the command intrusted to him that he had this power.

§ 149.

Time when a truce begins.

A truce is binding on the parties to it from the time when they have agreed to its terms, but on private persons from the time when intelligence of it can have reasonably reached them. For injuries inflicted in the interval the sovereign of the injurer is responsible.* When a general suspension of arms is agreed upon, it is not unusual to provide that it shall take effect in different portions of the theatre of war or parts of the world at different times, so as to afford opportunity to give notice of it to all who are concerned in, or whose business is affected by the war.

What can be done in a truce?

A truce being in itself a mere negation of hostilities, it is a little difficult to say what may, or may not, be done during its continuance. The following rule, if we are not deceived, expresses the views of most text-writers: that the state in which things were before the truce is so far to be maintained that nothing can be done to the prejudice of either party by the other, which could have been prevented in war, but which the truce gives the power of doing. But may a besieged place, during a truce, repair its walls and construct new works? This, which Wheaton after Vattel denies, is affirmed by Heffter (u. s.), after Grotius and Puffendorf.† Heffter also declares it to be unquestioned that the besieger cannot continue his works of siege, thus giving to the besieged in any partial truce the advantage over his foe. The question is whether to strengthen works of offence or of defence is an act of hostility, and is consistent with a promise to suspend hostilities. It would appear that neither party can act thus in good faith, unless it can be shown that the usages of war have restricted the meaning of truce to the suspension of certain operations. The rule then laid down by Vattel, and which he

* Heffter, § 142.

† Grotius, III. 21, § 7; Puffend. VIII. 7, § 10. Cocceii on Grot. u. s. § 10, denies it. So Vattel, III. 16, § 247; Wheaton, El. IV. 2, § 22.

is obliged to qualify by several others, namely that each may do among themselves, that is, within their own territories or where they are respectively masters, what they would have the right to do in peace, is true only of the general operations of war. A power may use the interval in collecting its forces, strengthening its works which are not attacked, and the like. But, when we come to the case of besieged towns, the question is of what are the two parties masters, and various quibbles might be devised to allow either of them to do what he pleased. The governor of a town, says Vattel, may not repair breaches or construct works which the artillery of the enemy would render it dangerous to labor upon during actual siege, but he may raise up new works or strengthen existing ones to which the fire or attacks of the enemy were no obstacle. Why, if this be so, may not the besiegers strengthen their works which are not exposed to the guns of the fortress?

End of a truce.

When a truce is concluded for a specified time, no notice is necessary of the recommencement of hostilities.* Every one who lingers freely in the enemy's country or within his lines, after this date, is obnoxious to the law of war. But forced delay on account of illness, or other imperative reason, would exempt such a one from harsh treatment.

§ 150.

Peace, what?

A peace differs not from a truce essentially in the length of its contemplated duration, for there may be very long armistices and states of peace continuing only a definite number of years. The ancients often concluded treaties of peace which were to expire after a certain time: thus one of the oldest monuments of the Greek language contains a treaty of alliance for a century between Elis and a town of Arcadia; the Acarnanians concluded a treaty of peace and alliance for the same number of years; and a thirty years'

* The Romans gave such notice to the Vejentes (Livy, IV. 30) by the usual ceremony. (§ 115.) But they seem to have rarely been at peace with the Etruscan States, truce taking its place, and so adopting its ceremonies.

peace between Athens and Sparta was not half finished when the Peloponnesian war broke out. But, while an armistice is an interval in war and supposes a return to it, a peace is a return to a state of amity and intercourse, implying no intention to recommence hostilities. An armistice again leaves the questions of the war unsettled, but a peace implies in its terms that redress of wrongs has been obtained, or that the intention is renounced of seeking to obtain it.

Treaties of peace in general.

The conclusion of a peace being one of the most important acts of sovereignty, it is naturally carried on with all the formalities with which the most solemn treaties of other kinds are adjusted. Sometimes the general basis on which the two parties will consent to be at peace is laid down long before the details are arranged. The first agreements are called preliminaries, and a peace at this stage is a preliminary peace in contrast with the definitive peace. The preliminary peace is binding from the time it is signed, although its provisions may be altered, by mutual consent, before the final negotiations are completed. As examples of such preliminary treaties, we may mention the treaty of Vienna, in 1735, the peace of Breslau, of June 11, 1742, that of Aix-la-Chapelle, of April 30, 1748, that of Paris between England and the United States, Nov. 30, 1782, and that of Versailles between Great Britain on the one part, and France and Spain on the other, Jan. 20, 1783. (Append. II. under the years.)

Sometimes after a treaty has been drawn up, separate articles are added, which are declared to be as binding as the treaty itself. These articles may be public or secret, the latter being kept from the world on account of their nature or the circumstances of the parties, although generally unearthed by foreign courts. When several powers unite in a treaty of peace, it is done either by the union of all as principals in one treaty; or by separate treaties of each with his enemy, in which case there is no common obligation, unless these treaties are made common by an express agreement; or finally a power becomes an accessory to a treaty already made, thus taking on itself the rights and obligations of a principal.*

* De Martens, § 336.

"In a treaty of peace, also, the interests of powers can be included which took no direct part in the war, but were either auxiliaries, or at least had some interest or other in the war or the peace. It may be (1.) that one of the principal contracting powers stipulates something in their favor, whether by comprehending them in the treaty,—so that the peace and amity shall extend to them without thereby rendering them principal contracting powers,—or by inserting a particular point in their favor; in which case it is not necessary that they formally signify their acceptance. Or (2.) to the treaty may be added conventions concluded with or between such states, which conventions are declared to be parts of the principal document. Or (3.) third powers may be invited to accede, either with a view to obtain their consent or to do them honor. And, on the other hand, sometimes third powers protest formally against a treaty of peace, or against one or other of its articles, and hand over such act of protestation to the principal contracting powers." * Thus the Pope protested against the peace of Westphalia, and with the King of Spain against the final act of the congress of Vienna.

Every nation has a right to employ its own language in treaties whether of peace or made for any other purpose. The Latin was the language chiefly employed in treaties until the 18th century. The treaties of Westphalia, for instance, of Nymwegen, of Ryswick, and, in the next century, of Utrecht and Rastadt, were composed in it. The communications of Turkey with European powers are written in Turkish, but with a Latin or French translation accompanying them. The prevailing language of diplomacy in the 18th century, and since, has been the French, of the use of which between the states of the German Empire, the peace of Breslau, in 1742, is said to afford the first example. But of late the German powers use their own language more than formerly in their treaties with one another. England and the United States naturally employ their common tongue in intercourse with one another, and have been more or less in the practice of making use of both English and

* From De Martens, u. s.

French in treaties with other nations; but this practice has its inconveniences, for disputes can easily arise where two contemporary documents of equal authority differ, as will be apt to be the case, in their shades of thought. The original of the treaty of 1774 between Turkey and Russia is in Italian. In several treaties expressed in French a protest is inserted that the use of this language shall not be regarded as a precedent for the future. Such is the case with the treaty of Aix-la-Chapelle (1748), that of Paris (1763), and the final act of the congress of Vienna in 1815. Our treaty of alliance with France (1778), and the treaty of cession of Louisiana (1803,) contain each a declaration that although the treaty has been written in both French and English, the French copy is the original.

§ 151.

Restrictions on the power to make peace.

The same thing is true of treaties of peace as of all other conventions, that they are of no validity where the government exceeds its constitutional powers in making them. (Comp. § 99.) Besides this there is a moral restriction, where nations have been allies in war. If a treaty of alliance requires the parties to it to co-operate in war until a certain end is gained, nothing but an extreme necessity, such as the hopelessness of future exertion, can authorize one of the parties to make a peace with the common enemy. Even if the terms of alliance for the purposes of war are less definite, it is dishonorable for an ally, above all for a principal party, to desert his confederates and leave them at the mercy of the foe. Allies may make, each his own peace, and obtain special concessions, but they are bound in good faith to act together, and to secure one another, as far as possible, against a power which may be stronger than any of them separately.*

* Vattel IV., 2, § 15, 16.

§ 152.

Although a peace is a return to a state of amity, and, among civilized nations, of intercourse, the conditions on which intercourse is conducted may not be the same as before the war. If a treaty contained no other agreement than that there should be peace between the parties, perhaps there would be a fair presumption that everything was settled again on its old basis, the cause of war alone being still unsettled. But treaties usually define anew the terms of intercourse. The general principles which govern the renewal of intercourse cannot be laid down, until it is first known what the effect of a war is upon previous treaties.

Effect of treaties of peace.

A war then puts an end to all previous treaties, except (1.) so far as they restrict the action of the war itself. Stipulations, which contemplate a state of war, are evidently not annulled by a state of war, otherwise they are in themselves nugatory and incapable of fulfilment. They are binding, that is, in war, just as ordinary treaties are binding in peace. If one party violate them, the other may practise retorsion (§ 114), or regard them as no longer in force.* Thus an agreement not to employ privateers in war, or not to levy contributions, or not to use submarine torpedoes, or to allow each other's commercial marine undisturbed use of the seas for certain purposes, is good through all time, unless dissolved by mutual agreement. But all other arrangements formerly existing, especially of the nature of privileges conceded by either party to the other, it is optional to resume or not. If nothing is said in the treaty about them, they are understood to have expired. Thus, our former privilege of using certain coasts belonging to Great Britain for the purpose of drying fish, was cut off by the war of 1812, and as no notice was taken of it in the treaty of Ghent (Append. II. and § 55), it had no existence.

2. Another exception to the rule that war puts an end to treaties, is found in those agreements, which are in their own nature perpetual. Thus, after the war of 1812, no new recog-

* Comp. Heffter, § 122.

nition of our independence by Great Britain was necessary. Even if the war and the treaty of Ghent had not been recognitions of our national existence as a war-making and peace-making power, the acknowledgment of our independence a generation before, was an admission that we formed a permanent state. So, too, cessions of territory, adjustments of boundaries and the like, so far as the war does not relate to them, are by their nature arrangements made once for all, not liable to be called into question in every new dispute; and the state within such limits is a perfect moral person.*

3. It is held by Vattel, that a new war for a new cause, not involving a breach of existing treaties, does not put an end to the rights acquired by such treaties, which are thus only suspended, to come into validity again when peace returns, whether confirmed by it or not. This rule, which would be a very important one if admitted, and yet, perhaps, one attended with practical difficulties, is not, so far as we are informed, insisted on by later text-writers, nor introduced into the code of nations. The general practice is, in a new treaty after a war, to make mention of all the old ones which the parties wish to keep in force, and which thus become incorporated in it. Nations ought by all means to do this in order to prevent misunderstandings, and cut off occasions for new wars.

4. Such is the case as far as public rights are concerned. But private rights, the prosecution of which is interrupted by war, are revived by peace, although nothing may be said upon the subject; for a peace is a return to a normal state of things, and private rights depend not so much on concessions, like public ones, as on common views of justice. And here we in-

* Comp. Vattel, II. § 192, and Wheaton, El. III. 2, § 9, who calls such arrangements *transitory* conventions, as distinguished from treaties.—The principle laid down in the text is well expressed in the treaty between the United States and Mexico, made in 1848 (Art xxii.): "And it is declared that neither the pretence that war dissolves all treaties nor any other whatever shall be considered as annulling or suspending the solemn covenant contained in this article. On the contrary, the state of war is precisely that for which it is provided; and during which its stipulations are to be as sacredly observed as the most acknowledged obligations under the law of nature or nations."

clude not only claims of private persons, in the two countries, upon one another, but also claims of individuals on the government of the foreign country, and claims—private and not political—of each government upon the other existing before the war.

§ 153.

5. The effect of a treaty on all grounds of complaint for which a war was undertaken, is to abandon them. Or, in other words, all peace implies *amnesty*, or oblivion of past subjects of dispute, whether the same is expressly mentioned in the terms of the treaty, or not. They cannot, in good faith, be revived again, although a *repetition* of the same acts may be a righteous ground of a new war. An abstract or general right, however, if passed over in a treaty, is not thereby waived.*

6. If nothing is said in a treaty to alter the state in which the war actually leaves the parties, the rule of *uti possidetis* is tacitly accepted. Thus, if a part of the national territory has passed into the hands of an enemy during war, and lies under his control at the peace or cessation of hostilities, it remains his, unless expressly ceded.

7. So, too, if a fortress or port is ceded by treaty, it must be ceded in the state in which the treaty finds it. Good faith requires that it should not be dismantled or blocked up after that event.

8. When a treaty cedes to a conqueror a part of the territory of a nation, the government is under no obligation to indemnify those who may suffer by the cession.† What the conqueror acquires in such a case is the sovereignty. The old laws continue until repealed by the proper authorities. Private rights remain, or ought to remain, unimpaired.

The question may be asked, whether the party making such a cession of inhabited territory is under any pledge to secure the new comer in possession. Or in other words, must the former do anything beyond renouncing his rights of sovereignty

* Comp. Klüber, § 324; Wheaton, IV. 4, § 3.

† Kent, I. 178, Lect. VIII.

over the territory, and leaving it free and open to the new sovereign. To us it appears that this is all he is bound to do. If, then, the inhabitants should resist and reject the new sovereign, as they have an undoubted right to do,—for who gave any state the right to dispose of its inhabitants,—the question now is to be settled between the province or territory and the conqueror. (Comp. § 52.)

§ 154.

A treaty of peace begins to bind the parties when it is signed (§ 107, § 149), and to bind individuals of the two belligerent nations when they are notified of its existence. (Comp. § 149.) Injuries done meanwhile must be made good by the state to which the person committing the injury belongs. But it is held that captures, made after a peace, but before the captor has become aware of it, subject him to a civil suit for damages, and that he must fall back on his government to save him harmless. It is also held that a capture, made before the time for the cessation of hostilities at a particular spot, but with a knowledge that the peace has been concluded, is unlawful, and must be restored; the reason for which rule is, that the limit of time is intended to cover hostile acts performed in ignorance of the new pacific relation.

CHAPTER II.

OF THE RELATIONS BETWEEN BELLIGERENTS AND NEUTRALS.

SECTION I.—*Of the Obligations and Rights of Neutral States.*

§ 155.

Doctrine of neutrality of modern growth.

THE rights of neutrals have grown up to be an important part of international law in modern times. The ancients put the rights of war foremost, and the neutral stood chiefly in the passive relation of non-interference. This was owing, in part, to the fact that a system of confederations united the states of antiquity together in war, so that few prominent powers stood aloof from the struggles in which their neighbors were engaged, and in part to the small importance of neutral interests. Things have put on a new shape with the growth of wide intercourse especially by sea, and with the spread of one code of public law over so many powerful states of the world, who, when they have stood aloof from war, have created for themselves rights, or secured the acknowledgment of existing ones. Now, when a war arises between two states, the interests of all neutrals are more affected than formerly; or, in other words, neutral power has increased more than war power, and the tendency is more and more towards such alterations of the code of war as will favor neutral commerce. A change evidently in the direction of peace and of Christian civilization.

The increasing importance of questions connected with neutrality is shown by the small space which Grotius gives to it, compared with his immense copiousness on many now minor questions. He devotes a short and trifling chapter to those who are "medii in bello" (III. 17), and a section to those who are not parties to a war, and yet supply aid to the combatants (III. 1, § 5.) This, if we are not deceived, is nearly the extent of his doctrine of neutrality. Take up now any of the leading publicists of the last hundred years, and you will find the chapters devoted to this doctrine second to few or none others in fulness and importance.

Neutrals, who?

A neutral state is one which sustains the relations of amity to both the belligerent parties, or negatively is a *non hostis*, as Bynkershoek has it, one which sides with neither party in a war.

Gradations of neutrality.

There are degrees of neutrality. *Strict* neutrality implies that a state stands entirely aloof from the operations of war, giving no assistance or countenance to either belligerent. *Imperfect* neutrality may be of two kinds: it may be *impartial*, inasmuch as *both* belligerents have equal liberty to pursue the operations of war, or certain operations, such as transit of troops, purchase of military stores, enlistments of soldiers or seamen, within the neutral's territory; or *qualified* by an anterior engagement to one of the parties, as by a covenant to furnish a contingent of troops, or to place a certain number of ships at his disposal. It is manifest that agreements like these partake of the nature of alliance. The other belligerent then is free to decide whether he will regard such a state as neutral or as an ally of his enemy. If the assistance to be rendered is trifling, and has no reference to a particular case or a war with a particular nation, it will probably be overlooked; otherwise it will expose the nation furnishing the assistance to the hostility of the other. Such was the agreement of Denmark, put into effect in 1788, in a war between Sweden and Russia, to furnish certain limited succors to the latter. Such, also, are the exclusive privileges, which may have been granted beforehand, of admitting the armed vessels and prizes of one of the belligerents into the neutral's ports.

Permanent neutrality?

A state may stipulate to observe perpetual neutrality towards some or all of its surrounding neighbors, on condition of having its own neutrality respected.

It thus strips itself of its own power of sovereignty, so far forth that it cannot declare war against any of these states except for the act of violating this neutrality. Such is the position of Switzerland,—including the provinces of Chablais and Faucigny and all the territory of Savoy, north of Ugine,*—and of Belgium, whose neutrality and inviolability of territory were formally recognized;—that of the first by the declaration of the allied powers, of March 20, 1815, which the federative authorities soon afterwards accepted, and that of the latter by the five great powers on its final treaty with Holland in 1831. The reasons for these arrangements were the welfare of the minor states before mentioned, and the preservation of the peace of Europe: Switzerland furnishes pathways for armies between France and Italy, and Belgium is interposed as a barrier between France and Germany. The free town of Cracow also enjoyed for a while a kind of guaranteed neutrality, before it lost its liberties in 1846.

Armed neutrality.

The position of the neutral gives rise to rights, which may be defended against attempted aggressions of a belligerent by armed forces, and several neutrals may unite for this purpose. This is called an armed neutrality, of which the two leagues of the Baltic powers in 1780 and 1800 furnish the most noted instances. But it may be doubted whether the term neutrality can be applied to leagues like this, which not only armed themselves for self-defence, but laid down principles of public law against the known maxims of one of the belligerents, which they were ready to make good by force. (§ 174, § 191.)

§ 156.

Obligations of neutrals.

In most wars nations are bound to be neutral, as having no vocation to judge in the disputes of other states, and as being already friends to both parties. The obligations must be fixed and known, in order to prevent the neutral from slipping into a position, to which war between his

* The neutrality of these Sardinian districts does not cease in consequence of their recent cession to France.

friends, if he do not keep his ground, must force him. "The enemies of our friends," says Bynkershoek (Quæst. J. P., I. 9), "are to be considered in a twofold light, as our friends and our friends' enemies. If you consider them as friends, we may rightfully aid and counsel them, and may supply them with auxiliary troops, arms, and other things which war has need of. But as far as they are our friend's enemies, it is not permitted to us to do this, for thus we should prefer one to the other in war, which equality in friendship,—a thing to be especially aimed at,—forbids. It is better to keep on friendly terms with both, than to favor one of the two in war, and thus tacitly renounce the other's friendship." The principles from which we start seem to be clear enough; at the same time, for the reason that neutrality is a thing of degrees, and that the practice of nations has been shifting, it is a little difficult to lay down with precision the law of nations in regard to it, as it is at present understood. That law seems to be tending towards strict neutrality.

Neutrals must be impartial.

A just war being undertaken to defend rights, each sovereignty must, as we have seen, decide for itself whether its war be just and expedient. It follows that powers not parties to the war must treat both belligerents alike as friends. Hence no privilege can be granted or withheld from one and not equally from the other. Thus, if transit, or the entrance into harbors of ships of war, for the purpose of refitting or of procuring military supplies, or the admission of captured prizes and their cargoes is allowed to the one belligerent, the other may claim it also. Otherwise a state aids one of its friends in acts of violence against another, which is unjust, or aids a friend in fighting against another party, which is to be an ally and not a neutral.

§ 157.

But impartiality is not enough.

But the rule of impartiality is not enough. The notion of neutrality, to say nothing of the convenience of the neutral and his liability to be drawn into the war, demands something more. It is not an amicable act, when I supply two of my friends with the means of doing injury, provided I do as much for one as for the other. Such a relation is not that of a *medius inter hostes*, but of an *impartial enemy*, of a *jack on both sides.* Moreover, it is impartiality in form only, when I give to two parties rights within my territories, which may be important for the one, and useless to the other. The United States in a war between Great Britain and Russia might allow both parties to enlist troops within its borders, but what would such a privilege be worth to Russia? And, indeed, almost every privilege conceded by neutrals would be apt to inure more to the benefit of one than of the other of two hostile nations. A rule of greater fairness would be to allow nothing to the belligerents, which either of them would object to, as being adverse to his interests; but this rule would be subjective, fluctuating, and probably impracticable. A rule, again, expressive of strict neutrality, would prohibit the neutral from rendering any service specially pertaining to war, or allowing his territory to be used for any military purpose by either belligerent. This, if we add the qualification, "unless engagements previous to the war concede some special assistance to one of the parties, which assistance is not of importance enough to convert a neutral into an ally," would nearly express what is the present law and usage of nations.

§ 158.

But it is necessary to descend to particulars. We shall consider, first, what duties neutrality does not preclude; secondly, what it binds the neutral not to do or allow; and then shall take up by themselves certain actions which are open to doubt.

Neutrals must be humane to both parties.

1. The neutral ought to discharge the duties of humanity to both belligerents, for these are still due even to an enemy, and are due to persons of no nationality. It is clear that a ship of war in distress may during war run into a neutral port, unless there is some special reason to prevent it. So asylum is allowed within neutral territory and waters to a defeated or fugitive belligerent force,

and the victor must stop his pursuit at the borders. The conditions, however, according to which refugees shall be received, are not absolutely settled. In the case of troops fleeing across the borders, justice requires that they shall be protected, not as bodies of soldiers with arms in their hands, but as individual subjects of a friendly state: they are, we believe, in practice generally disarmed, and supported in their place of shelter at the expense of their sovereign. The other course would be unfriendly, as protected soldiers might issue forth from a friend's territory all ready for battle; and would also tend to convert the neutral soil into a theatre of war. In the case of ships of war running into neutral waters in order to escape from an enemy, to demand that they shall either be disarmed, like fugitive troops, or return to the high seas, seems to be a harsh measure, and unauthorized by the usages of nations. An instance of such harshness occurred in the recent war between Schleswig-Holstein and Denmark. A small war-steamer, belonging to the former party, ran for safety, in July, 1850, into the waters of Lübeck, which was on friendly terms with both belligerents. The senate of Lübeck had given orders that vessels of war of either party, appearing within its jurisdiction, must lay down their arms, or depart beyond cannonshot from the coast. The lieutenant commanding the steamer chose the latter alternative. In justification of its conduct, which was impartial, Lübeck only plead that the neutral, in regard to the rules of hospitality, must consult its own interests, and that small states, in order to have their character for neutrality respected, must "observe in everything which relates to war itself the stricter rules of neutrality." They would receive, they said, vessels of the belligerent parties, only when escaping the perils of the seas, and then only whilst such perils lasted. The analogy from the practice of disarming fugitive troops does not hold here. If the ship is driven out at once, it goes where a superior force is waiting for it; if it remains disarmed, the expense and inconvenience are great.*

* Von Kaltenborn, author of the "Vorlaüfer des Hugo Grotius," published at Hamburg, in 1850, a brochure, entitled "Kriegsschiffe auf neutralem Gebiete," from

§ 159.

The same spirit of humanity, as well as respect for a friendly power, imposes on neutrals the duty of opening their ports to armed vessels of both belligerents, for purposes having no direct relation to the war, and equally likely to exist in time of peace. Cruisers may sail into neutral harbors for any of the purposes for which merchant vessels of either party frequent the same places, except that merchant vessels are suffered to take military stores on board, which is forbidden generally, and ought to be forbidden to ships of war.

May admit vessels of war of the belligerents.

2. The general practice of nations, dictated perhaps by comity, has hitherto permitted cruisers to bring their prizes into neutral ports. We have already seen that this is not obligatory on neutrals, and sound policy demands that it be prohibited.*

§ 160.

On the other hand, it is a violation of neutrality for a neutral state to lend money, or supply troops (with the exception already mentioned), or open harbors for hostile enterprises; or to allow the presence of any individual or any vessel pertaining to a belligerent state within his territory, when believed to be stationed there for the purpose of carrying out a hostile undertaking; or to suffer its subjects to prepare, or to aid in preparing or augmenting any hostile expedition against a friendly power, as for instance to build, arm, or man ships of war with such a purpose in view, or to build them with this intent so far, as to make them ready for an armament to be put on board upon the high seas or in some neutral port. Nor can he allow his courts to be employed in deciding upon the validity of captures made by belligerent vessels.

What neutrals may not do.

which these facts are drawn; and which, while occupied with an examination of this particular case, contains an excellent summary of the rights and duties of neutrals on their own territories.

* That is, captures in war ought to be attended with so many inconveniences as to check the spirit of plunder.

Nor, again, can he during a war be the acquirer by purchase or otherwise of any conquest made by either of the parties without deserting his unbiassed neutral position.

If a neutral power violates its obligations in these respects or winks at hostile proceedings, such conduct may afford ground even for war. If it is careless in not preventing damage to a friend from the undertakings of its subjects, it is liable for the loss thence resulting. (§ 163.) Nor can it plead the inefficiency of its laws, or want of sufficient law, for all nations are bound to enforce the law of nations, within their own limits. (§ 29, 207.) It ought to be said, however, that the base arts of merchants and shipbuilders will often prevent governments from obtaining due evidence of the existence of such hostile designs; and that the distinction between what is merely contraband of war,—as a ship of war made for sale, if that be a fair instance,—and that which is a hostile expedition, is sometimes so nice, that the present law of nations, and municipal law enforcing it, must allow many wrongs done to neutrals to slip through their fingers. Might not something be gained, if, during wars between friendly states, builders and armers of vessels were required by neutral governments to give security to double the value that these were not intended to be used in hostile expeditions? * (Comp. § 178, note.)

Cases doubtful or disputed. Passage of troops.

It was formerly thought that the neutral might allow the transit of belligerent troops through his territory, the passage of ships engaged in the service of war through his waters, and the preparation of hostile expeditions in his harbors, if he granted the same to both sides. All now admit that the neutral may refuse any of these privileges, and must be the sole judge in the case, although Vattel inclines to think that innocent transit in extreme cases may even be carried through with force.† Many publicists still

* For the conduct of our government in preventing hostile expeditions, and in making reparations for wrongs committed by them, when they had had their origin in our ports, see a pamphlet entitled "English Neutrality," by G. P. Lowrey, New York, 1863.

† Vattel, III. 7, §§ 119–135.

view the allowance of transit as reconcilable with the notion of neutrality, and a number of treaties have expressly granted it to certain states. Heffter, who held this view in his first edition, has in the third (§ 147) justly taken the opposite side. His reasons for his later opinion against allowing transit are, that for the most part an actual gain accrues from it to one party, and that it will rarely happen that both can avail themselves of it during a war, with equal advantage. (Comp. § 157.)

§ 161.

The neutral furnishing troops.

The practice of neutrals to furnish troops to belligerents, or to allow them to enlist troops on neutral ground, was formerly common and allowed.* Thus six thousand Scotchmen joined the army of Gustavus Adolphus. The Swiss, like the Arcadians of old, for centuries furnished troops to many foreign sovereigns, not without detriment to the national character, as Zwingli and other patriots have felt, and still in recent times they have hired out soldiers to some of the Italian states. Several old treaties gave France the preference over other nations in levying Swiss troops, and that of 1521 allowed her to enlist a number not exceeding 1,600, who could not be recalled by the authorities at home so long as France was at war. A treaty of this kind was made as late as 1803. Heffter thinks, however, that since the neutrality of 1815, they would not be justified in agreeing to furnish troops to one European power against another after the outbreak of a war. Many treaties made in the last three centuries have renounced the power thus to furnish troops, or have put an end to foreign enlistment, while a number of an opposite import have permitted the one or the other. By the treaty of Münster in 1648—we quote the words of Mr. Manning (p. 174), "it was agreed that none of the contracting parties should afford to the enemies of the other arms, money, soldiers, provisions, harbor or passage, the right being however reserved to the individual states of the empire to serve as mercenaries according to the constitutions of the Empire." This custom has now a linger-

* See Manning, Book III. 1. p. 166–181.

ing existence: it is forbidden in some countries by law, and is justly regarded as a violation of neutrality.

§ 162.

What may a neutral's subjects do?

International law does not require of the neutral sovereign that he should keep the citizen or subject within the same strict lines of neutrality, which he is bound to draw for himself. The private person, if the laws of his own state or some special treaty does not forbid, can lend money to the enemy of a state at peace with his own country for purposes of war, or can enter into its service as a soldier, without involving the government of his country in guilt. The English courts, however, and our own deny that any right of action can arise out of such a loan, on the ground that it is contrary to the law of nations. (Phillimore, III. § 151, case of Kennett v. Chambers, 14 Howard, U. S. Rep., 38.) The practice of individuals belonging to a neutral nation serving in foreign wars * was formerly widely diffused and admitted throughout Europe, and is not of easy prevention, if prohibited, for at the worst the individual may renounce his country. It is only when a great pressure into the armies of one of the belligerents is on foot, that the neutral can be called on to interfere. In the case of private armed vessels the usage is different. It is now regarded as a breach of neutrality to allow a subject to accept letters of marque and equip armed vessels, in order to prey on the commerce of a belligerent friend; although it would be impossible, as on the land, to prevent individuals from going abroad for this purpose.

§ 163.

Rights of neutrals.

Neutrals have a right, 1. To insist that their territory shall be inviolate and untouched by the operations of war, and their rights of sovereignty uninvaded. And if violations of their rights are committed, they have a

* Sometimes neutrals have even sent military officers to countries where war was waging, that they might learn the art of war. To send an experienced general on such an occasion, or to exempt him from penalties for accepting service abroad, would come nigh to giving assistance to one of the parties. (Hautefeuille, I. 258, ed. 2.)

right to punish the offender on account of them, or to demand satisfaction from his government. They are in a manner bound to do this, because otherwise their neutrality is of no avail, and one of the belligerents enjoys the privilege of impunity.

Case of the Caroline.

In 1837, the Caroline, a steamboat employed by Canadian insurgents in carrying passengers and munitions of war from our borders to the opposite shore, was captured and destroyed within our waters,—the leader of the expedition against it having expected to find it within British territory. In the correspondence between the governments to which this act gave rise, Mr. Webster said that such a violation of neutrality could be justified only by a "necessity of self-defence, instant, overwhelming, having no choice of means, and no moment of deliberation." Lord Ashburton contended that this was just such a case of necessity, but regretted that some explanation and apology for the occurrence was not immediately made. And so the matter ended.

No cruiser is authorized to chase a vessel within or across neutral waters, and all captures so made, or made in violation of the neutral laws for maintaining neutrality, must be regarded as illegal with respect to the neutral, although not illegal with respect to the enemy.* If such a prize is brought into any of the neutral's ports, he is authorized to seize and restore it. If it be carried into a port of another country, he has a right to demand its restoration, and the prize court of the belligerent is bound to respect the objection. If the neutral fails to exercise his rights in these respects, the government of the cruiser which has been thus captured may complain or even retaliate. The vessel committing the violation of neutrality may be seized, either within the waters of the neutral, or after pursuit on the high seas, and, when captured, may be tried before the proper court for the offence. Or its government, if the neutral prefer, or is forced to take that mode of redress, may be required to give satisfaction in regard to the injury

* Comp. Wildman, II. 147.

§ 164.

2. Neutrals can claim from the belligerents, during war, all that respect for their flag, for their representatives, for their property, and the property of their citizens or subjects, when employed in the lawful operations of war, to which they have a right during peace. To preclude the ambassadors of the neutral from egress and ingress into enemy's territory is unfriendly, although the enemy's envoys to the neutral may be seized except on neutral soil or ships. (§ 93.) The property of neutrals has sometimes been wrongfully seized for government purposes in cases where necessity was plead for so doing, but not without the prospect held out of compensation. And this, which Louis XIV. is said to have pronounced to be a right, has been extended to their seamen. The right of preemption in war will be considered in another place. And the restrictions on neutral trade will be the subject of a separate chapter.

§ 165.

Municipal laws enforcing neutrality.

Every nation is bound to pass laws whereby the territory and other rights of neutrals shall be secured, and has a right to secure itself in the same manner. Nor is there any deficiency of such laws in Christendom. Thus Great Britain, by an act passed in 1819, forbade British subjects to enter the service of foreign states under penalty of fine and imprisonment, although such an act of individuals, as we have seen, is not a violation of neutrality. The United States by various acts, as by those passed in 1794, 1818, and 1838, have endeavored to prevent injuries to neutral and friendly powers, as well as violations of our own rights, whether by citizens or foreigners. Thus (1.) it is made a misdemeanor for a citizen to accept or exercise within our territory a commission from a foreign power in a war against a state at peace with us. (2.) It is unlawful for any one to enlist, or induce another person within our borders to enlist, or engage him to go abroad to enlist in foreign service against a friendly power; or to institute within our territory any military expedition by land or sea, against any such power; or to augment the force of any vessel having such hostile intent; and the vessels engaged in such an enterprise by sea are subject to forfeiture. (3.) No belligerent vessels are allowed to provide themselves with military stores, or with anything not equally applicable to commerce and to war. When vessels of the two belligerents are in our harbors together, they are forbidden to depart within twenty-four hours of one another. And the President is empowered to use force to send out of the waters of the United States such vessels as ought not to remain within our limits, as well as to compel the observance of our neutrality laws in general.* In short our laws are not bad. May no administration or officials ever make a purposely ineffectual display of maintaining these laws, and connive at their violation in secret!

§ 166.

Case of the British ambassador in 1856.

During the late Crimean war it came to light that certain British consuls were persuading persons within our bounds to go out of the United States in order to enlist in that service, and that the minister at Washington was aiding therein. It could not be complained of, if the United States government showed displeasure at such proceedings, demanded his removal, and even ceased to hold communication with him as the agent of the British government. In what, now, did his offence consist, in a breach of our law only or in a violation of international law? In answer it may be said, that if the earlier usage is to decide, there was no direct breach of international law; if the more modern, there was a breach. But supposing this to be doubtful, in breaking our laws of neutrality, which have the peculiar character of supporting the laws of nations, and that too when he was the representative of another sovereignty, he attacked the sover-

* Kent, I. 122, 123, Lect. VI., whom I have used in this summary of our neutrality laws. For captures made by ships that have committed a breach of our neutrality laws, comp. § 163. Illegal augmentation of force affects captures made on the cruise for which the augmentation took place, but not afterward. (7 Wheaton Rep. 348.)

ereignty of the nation and in this way came in conflict with law international, which aims to secure the sovereignty of all the nations who acknowledge it. And even if our law could have been evaded by inducing men to go abroad for another object, and there persuading them to enlist in a war against one of our friends, there would still have remained ground of complaint against the agents in such a scheme, as disturbers of our relations with a friendly power.

§ 166 *b*.

Relation of neutrals to the parties in an internal war.

A foreign power, as we have seen (§ 40, § 41), may assist a state to repress a rebellion, but may not assist revolters themselves, but, when these have fairly created a new government, may enter into relations with it, without unfriendliness towards the original state. Meanwhile, until the fact of a new state is decided by the issue of the struggle, the position of neutrals is a delicate one, and one to which little attention has been paid by writers on the law of nations. *Theoretically* we say, (1.) The relation, if the foreign power stands aloof, is not that of neutrality between states, but of neutrality between parties *one of which is a state, and the other trying to become a state.*

(2.) The foreign power, therefore, cannot plead the laws of neutrality, for treating both parties alike, for the one is an acknowledged state, the other is not. Thus whatever favors it has granted to the cruisers of the friendly state it is not bound to grant to the revolters, or rather, it is bound not to grant to them the same privileges, for by so doing, it admits their right to prey on the commerce of its friend,—which only states can do.

(3.) In a certain sense the foreign power must regard the revolters as belligerents, entitled to all those rights which humanity demands, as that of asylum for troops or vessels in distress, or fleeing from a superior power,—the same sorts of rights which would be granted to political exiles. The vessels of such revolters cannot be regarded as piratical, for their motive is to establish a new state, while that of pirates is plunder. A pirate never ends his war with mankind, they fight for peace.

(4.) What measures can the state at war with a part of its subjects take in regard to foreign trade with revolted ports? To say that it cannot apply the rules of blockade, contraband and search, because the ports are *its own*, is mere pettifogging. But can it close these ports by an act of the government, as it once opened them? At first view it seems hard to refuse this right to a nation, but the better opinion is that foreigners, by having certain avenues of trade open to them, have thereby acquired rights. (§ 28.) The nation at war within itself must overcome force by force, but this method of closing ports supersedes war by a stroke of the pen. It is the fact of obstruction in the ordinary channels of trade which foreign nations must respect. If the state in question cannot begin and continue this fact, it must suffer for its weakness.

But international law does not make all these distinctions. The colonies of Spain, as yet unrecognized, were regarded by us as "belligerent *nations*, having, so far as concerns us, the sovereign rights of war, and entitled to be respected in the exercise of those rights?" And so England and France act in the war which is now upon us. (7 Wheaton Rep. 337.)

Section II.—*Of the Rights and Liabilities of Neutral Trade.*

§ 167.

Importance of question touching rights of neutral trade.

Having considered the relations between belligerent and neutral *states*, we now proceed to inquire how war affects the commerce of neutral *persons*, or the rights and liabilities of neutral trade. This is a subject of greater practical importance, perhaps, than any other in international law; for if the rule restricting the freedom of neutral trade verges to the extreme of strictness, the evils of war are very much increased, and its non-intercourse is spread over a wider field. It is also a subject in which the jarring views of belligerents and of neutrals have hitherto prevented fixed principles on many points from being reached, so that neither have different nations agreed in their views, nor has the same nation at different times been consistent, nor have text-writers advocated the same doctrines. Yet the history of opinion and practice will lead us to the cheering conclusion that neutral rights on the sea have been by degrees gaining, and to the hope that hereafter they will be still more under the protection of international law than at any time past.

§ 168.

Who are neutrals and what is neutral property.

The nationality of individuals in war depends not on their origin or their naturalization, but upon their domicil. He is a neutral who is domiciled of free choice in a neutral country, and he an enemy who is domiciled in an enemy's country. Hence

1. As domicil can be easily shaken off, a person in the prospect of war, or on its breaking out, may withdraw from the enemy's to another country with the intention of staying there, and thus change his domicil. If he should return to his native country, fewer circumstances would be required to make out intention than if he betook himself to a foreign territory. If against his will and by violence at the breaking out of war he was detained in the belligerent country, his longer stay would be regarded as the forced residence of a stranger, and probably all disadvantageous legal consequences of his domicil there would cease.

2. If a country is conquered during a war, its national character changes, although it may be restored again at peace, and so the nationality and liabilities of its inhabitants engaged in business change.

3. But a person having a house of commerce in the enemy's country, although actually resident in a neutral country, is treated as an enemy so far forth as that part of his business is concerned, or is domiciled there *quo ad hoc*. On the other hand, a person having a house of commerce in a neutral country and domiciled among the enemy, is not held to be a neu-

tral. This is the doctrine of the English courts, adopted by the American. "It is impossible," says Dr. Wheaton (El. IV. 1, § 20), "in this not to see strong marks of the partiality towards the interests of captors, which is perhaps inseparable from a prize code, framed by judicial legislation in a belligerent country, and adopted to encourage its naval exertions."

In general property follows the character of its owner. Thus neutral ships are ships owned by neutrals, that is by persons domiciled in a neutral country, and the same is true of goods. Hence in partnerships, if one owner is a neutral and the other an enemy, only the property of the latter is liable to capture. But here we need to notice, 1. That ships cannot easily transfer their nationality on a voyage, the act of so doing being presumptive evidence of a fraudulent intention to screen them from the liabilities of their former nationality.

2. That when a ship sails under a hostile flag, she has, by whomsoever owned, a hostile character.

3. If a neutral's ship sails under an enemy's license to trade, she becomes hostile; for why should she have the advantages of a close connection with the enemy without the disadvantages?

4. If a neutral is the owner of soil in a hostile country, the produce of such soil, exported by him and captured, is considered hostile. This is on the principle that the owner of soil identifies himself, so far forth, with the interests of the country where his estate lies.*

§ 169 *a*.

General principles as to liability to capture.

When a war arises, one of three things must take place. Either the neutral trade may go on as before, and belligerents have no right whatever to injure or limit it in any manner; or the belligerents may, each of them, interdict any and all trade of neutrals with the other; or there are certain restrictions which may be imposed on neutral trade with justice, and certain other restrictions, which must be pronounced unjust.

1. Few have contended that the trade of neutrals ought to

* Comp. Wheaton, El. IV. 1, §§ 17–22; Kent, I. 74, Lect. IV.

be entirely unfettered, for a part of that trade may consist in supplying one foe with the means of injuring the other, and the siege or blockade of strong places would be nugatory, if neutrals could not be prevented from passing the lines with provisions. Will it be said that such trade is impartial,—that it favors one party in a war no more than the other? It would be better to say that it is partial now to one side and now to the other, and that a series of assistances, rendered to a party in a struggle, although they might balance one another,—which would not generally be true in fact,—are unjust, because they only put off or render fruitless the effort to obtain redress, with which the war began.

2. On the other hand it will not be claimed that a belligerent may justly forbid neutrals to carry on every kind of trade with his enemy. I may have a right to distress my foe in order to bring him to a right mind and procure redress, but what right have I to distress my friend, except so far as he takes the part of my foe, and thus ceases to be my friend. Will it be said that all trade with one foe is a damage to the other, and may therefore be broken up? No doubt it is indirectly an injury, but indirect results of lawful business no more justify interference, than the advance of one nation in wealth and industry justifies others in endeavoring to cripple its resources. The neutral might with as much *justice* declare war, because the belligerent injured him by a fair operation of war,—by blockading the port of his foe for instance,—as a party to a war require that all trade should bend to his convenience. And besides this, the same *humanity* which allows internal trade to remain undisturbed during an invasion, ought to leave the neutral's commerce in some degree free to take its wonted course.

3. It is therefore allowed on all hands that some restrictions may be imposed on neutral trade, not such as a belligerent may select, but definite and of general application. The law of nations on this subject has been viewed as a kind of compromise between neutral and belligerent right. Neutrals may legitimately carry on all sorts of trade, and belligerents may inter-

rupt all. Hence nations have waived their rights and come to a certain middle ground, where some rights of both parties are saved and some thrown overboard. But this view seems to be objectionable, as making the actual neutral rights to arise out of a state of things which is a jural impossibility. It cannot at the same time be true that neutrals should enjoy a particular trade, and belligerents obstruct that trade. There must be kinds of trade which neutrals have a right to engage in, and herein belligerents are obliged to leave them undisturbed. Otherwise the law of nations has no jural foundation.

When we ask, however, what degree of restriction may be justly applied to neutral trade, we feel a want of a definite principle to guide us in the answer: we are forced to say somewhat vaguely that the restrictions must be *such* as to keep neutral trade from directly assisting either party in the armed contest, and the *smallest possible*, consistent with the ends which a just war involves.

If these views are correct, it is wrong for the neutral and for his subjects to engage in certain kinds of trade during a war, as truly as it is right for him to engage in certain others. If, for instance, he holds the same doctrine with the belligerent in regard to contraband of war, he would violate the rights of one friend by supplying another with such articles. And yet we by no means affirm that it is the duty of the neutral nation to prevent such trade on the part of individuals by vigilance and penalty. All that can be required of him is, especially when his opinions on the justice of the war may vary greatly from those of his belligerent friend, that he should be passive, while one friend tries to obtain what he calls redress from another. The rules of war are to be put in force by the parties immediately concerned: he is not under obligation to add to his trouble and expense by a new commercial police.

The restrictions on neutral trade known to international law have related for the most part

1. To the conveyance of hostile goods in neutral ships, and of neutral goods in hostile ships, or to the relation between goods and vessels having different nationalities;

2. To the conveyance of certain kinds of articles, having a special relation to war;

3. To conveyance to certain places specially affected by the operations of war; and sometimes

4. To a trade closed before a war, but open during its continuance.

And in order to carry those restrictions into effect, a right of examination or visit must be exercised upon vessel, goods, or both.

§ 169 *b*.

We now proceed to the rules of international law, in regard to the liability to captures of ships and goods engaged in ordinary trade.

Nationality of goods and vessel as making them liable or not liable to capture.

We may say, in general, that until very recent times two rules have contended with one another, —the rule that *the nationality of property on the sea determines its liability to capture*, or neutral property is safe on the sea and enemy's property may be taken wherever found, and the rule that *the nationality of the vessel determines the liability to capture*, or that the flag covers the cargo. By the first rule the neutral might safely put his goods into any vessel which offered itself, but could not convey the goods of his friend, being one of the belligerents, without the risk of their being taken by the other. By the second, when once the nationality of the ship was ascertained to be neutral, it went on its way with its goods in safety, but if it belonged to the enemy it exposed neutral goods on board, as well as other, to be taken. This latter rule consists of two parts, that free ships make free goods, and that enemy's ships make goods hostile, but the two are not necessarily, although parts of the same principle, connected in practice; the former may be received without the latter.

It was a thing of secondary importance both for the neutral and for a belligerent, being a naval power, how the rules should shape themselves in regard to the neutral's goods in hostile bottoms. And his own goods on board his own vessel were freely admitted to be safe. Hence justice and a spirit of concession to the neutral united in favor of the rule that *his goods were safe, by whatever vessel conveyed;* although not safe from sundry inconveniences,—from search and from capture of the hostile conveyance.

On the other hand, it was of great importance to the belligerent that the flag should not cover his enemy's goods, or that free ships should not make goods free; for thus, much of his power at sea to plunder or annoy his enemy would be taken away. To the neutral the opposite rule, that free ships should make goods free, was of great importance; for the carrying trade, a part of which war would in other ways throw into his hands, would thus be vastly augmented. But the belligerent's interests on the whole prevailed. The nations, especially Great Britain, which had the greatest amount of commerce, had also the greatest naval force, with which they could protect themselves and plunder their foes, and therefore felt small need in war of hiding their goods in the holds of neutral ships. Thus for a long time the prevailing rule was, that *neutral goods are safe under any flag*, and *enemy's goods unsafe under any flag* But at length neutral interests and the interests of peace preponderated; and the parties to the treaty of Paris in 1856, Great Britain among the rest, adopted for themselves the rule which will be valid in all future wars, and is likely to be universal, that free ships are to make goods free. Likely to be universal, we say, unless a broader rule shall exempt all private property on the sea engaged in lawful trade from capture.

§ 170.

Treatment of vessels conveying hostile goods.

The ship of a neutral in which hostile goods are found, has been sometimes, particularly by French and Spanish ordinances, treated as if engaged in a guilty business, and visited with confiscation. But modern practice, whilst it seized the enemy's goods, has been in favor of paying freight to such neutral, that is, *not* freight *for the part* of the voyage performed, *but for the whole*, capture of the goods being regarded as equivalent to delivery. But a neutral ship engaged in the enemy's coasting trade cannot claim freight for hostile goods on board, because it has put itself into the position of a hostile vessel.*

Freight on neutral goods in captured enemy's vessels.

On the other hand, when a hostile vessel is taken with the neutral's property on board, the captor is entitled to freight, if the goods are carried to their port of destination. But if "the goods are not carried to their original destination within the intention of the contracting parties, no freight is due." †

Coast-fisheries of foes protected in war by some nations.

Hostile ships, with whatever goods on board, have been uniformly regarded as prizes of war. But from the operations of war one class of vessels, engaged in an eminently pacific employment, and of no great account in regard to national resources, has often been exempted; we refer to vessels engaged in coast-fisheries. It appears that this exemption was allowed centuries ago. Froissart is cited as saying in his Chronicle that "fishermen on the sea, whatever war there be in France and England, do no harm to one another: nay, rather, they are friends and aid one another in case of need." The liberty of the enemy's fishermen in war has been protected by many French ordinances, and the English observed a reciprocal indulgence; but in 1798, during the French revolution, the latter government ordered its cruisers to seize French and Dutch fishermen and their smacks. Soon after, on remonstrance from the first consul of France, the order was withdrawn, as far as the coast-fisheries in the strict sense were concerned; and during the wars of the empire, this peaceful and hardy class of laborers enjoyed exemption from capture. In the instructions given by the French minister of marine to naval officers in 1854, at the outbreak of the late war with Russia, we find the same rule followed. "You must put no hindrance," say the instructions, "in the way of the coast-fishery even on the coasts of the enemy, but you will be on your guard that this favor, dictated by an interest of humanity, draws with it no abuse prejudicial to military or maritime operations. If you are employed in the waters of the White sea, you will allow to continue without interruption

* Comp. Wildman, II. 154.

† Id. II. 162.

(repression in case of abuse excepted) the exchange of fresh fish, provisions, utensils and tackling, which is carried on habitually between the peasants of the Russian coasts of the province of Archangel and the fishermen of the coasts of Norwegian Finmark." Such has been the practice of some of the principal Christian nations in protecting the coast-fisheries of enemies, but as yet this usage cannot be called a part of international law.*

§ 171.

Justice of the rules respecting neutral trade considered.

Having seen what is the actual state of international law in regard to neutral trade, we may now inquire whether any definite rule of justice applicable to such trade can be laid down.

Admitting for the present that capture of private property on the sea is justifiable, we ask which of the two principles is comformable to justice, that which makes capture depend on the nationality of the conveyance, or that which makes it depend on the nationality of the property, whether ship or goods? Here we find

1. That the conveyance or vessel has been claimed to be territory, from which it would follow that, by interfering with neutral vessels, the sovereignty of neutral nations was invaded. But the claim is false, as has already been shown (§ 54), and seems to have been devised just to cover this particular case, just to screen neutral ships. It is not a claim admitted in the law of nations: ships are liable to search on the ocean, and are under the jurisdiction of the nation in whose ports they lie, to neither of which liabilities territory is exposed. How can the sea itself be the territory of no one, and a vehicle moving over it have the properties of *terra firma?* A deserted ship is not claimed to be territory. A ship with a crew on board is under the protection and jurisdiction of its country, where no other jurisdiction interferes; that is, may have certain properties of territory, but not all properties. On the other hand, if ships were territory, it is clear that all the operations of war which

* Comp. Ortolan, II. 44.

affect neutral vessels must be given up, blockade and the prevention of contraband trade, as much as any other.

2. It seems to be in accordance with justice, that the nationality of the property should determine the rules of capture. The only ground for taking certain things away from private persons is, that they belong to the enemy, or that they aid the enemy's operations in war. If they are taken because they belong to the enemy, vessels and goods ought to share the same fate: they are equally private property, and differ in no essential respect. If they are exempt from capture because they belong to neutrals, ships, and goods on board any ship ought to be exempt. The rule thus is just, clear, and logical.

3. The neutral has certainly a right to take his friend's goods on board his ship, and an equal right to put his own on board his friend's ship; nor will the fact that this friend has an enemy alter the case. Here the war-right of this enemy may subject him to great inconvenience, but neither his property nor his wages, in the shape of freight, ought to be taken from him. He is not guilty: why should he suffer other than those incidental evils which war brings with it, and a part of which are inevitable?

4. The establishment of the rule that free ships make goods free, is a gain for humanity and a waiver of justice. Hence we hail it as inaugurating an era more favorable to peace. All this on the admission that private property may rightfully be taken on the ocean: if it cannot be, or it is expedient that it should not be, the same rule is a movement in the right direction.*

* Mr. Reddie (in his Researches in maritime international law, I. p. 468, cited by Ortolan, for I have not access to the work), remarks that it is doubtful whether the neutral gains anything by the rule, "free ships, free goods." For the carrying trade of hostile property must come to an end, as soon as peace is made, and the neutral's capital must then be turned into another channel. But if the belligerent's property be liable to seizure, goods as well as ship will belong to the neutral, and his capital thus invested will stimulate all branches of home industry, and probably be longer able to retain the channel which was opened to it by the war. There is something in this, but most wars are too short to keep the powers at war from returning to their old usages of trade at the peace. Besides, the annoyance of the neutral is a very great evil, and his loss may be great.

§ 172.

In the course of the centuries during which international law has been growing up, rules have been fluctuating as it respects the liabilities of neutral trade, and conventional law has often run counter to prevailing rules. We propose here to give some brief historical illustrations of the former law and practice.

Former practice in regard to neutral trade.

First, the leading results of a historical examination seem to be something like the following:

1. That of old in mediæval Europe there probably was a feeling that neutral trade might be made unlawful by either belligerent at any time, and that the permission of such trade was looked upon as a concession. This explains the custom of confiscating the neutral ship with hostile goods on board, which was more or less prevalent.

2. That from the time when commerce by sea began to be a great interest, neutrals could carry hostile goods on their ships with the liability of only such goods to capture, and generally without risk to the vessel, save of detention, search, and change of course; and could put their own goods on hostile ships without danger of confiscation.

3. That treaties and ordinances during the 17th and 18th centuries often modified what may be called the prevailing usage, and differed so much from one another, as to show that no principle ran through them. Many of the treaties gave large freedom to neutral carriers, and some ordinances, especially in France and Spain, established a very harsh rule towards them. In general, where by treaty free ships made goods free, this was coupled with the rule, that hostile ships made goods hostile, or the nationality of the vessel determined the character of the transaction.

4. That from the last quarter of the 18th century neutral nations endeavored to force on the world the rule, "free ships, free goods," which was resisted, and prevented from entering into the law of nations by Great Britain, the leading maritime power.

5. That since the peace of 1815, in Europe, the importance of pacific relations and the power of capital have brought about a change of views in regard to international policy, until the rule above mentioned has nearly prevailed, and there are not wanting indications of a still larger liberty of maritime commerce.

§ 173.

Historical illustrations.

One of the earliest provisions of mediæval Europe within our knowledge, is to be found in a treaty between Arles and Pisa, of the year 1221. It is there provided, that in case any goods of Genoese or other public enemies of Pisa are found in a ship with men of Arles, the men of Arles shall not make them their own, or defend them on their own account; and that during the continuance of the war between Pisa and Genoa, it may be lawful for the Pisans to treat men of Arles, if found on Genoese vessels, and their goods, as if Genoese, and to retain such goods when taken without restoring them, or causing them to be restored.*

Consolato del mare.

This, however, may have been a temporary and exceptional convention between the two cities. But a little later, at the end of the 13th or beginning of the 14th century, we meet with a code of wide influence, the *Consolato del mare* (comp. App. I.) which is remarkable, as being the only ancient sea-code that speaks of neutral rights in war. In chapter 231 of this code (Pardessus, II. 303–307), it is provided, that if a ship that is captured belongs to friends, and the merchandise on board to enemies, the commander of the cruiser may force the master of the captured vessel to bring him the hostile goods, and even to keep them in his own vessel, until

* Pardessus, Collection des lois mar. II. 303, refers to this treaty, which is to be found in Muratori's Antiq. Ital. IV. Col. 398, as illustrating the usage that the merchandise of a friend, although put on board an enemy's vessel, ought to be respected. But it shows just the contrary. The text of the latter part is "si forte aliquis Arelatensis cum Januensi, donec guerra inter Pisanos et Januenses fuerit, a Pisanis inventus fuerit, in eorum navibus, eundo vel redeundo, liceat Pisanis . . . Arelatensibus [that is, Arelatenses] et res eorum tamquam Januensium offendere et capere, et capta retinere, et non reddere nec reddi facere."

it is brought into a place of safety; but it is to be understood that the captured ship be carried in tow to a place where there shall be no fear of enemies,—the commander of the cruiser paying, however, all the freight due for carrying the cargo to the place of unloading, etc.

Another provision of the same chapter is to the effect that, if the ship taken be hostile with a cargo belonging to friends on board, the merchants in the ship, and to whom the cargo in whole or in part pertains, ought to arrange with the captain of the captor to ransom the prize, and that he ought to offer it to them at a reasonable price. But if the merchants will not make a bargain, he is to have the right to send it into the port where his vessel was equipped, (?) and the merchants are obliged to pay the freight,—just as if he conveyed the goods to the port of destination,—and nothing more than that freight. The code then goes on to speak of injuries suffered by the neutral merchants from the arrogance or violence of the captor, in which case, besides being relieved from paying freight, they shall receive compensation.*

According to Mr. Manning, all the treaties before the 17th century coincide with the *Consolato del mare*, in regard to the liability to capture of enemies' goods on board neutral vessels. In 1417, an engagement between Henry V. of England and the Duke of Burgundy (*Jean-sans-peur*), contained the stipulation that goods of Flemings, who were the duke's subjects, on board ships of Genoa, then at war with England, should be forfeited, if captured, as lawful prize. "This is the only instance I have met with," says Mr. Manning, "in which the claim, that neutral goods found in an enemy's ship are liable to capture as lawful prize, has ever been asserted or even been specified by this country, unless in return for the stipulation that enemies' goods are free in a neutral ship."

* Mr. Manning cites this as chap. 273, others as chap 276.—In the remainder of these historical illustrations, and in those pertaining to contraband, blockade, and search, I have been greatly assisted by Mr. Manning's work.

§ 174.

In the 17th century, and onward, until toward the end of the 18th, no general rule runs through conventional law: the same states are found to make treaties of directly opposite character at the same epoch. The Dutch, being the principal carriers of Europe, aimed to put their trade on a footing of security; and the first treaty between Christian powers containing the principle, "free ships, free goods," was one between the United Provinces and Spain in 1650. We say between Christian powers, because a treaty of France with the Porte, in 1604, contained the same provision. In 1654 England, in a treaty with Portugal, for the first time agreed that the ship should cover the cargo; while in a treaty of the same year with the Dutch republic, the old rule touching the liabilities of hostile goods continued. Again, in the treaty of Breda, made by these same two powers, in 1667, free ships make free goods for the first time in their diplomatic intercourse, while a treaty of England with Denmark makes no change in the old usage. By the treaty of the Pyrenees, in 1659, renewed in 1668, France and Spain agreed that the cargo should follow the liabilities of the ship, whether neutral or hostile, of which rule the Dutch secured the benefit in their intercourse with these two states in 1661. Many treaties of the close of Century XVII. enlarge the privileges of neutrals, as that of Nymwegen in 1678, and of Ryswick in 1697, as far as France and the Dutch were concerned. In the commercial treaties connected with the peace of Utrecht in 1713,* the analogy of the peace of the Pyrenees was followed, in making all goods in neutral bottoms free, and in hostile liable to capture. A similar stipulation appears afterwards in a treaty of 1762, between Russia and Sweden, and in that of France with the United States, when she acknowledged their independence, in 1778. Thus, while earlier usage and many treaties protected neutral property, wherever found, but not enemies' property, many important treaties of the century before 1780, gave freedom to the neutral ship and to whatever it contained, but not to neutral goods on an enemy's vessel.

* See Dumont, VIII. 1, p. 348, Arts. XVII., XVIII.

The law of France, meanwhile, followed by that of Spain, was severe towards neutrals with whom no treaty existed. The edict of Henry III., given out in 1584, formally confiscates neutral goods on enemies' vessels, as well as enemies' on neutral vessels. The maritime ordinance of Louis XIV., framed in 1681, went farther still. It contains the following article: "All ships laden with the goods of our enemies, and the merchandise of our subjects or allies found in an enemy's vessel, shall be lawful prize." By allies here, not allies in war, but neutrals were aimed at, as it appears by an *arrêt* made a few years afterward. Things continued thus until in 1744, under Louis XV., a regulation freed neutral *ships* from the infection of the hostile cargo, but the same enactment ordained that neutral goods, the growth or fabric of enemies, should be confiscated. Again, in 1778, under Louis XVI., a regulation contained an implied sanction of the maxim, that the neutral flag covers the cargo, coupling it, however, like the treaty of the Pyrenees and others, with the opposite, that the hostile flag exposes the cargo; and these maxims have governed the conduct of France towards neutrals since then until recent times, with the exception of her retaliatory measures under Napoleon towards England, the effects of which fell heavily on neutrals. Spain, in 1702 and 1718, followed the legislation of the elder Bourbon line, and in 1779 adopted the relaxation proclaimed in France the year before.*

First armed neutrality.

The armed neutrality set on foot in 1780 was a plan to escape from the severe but ancient way of dealing with neutrals which Great Britain enforced, by advancing certain milder principles of international law. These were, that neutral vessels had a right to sail in freedom from harbor to harbor and along the coasts of belligerents; that the property of enemies not contraband of war on neutral ships should be free; that a port is blockaded only when evident danger attends on the attempt to run into it; that by these principles the detention and condemnation of neutral ships should be determined; and that, when such vessels had

* Comp. Ortolan, II. 86, et seq., esp. 93

been unjustly used, besides reparation for loss, satisfaction should be made to the neutral sovereign. The parties to this league engaged to equip a fleet to maintain their principle, and were to act in concert. These parties were, besides Russia, which announced the system to the powers at war, and invited other neutrals to coöperation, Denmark, Sweden, the Dutch provinces, Prussia, Austria, Portugal, and Naples. Two of the belligerents, France and Spain, concurred, but the other, England, replied that she stood by the law of nations and her treaties. England had reason to complain of this league, because some of the parties, then at peace with her,—Sweden and Denmark,—were at the time held by treaty with her to just the contrary principle; while others had even punished neutral ships for what they now claimed to be a neutral right. The first armed neutrality did little more than announce a principle, for no collision took place between them and Great Britain; but it formed an epoch, because in no previous arrangement between Christian states had the rule, "free ships, free goods," been separated from the opposite, "unfree or hostile ships, hostile goods." In the peace of Versailles, which in 1783 terminated the war between England and France growing out of our revolution, the two powers returned to the stipulations of the peace of Utrecht which have been mentioned above.

In the opening years of the French revolution England recovered her influence over the powers of Europe, and several of them abandoned or suspended the rule for which in great measure, the armed neutrality was formed. And the national convention of France, in 1793, decreed that enemy's goods on board neutral vessels, but not the vessels themselves, should be lawful prize, and that freight should be paid to the captor.

Treaties of the United States.

The United States, in treaties with foreign powers, have generally aimed to extend the rights of neutral carriers as far as possible. In some conventions, however, as in that with Spain in 1819, with Columbia in 1824, with Central America in 1825, a somewhat cumbrous rule of reciprocity has been followed, namely, that free ships shall make goods free, only so far as those powers are concerned which recognize the principle. But in the treaty with England, in 1795 (comp. § 118), it is agreed that the property of enemies on neutral vessels may be taken from them. And in one made with France in 1800, the maxim that hostile ships infect the cargo goes along, as was then not unusual, with the freedom of neutral vessels.

Second armed neutrality of 1800.

Twenty years after the first armed neutrality a second was formed, to which Russia, the Scandinavian powers and Prussia were parties; and which derived the pretext for its formation from differences of opinion concerning convoy (§ 191), as well as from certain violations of neutral rights by English cruisers in the case of a Swedish vessel. The platform of this alliance embraced much the same principles as that of 1780, together with new claims concerning convoy. But nothing was gained by it saving some trifling concessions from Great Britain (§ 191, u. s.), while Russia, Denmark and Sweden, ere long gave in their adherence to the English views of neutral liabilities.

§ 175.

Rules of the peace of Paris in 1856.

During the years between 1814 and 1854, which were disturbed by no important European war, the rules of war respecting neutral trade were of no immediate importance. On the breaking out of the short but important Crimean war, notice was given by Great Britain and France, that for the present the commerce of neutrals with Russia would not be subjected to the strict operation of the rights of war as commonly understood.* At the peace of

* The concurrent declarations of England and France in their English dress were as follows, under date of March 28–29, 1854.

"Her Majesty, the Queen of the United Kingdom of Great Britain and Ireland, having been compelled to take up arms in support of an ally, is desirous of rendering the war as little onerous as possible to the powers with whom she remains at peace.

"To preserve the commerce of neutrals from all unnecessary obstruction, Her Majesty is willing for the present to waive a part of the belligerent rights appertaining to her by the law of nations.

"It is impossible for Her Majesty to forego the exercise of her right of seizing

Paris in 1856, the principles foreshadowed in the declaration of the belligerents, which appear in the note below, were embodied in a declaration to which all the parties to the treaty subscribed. We have often spoken of these declarations, which form an epoch in the history of international law, but we here insert them in full, although but one of them refers to our present subject.

1. Privateering is and remains abolished. (§ 122.)

2. The neutral flag covers enemy's goods, with the exception of contraband of war.

3. Neutral goods, with the exception of contraband of war, are not liable to capture under an enemy's flag.

4. Blockades, in order to be binding, must be effective; that is to say, maintained by a force sufficient really to prevent access to the coast of an enemy.

Other powers were to be invited to accede to these articles, but only in solidarity and not separately. The third and fourth being already received by Great Britain, the abandonment of privateering must be regarded as her motive for waiving her old and fixed doctrine in regard to the liability to capture of hostile goods on board a neutral vessel. The minor powers of Europe, whose interests lie on the side of neutral privileges, have already acceded or are likely to accede to this declaration. The negative reply of the United States to an invitation to do the same, with its reasons, has been already given in § 122. If the larger exemption of all innocent private property from the liabilities of war, to which the United States offers to be a party, should become incorporated in the law of

articles contraband of war, and of preventing neutrals from bearing the enemy's despatches, and she must maintain the right of a belligerent to prevent neutrals from breaking any effective blockade, which may be established with an adequate force against the enemy's forts, harbors or coasts.

"But Her Majesty will waive the right of seizing enemy's property, laden on board a neutral vessel, unless it be contraband of war.

"It is not Her Majesty's intention to claim the confiscation of neutral property, not being contraband of war, found on board enemy's ships, and Her Majesty further declares that, being anxious to lessen as much as possible the evils of war, and to restrict its operations to the regularly organized forces of the country, it is not her present intention to issue letters of marque for the commissions of privateers."

nations, her attitude will have been one of great advantage to the world. If not, her plea of self-defence in keeping up the system of privateering will probably be regarded in another age as more selfish than wise.

§ 176.

Opinions of publicists, etc.

Until about the middle of the eighteenth century writers on the law of nations for the most part held, that neutral goods were safe in any vessel, and hostile liable to capture in any vessel. Some of the earlier writers, as Grotius, Zouch and Loccenius, go beyond this rule in severity towards the neutral ship, and seem to think that if the owners admitted hostile property on board, the vessel might be made prize of. They also lay it down that goods on hostile vessels belong presumptively to the enemy, but may be saved from harm on proof to the contrary. Bynkershoek in 1737, and Vattel in 1758, state the doctrine as it has been understood by those who maintain that enemy's goods on neutral vessels but not neutral on enemy's vessels are lawful prize. The latter expresses himself thus: "If we find an enemy's effects on board a neutral ship, we seize them by the rights of war; but we are naturally bound to pay the freight to the master of the vessel who is not to suffer by such seizure. The effects of neutrals found in an enemy's ship are to be restored to the owner, against whom there is no right of confiscation; but without any allowance for detainer, decay, etc. The loss sustained by the neutrals on this occasion is an accident, to which they exposed themselves by embarking their property in an enemy's ship; and the captor, in exercising the rights of war, is not responsible for the accidents which may thence result, any more than if his cannon kills a neutral passenger who happens unfortunately to be on board an enemy's vessel." Mr. Manning cites Moser (1780) and Lampredi (1788) to the same effect. English authorities are unanimous in declaring these to be rules of international law. Our supreme court, and our principal writers on this branch, take the same ground. Chancellor Kent says: "The two distinct propositions, that enemy's goods found on board a neutral ship may be lawfully seized as prize of war, and that the goods of a neutral found on board an enemy's vessel are to be restored, have been explicitly incorporated into the jurisprudence of the United States, and declared by the supreme court to be founded on the law of nations. I should apprehend the belligerent right to be no longer an open question; and that the authority and usage on which that right rests in Europe, and the long, explicit, and authoritative admission of it by this country, have concluded us from making it a subject of controversy; and that we are bound in truth and justice to submit to its regular exercise, in every case, and with every belligerent power who does not freely renounce it." * Again, Dr. Wheaton says: "Whatever may be the true, original, abstract principle of natural law on this subject, it is undeniable that the constant usage and practice of belligerent nations, from the earliest times, have subjected enemy's goods in neutral vessels to capture and condemnation, as prize of war. This constant and universal usage has only been interrupted by treaty-stipulations, forming a temporary conventional law between the parties to such stipulations." "The converse rule, which subjects to confiscation the goods of a friend on board the vessels of an enemy, is manifestly contrary to truth and justice." †

The opposite doctrine, in regard to enemy's goods on neutral vessels, was first maintained by a Prussian commission appointed to look into the complaints of certain merchants who had had French goods taken out of their vessels by English cruisers in 1744. They venture to affirm that such conduct is

* I. 129–131, Lect. VI.

† El. IV. 3, §§ 19, 21. It may be added that the United States, in their diplomatic intercourse with foreign governments, have long claimed it to be a neutral right that free ships should make free goods. Mr. Marcy, in 1854, in a note to the British envoy at Washington, expresses the President's satisfaction that "the principle that free ships make free goods, which the United States have so long and so strenuously contended for as a neutral right, is to have a qualified sanction" in the war of England and France with Russia. He means probably no more than that this is a fair and just claim of neutrals, not that it is an admitted one, or a part of actual international law. And such we believe to have been the ground previously taken.

not only contrary to the law of nations, but also to all the treaties which were ever concluded between maritime powers,—two propositions which are equally untenable. In 1759, Martin Hübner, a professor at Copenhagen, claimed that this principle ought to be admitted into international law; and chiefly on two grounds, *first* that neutral ships are neutral territory, and again that commerce is free to neutrals in war as well as in peace; since war ought not to injure those who are not parties in the contest. In more recent times several writers on the law of nations have taken the same position. Thus Klüber says, "On the open sea every ship is exterritorial in reference to every state except its own: a merchant ship is to be looked on as a floating colony. Therefore a belligerent power on the open sea ought to be permitted neither to visit a neutral vessel, nor to take hostile goods out of it, still less to confiscate the ship on account of the goods found in it." And again, "A belligerent power ought to be allowed as little to confiscate neutral goods found on an enemy's vessel, as if they had been met with on the soil of the enemy's territory." De Martens holds to the freedom of neutral ships.* Ortolan, while rejecting this ground, turns to sounder principles of natural justice. "If the goods," says he, "put on board a neutral vessel have not, of themselves, a hostile character, that the neutral should take pay for his ship and for the labor of his sailors, has nothing in it irreconcilable with the duties of neutrality. Why then should a belligerent obstruct such trade by seizing the cargo? Is it not legitimately in the hands of friends, who have made and have had the right to make a bargain to carry it for pay to a place agreed upon, and who, apart from the freight, have an interest in securing its preservation, since on this may depend the success or failure of the commercial enterprise in which they are engaged? And in hindering, by the confiscation of goods transported, this commerce of freight and commission, do not belligerents abuse the principle, which permits them to capture enemy's property on the sea, by pushing this prin-

* Klüber, § 299, p. 354, ed. in German of 1851. De Martens, § 316, vol. II. 322, Paris ed. of 1858.

ciple into consequences which unjustly attack the independence and essential rights of friendly nations?" He adds, that the practice of paying freight for the goods thus taken out of neutral ships contains a kind of confession that the neutral has sustained an injury, whilst yet the payment of freight is by no means an adequate compensation for all their losses.

§ 177.

Neutral property in armed enemies' vessels.

While the neutral can put his goods on the merchant vessel of either of the belligerents in safety, it has been made a question whether he can make use of their armed vessels for that purpose. The English courts have decided against, and the American courts in favor of the neutral's using such a conveyance for his goods. On the one hand it may be said, that in this act an intention is shown to resist the right of search, and the inconveniences of capture, and of transportation to a port such as the captor may select. On the other hand, the neutral, his goods being safe already, has perhaps no great motive to aid in resistance, for the complete loss of his goods is endangered by an armed engagement. If, however, the neutral can be shown to have aided in the arming of the vessel, it is just that he should suffer.

The decision of this case, as Chancellor Kent observes,* is of very great importance. Yet with the discontinuance of privateering such cases would cease, for few ships will be armed with the purpose to resist ships of war.

§ 178.

Contraband of war.

Contrabannum, in mediæval Latin, is *merces banno interdictæ*. (Du Cange.) *Bannus*, or *bannum*, represented by our *ban*, and the Italian *bando*, denoted originally an edict, a proclamation, then an interdict. The sovereign of the country made goods contraband by an edict prohibiting their importation or their exportation. Such prohibitions are found in Roman law. A law of Valentinian and his colleagues (Cod. IV. 41, 1), forbids the exportation of wine,

* I. 132, Lect. VI.

oil, and fish-sauce (*liquamen*) to barbarian lands, and another of Marcian (ibid. 2), the selling of any arms or iron to barbarians, the latter on pain of confiscation of goods and death. Several Popes threatened with the ban the conveyance of arms to infidels, and similar prohibitions are found in some of the ancient maritime codes. Contraband of war perhaps denoted at first that which a belligerent publicly prohibited the exportation of into his enemy's country, and now, those kind of goods which by the law of nations a neutral cannot send into either of the countries at war without wrong to the other, or which by conventional law the states making a treaty agree to put under this rubric.*

If there was a famine in one of the countries at war, and a friendly power should send provisions thither, either at the public expense or for a compensation, the act would be a lawful one. But if the neutral, instead of wheat, should send powder or balls, cannon or rifles, this would be a direct encouragement of the war, and so a departure from the neutral position. The state which professed to be a friend to both has furnished one with the means of fighting against the other, and a wrong has been done. Now the same wrong is committed when a private trader, without the privity of his government, furnishes the means of war to either of the warring parties. It may be made a question whether such conduct on the part of the private citizen ought not to be prevented by his government, even as enlistments for foreign armies on neutral soil are made penal. But it is difficult for a government to watch narrowly the operations of trade, and it is annoying for the innocent trader. Moreover, the neutral ought not to be subjected by the quarrels of others to additional care and expense. Hence by the practice of nations he is passive in regard to violations of the rules concerning contraband, blockade and the like, and leaves the police of the sea and the punishing or reprisal power in the hands of those who are most

* The explanation of contrabannum from the *church ban* laid on the carrying of arms, etc., to the enemies of Christianity, seems to be less worthy of acceptation than that given in the text.

interested, the limits being fixed for the punishment by common usage or law.

It is to be observed, that the rules concerning contraband relate to neutrals exporting such articles to a country at war. There is nothing unlawful, when merchant vessels of either of the belligerents supply themselves in a neutral mart with articles having the quality of contraband. Here, again, the neutral is passive, and leaves the law of nations to be executed by others, who would make all the property, if captured, prize of war.*

* Comp. § 162. A formal way of stating the relations of a neutral country to contraband trade, taken by some textwriters, is found in the proposition, that such a transaction cannot occur on neutral territory, that is, that it begins, when the articles, called contraband, are brought upon the high sea, or within the enemy's limits on the land. All admit that when the act of exportation from the neutral territory begins, an act of violation of neutrality on the part of some one commences. The question may still be asked whether the government of the neutral is not bound to interfere, when it has evidence that its subjects are thus aiding a belligerent against a friend, and is not bound also to acquaint itself with such evil intentions. In the present state of the law of nations this is not felt to be obligatory, although such trade is immoral, and tends to produce lasting national animosities. A juster and humaner policy would make all innocent trade with the enemy free, and require a neutral to pass stringent and effectual laws against contraband trade. Phillimore (III. §§ 230–233) denies that such articles can even be lawfully sold to the belligerent, within the territory of the neutral. "If it be the true character of a neutral," says he, "to abstain from every act which may better or worsen the condition of a belligerent, the unlawfulness of any such sale is a necessary conclusion from these premises. For what does it matter where the neutral supplies one belligerent with the means of attacking another? How does the question of locality, according to the principles of eternal justice and the reason of the thing, affect the advantage to one belligerent or the injury to the other accruing from this act of the alleged neutral?" He goes on to say with justice that foreign enlistments stand on the same ground with the sale of munitions of war. If they are prohibited and made penal, as they are extensively, why should not these be so also? And he regrets that Judge Story should have said (case of the Santissima Trinidad, 7 Wheaton, 340), "there is nothing in our laws or in the law of nations that forbids our citizens from sending armed vessels as well as munitions of war to foreign ports for sale. It is a commercial adventure which no nation is bound to prohibit; and which only exposes the persons engaged in it to the penalty of confiscation." I too regret that Story should have to say this, if it be true. The same fact prevails everywhere as to munitions of war. But as to armed vessels of war and even vessels made ready for an armament, are they not too decisively the beginning of a hostile expedition to be allowed by any nations that prohibit such expeditions from issuing out of their territories?

§ 179.

It is admitted, that the act of carrying to the enemy articles directly useful in war is wrong, for which the injured party may punish the neutral taken in the act. When, however, we ask what articles are contraband, the answer is variously given. Great maritime powers, when engaged in war, have enlarged the list, and nations generally neutral have contracted it. Treaties defining what is contraband have differed greatly in their specifications; the same nation in its conventions with different powers at the same era, has sometimes placed an article in the category of contraband, and sometimes taken it out. Writers on the law of nations, again, are far from uniformity in their opinions. To make the subject more clear, it is necessary to enter into a consideration of different classes of articles.

What goods are contraband

1. Articles by general consent deemed to be contraband, are such as appertain immediately to the uses of war. Such are, in the words of a treaty of the year 1800, between England and Russia, cited by Mr. Manning, "cannons, mortars, fire-arms, pistols, bombs, grenades, bullets, balls, muskets, flints, matches, powder, saltpetre, sulphur, cuirasses, pikes, swords, belts, cartouch-boxes, saddles, and bridles, beyond the quantity necessary for the use of the ship." In the instructions of the French government to the officers of the navy in the Crimean war, given in March 1854, the articles enumerated are "bouches et armes à feu, armes blanches, projectiles, poudre, salpêtre, soufre, objets d'équipment, de campement et de harnachement militaires, et tous instruments quelconques fabriqués à l'usage de la guerre." The following enumeration recurs in several treaties between the United States and Spanish American Republics: "1. Cannons, mortars, howitzers, swivels, blunderbusses, muskets, fusees, rifles, carbines, pistols, pikes, swords, sabres, lances, spears,

in the usage of nations?

The views of Phillimore, although be may confound the duty of a neutral state and that of a citizen of such a state, do him great honor. If contraband trade in any article can be prevented within the borders of the neutral, he is bound, in right reason, but not by the present law of nations, to prevent it.

halberts, hand-grenades, bombs, powder, matches, balls, and all other things belonging to the use of these arms. 2. Bucklers, helmets, breastplates, coats of mail, infantry belts, and clothes made up in a military form and for a military use. 3. Cavalry belts, and horses with their furniture. 4th, and generally, all kinds of arms and instruments of iron, steel, brass, and copper, or of any other material, manufactured, prepared, and formed expressly to make war by sea or land." *

2. Horses have been mentioned as being contraband in very many treaties extending down into this century. "All the principal powers have so looked upon them at different times," says Mr. Manning, "with the exception of Russia."

3. In a few treaties belonging to the seventeenth century unwrought metals and money have been so regarded. In others, money is expressly excepted, as in that of Utrecht, in 1713; that of England with France, in 1786; and that between Spain and the United States, in 1795.

4. Naval stores and materials for ship-building have been declared to be contraband in many treaties, and in some others have been excepted from the list. The treaty of 1794, between Great Britain and the United States, after declaring several kinds of naval stores to be contraband, adds that "generally, whatever may serve directly to the equipment of vessels, unwrought iron and fir-planks only excepted," shall partake of this quality. Chancellor Kent says, that the government of the United States has frequently conceded that materials for the building, equipment, and armament of ships of war, as timber and naval stores, are contraband. (I. 137.) The English prize courts, in the case of such articles, and of provisions, have been led to adopt a set of rules of which we shall speak a little below.†

* As in the treaty with Colombia, Oct. 3, 1824, with Venezuela, Jan. 20, 1836, with Guatemala, March 3, 1849, with New Granada, June 10, 1848, San Salvador, Jan. 2, 1850, with Mexico, April 5, 1851. In the two last a fifth clause makes contraband "provisions that are sent into a besieged or blockaded place."

† Ships ready made and capable of use for purposes of war, have not occupied the attention of treaty-making powers. Hübner declares them contraband. Heffter is of the same judgment. (§ 157, *b.*) Phillimore says "that the sale of a ship *for*

5. Provisions are not in themselves contraband, but, according to a number of text-writers, as Grotius, Vattel, and several modern, especially English authorities, may become so, where there is a prospect of reducing the enemy by famine. The usage in regard to them has been shifting. Queen Elizabeth's government forbade the Poles and Danes to convey provisions to Spain, on the ground, that by the rights of war an enemy might be reduced by famine. The conventions, which, at various times in the 17th and 18th centuries, declared that they were not contraband, show at least a fear that belligerent nations would treat them as such. At the outburst of the war succeeding the French revolution, when France was almost in a state of famine, conventions were made between Great Britain on the one hand, and Russia, Spain, Portugal, Prussia, and Austria, on the other, which restricted the conveyance from their respective ports into France, of naval and military stores, and of provisions,—whether cereal grains, salt-fish, or other articles. The French convention, also, in the same year, 1793, in which these treaties were made, declared that cargoes of neutral ships, consisting of grain, and destined for a hostile port, might be seized for the use of France, on the principle of preëmption, of which we shall presently speak. These measures, in regard to provisions especially, were earnestly resisted by Denmark and the United States, which were then the leading neutral powers. The treaty of 1794, between England and the United States, contains an admission that provisions and other articles, not generally contraband, might become

purposes of war is the sale of the most noxious article of war. The sale by a neutral of any ship to a belligerent is a very suspicious act in the opinion of the English and North American prize courts, and one which the French prize courts refuse to recognize." And he goes on to cite a case in which a ship adapted to purposes of war was sent with goods on board to a belligerent port under instructions to have her sold if possible, and was condemned. (III. p. 360.) Hautefeuille, on the other hand, says that he cannot understand how a *mere* vessel, as yet unarmed, whatever may be its destination, is an article of contraband. (II. 145.) "It is nothing but a vehicle." And so sulphur and saltpetre are nothing but commodities; they are incapable as yet of a military use. Our authorities would no doubt regard such vessels as contraband. (Story, in 7 Wheaton, 340.)

such according to the existing law of nations, and proceeds to prescribe that if seized they shall be paid for, or, in other words, allows, as between the contracting parties, of the practice of preëmption.

§ 180.

Results for determining what articles are contraband.

In view of these historical statements, showing the varying practice of nations in regard to certain articles, we may say

1. That nothing can justly be regarded as contraband, unless so regarded by the law of nations, or by express convention between certain parties. The definition of contraband must be *clear* and *positive.* For as belligerents are authorized to inflict severe evils on neutrals trading in contraband articles, it is plain that *they alone* cannot define in what contraband consists. The heavy penalty implies a heavy crime understood to be such, when the penalty was allowed. There must be certain kinds of articles, such as afford direct assistance, *not to the enemy, but to the enemy's military operations*, and *known beforehand*, and hence implying a departure from the spirit and rules of neutrality, which can be seized and confiscated. Or, since the articles of *direct use* in war may change from age to age, at the most, new articles,—as for instance in these days of war-steamers, steam-engines, coals, and the like,—can justly come into this list, *only* when there is satisfactory proof that they are for the direct uses of war. And this, of course, only where treaty has not specified certain definite articles, and such alone.

Occasional contraband.

2. The doctrine of occasional contraband or contraband according to circumstances, is not sufficiently established to be regarded as a part of the law of nations. Naval stores and provisions are the articles which come here under our notice: now as these may form the principal exports of a nation, it is plain that by this rule the neutral's trade may be quite destroyed. The rule would thus be excessively harsh, if the usual penalty hanging over contraband were inflicted. To mitigate this severity and in a certain sense

to pacify neutrals, the British prize judges, especially Sir William Scott, adopted certain discriminating rules, according to which the articles in question partook more or less of the contraband character. Thus, if the produce of the country from which they had been exported, or in an unmanufactured state, or destined to a commercial port, they were viewed with greater indulgence than if shipped from a country where they were not grown, or in a manufactured state, or destined to a naval station. Sir William Scott afterwards withdrew his indulgence from naval stores destined to a commercial port, on the ground that they could be used there to equip privateers, or be transported to a port of naval equipment.* And in some cases a yet milder rule was adopted by Great Britain—that of preëmption, of which we shall speak by itself.

§ 181.

Is it just, and sanctioned by usage?

In regard, now, to this doctrine of occasional contraband, we say *first*, that it is *unjust* to neutrals. If it be doubtful whether an article pertains to the class of contraband or not, the penalty attached to this class of articles ought certainly not to be levied upon it. It is either contraband or not, and is not so, if there is a doubt to what class it belongs. To visit it with a half-penalty, because it is of doubtful character, is like punishing on a lower scale a crime half proven.

Secondly. Does usage sanction occasional contraband? So far as I can see, the most that can be said is, that belligerents have sometimes put doubtful articles into the list of contraband, and neutrals have sometimes submitted to it; but that no clear practice appears to have prevailed.

Thirdly. The authority of the older text-writers is more in favor of such a distinction. In an often-cited passage of Grotius (III. 1, § 5), after dividing things in the hands of those who are not enemies, into such as have a use in war alone, such as have no use in war, and such as have a use in war and aside from war, he says that in regard to this third class of articles

* Comp. Wheaton, El. IV. 3, § 24, p. 519.

ancipitis usus; "si tueri me non possum, nisi quæ mittuntur intercipiam, necessitas, ut alibi exposuimus, jus dabit, sed sub onere restitutionis, nisi causa alia accedat." His commentator, Samuel de Cocceii, on this passage observes, that "necessity gives no right over the goods of another, so that if my enemy is not aided by such articles, I cannot intercept them, although I may be in want of them. On the other hand, if the power of the enemy is thereby increased, I can take them, albeit I may not need them myself." * Bynkershoek, although he differs from Grotius as to the rule of necessity, and regards a commerce in the raw materials of war as not illicit, yet thinks they may be prohibited, if the enemy cannot well carry on war without them. (Quæst. J. P. I. 10.) And Vattel decides that even provisions are contraband in certain junctures, when we have hopes of reducing an enemy by famine.

Opinions in respect to it.

Modern English writers and Chancellor Kent give their sanction to the doctrine of occasional contraband, while Wheaton, without expressing a positive opinion, seems averse to it. Several continental authors of repute either deny it to be a part of the law of nations, or admit it with cautious reserve. Heffter says (§ 160), "never have belligerents been allowed, alone and according to their good pleasure, to make restrictions of this kind, although when possessed of power enough, they have assumed to do this." And he adds in regard to doubtful articles, that belligerents can take measures against neutrals exporting them, only when a destination for the enemy's government and military forces can be ascribed to them on sufficient grounds. Ortolan (II. 179) denies that provisions and objects of prime necessity can ever be considered contraband, but concedes that a belligerent may declare objects to be contraband which are not usually such, when they become what he calls contraband in disguise, as the parts of military machines conveyed separately, and ready to be put together. His countryman, Hautefeuille (Droits des nations neutres, II. 419 †), maintains that no products of use in peace and war both can in any case be contraband, "and

* Lausanne ed. of Grotius, vol. III., p. 602. † 1st ed. Comp. II. 157 2d ed.

that nothing else is contraband but arms and munitions of war actually manufactured, proper, immediately, and without any preparation or transformation by human industry, to be employed in the uses of war, and not capable of receiving any other destination." Klüber, after saying (§ 288) that naval stores and materials are not to be reckoned contraband, adds, that in case of doubt as to the quality of particular articles, the juristic presumption inclines to the side of natural right, which allows the natural freedom of trade. De Martens says (§ 318), that "where no treaties intervened, the powers of Europe, when they were neuter, maintained long before 1780 [the date of the first armed neutrality], that only articles of direct use in war could be considered and treated as contrabands by belligerents." The United States, it is believed, has steadily taken this ground in regard to provisions, although not in regard to naval stores.

The doctrine of occasional contraband received its widest extension in the war of England against revolutionary France. The British representative to our government claimed in 1793 and 1794, that by the law of nations all provisions were to be considered as contraband, in the case where the depriving the enemy of these supplies was one of the means employed to reduce him to reasonable terms of peace, and that the actual situation of France was such as to lead to that mode of distressing her, inasmuch as she had armed almost the whole laboring class of the people for the purpose of commencing and supporting hostilities against all the governments of Europe.* If a government had armed nearly its whole laboring population, the laws of political economy would probably reduce it to weakness far sooner than the cruisers of its enemy would have that effect.

§ 182.

Preëmption.

3. The harshness of the doctrine of occasional contraband brought into favor the rule of preëmption, which was a sort of compromise † between the belliger-

* Kent, I. 137, Lect. VII.

† So Sir W. Scott calls it in Robinson's Rep. I. 241.

ents (if masters of the sea) and the neutrals. The former claimed that such articles may be confiscated, the latter that they should go free. Now as the belligerent often wanted these articles, and at least could hurt his enemy by forestalling them, it came nearest to suiting both parties, if, when they were intercepted on the ocean, the neutral was compensated by the payment of the market price, and of a fair profit.

This rule, which was more especially applied by the English prize courts shortly after the French revolution, would be a relaxation of the severe right of war, if the doctrine of occasional contraband could be established, and as such, a concession to neutrals. But it does not, as an independent rule, possess sufficient support from usage and authority. There are two sources from which arguments in its support have been derived. (1.) An old practice of European governments was to seize the grain or other necessary articles found in the hands of foreigners in their ports, on promise of compensation, which naturally would be slow in coming. Many treaties of century XVII. put an end to this half-barbarous exercise of sovereignty between the contracting powers, and it is believed to be unknown to the law of nations, unless (2.) under the form of a rule of necessity. Such a rule in a broad sense would authorize, whether in war or peace, the taking of property from subjects or foreigners, if self-preservation required it. A more limited necessity is contemplated in the passage of Grotius already cited, as pertaining to a belligerent, and justifying him in detaining the goods of those who are not enemies, if otherwise he cannot defend himself. Omitting to inquire whether nations have any such right, which if it exist can arise only in extreme cases, we need only say that modern preëmption is limited in extent to cargoes of neutrals bound to the enemy's ports, and is practised to distress the enemy, not to relieve an imminent distress of one's own. "I have never understood," says Sir William Scott, "that this claim [of preëmption] goes beyond the case of cargoes avowedly bound for enemy's ports, or suspected on just grounds, to have a concealed destination of that kind."

The English practice in cases of preëmption is to pay a reasonable indemnification, and a fair profit on the commodity intercepted, but not to pay the price which could be obtained in the enemy's ports. In a treaty with Sweden of 1803, it was arranged, that in seizures of this kind the price of the merchandise should be paid, either as valued in Great Britain or in Sweden at the option of the proprietor, with a profit of ten per cent., and an indemnity for freight and expenses of detention. In the treaty of 1794, already referred to, between Great Britain and the United States, it is said, "that whereas the difficulty of agreeing on the precise cases, in which provisions and other articles of contraband may be regarded as such, renders it expedient to provide against the inconveniences and misunderstandings which might thence arise, . . . whenever any such articles so becoming contraband according to the existing law of nations, shall for that reason be seized, . . . the captors, or in their default, the government, under whose authority they act, shall pay the full value . . . with a reasonable mercantile profit thereon, together with the freight and also the damages incident to such detention." The expression "becoming contraband according to the existing law of nations," left the question, What the law of nations decided, an open one: if the United States, for instance, denied that certain articles seized as contraband were legally such, they could not yield their opinion, and preëmption itself in such cases might be a cause of complaint and even of war. This was an unfortunate halfway admission, which left everything unsettled, and yet justified the other party to the convention in their measures of detention on the seas.

English practice of preëmption.

§ 183.

If the contraband articles are clearly intended for the enemy's use, especially if they are more in quantity than the ship's company need, they are subject to confiscation on being captured, and no freight is paid for them to the transporter.* Ancient French ordinances, be-

Penalty for contraband trade.

* The words "for the enemy's use" are not sufficiently precise, as they might

fore the ordinance of 1681, prescribed a much milder course: the value of the contraband articles, at the estimate of the admiral or his lieutenant, was to be paid after bringing the ship so freighted into port. Ancient usage, in general, made the ship also liable to confiscation: the commercial treaty of Utrecht, in 1713, points at this where it says, that "the ship itself, as well as the other goods found therein, are to be esteemed free, neither may they be detained on pretence of their being, as it were, infected by the prohibited goods, much less shall they be confiscated as lawful prize." The modern rule, pretty uniformly acknowledged, seems to be, that the ship and goods not contraband go free, except where one or both pertain to the owner of the contraband articles, or where false papers show a privity in carrying them.* The justice of confiscating the ship in both these cases is plain enough, for there is an evident intention of violating, by means of the vessel, the duties of neutrals. Whether, when the rest of the cargo belongs to the same owner, it should be thus severely dealt with, may be fairly doubted. Bynkershoek (Quæst. J. P. I. 12) decided in favor of confiscation, "ob continentiam delicti;" and Sir William Scott gives as his reason for a similar opinion, "that where a man is concerned in an illegal transaction, the whole of his property involved in that transaction is liable to confiscation." The penalty ceases, after the voyage with the objectionable goods on board is performed.

In two other cases the confiscation of the ship has sometimes been enforced,—when the contraband goods make up three quarters of the value of the cargo, and when the owner of the vessel is bound, by special treaties of his government with that of the captor, to abstain from a traffic of this description. The first resolves itself into a rule of evidence in regard to the complicity of the ship, and need not be made a distinct

include articles sent from one neutral port to another, but clearly intended to be reshipped from thence to a belligerent place. Even this indirect trade in munitions of war some would regard as contraband trade, but not, we apprehend, on good grounds.

* Of course where the ship is fitted for the naval warfare of the enemy, it is liable to confiscation on another ground.

case; the other assumes, without reason, that the owner of the vessel must have a knowledge of the cargo, and is not generally acknowledged.

Treaty modifying the penalty.

Among treaties modifying the penalty in cases of contraband, that between the United States and Prussia, which Franklin negotiated in 1785 (comp. § 122), and the article of which relating to this subject was inserted in the new treaty of 1799, deserves especial mention. It is there provided, with regard to military stores, that the vessels having them on board may be detained "for such length of time as the captors may think necessary to prevent the inconvenience or damage that might ensue from their proceeding, paying, however, a reasonable compensation for the loss such arrest shall occasion to the proprietors; and it shall further be allowed to use in the service of the captors the whole, or any part of the military stores so detained, paying the owners the full value of the same, to be ascertained by the current price at the place of its destination. But in a case supposed of a vessel stopped for articles of contraband, if the master of the vessel stopped will deliver out the goods supposed to be of a contraband nature, he shall be admitted to do it, and the vessel shall not in that case be carried into any port, nor further detained, but shall be allowed to proceed on her voyage."

§ 184.

Neutral conveyance of enemy's troops and despatches.

If the obligations of neutrality forbid the conveyance of contraband goods to the enemy, they also forbid the neutral to convey to him ships, whether of war or of transport, with their crews, and still more to forward his troops and his despatches. These have sometimes been called contraband articles, which name a treaty of England with Sweden in 1691 expressly gives to soldiers together with horses and ships of war and of convoy.* They have been called, again, "contraband par accident." But in truth, as Heffter remarks, they are something more than contraband, as connecting the neutral more closely with the enemy. A contra-

* Marquardsen, der Trent-Fall, p. 51.

band trade may be only a continuation of one which was legitimate in peace, but it will rarely happen that a neutral undertakes in time of peace to send troops of war to another nation, and the carrying of hostile despatches implies a state of war. These two kinds of transport deserve a more extended discussion.

1. The conveyance of troops for a belligerent has long been regarded as highly criminal. In the commercial treaty of Utrecht of 1713 (Dumont, VIII. I. 345), between France and Great Britain, it is provided that the liberty granted to goods on a free or neutral ship "shall be extended to persons sailing on the same, in such wise that, though they be enemies of one or both the parties, they shall not be taken from the free ship, unless they be military persons, actually in the service of the enemy." Many modern treaties contain the same exception from the protection of the neutral flag and in nearly the same words; as for instance those of 1785 and 1800 between France and the United States, and those of the latter with Guatemala, San Salvador, and Peru.* Our formula of exception is "unless they are officers or soldiers, and in the actual service of the enemy." As for the number of persons of this sort, so transported, which will involve a vessel in guilt and lead to its condemnation, it may perhaps be said that a soldier or two, like a package or two of contraband articles, might be overlooked; but it is held that to forward officers, especially of high rank, or even a single officer, would subject the neutral vessel to confiscation. (The Orozembo, Robinson's Rep. VI. 434, Phillim. III. § 272.) A modern case shows the rigor of the English courts in regard to such transportation. The Bremen ship Greta was condemned in 1855 during the Crimean war, by a prize court at Hong Kong, for carrying 270 shipwrecked Russian officers and seamen from a Japanese to a Russian harbor, —although had this conduct been dictated by mere humanity, condemnation could not have taken place.†

2. No rule of international law, forbidding the conveyance of hostile despatches, can be produced, of an earlier date than

* Marquardsen, u. s. p. 61.

† Marquardsen, u. s. p. 59.

the first years of the present century. Sir William Scott (Lord Stowell) seems to have struck out this rule, as a deduction, and we may say, as a fair deduction from the general obligation of neutrality. The general doctrine of the English courts is this: Despatches are official communications of official persons on the public affairs of government. Letters of such persons concerning their own private affairs, and letters written by unofficial persons are not despatches. Communications from a hostile government to one of its consuls in a neutral country, unless proved to be of a hostile nature, and despatches of an enemy's ambassador resident in a neutral country are excepted from the rule, on the ground that they relate to intercourse between the hostile state and a neutral, which is lawful, and which the other belligerent may not obstruct. The comparative importance of the despatches, if within the rule, is immaterial.

In order to make the carrying of enemy's despatches an offence, the guilt of the master must be established. If the despatches are put on board by fraud against him, no penalty is incurred by the ship. If he sails from a hostile port, and especially if the letters are addressed to persons in a hostile country, stronger proof is needed that he is not privy to a guilty transaction than if the voyage began in a neutral country, and was to end at a neutral or open port.

If the shipmaster is found guilty of conveying hostile despatches, the ship is liable to condemnation, and the cargo is confiscable also, both "ob continentiam delicti," and because the agent of the cargo is guilty. But if the master is not such an agent, his guilt will not extend beyond the vessel.

This rule, in its general form, if not in its harsher features, may be said to have passed into the law of nations. Not only the declarations of England and France, made in the spring of 1854 (§ 175, note), but the contemporaneous ones of Sweden and of Prussia sanction it, and the government of the United States in one instance has accepted it as a part of the law of nations. It is received as such by text-writers of various nationalities, by Wildman and Phillimore, by Wheaton, by Heffter, Marquardsen, and other German writers, by Ortolan and Hautefeuille. The last named publicist gives a modification of the rule, which though of private authority, deserves serious attention. Despatches can be transported, says he, from one neutral port to another, from a neutral to a belligerent, or from a belligerent to a neutral, or finally from one belligerent port to another. In the three first cases the conveyance is always innocent. In the last it is guilty only when the vessel is chartered for the purpose of carrying the despatches; but when the master of a packet boat or a chance vessel takes despatches together with other mail matter according to usage, he is doing what is quite innocent, and is not bound to ascertain the character of the letters which are put on board his vessel. Whatever may be thought of this, it may be seriously doubted whether a neutral ship conveying mails according to usage or the law of its country can be justly treated as guilty for so doing. The analogy from articles contraband of war here loses its force. When a war breaks out a captain ought to know what articles he has on board, but how can he know the contents of mailed letters?

The case of the Trent, in which this and several other principles of international law were involved, may here receive a brief notice. This vessel, sailing from one neutral port to another on its usual route as a packet ship, was overhauled by an American captain, and four persons were extracted from it on the high seas, under the pretext that they were ambassadors, and bearers of despatches from the Confederate government, so called, to its agents in Europe. The vessel itself was allowed to pursue its way, by waiver of right as the officer who made the detention thought, but no despatches were found. On this transaction we may remark, (1) that there is no process known to international law by which a nation may extract from a neutral ship on the high sea a hostile ambassador, a traitor or any criminal whatsoever. Nor can any neutral ship be brought in for adjudication on accouut of having such passengers on board. (2.) If there had been hostile despatches found on board, the ship might have been captured and taken into port; and when it had entered our waters, these four men, being citizens charged with treason, were amenable to our laws. But there appears to have been no valid pretext for seizing the vessel. It is simply absurd to say that these men were living despatches. (3.) The character of the vessel as a packet ship, conveying mails and passengers from one neutral port to another, almost precluded the possibility of guilt. Even if hostile military persons had been found on board, it might be a question whether their presence would involve the ship in guilt, as they were going from a neutral country and to a neutral country. (4.) It ill became the United States,—a nation which had ever insisted strenuously upon neutral rights,—to take a step more like the former British practice of extracting seamen out of neutral vessels upon the high seas, than like any modern precedent in the conduct of civilized nations, and that too when she had protested against this procedure on the part of Great Britain and made it a ground of war. As for the rest, this affair of the Trent has been of use to the world, by committing Great Britain to the side of neutral rights upon the seas.*

§ 185.

Trade closed in peace, but opened in war.

Certain kinds of trade, as the coasting and colonial, have been by the policy of most nations confined to national vessels in time of peace; and neutrals have been allowed to participate in them only when war rendered the usual mode of conveyance unsafe. It would appear, that to make such trade lawful, licenses were granted to particular vessels, and the belligerent captor could, with justice,

* For the subjects embraced within this section see Marquardsen (prof. at Erlangen) der Trent-Fall, Erlangen, 1862.—For the conveyance of troops and of despatches most of the modern text-writers may be consulted, as Wheaton, IV. 3, § 25; Heffter, § 157 *b*; Ortolan, II. 213; Wildman, II. 234–244; Phillimore, III. § 273. The cases, which have principally determined the law in the matter of despatches, are those of the Atalanta, 6 Robinson's Rep. 440, Carolina, ibid. 465, and Madison, Edwards' Rep. 224. The Atalanta brought despatches from the French governor of the Isle of France to the French minister of marine, and was condemned; the Carolina, from the French ambassador in the United States, a neutral country, to his home government, and was released.—For the course which the United States should have taken from the first news of the Trent affair, in consistency with our past principles, comp. Mr. Sumner's speech in the Senate of the United States in Jan. 1862.

take the ground that the vessel under license had identified itself with the enemy. In the seven years' war, declared in 1756, the British government and courts maintained that this kind of trade was prohibited by the law of nations: hence the principle, that a neutral could not lawfully engage, during war, in a trade with the enemy, from which he had been shut out in peace, is called the rule of 1756. The rule was protested against in 1780 by the first armed neutrality, so far as coasting trade was concerned; but in 1793 and onwards was enforced by the British government; although, now, the trade was no longer carried on by special license, but was opened to all neutral vessels. The grounds on which the rule stood were, that the neutral interfered to save one of the belligerents from the state of distress to which the arms of his foe had reduced him, and thus identified himself with him. The neutral states have never allowed that the rule forms a part of the international code. "Its practical importance," Dr. Wheaton observes, "will probably hereafter be much diminished by the revolution which has taken place in the colonial system of Europe.*

§ 186.

Blockade.

The word blockade properly denotes obstructing the passage into or from a place on either element, but is more especially applied to naval forces preventing communication by water. With blockades by land or ordinary sieges neutrals have usually little to do.

What places can be blockaded.

A blockade is not confined to a seaport, but may have effect on a roadstead or portion of a coast, or the mouth of a river. But if the river is a pathway to interior neutral territories, the passage on the stream of vessels destined for neutral soil cannot be impeded. It has been asserted, that no place could be put under blockade, unless it were fortified; but the law of nations knows no such limitation.†

There is a general agreement that it is unlawful for a neu-

* Wheaton, El. IV. 3, § 27, at the end.

† By Lucchesi-Palli, p. 180, of the French translation of the Italian work, cited by Ortolan, II 299.

tral vessel knowingly to attempt to break a blockade, whether by issuing from or entering the blockaded place. Such an act, especially of ingress, tends to aid one of the belligerents in the most direct manner against the designs of the other, and is therefore a great departure from the line of neutrality. And a similar act on land would involve the loss of the most innocent articles intended for a besieged town. M. Ortolan places the obligation to respect a blockade on the ground that there is an actual substitution of sovereignty, that is, that one belligerent has possession by occupancy of the waters of the other. But this is a formal way of defending the right of blockade, and may be found fault with, perhaps, for the reason that sovereignty over water along a coast is merely an incident to sovereignty on the adjoining land, which the blockader has not yet acquired. The true ground of the right is simply this, that the belligerent has a right to carry on a siege; and that his act of commencing such a siege places neutrals under an obligation not to interfere with his plans. If the sea were a common pathway to the very coast this right would still subsist.

Why is a breach of blockade unlawful?

Blockades may be considered in regard to their objective validity, to the evidence which the neutral ought to have of the fact, or their subjective validity, to the conduct which constitutes a breach of blockade and its penalties, and to the history of attempts to stretch the notion of blockade beyond the limits prescribed by international law.

A valid or lawful blockade requires the actual presence of a sufficient force of the enemy's vessels before a certain place on the coast. By presence is intended *general* presence, or presence so far as the elements do not interfere, so that the dispersion for a time of the blockading squadron by a storm is not held to amount to its being broken up. For this there must be abandonment of the undertaking. What *a sufficient force* is, cannot be determined with logical rigor. It may be said to be such a force as will involve a vessel attempting to pass the line of blockade in considerable danger of being taken.

1. What is a valid blockade?

Treaties have sometimes determined the amount of force necessary to make a blockade valid. Thus a treaty of 1742, between France and Denmark, declares that the entry of a port, to be blockaded, must be closed by at least two vessels, or by a battery of cannons placed on the coast, in such sort that vessels cannot get in without manifest danger. A treaty of 1753, between Holland and the two Sicilies, requires the presence of at least six vessels of war, at the distance of a little more than cannon-shot from the place, or the existence of batteries raised on the coast, such that entrance cannot be effected without passing under the besieger's guns. A treaty of 1818, between Russia and Denmark, repeats in substance the provisions of the first named treaty.

Paper or cabinet-blockades unlawful.

It results from this, that all paper or cabinet-blockades, whether declarations of an intention to blockade a place without sending an adequate force thither, or the mere formality of pronouncing a tract of coast under blockade, are an undue stretch of belligerent right, and of no validity whatever. Such grievous offences against the rights of neutrals have come, it is to be hoped, to a perpetual end, since the nations which offended most signally in this respect were parties to the declaration accompanying the peace of Paris (April 16, 1856), that "blockades in order to be binding must be effectual, that is to say, maintained by a force, sufficient in reality to prevent access to the coast of the enemy." (§ 175.)

§ 187.

2. Evidence of the existence of a blockade.

As a blockade arises from some positive act and not from a mere intention, as it is a temporary, and, it may be, an often-repeated measure, and as a neutral, is, in general, innocent in endeavoring to enter any port in his friend's territory, it is manifest that in order to become guilty, he must have had the means of obtaining due notice of the new state of things which a blockade has occasioned.

What is due notice?

The best notice is, when a vessel approaching a port, or attempting to enter it, is warned off by a ship pertaining to the blockading squadron. In many special treaties this is required. In that of 1794, between Great Britain and the United States, it is provided, that whereas vessels frequently "sail for a port or place belonging to an enemy without knowing that the same is either besieged, blockaded, or invested, it is agreed that every vessel so circumstanced may be turned away from such port or place; but she shall not be detained, nor her cargo, if not contraband, be confiscated, unless, after notice, she shall again attempt to enter." Similar stipulations exist in treaties between France and the governments of Spanish America.*

Justice to neutrals requires that their ships should not be subject to the risk and delays of a voyage to a port, where they may be debarred admission. The universal practice, is, therefore, to communicate the news of a blockade to neutral governments, upon whom lies the responsibility of making it known to those who are engaged in commerce. And if such notice be given, similar notice must be given of the discontinuance of a blockade, as far as possible. For a wrong is done to neutrals, if they are left to find out as they can that a blockade is terminated, since a long time may elapse before it will be considered safe to return to the old channel of commerce.

There is a difference of practice in regard to the amount of notification which neutrals may claim. The French hold, if we mistake not, that both a notice from the government of the belligerent, and notice from a blockading vessel, at or near the port, are necessary, so that a vessel will not incur guilt by coming to a port in order to ascertain whether a blockade, made known in the diplomatic way, is still kept up. The English authorities make two kinds of blockade, one a blockade *de facto*, which begins and ends with the fact, and which will involve no vessel attempting to enter a harbor in guilt, unless previously warned off; and the other a blockade, by notification, accompanied by the fact. In the latter case, the presumption is that the blockade continues until notice to

* Wheaton, El. IV. 3, § 28, p. 544; Ortolan, II. 305, seq.—Treaties of France, with Brazil (1828), Bolivia (1834), Texas (1839), Venezuela (1843), Equador (1843), and others more recent, contain such provisions.

the contrary is given by the blockading government. Hence ignorance of the existence of the blockade cannot ordinarily be plead as an excuse for visiting the blockaded port, but the voyage itself is evidence of an intention to do an unlawful act. This seems to be quite reasonable: notice to the neutral state must be regarded as notice to all shippers who are its subjects, and if the rule of evidence presses hard in a few cases, the blockading government is not in fault. But the notice must be given to all neutral powers in order to reach their subjects: general notoriety, as by news travelling from one country to another, is not sufficient notice.*

Equity requires that the neutral should have had time to receive notice of a blockade. Hence, a ship from a distance, as from across the Atlantic, may attempt to enter a port actually invested, without exposing itself to penalties.

It cannot be said in justice, that a shrewd suspicion of a blockade is enough to make a vessel guilty in sailing for a certain port, for a known or a knowable fact must precede guilt. On the other hand, a fair possibility derived from the expectation of peace, or from other sources, that a blockade is raised, may justify a vessel in sailing contingently for the port in question with the intention of inquiring at the proper place into the fact.

3. When is a blockade discontinued?

A blockade ceases, whenever the vessels which constitute it are withdrawn, whether with or without compulsion from the enemy, so that the undertaking is for the time, at least, abandoned. If the vessels return after leaving their stations, the commencement of a new blockade requires the same notification as before. Common fame in regard to the breaking up of a blockade will justify a neutral in sailing for the blockaded port, although, as we have seen, it is not sufficient notice to him: he ought to have more evidence of an interference with the normal state of things than he needs to have of a return to it.

* Comp. Wheaton, IV. 3, § 28; Phillimore, III. 385; Ortolan, II. 301 et seq.

§ 188.

A vessel violates the law of blockade by some positive act of entering or quitting, or by showing a clear and speedy intention to enter a blockaded port. A remote intention entertained at the outset of the voyage, for instance, might be abandoned, and the seizure of such a vessel on the high seas would be unlawful. It must be at or near the harbor, to be liable to penalty. The penalty is confiscation, and it falls first on the ship as the immediate agent in the crime. The cargo shares the guilt, unless the owners can remove it by direct evidence. The presumption is, that they knew the destination of the vessel, for the voyage was undertaken on account of the freight. If ship and cargo are owned by the same persons, the cargo is confiscated of course.

4. Penalty for breach of blockade.

The penalty for a breach of blockade is held to continue upon a vessel until the end of her return voyage, and to have ceased, if she were captured after the actual discontinuance of the blockade. The reasons for the former rule may be that the voyage out and back, is fairly looked on as *one transaction*, the return freight being the motive in part for the act, and that time ought to be allowed to the blockading vessels to pursue and capture the offender. The reason for the latter is, that the occasion for inflicting the penalty ceased with the blockade.

Duration of liability to penalty.

Besides this penalty on cargo and vessel, the older text-writers teach that punishment may be visited upon the direct authors of a breach of blockade.* Even de Martens (§ 320), declares that corporal pains, by the positive law of nations and by natural justice, may be meted out to those who are guilty of such breach. But the custom of nations, if it ever allowed of such severities, has long ceased to sanction them.

* Grotius, III. 1, § 5, 3; Bynkersh. Quæst. J. P. I. 11; Vattel, III. 7, § 117.

§ 189.

5. Attempts to stretch the doctrine of blockade.

The natural inclination of belligerents to stretch their rights at sea at the expense of neutrals, appears in attempts to enlarge the extent of blockades over a tract of coast without a sufficient force; and at no time so much as at the end of the eighteenth and beginning of the nineteenth century. In the war of France and Spain with Great Britain during the American revolution, those nations extended the notion of blockade unduly,* which led to the declaration of Russia in 1780,—afterwards made one of the principles of both the armed neutralities,—that the blockade of a port can exist only, " where, through the arrangements of the power which attacks a port by means of vessels stationed there and sufficiently near, there is an evident danger in entering."

The far more important aggressions on neutral rights between the years 1806 and 1812, are too closely connected with the affairs of our own country to be passed over in silence. These aggressions, under the continental system, as it was called, may be traced back to measures adopted towards the close of the last century, the object of which was to cripple the commerce of England. Thus, in 1796, the ports of the ecclesiastical state and Genoa, and in 1801, those of Naples and Portugal were closed to British vessels, by special treaties with the French republic.

Prussian decrees.

In 1806, Prussia, then in vassalage to Napoleon, but at peace with England, and being now in temporary possession of Hanover, issued a decree announcing that the ports and rivers of the North Sea were closed to English shipping, as they had been during the French occupation of Hanover. By way of retaliation, the British government gave notice to neutral powers, that the coast from the Elbe to Brest was placed in a state of blockade, of which coast the portion from Ostend to the Seine was to be considered as under the most rigorous blockade, while the remainder was open to

* Klüber, § 303.

neutral vessels not laden with enemies' goods, nor with goods contraband of war, nor guilty of a previous violation of blockade, nor sent from the ports of enemies of the British government.

Berlin decree.

This measure led to the Berlin decree of Bonaparte, bearing the date of November 21, 1806. In this decree, issued from the capital of subjugated Prussia, after reciting the infractions of international law with which England was chargeable, the Emperor declares the British islands to be under blockade, and all commerce with them to be forbidden, English manufactures to be lawful prize, and vessels from ports of England or her colonies to be excluded from all ports, and to be liable to confiscation, if they should contravene the edict by false papers.

First orders in council.

The Berlin decree "rendered every neutral vessel going from English ports with cargoes of English merchandise, or of English origin, lawfully seizable by French armed vessels.* The British government was not slow in its retaliation. By an order of council, dated Jan. 7, 1807, it was declared "that no vessel should be permitted to sail from one port to another, both of which ports should belong to or be in the possession of France or her allies, or should be so far under their control, that British vessels might not trade thereat." And by a second order of council, dated Nov. 11, 1807, it was declared that, as the previous order had not induced the enemy to alter his measures, all places of France, her allies and their colonies, as also of states at peace with Great Britain and yet excluding her flag, should be under the same restrictions as to commerce, as if they were blockaded by British forces. All commerce in the productions of such states was pronounced illegal, and all vessels so engaged, with their cargoes, if taken, were to be adjudged lawful prize. But neutrals might trade with the colonies, or even with the ports of states thus under the ban, for goods to be consumed by themselves, provided they either

Second orders in council.

* Words of M. Champagny, French minister of foreign relations, Oct. 7, 1807.

started from or entered into a British port, or sailed directly from the enemies' colonies to a port of their own state. Moreover, as certain neutrals had obtained from the enemy "certificates of origin" so called, to the effect that the cargoes of their vessels were not of British manufacture, it was ordered that vessels, carrying such certificates, together with the part of the cargo covered by them, should be confiscated, as the prize of the captor. A supplement to this order declared that ships sold by the enemy to a neutral would be deemed illegally sold, and be considered lawful prize, while another supplement regulated the manner in which neutrals must carry on their commerce, and prescribed licenses, without which trade in certain articles would be held unlawful.

Milan decree.

Against these orders the French Emperor fulminated the Milan decree of Dec. 17, 1807, declaring that every vessel which submitted to be searched by an English cruiser, or to make a voyage to England, or to pay a tax to the English government, had lost the right to its own flag, and had become English property; that such vessels, falling into the hands of French cruisers, or entering French ports, would be regarded as lawful prize; and that every vessel holding communication with Great Britain or with her colonies, if taken, would be condemned.

Measures of the U. States.

These arbitrary extensions of the right of war, by which neutral rights were sacrificed to the retaliation of the belligerents, were calculated to grind to pieces the few remaining neutral powers. Our country, being the principal state in this condition, made strong complaints, the disregard of which led to more positive measures. In December, 1807, an embargo was laid on commercial vessels in the ports of the United States, and in March, 1809, was passed an act prohibiting intercourse with France and England, until their restrictions on neutral commerce should be removed; which act was to continue in force towards either country, until it should revoke its obnoxious decrees.

This led to some relaxation on the part of Great Britain.

By an order in council of April 20, 1809, the ports of Holland, France, and Northern Italy, were to be placed under blockade, while the rest of the coast, embraced under previous orders, was opened to neutral commerce. Napoleon, as yet, however, relaxed his system of measures in no degree. In 1810, he ordered all British manufactures found in France to be burnt, and the same regulation extended to the states under French supremacy. This would seem to show that the prohibition of trade with England was not rigidly enforced, which was owing in part to the deficiency of the French naval force, and in part to the great demand for British manufactures and the venality of revenue officers. On the other hand, the English, being masters of the sea, were able to make their orders in council good against neutral commerce. It would seem that there was an understanding between the French government and our own, that the Berlin decree should not be put into force against our vessels.

British orders in council of April, 1809.

Such continued to be the state of things until 1812, when the French government annulled its obnoxious decrees, and the British, upon being made acquainted with the fact, rescinded their retaliatory orders, as far as concerned American goods on American vessels. This took place June the 23d,—not in time to prevent the war with Great Britain, which the United States had already begun in the same month, and a principal pretext for which was these same orders in council.

§ 190.

In order to enforce the right of preventing neutrals from conveying hostile or contraband goods on their ships, and from breaking blockade, it is necessary that the belligerents should be invested with the right of search or visit. By this is intended the right to stop a neutral vessel on the high seas, to go on board of her, to examine her papers, and, it may be, even her cargo,—in short, to ascertain by personal inspection that she is not engaged in the infraction of any of the rights above enumerated.

The right of search.

The right of search is by its nature confined within narrow

Confined within narrow limits.

limits, for it is merely a method of ascertaining that certain specific violations of right are not taking place, and would otherwise be a great violation, itself, of the freedom of passage on the common pathway of nations. *In the first place*, it is *only a war right.* The single exception to this is spoken of in § 194, viz. that a nation may lawfully send a cruiser in pursuit of a vessel which has left its port under suspicion of having committed a fraud upon its revenue-laws, or some other crime. This is merely the continuation of a pursuit beyond the limits of maritime jurisdiction with the examination conducted outside of these bounds, which, but for the flight of the ship, might have been conducted within. *In the second place*, it is applicable to merchant ships alone. Vessels of war, pertaining to the neutral, are exempt from its exercise, both because they are not wont to convey goods, and because they are, as a part of the power of the state, entitled to confidence and respect. If a neutral state allowed or required its armed vessels to engage in an unlawful trade, the remedy would have to be applied to the state itself. To all this we must add that a vessel in ignorance of the public character of another, for instance, suspecting it to be a piratical ship, may without guilt require it to lie to, but the moment the mistake is discovered, all proceedings must cease. (§§ 54, 195.) *In the third place*, the right of search must be exerted in such a way as to attain its object, and nothing more. Any injury done to the neutral vessel or to its cargo, any oppressive or insulting conduct during the search, may be good ground for a suit in the court to which the cruiser is amenable, or even for interference on the part of the neutral state to which the vessel belongs.

Duty of submitting to a search.

It is plain, from the reality of the right of search, that an obligation lies on the neutral ship to make no resistance. The neutral is in a different relation to the belligerents than the vessels of either of them to the other. These can resist, can run away, unless their word is pledged, but he cannot. Annoying as the exercise of this right may be, it must be submitted to, as even innocent persons are bound to submit to a search-warrant for the sake of general justice. Any resistance, therefore, or attempt to escape, or to get free from the search or its consequences, by force, if they do not bring on the destruction of the vessel at the time, may procure its confiscation, even though it had been engaged in a traffic entirely innocent.

Treaties often regulate the right of search.

This delicate right is often regulated by treaties prescribing the distance at which the visiting vessel shall remain from the vessel to be visited, which is in general not within cannot-shot; the number of persons to undertake the examination, as that only two besides the oarsmen shall pass to the merchant vessel; and the amount of evidence, which shall satisfy,—as that the ship itself shall not be searched, if the proper papers are on board, unless there is good ground for suspicion that these papers do not give a true account of the cargo, ownership, or destination.

§ 191.

Is there a right of convoy?

A search at sea is exceedingly annoying, not only because it may affect an innocent party, and may cause expensive delays, but also because those who are concerned in it are often insolent and violent. What can be expected of a master of a privateer, or of an inferior officer in the navy, urged perhaps by strong suspicion of the neutral's guilt, but that he will do his office in the most offensive and irritating manner? To prevent these annoyances, governments have sometimes arranged with one another, that the presence of a public vessel, or convoy, among a fleet of merchantmen, shall be evidence that the latter are engaged in a lawful trade. But neutrals have sometimes gone farther than this, they have claimed, without previous treaty, that a national ship convoying their trading vessels, shall be a sufficient guaranty that no unlawful traffic is on foot. The beginnings of such a claim proceeded from the Dutch in the middle of the 17th century, but the first earnest and concerted movement on the part of neutrals for this end, was made near the end of the last century, at which time, also, the principal

Historical illustrations.

maritime powers, excepting Great Britain, made treaties establishing the right of convoy between themselves. From this starting point, neutrals went on to claim that this right ought to be regarded as a part of the law of nations, and to employ force, when Great Britain exercised, without respect to the convoy, the right of search on the old plan. In 1798, the convoy of a fleet of Swedish merchantmen, having, in conformity with instructions, taken a British officer out of one of the vessels of commerce, the whole fleet was captured, and Sir William Scott, in the British admiralty court, decided that the act of violence subjected all the vessels to condemnation.* Not long after this, in 1800, a Danish frigate in the Mediterranean, acting as a convoy, fired on the boats sent from British frigates to examine the merchant vessels under its protection. The act was repeated in July of the same year by another frigate of the same nation, then neutral but ill-affected towards England. The frigate, named the Freya, with six trading vessels under its care, met six British ships of war, when the refusal of a demand to search the merchantmen led to acts of hostility, which resulted in the surrender of the Danish national vessel. In consequence, however, of negotiations between the two governments, the ship was released, and it was agreed, on the part of the Danes, that the right of convoy should not be exercised, until some arrangement should be made touching this point.

These collisions were one of the reasons for the formation of the *second armed neutrality* of 1800. In that league the contracting powers (Russia, Sweden, Denmark, and Prussia) laid down the following basis of a right of convoy, and of visit generally: (1.) That the right of visit, exercised by belligerents on vessels of the parties to the armed neutrality, shall be confined to public vessels of war, and never committed to privateers. (2.) That trading vessels of any of the contractants, under convoy, shall lodge with the commander of the convoying vessel their passports and certificates or sea-letters, drawn

* Case of the Maria, 1 Robinson's Rep. 340–379.

up according to a certain form. (3.) That when such vessel of convoy and a belligerent vessel meet, they shall ordinarily be beyond the distance of cannon-shot from one another, and that the belligerent commander shall send a boat to the neutral vessel, whereupon proofs shall be exhibited both that the vessel of convoy has a right to act in that capacity, and that the visiting vessel in truth belongs to the public navy. (4.) This done, there shall be no visit, if the papers are according to rule. Otherwise, the neutral commander, on request of the other, shall detain the merchantmen for visits, which shall be made in the presence of officers selected from the two ships of war. (5.) If the commander of the belligerent vessels finds that there is reason in any case for further search, on notice being given of this, the other commander shall order an officer to remain on board the vessel so detained, and assist in examining into the cause of the detention. Such vessel is to be taken to the nearest convenient port belonging to the belligerent, where the ulterior search shall be conducted with all possible despatch.*

The armed neutrality was succeeded by retaliatory embargoes, and on the 2d of April, 1801, the battle of Copenhagen prostrated the power of Denmark. Conventions were soon afterwards effected between Great Britain and the northern powers, by which they gave up the principle of "free ships, free goods;" and she acceded to their rules of convoy, stipulating also, in addition to the articles we have given above, that detention without due cause, and all acts of wrong, should render the commander of the belligerent force not only liable for damages to the proprietors of the vessels, but obnoxious to punishment.

The right of convoy, although not entitled to take a place in the international code, apparently approaches such a destiny, inasmuch as it is now engrafted into the *conventional* law of almost all nations. Whether, as some put it, the word of honor of the commander of the convoying vessel ought to be

* Cited from Heffter, § 170, note 2. See append. II. p. 397.

sufficient proof, may fairly be doubted. The French orders to their naval officers, issued in 1854, for the war with Russia, deserve notice for contemplating this point. "You shall not," say they, "visit vessels which are under the convoy of an allied or neutral ship of war, and shall confine yourselves to calling upon the commander of the convoy for a list of the ships placed under his protection, together with his written declaration that they do not belong to the enemy, and are not engaged in any illicit commerce. If, however, you have occasion to suspect that the commander of the convoy has been imposed upon [que la religion du commandant du convoi a été surprise], you must communicate your suspicions to that officer, who should proceed alone to visit the suspected vessel."

§ 192.

Justice of the right of convoy.

On the ground of justice this right cannot be defended. It is said that the commander of the convoying vessel represents the state, and the state guarantees that nothing illicit has been put on board the merchantmen. But how can the belligerent know whether a careful search was made before sailing, whether the custom-house did not lend itself to deception? It is only by comity that national vessels are allowed their important privileges; how, except by a positive and general agreement, can those privileges be still further extended, so as to limit the belligerent right of search? But on the ground of international good-will the right is capable of defence, and, so far as we can see, except where the protected fleet is far separated by a storm from its guardian,—in which case, we suppose the ordinary right of search must be resumed,—can be exercised in the interests of belligerents as well as neutrals.

§ 193.

Neutrals under belligerent convoy.

A novel case in international law arose, when, in 1810, Denmark, being at war with England, issued an ordinance, declaring to be lawful prize such neutral vessels, as had either in the Baltic or the Atlantic made use of English convoy. A number of vessels from the United States, bound to Russia, had placed themselves under English protection, and on their return, were seized and condemned in Denmark, not for resistance to search, nor for the character of their traffic, but for violating an ordinance to them unknown. The arguments of our negotiator setting forth the injustice of this proceeding, are given at large in Dr. Wheaton's Elements (IV. 3, § 32, 556–566), and Mr. Manning has expressed a brief opinion on the contrary side, in favor of the Danish rule. (III. 11, p. 369.) The ships appear to have been engaged in an innocent trade, and to have dreaded the treatment they might meet with from French cruisers, but not to have sought to avoid the allies of the French, the Danes. The case was a peculiarly hard one, when they were condemned; and this Denmark admitted in 1830, by paying an indemnity to our government for the sufferers. As for the principle on which the case is to be decided, it seems to run between making use of the enemy's flag, and putting one's goods on board an armed enemy's vessel. The former is done to enjoy certain privileges, offered by a party at war, which could not otherwise be secured; the latter may be done without complicity with the intentions or conduct of the captain of the armed ship, or may be done with the design of having two strings to one's bow,—of availing one's-self of force or not, as circumstances shall require. Upon the whole, the intention to screen the vessels behind the enemy's guns, is so obvious, that the act must be pronounced to be a decided departure from the line of neutrality, and one which may justly entail confiscation on the offending party.

§ 194.

Search during peace to execute revenue laws.

It is admitted by all, that within the waters which may be called the territory of nations, as within a marine league, or in creeks and bays, the vessel of a friendly state may be boarded and searched on suspicion of being engaged in unlawful commerce, or of violating the laws concerning revenue. But further than this, on account of the ease with which a criminal may escape beyond the proper sea-line of a country, it is allowable to chase such a vessel into the high sea, and then execute the arrest and search which flight had prevented before. Furthermore, suspicion of offences against the laws taking their commencement in the neighboring waters beyond the sea-line, will authorize the detention and examination of the supposed criminal. An English statute "prohibits foreign goods to be transhipped within four leagues of the coast without payment of duties; and the act of congress of March 20, 1799, contained the same prohibition; and the exercise of jurisdiction to that distance, for the safety and protection of the revenue laws, was declared by the supreme court in Church *v.* Hubbard (2 Cranch, 187), to be conformable to the laws and usages of nations." (Kent, I. 31, Lect. II.)

§ 195.

Search on suspicion of piracy.

That kind of right of search, which we have just considered, is an accident of sovereignty in a state of peace, but is confined in its exercise to a small range of the sea. The right of search on suspicion of piracy, however, is a war-right, and may be exercised by public vessels anywhere except in the waters of another state, because pirates are enemies of the human race, at war with all mankind. The supreme court of the United States has decided that ships of war acting under the authority of government to arrest pirates and other public offenders, may "approach any vessels descried at sea for the purpose of ascertaining their real character." * And thus even public vessels, suspected of piracy, may be called to account upon the ocean. Whether the detention of a vessel unjustly suspected of piracy may not be a ground for a claim of damages may be made a question.

* Case of the Marianna Flora, 11 Wheaton, 43.

§ 196.

As the slave-trade is not as yet piracy by the law of nations, but only by the municipal and conventional law of certain nations (§ 138), no state can authorize its cruisers to detain and visit vessels of other states on suspicion of their being concerned in this traffic, because the right of detention and visit is a war-right. Every state may, to carry out its laws and the laws of humanity, detain and search its own vessels in peace also, but if, in so doing, mistakes are committed, the commander of the searching vessel is responsible, and damages may be demanded.

Search of foreign vessels suspected of being slavers unauthorized,

§ 197.

Such right, however, of reciprocal detention and visitation upon suspicion of being engaged in the slave-trade has been conceded by a considerable number of treaties between the principal powers of Europe. Previous to the downfall of Bonaparte there had been a falling off of the traffic in slaves; for Great Britain, who had prohibited her own citizens from the traffic, prevented also her enemies from engaging in it by her command of the seas; it had, moreover, long been forbidden under heavy penalties by the United States; and there were then on this side of the water few motives for engaging in so dangerous an employment. At the peace, although the sentiment of Europe was expressed against the slave-trade, the nations most interested in resuming it, France, Spain and Portugal, refused to give it up at once, alleging that their colonies needed to be replenished with slave-laborers, while those of England were fully stocked. The first concession of the right of search is to be found in the treaty between Portugal and England made July 28, 1817,—which, however, related only to the trade north of the equator; for the slave-trade of Portugal within the regions of western Africa, to the south of the equator, continued long after this to be carried on with great vigor. By this treaty, ships of war of each of the nations

but conceded by treaties between most of the nations of Europe,

as England and Portugal in 1817.

might visit merchant vessels of both, if suspected of having slaves on board, acquired by illicit traffic. By the treaty of Madrid, of the same year, Great Britain obtained from Spain, for the sum of four hundred thousand pounds, the immediate abolition of the trade, north of the equator, its entire abolition after 1820, and the concession of the same mutual right of search, which the treaty with Portugal had just established. The precedent was followed by a treaty of Great Britain with the Netherlands, in 1818, which also contemplated the establishment of a mixed commission to decide upon the cases of vessels seized on suspicion of slave-trading. Stipulations somewhat similar were made between Sweden and Great Britain in 1824.

Treaty of Madrid, 1817.

Other treaties in 1818, 1824.

In 1831 and 1833, conventions between France and Great Britain included one more power in arrangements for mutual search. But the right of search was only admissible on the western coast of Africa from Cape Verd (15° North Lat.) to the tenth degree of south latitude, and to the thirteenth degree of west longitude from the meridian of Paris, and also around Madagascar, Cuba, and Porto Rico, as well as on the coast of Brazil to the distance into the sea of twenty leagues. It was agreed, however, that suspected vessels, escaping beyond this range of twenty leagues, might be detained and visited if kept in sight. As to steps subsequent to capture no mixed commission was allowed, but the captured vessel was to be tried in the country to whose jurisdiction it belonged, and by its courts.

Conventions in 1831, 1833, between France and G. Britain.

By the quintuple treaty of December 20, 1841, to which Great Britain, Austria, Prussia, Russia, and France, were parties, all these powers, excepting the latter, conceded to one another the mutual right of search within very wide zones of ocean between Africa and America, and on the eastern side of Africa across the Indian ocean. France, however, owing to popular clamor, and the dislike entertained by almost the entire chamber of deputies toward the right of search, withheld her ratification and adhered to her arrangements of 1831 and 1833, above spoken of, until the

Quintuple treaty of 1841.

year 1845. In that year she withdrew her consent to the mutual right of search altogether,—as the terms of the conventions allowed her to do,—but stipulated to coöperate with Great Britain in suppressing the slave-trade by sending a squadron to the coast of Africa. Each power engaged to keep twenty-six vessels on the coast for this service, at first, but the number on the part of France was afterward to be reduced to one half. This is believed to be the existing arrangement.

France, in 1845, withdraws her consent to a right of search.

§ 198.

The treaty of Ghent, which terminated the war between the United States and Great Britain on the 24th of December, 1814, contains the following article: "Whereas the traffic in slaves is irreconcilable with the principles of humanity and justice; and whereas both His Britannic Majesty and the United States are desirous of continuing their efforts to promote its entire abolition, it is hereby agreed that both the contracting parties shall use their best endeavors to accomplish so desirable an object." The act passed by Congress in 1818, which increased the penalties hanging over this traffic and extended their application; that of 1819, which authorized the sending of armed vessels to the coast of Africa, and the confiscation of slave-trading ships belonging to citizens or foreign residents, together with the effects on board; and the act of 1820, by which the slave-trade, wherever carried on, was declared to be piracy both for all persons on American craft so employed, and for American citizens serving on board vessels of any nationality,—these several acts show that the United States were sincerely endeavoring "to accomplish so desirable an object" as the entire abolition of this infamous traffic.

Obligations of the U. States in regard to the slave-trade.

But the trade continued notwithstanding such legislation, and it would appear that vessels and crews from the United States were concerned in it, acting in the interest of Cubans, but especially of Portuguese in Brazil. The British government, therefore, from time to time, urged on that of the United

States the adoption of more effectual measures to comply with the stipulations of the treaty of Ghent. In particular it urged that the two nations should concede to each other the right of search, with the single object in view of ascertaining whether a suspected vessel was really concerned in the slave-trade. To this the United States uniformly declined giving their assent. The right of search was an odious one even in war, and peculiarly odious, because British cruisers had exercised it in an overbearing and illegitimate way, when the United States were a neutral nation. It would, if admitted, naturally involve a mixed court for deciding cases of capture, which court, stationed in a foreign country, and composed of judges not all of them amenable to our laws, did not afford to native citizens brought before it those securities, which are guaranteed to them by the constitution.

Resolution of Feb. 28, 1823.

Meanwhile, in February, 1823, by a vote of one hundred and thirty-one to nine, the House of Representatives passed the following resolution: "That the President of the United States be requested to enter upon and to prosecute, from time to time, such negotiations with the several maritime powers of Europe and America, as he may deem expedient for the effectual abolition of the African slave trade, and its *ultimate denunciation as piracy under the law of nations* by the consent of the civilized world." The Secretary of State, John Q. Adams, in transmitting this resolution to the British negotiator, says that "the President has no hesitation in acting upon the expressed and almost unanimous sense of the House of Representatives, so far as to declare the willingness of the American Union to join with other nations in the common engagement to pursue and punish those who shall continue to practise this crime, and to fix them irrevocably in the class and under the denomination of pirates."

Most unfortunately the international arrangements here contemplated were not carried into effect. The British government conceived, as we presume, that it would be very difficult to bring the other nations into similar agreements, and in fact did not, itself, carry through parliament a law making the slave-trade piracy until March 31, 1824. Again, therefore, the old plan of mutual search was urged; but, although there was some little expectation that an agreement might be reached, on the basis of delivering over captured vessels to the jurisdiction of their own country, and of holding the captor responsible for any improper acts to the tribunal of the captured party, yet no definite result came from the correspondence between Mr. Adams and the British minister at Washington. This correspondence deserves especial attention from the ability with which the Secretary of State discusses the right of search.

Negotiations in England. Convention of 1824.

The negotiations were now transferred to England, where, on the 13th of March, in 1824, the two governments, by their representatives, signed a convention which nearly accomplished the object at which they had been aiming. By this convention the officers of certain public vessels, duly instructed to cruise on the coasts of Africa, America, and the West Indies, were authorized to detain and examine vessels suspected of being engaged in the illicit traffic in slaves. If, after search, such vessels were found to be so employed, they were to be delivered up to the officers of a vessel of the same nationality, who might be on the station; or, if there were no cruisers nigh, were to be conveyed to the country to which such slavers belonged, or to one of its dependencies, and placed within the reach of its tribunals. Officers exercising the right of search in a vexatious or injurious manner, were to be personally liable in costs and damages to the masters or owners of vessels detained and visited. In all cases of search the boarding officers were to give certificates to the captains, identifying themselves, and declaring their object to be simply and solely that of ascertaining whether the merchantman was engaged in the slave-trade. Other provisions secured the right of challenging witnesses, and the payment of their expenses. The tenth article we give in its own words: "The high contracting parties declare that the right, which, in the foregoing articles, they have each reciprocally conceded, of detaining, visiting, capturing, and delivering over for trial the merchant vessels of the other engaged in the

African slave-trade, is wholly and exclusively grounded on the consideration of their having made that traffic piracy by their respective laws; and further, that the reciprocal concession of said right, as guarded, limited, and regulated by this convention, shall not be so construed as to authorize the detention or search of the merchant vessels of either nation by the officers of the navy of the other, except vessels engaged, or suspected of being engaged, in the African slave-trade, or for any other purpose whatever than that of seizing and delivering up the persons and vessels, concerned in that traffic, for trial and adjudication by the tribunals and laws of their own country; nor be taken to affect in any other way the existing rights of either of the high contracting parties. And they do also hereby agree, and engage to use their influence, respectively, with other maritime and civilized powers, to the end that the African slave-trade may be declared to be piracy under the law of nations."

Amended by Senate of U. S; then rejected by G. Britain.

When this convention came before the Senate of the United States they amended it as follows: (1.) Either party might renounce the convention after six months' notice. (2.) The cruising of vessels on the search for slavers was limited to Africa and the West Indies, *America* being stricken out. (3.) Article VII. of the convention speaks of trying for piracy citizens or subjects of either country found on board a vessel not "carrying the flag of the other party, nor belonging to the citizens or subjects of either, but engaged in the illicit traffic of slaves, and lawfully seized by the cruisers of the other party." This, also, was struck out by the Senate. Such cases would be those of American citizens on board of Portuguese or other slavers subject to search by special treaty with Great Britain, who were committing an offence capital by the laws of their own country, but not capital by those of the country of the vessel. The convention, thus mutilated, went back to England to be rejected, and so the affair ended.

§ 199.

The treaty of Washington, signed August 9, 1842, contains new arrangements in regard to the right of search which have served until of late as the rule of practice for the cruisers of the two countries. In article VIII. of that treaty occur the following words: "Whereas, notwithstanding the laws which have at various times been passed by the two governments, that criminal traffic is still prosecuted and carried on; and whereas the United States of America and Her Majesty, the Queen of the United Kingdom of Great Britain and Ireland, are determined that, so far as it may be in their power, it shall be effectually abolished; the parties mutually stipulate that each shall prepare, equip, and maintain in service, on the coast of Africa, a sufficient and adequate squadron or naval force of vessels, of suitable numbers and descriptions, to carry in all not less than eighty guns, to enforce separately and respectively the laws, rights, and obligations of each of the two countries for the suppression of the slave-trade: the said squadrons to be independent of each other; but the two governments stipulating nevertheless to give such orders to the officers commanding their respective forces as shall enable them most effectually to act in concert and coöperation, upon mutual consultation, as exigencies may arise, for the attainment of the true object of this article; copies of all such orders to be communicated by each government respectively." To this, article IX. adds, that "whereas, nothwithstanding all efforts that may be made on the coast of Africa for suppressing the slave-trade, the facilities for carrying on that traffic and avoiding the vigilance of cruisers, by the fraudulent use of flags and other means, are so great, and the temptations for pursuing it, while a market can be found for slaves, so strong, as that the desired result may be long delayed, unless all markets be shut against the purchase of African negroes, the parties to this treaty agree that they will unite in all becoming remonstrances with any and all powers, within whose dominions such markets are allowed to exist; and that they will urge upon all such powers the propriety and

Treaty of Washington in 1842.

duty of closing such markets forever." By article XI. it is provided that the eighth article shall continue in force five years after the ratification, and afterwards until either of the parties shall signify a wish to terminate it.

Practice under the treaty.

In carrying out the provisions of this treaty the squadrons of the two nations have acted in concert a good part of the time since 1842, and with considerable success. There are, however, serious difficulties in the way of putting an end to the slave-trade under this arrangement. The United States admit no right of search of vessels sustaining their national character. If, then, a British cruiser boards a vessel of the United States whose papers are right, no search can be made, notwithstanding the most flagrant suspicion. Should the boarded vessel, on the other hand, prove to be concerned in a lawful traffic, the cruiser is responsible for the damage of the detention. Unless, then, ships of the two nations "hunt in couples," or officers of one accompany the ships of the other, with authority to superintend the visit, the trade cannot wholly be prevented. Or rather such entire prevention will be impossible until the coast of Africa shall be skirted with Christian colonies, until its interior be stimulated into an industry which shall create a demand for labor at home, and until the slave-trade shall become piracy by the voice of all nations.

§ 200.

What does the right of search mean?

A question has arisen between the government of the United States and that of Great Britain as to the true notion of the right of search? Is there any difference between the right of visitation so called, and the right of search,—between the right to ascertain by an inspection of the ship's papers that she has the nationality which she claims, and the subsequent right of inspecting the vessel and cargo, for the purpose of ascertaining whether she has certain kinds of merchandise, as slaves for instance, on board, or whether her papers are fraudulent? The English doctrine touching this point is expressed by Lord Aberdeen in a note addressed to our minister in London, of which the following words are a part: "The right of search, except when specially conceded by treaty, is a purely belligerent right, and can have no existence on the high seas during peace. The undersigned apprehends, however, that the right of search is not confined to the verification of the nationality of the vessel, but also extends to the objects of the voyage and the nature of the cargo. The sole purpose of the British cruisers is to ascertain whether the vessels they meet with are really American or not. The right asserted has in truth no resemblance to the right of search, either in principle or in practice. It is simply a right to satisfy the party, who has a legitimate interest in knowing the truth, that the vessel actually is what her colors announce. This right we concede as freely as we exercise. The British cruisers are not instructed to detain American vessels under any circumstances whatever: on the contrary they are ordered to abstain from all interference with them, be they slavers or otherwise. But where reasonable suspicion exists that the American flag has been abused for the purpose of covering the vessel of another nation, it would appear scarcely credible . . . that the government of the United States, which has stigmatized and abolished the trade itself, should object to the adoption of such means as are indispensably necessary for ascertaining the truth."

A little later we find the English envoy at Washington in a communication from his government giving notice that Great Britain still "maintained and would exercise, if necessary, its own right to ascertain the genuineness of any flag which a suspected vessel might bear; that if, in the exercise of this right, either from involuntary error, or in spite of every precaution, loss or injury should be sustained, a prompt reparation would be offered; but that it should entertain for a single instant the notion of abandoning the right itself would be quite impossible."

Doctrine held by the United States.

The government of the United States, on the other hand, has maintained that there is no right of visiting a vessel, for the purpose of ascertaining its nationality and distinct from the right of search, known to the law of nations; that the right to visit, in order to be effectual, must in the end include search; that the right differs in no respect from the belligerent right of search; and that every case of detention of an American vessel for this purpose is a wrong, calling for reparation. These views are set forth by Mr. Webster, then Secretary of State, in a letter to the ambassador of the United States at London. "No such recognition," he there says [*i. e.* of the right claimed by England], "has presented itself to the United States; but, on the contrary, it understands that public writers, courts of law, and solemn treaties, have for centuries used the word 'visit' and 'search' in the same sense. What Great Britain and the United States mean by the 'right of search,' in its broadest sense, is called by continental writers and jurists by no other name than the 'right of visit.' Nor can the government of the United States agree that the term 'right' is justly applied to such exercise of power as the British government thinks it indispensable to maintain in certain cases." Again, "there is no right to visit in time of peace, except in the execution of revenue laws or other municipal regulations, in which cases the right is usually exercised near the coast, or within a marine league, or where the vessel is justly suspected of violating the law of nations by piratical aggression; but whenever exercised it is the right of search.

To Lord Aberdeen's declaration, that reparation would be made for injury sustained through the exercise of this right of visit, it is replied that, "if injury be produced by the exercise of a right, it would seem strange that it should be repaired as if it had been the effect of a wrongful act. The general rule of law certainly is, that in the proper and prudent exercise of his own rights, no one is answerable for undesigned injury. It may be said that the right is a qualified right, that is, a right to do certain acts of force at the risk of turning out to be wrong-doers, and of being made answerable for all damages. But such an argument would prove every trespass to be matter of right, subject only to just responsibility. It is as if a civil officer on land have process against one individual and through mistake arrest another; this arrest is wholly tortious. No one would think of saying it was done under any lawful exercise of authority, or that it was anything but a mere trespass, though an unintentional trespass. The municipal law does not undertake to lay down beforehand any rule for the government of such cases; and as little does the public law of the world lay down beforehand any rule for the government of cases of involuntary trespasses, detentions and injuries at sea, except that in both cases, law and reason make a distinction between injuries committed through mistake, and injuries committed by design, the former being entitled to fair and just compensation, the latter demanding exemplary damages, and sometimes personal punishment." In another passage the inquiry is made, "By what means is the ascertainment of the nationality of a vessel to be effected? Must it lie to? Or, if it pursue its voyage, may force be used? Or, if it resist force and is captured, must it not be condemned as resisting a right, which cannot exist without a corresponding obligation imposed on the other party? Thus, it appears that the right exercised in peace differs nothing, as to the means of enforcing it which must be adopted, from the right of search exercised in war, which the English government disclaims the use of. The government of the United States admits that its flag can give no immunity to pirates, nor to any other than regularly documented vessels, and it was upon this view of the whole case, that it cheerfully assumed the duties of the treaty of Washington."*

New discussion of the right of search in 1858, 1859.

This discussion took place between 1841 and 1843. Since then, in 1858, the British government having stationed cruisers near Cuba, for the purpose of preventing the slave-trade with that island, certain American vessels were visited on suspicion, and loud complaints arose. The Senate of the United States, thereupon, passed the following resolution: "that American vessels on the high seas in time of peace, bearing the American flag, remain under the jurisdiction of the country to which they belong; and, therefore, any visitation, molestation, or detention of such

* Comp. Wheaton's Hist. pp. 585–718 (from which we have freely drawn), and Webster's Works, Vol. VI., p. 329, et seq.

vessels, by force, or by the exhibition of force on the part of a foreign power, is in derogation of the sovereignty of the United States."

From the explanations which have since taken place, it does not appear that the British government was disposed to deny the right which this resolution implies. Knowing or believing slavers to have an American nationality, it has, at least since 1842, disclaimed the right to detain them, and finding them to be American, upon examination of their papers, it admits that it cannot search them without a violation of international law. What, then, is the point upon which the two governments differ. Is it that the flag shall always protect the vessel which carries it? We do not understand our government to take this almost absurd position, which would prevent, in fact, the execution of the treaties establishing the right of mutual search into which England has entered with Spain and Portugal, and would render nugatory all attempts to put down the slave-trade. Is it that if an American vessel is detained by mistake, no reparation shall ever be paid? But the contrary has been asserted by Lord Aberdeen and others who have spoken for the British government. The only questions between the two powers ought to be these: in ascertaining the nationality of a vessel under suspicion, what procedure shall be prescribed to the officer in charge of the matter, and if injury is done by the detention, in what way shall it be discovered and compensated? The English and French governments have agreed on a code of instructions relating to this subject which are identical, and that code has been submitted to our government for its adoption.*

New arrangements in 1862.

So stood the discussion between the two governments on the right of search down to 1860, when the first edition of this work was published. A new face was put on affairs by the treaty signed at Washington, April 7, 1862, and ratified at London, May 25, by which the two powers conceded the mutual right of search to public

* Speech of Lord Malmesbury, of Feb. 14, 1859.

vessels specially provided with instructions for that purpose, which are authorized to visit each other's merchant vessels, known or suspected of trading in slaves, but only within 200 miles of the African coast south of parallel 32, and within 30 leagues of Cuba. The searching officers are required to show their instructions, and give certificates of their rank, etc., to the visited vessel. Losses by arbitrary and illegal detention are to be made good, etc. Three mixed courts without appeal are established,—at New York, Sierra Leone, and the Cape of Good Hope. Certain indications of the character of vessels searched are mentioned as being presumptive evidence of intention to engage in the slave-trade, and as justifying detention, and precluding damages, for it. Vessels condemned by the courts above-mentioned are to be broken up, and sold unless used for public purposes. May this treaty prove an effectual bar to this wicked traffic in future.

§ 201.

Nationality of vessels a legitimate matter of inquiry in time of peace.

Viewing this subject now for a moment, not in the light of positive law, but in that of justice, we must admit the distinction between search which ends with ascertaining a vessel's nationality, and search which goes further, to be entirely reasonable, and deserving of recognition by the law of nations. There is no middle ground between the flags' being decisive proof of nationality and examining upon suspicion. Every nation has, in peace, the right of visiting its own vessels on the high seas, and it may be highly important so to do. By the nature of the case, mistakes must sometimes be made in attempting to exercise such a right, and as soon as they are discovered search is to be broken off. Suppose, again, that by special convention, two states were to give up, reciprocally, the right of search in war; and one of them were to be at war with some other country. Is it not evident that either such belligerent must abandon the right of search altogether, or ascertain for itself by inspection of papers, that particular vessels belonged to the country with which its agreement to abstain from search existed? If an injury grows out of detention, so may it grow out of detention on suspicion of piracy, where the examination may proceed far beyond the point of ascertaining the nationality of the vessel. If now a nation or its cruisers may be called to account for injuring the innocent while doing a lawful work, and if equitable claims for damage arising from detention are allowed, it is not easy to see what harm can spring from a police of the seas thus limited.

§ 202.

Rights to search for her seamen on neutral ships claimed by Great Britain.

"England asserts the right of impressing British subjects in time of war out of neutral ships, and of deciding by her visiting officers, who among the crews of such merchant ships are British subjects. She asserts this as a legal prerogative of the crown; which prerogative is alleged to be founded on the English law of perpetual and indissoluble allegiance of the subject, and his obligation under all circumstances, and for his whole life, to render military service to the crown whenever required." *

The exercise of this assumed right has formerly been the source of more embittered feeling among the inhabitants of the United States towards Great Britain, than any or all other causes. At different times since the French revolution, and especially before the war of 1812, attempts were made to remove by negotiation this ground of vexation and animosity. In 1803, a convention having this in view, came to the point of signature, but was broken off, because the British government insisted that it should not apply to the "narrow seas" near the British islands. The war of 1812, it is well known, was justified on this pretext after the orders in council had been rescinded. The claim was not alluded to in the treaty of Ghent, nor has Great Britain since abandoned it. The exercise of this right of search was peculiarly galling and severe, because mistakes might arise, or be claimed to arise, from similarity of names; and because emigrant sailors, whose families and hopes were on this side of the water, might be

* Mr. Webster's letter to Lord Ashburton, of Aug. 1842.

dragged away from the vessel in which they had shipped, and in which they would soon return to their homes.

The question of the indefeasibleness of the subjects' allegiance, is by no means closely connected with this so-called right. Admit the doctrine of indissoluble allegiance, this right will not follow. Reject it, and still it might be true that England might impress her subjects not naturalized in this country, if found on our vessels. But the right must be pronounced to have no foundation. A belligerent cruiser has no right to search a neutral on the high sea for any reason which does not involve the neutral's violation of his neutrality, *i. e.* his attempt to aid one of the parties at war. For every other purpose the ship is territory, so far forth, that it is under its territorial law, and no one on board can be invaded more than another. The laws of the land to which a vessel belongs, govern on the high seas, unless international law interferes. Is it, then, against the law of nations, is it even a wrong done to a country, if a sailor there born is taken on board a vessel as one of its crew? This will not be pretended. What, then, is to be thought of a right which invades the deck of a neutral vessel with force, in order to prevent that which a neutral may lawfully do, and which, it may be, the sailor in question might lawfully do, until this right was enforced against him, and which he was bound to do by contract? Moreover, it is not easy to see, if the right exists, why it is confined to a time of war, since it has nothing to do with the relations between the neutral and the enemy. It is really, then, a perpetual and universal right, if a right at all, and as legitimate on land as on the sea.

It is the recollection of the arrogance with which England, as the mistress of the seas, attempted to enforce this right, that has obstructed her in all effective arrangements with the United States for suppressing the slave-trade. Had this unhappy wound not been opened years since, it is not unlikely that her benevolent purposes towards Africa, would have found more earnest co-operation, and have borne full fruit.*

* Comp. Mr. Webster's admirable letter to Lord Ashburton, of Aug. 8, 1842,

CONCLUSION.

DEFECTS, SANCTIONS, PROGRESS, AND PROSPECTS OF INTERNATIONAL LAW.

§ 203.

INTERNATIONAL LAW, as we have viewed it, is a system of rules, adopted by the free choice of certain nations for the purpose of governing their intercourse with each other, and not inconsistent with the principles of natural justice. It has grown up by degrees, and has been submitted during its progress to sundry modifications. It is the most voluntary of all codes, but in other respects shares the character of national law. We propose, in this closing chapter, to consider briefly its defects, its sanctions, its progress hitherto, and its prospects for the future.

1. Defects of international law.

The principal deficiencies of international law grow out of its voluntary nature, and its being a law for the conduct of perfectly sovereign independent bodies. Hence its slow progress, since it takes time for modifications or improvements of it to pass from one nation to another; and hence, also, in part, the different views of it taken by different nations, some of which are in advance of their age, in a sense of justice or of true international policy. But the principal defect arising from this source is *the want of an authoritative exponent of its principles.* When individuals differ in regard to their rights, the law as interpreted by the courts decides at last between them. But no nation can set up its opinion on a doubtful question of international law as a rule for another. No text-writer has such

Its uncertainty.

given by Wheaton in his History, pp. 737–746, and in Webster's Works, Vol. VI., p. 318.

authority that all will abide by his judgment, not to say that he may need an interpreter himself; that new cases may arise which he has not contemplated; and that part of the law he has laid down may become obsolete. And thus, if nations have differed on some important question touching their rights, they have been prone, in the absence of any sovereign authority beyond themselves, to take the law into their own hands, —to commit their cause to the sword.

In regard, however, to the question what is actually international law, there seems no impossibility that a congress of men learned in that department should prepare a code, on which all Christian nations or the great body of them should agree. Such a congress has appeared to many to be highly desirable. That its decisions in the shape of a code should introduce entire certainty into the science, or that its own language would not give rise to new uncertainties, is not to be supposed; still many questions as to the rights of ambassadors, of neutral territory, and of war on land and on the sea, and the like, could be so far settled, that there would be fewer grounds of controversy, fewer unintended violations of the law between nations than hitherto. As for the interpretation of such a code in the general, and when it should bear on no present dispute, it is not unlikely that a uniform view would grow up among the publicists of all nations. And if additions or changes should be found necessary in the progress of human society, they could be made with more ease than the original code itself.

§ 204.

2. Its narrow limits.

Another defect of existing international law is the limited number of nations to which it is applicable. As it is a voluntary code, to which neither the half-civilized nor the barbarian parts of the world have given their assent, the Christian states who make it a law between themselves are in danger of acting as if no rules of justice bound them beyond their own circle, and as if nations which refused to abide by their rules of intercourse in any respect were to be treated as enemies. Formerly barbarous tribes were conquered under grant from the Pope to make Christians of them. Now great nations do not scruple to seize on islands or coasts with no sufficient pretext, or go to war because a nation of the East, in the exercise of its sovereignty, declines to trade with them. And when war breaks out in such cases, there is no obligation acknowledged to abide by the ordinary rules of humanity, or scarcely of justice. When Constantine was stormed, in 1837, by the French, besides the ordinary pillage of property by the troops, a scientific commission robbed the inhabitants of all the Arabic manuscripts they could lay their hands on.

No cure can be effectual for this evil, until a deeper moral sense and feeling of brotherhood shall dictate rules, humane and just, by which the vessels of civilized nations shall govern their intercourse with the weak and the barbarous parts of the world. Nor even then will lawless crews abstain from outrages, which will be avenged on the next ship, and thus new fuel be applied to kindle up the ferocity of savages. And for every outrage there will be a plea, which will prevail, because the savages cannot tell their own story. We have already remarked (§ 136), that rules of intercourse with such races of men cannot be conformed to our international code, and that punishments must often be summary with them, to be understood. But is justice, is humanity, to be thrown off, as being conventional? Can there be a doubt that, if all the ships of Christian states had dealt kindly and righteously with the islands of the sea, long ago they would have been far more open to Christianity and civilization than they are now.

§ 205.

3. No umpire in controversies.

Another obvious defect of international law, is its weakness in cases of controversy, arising from the sovereignty of nations, and from the fact that they have no national umpire to whom, in entire confidence, they can refer their disputes. It has, indeed, often happened, that a point of controversy has been referred to an arbitrator chosen for the occasion, and that thus wars have been prevented. But there seem to be difficulties in such a course, owing either to the arbitrator's imperfect acquaintance with the subject-matter referred to him, or to his inclination to "split the difference," whether through a desire to stand well with both parties, or through his inability to come to a sure decision.

It has been urged with great zeal by benevolent persons, anxious to put an end to war, that a congress of nations,—an international court,—can and ought to be instituted, to which all controversies should be submitted, and whose decisions would be, by the pledged word of the parties represented, final. There are great difficulties to be overcome, before such a court, with deputies from great and small states, under various forms of government, could be constituted with the requisite powers; and probably others no less formidable would attend its working, and the execution,—by force if necessary,—of its decisions. If such a court or congress could be created, we should hail the event as a sign of the peaceful spirit which was abroad, and which would give the body very little to do.

A congress to settle disputes.

§ 206.

A plan to prevent war was proposed by the Abbé St. Pierre, in 1729, in his "Abregé du projet de paix perpetuelle," of which, as well as of other similar plans, an extended account is given by Dr. Wheaton, in his history of the law of nations.* St. Pierre contemplated a perpetual alliance, or league, of which the states of Europe should be members, having in all, either singly or in groups, twenty votes. The allies should renounce the right of war, and submit their differences to the arbitration of the general assembly of the league, whose decision, if it carried three fourths of the votes, should be final. If one of the allies should refuse to abide by such decision, or make treaties in contravention of it,

Projects of peace between nations. 1. St. Pierre's.

* For St. Pierre's, comp. Part 2, § 17; for Bentham's, Part 3, § 21; for Kant's, Part 4, §§ 36, 37. Comp. also Kant, "zum ewigen Frieden," in his works, vol. 5, pp. 411–466 (ed. Leipz. 1838); and Ladd, in Prize Essays on a Congress of Nations, pp. 509–638. (Boston, 1840.)

or make preparations for war, the allies should arm against the refractory member with the view of reducing it to obedience. The representatives of the league were to be empowered to pass, by a plurality of votes, all laws necessary to carry the objects of the alliance into effect, but entire unanimity of the allies was required for changes in the fundamental articles of their confederation.

2. Jeremy Bentham's.

About the year 1789, and just before the great revolutionary outburst in Europe, Jeremy Bentham sketched a plan of a general congress, which was long afterwards published. The nations were first to be led to reduce and fix their military establishments in some fair ratio, and also to abandon their colonies, for which so much blood had been shed. Then a congress was to be established, consisting of two deputies from each state, the agency of which should consist in reporting and circulating its decrees, and in placing refractory states under the ban of Europe. Bentham was willing that a fixed contingent should be furnished by the several states for the purpose of enforcing the decrees of the court, but thought that public opinion and a free press would prevent the necessity of such an extreme measure.

3. Kant's.

In 1795, Immanuel Kant published a short essay inscribed "zum ewigen Frieden,"—"to perpetual peace." Some of his preliminary articles were the following: that no state should be merged by inheritance, exchange, sale or gift in another state; that standing armies should in time cease; that no state debts should be incurred with reference to external politics; that no state should interfere with force in the affairs of another. Then follow the definitive articles, the first of which is, that every state shall have a republican constitution, or one in which all the citizens share in the power of making laws, and deciding on questions of peace and war. The next is, that international law shall be based upon a confederation of free states; and finally, there is to be a citizenship of the world, limited to the notion of the free access of all men to, and their residence in any state upon the earth's surface. The congress which Kant proposes is not to be indissoluble, but is to be held and to be dissolved according to the pleasure of the members.*

For the advantages and the feasibleness, according to the views of the authors, of a general congress of nations, the prize essays may be consulted, which were called forth by premiums offered by friends of the American Peace Society, especially the sixth essay written by Mr. William Ladd.

Wm. Ladd's essay.

With regard to all such plans for securing perpetual peace, we must take into account (1.) the danger of dissolution, owing to the separate interests and party-feelings of the members; (2.) the danger that great states would control the congress, and make it their instrument; (3.) that if the congress had no means of enforcing its decrees, they would not be respected, and if they had, a general war would break out instead, as it might be, of a particular one.†

§ 207.

What, then, are the sanctions of international law? They are, *first*, within each separate state municipal laws confirming it, and making penal its violation. Such are the laws of the United States which protect the persons of ambassadors, or prohibit offences against neutral rights, and the like. (Comp. § 165.) *Secondly*, the moral sentiment of each and all the states which have consented to the existing international law. This is a considerable and an increasing force, one which comes into the recesses of palaces and cabinets; and which sometimes speaks in threatening tones against gross wrongs. *Thirdly*, war. Great as the evil of war is, it is not in the existing condition of mankind the greatest. It would have been a greater evil for the states of Europe to have surrendered their independence to Napoleon, than it was to recover it by the sacrifice of untold treasure and countless

Sanctions of international law.

* Comp. Wheaton's Hist. p. 754, and Kant's Rechtlehre, § 61, the end of the treatise.

† Comp. Bluntschli, Staatsr. II. 18.

lives. Nations are reformed by the sobering influences of war. Nations are exalted by contending in war for something which is good. Let not this dread sanction, then, be thought to be of no use. War often cures the internal maladies which peace has fostered.

§ 208.

Actual progress of intern. law.

But war often for a time exhausts and demoralizes, it sometimes perpetuates injustice, it is occasionally undertaken against the clearest provisions of the law of nations. Has, then, this law of nations, amid the violations of its code, on the whole made progress? To this question a negative answer can be given only by those who plant their argument on gross offences rising up here and there, as we look down history, but who do not enough take into account the general strain and spirit of the age.* When the question is made to embrace a large tract of time, and we search for progress between the eras while the codes of Greece and Rome were living ones, and the present day, no one can hesitate what answer to give to it. But has there been progress between the time of Grotius (1625), or the peace of Westphalia (1648), and the most modern times? An answer by a very competent authority—Dr. Wheaton—at the close of his history, sums up the principal heads of progress as follows:—

"That the pacific relations among nations have been maintained by the general establishment of permanent missions, and the general recognition of the immunities of public ministers.

"Although the right of intervention to preserve the balance of power, or to prevent the dangers to which one country may be exposed by the domestic transactions of another, has been frequently assumed; yet no general rules have been discovered by which the occasions which may justify the exercise of this right, or the extent to which it may be carried, can be laid down; and that it remains, therefore, an undefined and undefinable exception to the mutual independence of nations.

"The exclusive dominion, claimed by certain powers over particular seas has been abandoned, as an obsolete pretension of barbarous times; the

* Comp. for a gloomy view of the progress of international law the article (referred to in § 3) in the Edinburgh Review, No. 156, for April, 1843.

general use of the high seas, without the limits of any particular state, for the purposes of navigation, commerce, and fishery, has been conceded; and the right of search on the ocean limited to periods of war, except certain conventional arrangements applicable to the African slave-trade.

"The navigation of the river Scheldt, which was closed by the treaty of Westphalia, in favor of the commerce of Holland, has been re-opened to all nations; and the general right to navigate the Rhine, the Elbe, the Danube, and other rivers which separate or pass through different states, has been recognized as a part of the public law of Europe.

"The colonial monopoly, that fruitful source of wars, has nearly ceased; and with it the question as to the right of neutrals to enjoy in war a commerce prohibited in time of peace.

"The African slave-trade has been condemned by the opinion of all Christian nations, and prohibited by their separate laws, or by mutual treaty-stipulations between them.

"The practices of war between civilized nations have been sensibly mitigated, and a comparison of the present modes of warfare with the system of Grotius, will show the immense improvement which has taken place in the laws of war.

"Although there is still some uncertainty as to the rights of neutral navigation in time of war, a conventional law has been created by treaty, which shows a manifest advance towards securing the commerce of nations which remain at peace, from interruption by those which are engaged in war.

"The sphere, within which the European law of nations operates, has been widely extended by the unqualified accession of the new American states; by the tendency of the Mahommedan powers to adopt the public law of Christendom; and by the general feeling, even among less civilized nations, that there are rights, which they may exact from others, and consequently duties which they may be required to fulfil.

"The law of nations, as a science, has advanced with the improvements in the principles and language of philosophy; with our extended knowledge of the past and present condition of mankind, resulting from deeper researches into the obscurer periods of history, and the discovery of new regions of the globe; and with the greater variety and importance of the questions to which the practical application of the system has given rise.

"And lastly, that the law of nations, as a system of positive rules regulating the mutual intercourse of nations, has improved with the general improvement of civilization, of which it is one of the most valuable products."

To which we may add, that since Dr. Wheaton's history was written, in 1843,

Free navigation of nearly all the rivers of the world, under the jurisdiction of Christian states, has been conceded to those who dwell on their upper waters, if to no others;

That the Black Sea is open to all merchant vessels, and the navigation through the Danish Straits freed from onerous duties,

And that most of the leading nations of the world have agreed, that as between them, free ships shall make free goods, and that privateering shall cease.

§ 209.

Prospects of international law for the future.

Is there reasonable expectation that this progress will continue in future times? This question resolves itself into the broader one, whether true civilization built on sound morality and religion is destined to advance or to decline? If nations are to grow in moral enlightenment; if there is to be a faith that the great Ruler of nations has put them upon trial, as truly as individuals, so that no amount of power can save from punishment, or even from extinction, a nation, in which the feeling of justice is blunted by a long course of sinning; if opinion is destined to circulate so freely through the world that crimes committed against other and weaker states shall stamp disgrace on a nation through coming time, and a sense of character over the world shall be felt to be valuable; if national crimes shall appear to all to be hurtful to their perpetrators; if, finally, closer intercourse shall bring the nations more nearly to the same standard of justice, then will international law purify itself, until it reaches the perfection of justice attainable by man, and with this that degree of humanity and of renunciation of strict right which is compatible with the distinct sovereignty and special sphere of separate nations. That such advance will be made we believe, for we can see no limit to the influences of the moral and religious powers which the Author of Nature and of the Gospel has put into motion. And it is probable that the advance will be more rapid than heretofore, although by no means easy or unopposed.

§ 210.

From all that has been said it has become apparent that the study of international law is important, as an index of civilization, and not to the student of law only, but to the student of history. In our land especially it is important, on more than one account, that this science should do its share in enlightening educated minds. One reason for this lies in the new inducements which we, as a people, have to swerve from national rectitude. Formerly our interests threw us on the side of unrestricted commerce, which is the side towards which justice inclines, and we lived far within our borders with scarcely the power to injure or be injured except on the ocean. Now we are running into the crimes to which strong nations are liable. Our diplomatists unblushingly moot the question of taking foreign territory by force if it cannot be purchased; our executive prevents piratical expeditions against the lands of neighboring states as feebly and slowly as if it connived at them; we pick quarrels to gain conquests; and at length after more than half a century of public condemnation of the slave-trade, after being the first to brand it as piracy, we hear the revival of the trade advocated as a right, as a necessity. Is it not desirable that the sense of justice, which seems fading out of the national mind before views of political expediency or destiny, should be deepened and made fast by that study which frowns on national crimes?

Importance of the study of international law.

And, again, every educated person ought to become acquainted with international law, because he is a responsible member of the body politic; because there is danger that party views will make our doctrine in this science fluctuating, unless it is upheld by large numbers of intelligent persons; and because the executive, if not controlled, will be tempted to assume the province of interpreting international law for us. As it regards the latter point it may be said, that while Congress has power to define offences against the laws of nations, and thus, if any public power, to pronounce authoritatively what the law of nations is, the executive through the Secretary of State, in practice, gives the lead in all international questions. In this way the Monroe doctrine appeared; in this way most other positions have been advanced; and perhaps this could not be otherwise. But we ought to remember that the supreme executives in Europe have amassed power by having diplomatic relations in their hands, that thus the nation may become involved in war against its will, and that the prevention of evils must lie, if there be any, with the men who have been educated in the principles of international justice.*

I close this treatise here, hoping that it may be of some use to my native land, and to young men who may need a guide in the science of which it treats.

* I leave this § as it stood in the first ed., only remarking that all our aggressions have been directly or indirectly owing to the slave power; and that with the downfall of that power, to which we may look forward as certain, most of our temptations to injustice, and most of the influences which have blunted the consciences of a large part of the nation, will be removed.

APPENDIX I.

A BRIEF SELECTION OF WORKS AND DOCUMENTS BEARING ON INTERNATIONAL LAW.

A. Its Literature and History.

Von Ompteda. Literatur des gesammten, so wohl natürlichen als positiven, Völkerrechts. Regensburg (Ratisbon), 1785, 2 parts, continued by

Von Kamptz. Neue Literatur des Völkerrechts seit dem Jahre, 1784. Berlin, 1817.

Robert v. Mohl. Die Geschichte und Literatur der Staatswissenschaften. Erlangen, 1855–58, 3 vols. The first volume includes a monography on the more recent literature of the law of nations, containing valuable criticisms.

The works of Klüber and De Martens on the law of nations, in the edition of the former by Morstadt (1851), and of the latter by Vergé (1858), contain, each, a selection of authorities and helps in that science, and the notes to Heffter's Völkerrecht contain copious references to other writers.

Rob. Ward. Enquiry into the foundation and history of the law of nations in Europe from the time of the Greeks and Romans to the age of Grotius. London (and Dublin), 1795, 2 vols.

Henry Wheaton. History of the law of nations in Europe and America, from the earliest times to the treaty of Washington, 1842. New York, 1845. This work was first written and published in French, as an answer to a prize question proposed by the French academy of moral and political sciences, and was considerably enlarged when it appeared in its English dress.

Ed. Osenbrüggen. De jure pacis et belli Romanorum liber singularis. Leipzig, 1836.

K. Th. Pütter. Beiträge zur Völkerrechtsgeschichte und Wissenschaft. Leipzig, 1843.

Müller-Jochmus. Geschichte des Völkerrechts im Alterthum. Leipzig, 1848.

F. Laurent. Histoire du droit des gens. Ghent, 1850, Paris, 1851, 3 vols. The first volume treats of the Oriental nations, the second of the Greeks, the third of the Romans. Comp. Mohl's criticism, u. s. I. 374.

B. Documents, including Diplomatic History.

1. *The early maritime laws.*

These are chiefly contained in Pardessus' Collection des lois maritimes antérieures au xviiie siècle. Paris, 6 vols., 4to. 1828–1845.

The earliest of them, the laws of the Rhodians, belongs to century IX. To the twelfth century pertain the maritime laws contained in the Assises des bourgeois du royaume de Jerusalemme, the Rooles or Jugements d'Oleron, and the Jugemens de Damm, or Lois de West-Capelle. Damm in Flanders, the port of Bruges, began to be a town of importance before 1180. Its customs were principally copied from those of the isle of Oleron.* The Consolato del mare, composed at Barcelona in the Catalonian dialect, the most extensive and important of the sea-codes (comp. § 173), was collected in century XIV, and to the same century must be ascribed the first laws of Wisby on the island of Gothland, and the customs of Amsterdam; but the sea-code of Wisby belongs to the next century, and according to Hüllmann (Städtewesen des Mittelalters I. 182), was borrowed in part from the laws of Oleron and of Amsterdam. The laws of the Hanseatic league are of various dates, especially of the fourteenth and fifteenth centuries, and the Guidon de la mer was composed in the century next succeeding. The sea laws of Amalfi, of an earlier date, have been published by the Italian historian, Troya, under the title, "Capitula et ordinationes maritimæ civitatis Amalfitanæ." Vienna, 1844.

2. *Collections of Treaties.*

Dumont. Corps universel diplomatique, etc. Amsterdam and the Hague, 1726–1731; 8 vols., folio, most of them in two parts. A supplement to this work in 5 vols. folio (Amst. and the Hague, 1739) contains a history of ancient treaties by Barbeyrac (vol. 1), a supplementary collection of treaties from 838 to 1738,—Dumont having ended with 1731, by Rousset (vols. 2–3), and a "diplomatic ceremonial of the courts of Europe" (vols. 4–5), by the same author. Another supplement sometimes accompanying Dumont's work is entitled 'Histoire des traités de paix et autres négociations du xviie siècle, par Jean-Yves de St. Priest, Amst., 1735, 2 vols., fol.

Wenck (F. A. G.) Codex juris gentium recentissimi. Leipzig, 3 vols., 8vo., 1781–1795. This embraces a period of thirty-seven years, 1735–1772, and continues Dumont's work.

De Martens (G. F.) Recueil des principaux traités de paix, d'alliance, etc., depuis 1761, jusqu'à nos jours. The *Recueil* forms 8 volumes and reaches down to 1808, with 4 volumes of supplements. (2d ed. Götting. 1817–1835.) The *nouveau Recueil* by the same editor, continued by his nephew C. de Martens, by Saalfeld and Murhard, is in 16 vols., some of

* Warnkönig, in his Flandrische Staats-und Rechtsgeschichte, vol. I. Appendix, No. XLI gives an old text of the laws of Damm, instead of the modern and worthless one of Pardessus.

which are in several parts, so as to make 20 vols., and reaches from 1808 to 1839. The *nouveau Recueil général* edited by Murhard, and from the 14th vol. by Samwer, consists thus far of 17 vols. The first part of vol. 17 reaches into 1861. The *nouveaux Supplemens* by Murhard in 3 vols. supply what is deficient down to 1839. A register in two parts, entitled *Table générale* du Recueil des traités de G. F. de Martens, accompanies this work, and covers the period down to 1839. (All the volumes have been published at Götting. in various years.)

Schmauss (J. J.) Corpus juris gentium academicum (1096–1731), Leipz. 1730, 2 vols., 8vo.

Leibnitz. Codex juris gentium diplomaticus, and mantissa codicis juris gentium diplomatici. Containing not only treaties, but various other documents. 1693, 1700, Hanover.

Ch. de Martens et J. de Cussy. Recueil manuel et pratique des traités, conventions, etc. Of this selection, which is intended to embrace the treaties on which the relations of the world since 1760 are based, 7 vols. had appeared in 1857.

Most civilized nations have special collections of their own diplomatic transactions. We name a few:

Leonard. Recueil des traités, etc. faits par les rois de France, depuis près de trois siècles. Paris, 1693, 6 vols., 4to.

Rymer. Archiva regia reserata, sive foedera, etc. inter reges Angliæ et alios quosvis ab ineunte sæculo xiimo. Lond. 1703–1735, 20 vols., fol. The later volumes were prepared by Rob. Sanderson.

Collection of all the treaties of peace between Great Britain and other powers from 1648 till 1771. Lond., 1772. A second ed., by Ch. Jenkinson, afterwards earl of Liverpool, in 3 vols., carries them down to 1784.

Chalmers. A collection of maritime treaties of Great Britain and other powers. Lond., 1790. 2 vols., 8vo.

Lünig (J. C.) Teutsches Reichs-Archiv. Leipz., 1710–1722. 24 vols., fol.

Colleccion de los Tratados de Paz, Alianza, etc., by D. Jos. Ant. de Abreu y Bertonado. Madrid, 1740–1752. 12 vols., fol.

Cantillo. Tratados de Paz y de Comercio. Madrid, 1843.

Lünig (J. C.) Codex Italiæ diplomaticus. Frankf. and Leipz. 1725–1735. 4 vols., fol.

Elliott (J.) American diplomatic Code, containing treaties of the United States between 1778–1834. Washington, 1834.

The seventh volume of "Public Statutes at large of the United States of America," edited by R. Peters, Boston, 1848, contains, in two parts, treaties with foreign states and Indian tribes. (Vols. 7 and 8, new ed.)

For other collections of the treaties of particular states, Ompteda and the Appendix to Klüber's Völkerrecht may be consulted.

Klüber (J. L.) Acten des Wiener Congresses, in den Jahren, 1814 und 1815. Erlangen, 1815–1816. 6 vols., 8vo.

Ghillany (F. G.) Diplomatisches Handbuch. Nördlingen, 1854. 2 vols. Also in French, Paris and Brussels, 1856. A brief selection, omitting a number of the most important treaties.

3. *Diplomatic History.*

The Abbé de Mably. Droit public de l'Europe fondé sur les traités. Paris, 1717, 2 vols. Often reprinted, as in his works. Paris, 1821. 15 vols.

Koch. Abrégé de l'histoire des traités de paix, etc. Bâle, 1796–7. 4 vols. Recast by Schöll. Paris, 1817–18, in 15 vols.

Flassan. Histoire générale et raisonnée de la Diplomatie Française. Paris et Strasbourg. Second ed. 1811. The same author published a history of the Congress of Vienna at Paris in 1829.

Histoire des traités de paix, etc. par le Comte de Garden. Fourteen volumes appeared before 1859, and reach down from the peace of Westphalia to the peace of Paris in 1814. This is a revival of the works of Koch and Schöll. See Mohl's critique on this work (u. s. p. 345.)

Spalding (L.) The diplomacy of the United States. Being an account of the foreign relations of the country. Boston, 1826.

Mignet. Negotiations rélatives à la succession d'Espagne sous Louis XIV. Paris, 1835–42. 4 vols., 4to.

Other works on the history of diplomacy are mentioned and characterized by Von Mohl (u. s.) Here also the published correspondence of statesmen and ambassadors, and the works of the ablest historians are great helps. Here is the place to name collections of documents, which are often of great value in illustrating the *progress* of negotiations. Of this kind are the British and foreign state papers, of which 24 volumes had appeared in various years down to 1853; the Parliamentary papers of various years; the Portfolio, 6 vols., 1836–37; Diplomatic correspondence of the Amer. revolution, by J. Sparks, Boston, 1829–30, 12 vols.; Diplomatic correspondence of the United States from 1783 to 1789. Boston, 1838. 7 vols.

C. Treatises on the Law of Nations or on Titles of it.

(*a*) Among the forerunners of Grotius may be named Oldendorp, professor at Marburg. Isagoge, seu elementaria introductio juris naturae, gentium et civilis. Cologne, 1539.

Suarez, a learned Spaniard, professor at Alcala, Salamanca, etc. (1548–1617). De legibus et Deo legislatori.

Francis a Victoria, professor at Salamanca. In his Relectiones theologicæ, published at Lyons, 1557, the sixth part is entitled "de jure belli." See Hallam's introd. 2, 242, and Wheaton's hist. pp. 35–43.

Balthazar Ayala, a Spaniard, jndge advocate of the Spanish army in the Netherlands. De jure et officiis bellicis et disciplinâ libri tres. Antwerp, 1597. Comp. Hallam, 2, 244, and Wheaton, u. s., 43–49. The following passage cited by Hallam from this scarce work, speaks well for Ayala's soundness of thinking. "Bellum adversus infideles, ex eo solum quod infideles sunt, ne quidem auctoritate imperatoris vel summi pontificis indici potest; infidelitas enim non privat infideles dominio quod habent jure gentium; nam non fidelibus tantum rerum dominia, sed omni rationabili creaturæ data sunt."

Albericus Gentilis (1551–1611), son of an Italian who left his country upon embracing Protestantism. The son became professor of civil law at Oxford, in 1582, and published in the next year a treatise *de legationibus*—the first work, it is said, specially devoted to the rights of ambassadors. In 1588 came out at Oxford his work *de jure belli*, and still another is imputed to him by Ompteda, entitled de jure maris. Of Gentilis, Grotius says, in his prolegomena, § 38, "cujus diligentiâ sicut alios adjuvari posse scio et me adjutum profiteor."

Benedict Winckler († 1648), professor of law at Leipzig, then syndic of Lübeck. Principiorum juris libri tres. Leipz. 1615.

For the predecessors of Grotius in general, compare von Kaltenborn, "die Vorlaüfer des Hugo Grotius." Halle, 1848.

(*b*.) Grotius and subsequent writers to Moser.

Hugo Grotius, or de Groot (1583–1645.) After filling important offices in Holland, Grotius was involved in the strife between Maurice of Orange, the stadtholder, and the grand pensionary of Holland, Oldenbarneveld. When the latter was beheaded, Grotius was condemned to perpetual imprisonment, with confiscation of his goods, in 1619, but by a successful stratagem of his wife escaped from his confinement in 1621. The next ten years he spent in learned leisure in France, and the rest of his life in the service of Sweden, for a large part of the time as ambassador at the French court. Grotius was equally eminent in classical scholarship, biblical criticism, the defence of the truth of revelation, and the law of nations. He wrote also on history, law, and theology. During his exile in France was composed and published his work entitled, "de jure belli et pacis libri tres, in quibus jus naturæ et gentium, item juris publici præcipua explicantur." The first edition was published at Paris, 1625. Of the numberless editions which have since appeared, are deserving of mention, 1. That published at Amsterdam in 1720, in 2 vols., with the notes of Grotius, J. F. Gronovius, and of the editor, J. Barbeyrac, a professor at Groningen. 2. H. Grotii etc. cum commentariis Henr. liberi baronis de Cocceji, nunc ad calcem cujusque capitis adjectis, insertis quoque observationibus Sam. lib. bar. de Cocceji, Lausanne, 1751, 5 vols., 4to. These commentaries had been published before by themselves. An abridged translation with notes was published in 1854, at Cambridge by Dr. Whewell. An excellent estimate of the work of Grotius may be found in Hartenstein's "Darstellung der Rechtsphilosophie des H. Grotius," in the first vol. of the transactions of the philological and historical class of the royal Saxon Academy, Leipz. 1850.

In some editions of the works of Grotius, as in Barbeyrac's, there is annexed a short treatise of his written in 1609, and entitled *mare liberum.* In reply, the most learned Englishman of his time, John Selden, published his *mare clausum* (1635), in vindication of the claims of Great Britain to sovereignty over the seas which surround the British islands.

Zouch (1590–1660), professor of civil law at Oxford, and judge of the High Court of Admiralty. Juris et judicii fecialis, sive juris inter gentes et quæstionum de eodem explicatio. Oxford, 1650. Comp. Wheaton, Hist. pp. 100–103, and the table of contents in Ompteda, 1, § 64.

Samuel von Puffendorf, or Pufendorf (1631 or 32–1694), professor at Heidelberg of the law of nature and nations (1661), then at Lund in Sweden (1670) historiographer of the king of Sweden, and one of his council (1686), privy councillor of the elector of Brandenburg (1688). His works which concern us are,

1. Elementorum jurisprudentiæ universalis libri duo. The Hague, 1660, a work of his youth. In this work, says Ompteda, he has the same course of thought, which appeared in his later works. The natural jus gentium is included in the wider science of jus naturæ, and requires no special elaboration. Besides this there is no voluntary or positive law of nations, since those usages which nations extensively observe in regard to war carry no binding force with them, and by their violation no duties, properly so called, are violated. The inviolability of ambassadors, and their other privileges, are derived, partly from the general law of nature, partly from the free act and policy of the nation accepting the ambassador, and can be refused at the pleasure of such nation without injury to the ambassador's sovereign.

2. De jure naturæ et gentium libri octo, Lund. 1672, and often. This is his principal work. A French translation, with notes, by Barbeyrac, appeared at Amsterdam in 1706, and an English translation in 1717.

3. De officiis hominis et civis. 1673. This is a mere extract from No. 2. Comp. Wheaton, 88–99. Leibnitz said of Puffendorf that he was "vir parum juris consultus et minime philosophus." Too high a rank is given to him by Sir James Mackintosh, in his discourse on the law of nature and nations.

Samuel Rachel (1628–1691), professor first at Helmstadt, then at Kiel. De jure naturæ et gentium dissertationes duo. Kiel, 1676. This work is remarkable as opposing the views of Puffendorf, and as giving rise to a controversy between two sects of German jurists towards the close of

Cent. XVII. "The one sect," says Dr. Wheaton (p. 103), "adhering to Puffendorf, denied the existence of any other law of nations than the law of nature, applied to independent communities; whilst the latter adopted the doctrine of Rachel, founding the law of nations upon the law of nature, as modified by usage and express compact." Rachel's definition of the law of nations is "jus plurium liberarum gentium, pacto sive placito expresse aut tacite initum, quo utilitatis gratiâ sibi invicem obligantur." For an analysis of his work see Ompteda, § 74.

J. W. Textor, professor of law at Altorf, then at Heidelberg (1637–1701). Synopsis juris gentium, Bâle, 1680. He embraced Rachel's views.

Christian Thomasius (1655–1728), taught at Leipzig, then in 1694 became a professor in the new university of Halle. Fundamenta juris naturæ et gentium. Halle, 1705, (1st Ed.) A learned and influential defender of the views of Puffendorf.

Adam F. Glafey (1682–1754), keeper of the Archives at Dresden. Vernunft und Völkerrecht. Frankfurt, 1723.

Christian von Wolf (1679–1754), one of the most noted philosophers of his day, professor at Halle in 1706, dismissed from his place by the king of Prussia on account of the theological odium excited against him, then at Marburg, and from 1740 onward again at Halle, being restored to favor. He wrote a system of the law of nature in nine large quartos, of which the last volume treats of the law of nations; and also in 1749, when he was seventy years old, published his "jus gentium methodo scientifica pertractatum, in quo jus gentium naturale, ab eo quod voluntarii, pactitii et consuetudinarii est, accurate distinguitur." Halle, 1749. Of this, his "institutiones juris naturæ et gentium," Halle, 1750, translated also into German and French, is an abridgment. "It is not easy," says Wheaton, "to infer from the title of the former work precisely what the author understood to be comprehended under the term *voluntary* law of nations, as distinguished from the *conventional* and *customary* law of nations. Grotius had used the term *jus gentium* voluntarium in a comprehensive sense, as including all those foundations of international law which could not properly be referred to the law of nature, but depended upon the voluntary consent of all or many nations." In his prolegomena, Wolf says that "the voluntary law of nations derives its force from the *presumed* consent of nations, the conventional from their *express* consent; and the consuetudinary, from their *tacit* consent." This presumed consent he derives from the fiction of a natural commonwealth to which all nations belong, governed by laws which are modifications of natural law, fitted for such a society of nations, and are obligatory on each member as the laws of a state are on its individual members. He barely assumes the existence of such a commonwealth of nations, and does not show how or when the nations of the world became thus united. Wolf, adds Wheaton, supposes himself to differ from

Grotius as to a voluntary law of nations, in two particulars. The first is, that Grotius regards it as a positive law, obligatory on account of the general consent of the nations or of certain nations, while Wolf considers it to be a law imposed by nature, to which no nation may refuse its assent. The second, that Grotius confounds the voluntary with the customary law of nations, whereas the former is of universal obligation, while the latter prevails between particular nations, having been established by tacit consent. (Comp. Wheaton, 176–183.) Wolf's works have become obsolete with his philosophy, but his materials have been worked over by a disciple,

Emmerich de Vattel (1714–1767), a Swiss, who for many years was in the service of the Saxon court, and published at Leyden, in 1758, le Droit des gens, ou principes de la loi naturelle appliqués à la conduite des nations et des souverains. This work, on account of its clearness and smoothness, has long been a favorite with statesmen, and has been translated into the principal languages of Europe. The best edition of it is that published at Paris in 1838, with notes by Pinheiro-Ferreira.

De Real. La science du gouvernement. Paris, 1754 and 1764. In eight volumes, the fifth of which contains the law of nations.

J. G. Heineccius (1681–1741), professor at Halle, etc. Elementa juris naturæ et gentium. Halle, 1738, translated into English, 1742, by G. Turnbull. He understands by jus gentium, says Ompteda, the rights which find their application to societies of every sort, and treats only in a cursory way of the rights of nations.—Another work of his was a Dissertation de navibus ob mercium illicitarum vecturam commissis. Halle, 1721 and 1740; also transl. into German and Dutch.

J. J. Burlamaqui, professor of law in Geneva, and member of the council there (1694–1748.) Principes du droit naturel. Geneva, 1747. Transl. also into English.

Thomas Rutherforth, professor at Cambridge, archdeacon of Essex. Institutes of natural law. London, 1754.

Cornelius von Bynkershoek (1673–1743), member and president of the supreme court of Holland. He has written no systematic work, but the following dissertations, contained in the second volume of his Opera Omnia (Leyden, 1767)—De dominio maris (1702)—De foro legatorum (1721) and Quæstiones juris publici (1737), place him among the highest authorities.

Charles Jenkinson, afterward Lord Liverpool. Discourse on the conduct of the government of Great Britain in respect to neutral nations, 1757. Relates to the 'rule of 1756,' so called. Comp. § 185.

Martin Hübner. De la saisie des bâtimens neutres, etc. The Hague, 1759, 2 vols. For a critique on this work, comp. Wheaton, Hist. 219–220.

(*c*.) Moser and writers since his day. From this time the positive and practical tendency has prevailed,—in some writers to the neglect of the principles of general justice.

1. *Systematic Works.*

John Jacob Moser (1701–1786), professor at Tübingen, then at Frankfort-on-the-Oder, founder in 1749 of an academy for the political instruction of young nobles, then in the service of the estates of Würtemberg, during which employment he was imprisoned by the Duke and kept in confinement five years. A most voluminous publicist, thoroughly practical, with no great depth or philosophical power, the father of the positive method. For an estimate of this excellent man, see Von Mohl, Gesch. II. 402. His principal works are Versuch des neuesten Europäischen Völkerrechts in Friedens-und-Kriegszeiten, etc. Frankfurt am Mayn, 1777–80, in twelve parts; Beyträge zu dem neuesten Europäischen Völkerrechts in Friedenszeiten, and the same in Kriegszeiten. Tübingen, 1778–1781. These two works are unfinished.

Günther (C. G.) Grundriss eines Europ. Völkerrechts, nach Vernunft, Verträgen, Herkommen, etc. Ratisb., 1779, 8vo.

Geo. Fred. de Martens (1756–1821). Professor at Göttingen, from 1808 in the service of the king of Westphalia, and then in that of Hanover. Of his numerous works two have already been mentioned. Another is entitled Précis du droit des gens moderne de l'Europe, fondé sur les traités et l'usage, Gottingue, 1789, transl. into German by the author, 1796, and into English by W. Cobbett, Philadelphia, 1795. The fourth edition in French appeared at Paris, 1831, in 2 vols., with notes by Pinheiro-Ferreira, who opposes the extreme positivism of De Martens and others. A fifth edition in French, with notes by Pinheiro-Ferreira and Vergé, appeared in 1855, and has been used for the present work.

Gerard de Rayneval (1736–1812). Institution du droit de la nature et des gens, etc. Paris, 1803, in 1 vol., 1851 in 2 vols.

Fried. Saalfeld. Handbuch des positiven Völkerrechts. Tübingen, 1833.

J. L. Klüber (1762–1835), professor at Erlangen, then at Heidelberg. Droit des gens moderne de l'Europe, Stuttgart, 1819, and in German as Europäisches Völkerrecht, nearly at the same time. The French work was reprinted in 1831, and the German, with notes by Morstadt, at Schaffhausen in 1851. Comp. what Manning says of this work, p. 41 of his Commentaries. He also, besides publishing the acts of the Congress of Vienna, wrote a work entitled Öffentliches Recht des deutschen Bundes und der Bundesstaaten, of which editions appeared in 1817, 1822, 1833.

Jul. Schmelzing. Systematischer Grundriss des praktischen europ. Völkerrechts. Rudolstadt, 1818–19, 3 vols.

Theod. Schmalz (1760–1831). Europ. Völkerrecht, Berlin, 1817.

C. S. Zachariæ (1769–1843). Vierzig Bücher vom Staate. Revised ed. Heidelberg, 1841, in 7 vols. Vol. 5 contains his Völkerrecht.

Jeremy Bentham (1749–1832). In vol. 8 of his works, published in 1839, occur several fragments on international law, serving as an outline of the science, in which he advocates bringing it into the form of a code and a common congress for the adjustment of differences between states. See Wheaton's critique (hist. pp. 328–344), and comp. § 206.

James Kent (1763–1847), Judge of the Supreme Court and Chancellor of the State of New York, then professor of law in Columbia College, city of New York. His nine lectures on the law of nations form the first part of his Commentaries on American law, which appeared first in 1826 and following years, and in repeated editions since.

Henry Wheaton (1785–1848), reporter of decisions of the Supreme Court of the United States, from 1827 for many years representing the United States at the courts of Copenhagen and Berlin. His elements of international law appeared first in 1836, at London and New York, in an enlarged third edition in 1846, and in a sixth in 1855. This is one of the standard works in our language. Dr. Wheaton's definition of international law makes it to consist of "those rules of conduct which reason deduces, as consonant to justice, from the nature of the society existing among independent nations; with such definitions and modifications as may be established by general consent." This definition removes the science from the nakedly positive ground, and gives full scope to comparisons between the existing law and the standard of justice.

William Oke Manning. Commentaries on the law of nations. London, 1839. This work is full on certain topics connected with maritime war, especially on the rights of neutrals, but omits other topics of importance, as the rights of ambassadors.

August W. Heffter, professor at Bonn, and then at Berlin. Das Europäische Völkerrecht der Gegenwart, Berlin, 1844, where also the third edition of 1855 appeared. This work has higher authority in Germany than any other on the science of which it treats.

Richard Wildman (Recorder of Nottingham). Institutes of international law. London, 1829, 2 vols.

Pinheiro-Ferreira. Cours de droit public interne et externe. Paris, 1830, 2 vols. The first part of vol. 2 treats of international law. A radical writer, who exaggerates the rights of the individual and the individual state.

J. M. de Pando. Elementos del Derecho Internacional. Madrid, 1843, 4to.

Polson. Principles of the law of nations. To which is added diplomacy by Thomas H. Horne. 2d ed. London, 1854.

Robert Phillimore, at one time M. P., Queen's advocate in the admiralty court, judge of the cinque ports. Commentaries upon International Law. 3 vols., 1854–1857, reprinted in Philadelphia: a fourth volume on private International Law or Comity appeared in London, in 1861. This work, which I had not the use of, while preparing the first edition of my Introduction, is the most extensive, thorough and learned work on the science in our language, if not in any language. Comp. the favorable critique of Mohl, I. 398. It has been his object,—the author says near the close of his work—"to strengthen or add to the previously existing proof that States, as well as Individuals of which they are the aggregate, have in their collective capacity, a sphere of duty assigned to them by God. He has endeavored to forward the great argument that there are International rights and therefore International Laws, convinced that every work, however humble, which tends to procure the recognition of these laws,—to show by reason, by history, by authority, that the interest and duty of states are eventually one,—that the substitution of might for right brings misery, not only on the oppressed but on the oppressor—deserves an indulgent reception from the world to which it is addressed."

H. W. Halleck, now major-general in the service of the United States. International Law; or, Rules regulating the intercourse of states in peace and war. San Francisco, 1861.

Travers Twiss (Regius professor of civil law at Oxford). The law of nations, considered as independent political communities. Oxford and London, 1863.

2. *Essays and Tracts*

on separate titles of the law of nations.

(*a.*) On ambassadors and consuls.

Of Albericus Gentilis and of Bynkershoek's treatise De foro legatorum we have already spoken.

Of works before the modern era we name here

Abraham Wicquefort (1598–1682), L'Ambassadeur et ses fonctions. Cologne, 1679, the Hague, 1680–81. The fourth edition appeared at Amsterdam in 1730, in two volumes, with Barbeyrac's notes, who added other pieces of Wicquefort's and a translation of Bynkershoek's above-named work. For Wicquefort himself comp. Ompteda, p. 541, Wheaton's hist. 234–246, and § 92. *a.* supra.

Moser (J. J.) Beiträge zu dem neuesten Europäischen Gesandschaftsrecht. Frankfurt, 1781.

David B. Warden (consul of the United States at Paris). On the origin, nature, progress and influence of the consular establishments. Paris, 1814, and in French, 1815.

A. Mirus. Das Europ. Gesandtschaftsrecht. Leipz. 1847, 2 vols.

Ch. de Martens. Guide diplomatique. Paris, 4th ed. 1852. Comp. § 94 supra, note.

F. de Cussy. Dictionnaire, ou manuel-lexique du diplomate et du consul. Leipz. 1846. Also by the same author, Réglemens consulaires des principaux états maritimes de l'Europe et de l'Amérique. Leipz. and Paris, 1851.

Garden, le Comte de. Traité complet de Diplomatie, ou théorie générale des relations extérieures des puissances de l'Europe. 3 vols., Paris, 1833.

Alex. de Miltitz, chamberlain of the king of Prussia, formerly ambass. at Constantinople. Manuel des Consuls. London and Berlin, 1837–1843, 2 vols., the second in two large parts. One of the most learned and exhaustive works ever written on any branch of the law of nations.

(*b.*) On private international law.

Joseph Story, Judge in the Supreme Court of the United States, professor in the law department of Harvard Univ. Commentaries on the conflict of laws, foreign and domestic. Boston, 1834, and a number of editions since. Comp. § 69.

Foelix. Traité du droit international privé. Paris, 1843. A collection of articles originally published in the author's Revue de Legislation. Third ed., with notes by Dumangeat. Par. 1856, 2 vols.

W. Burge. Commentaries on colonial and foreign laws, generally and in their conflict with one another and with the law of England. London, 1838, 4 vols.

F. C. de Savigny. The eighth vol. of his system des heutigen römischen Rechts. Berlin, 1849.

W. Schaeffner. Entwickelung des internationalen Privatrechts. Frankfurt, 1841.

M. H. Massé. The second vol. of his droit commercial is devoted to this subject.

The older writers may be found enumerated in Savigny, vol. 8, p. 9, and at the end of the work of Foelix. The more recent, down to 1855, are classified and subjected to a criticism by Mohl, I. 441–454.

(*c.*) Property of States, sovereignty over seas and rivers.

Eug. Ortolan. Des moyens d'acquérir le domaine international, etc. Par. 1851. Comp. Mohl, I. 419.

B. D. H. Tellgen. Disputatio de jure in mare imprimis proximum. Groningen, 1847.

Cremer van dem Bergh. Historia novarum legum de fluminum communium navigatione. Leyden, 1835.

Van Hoorn. Dissertatio de navigatione et mercatura in mari nigro. Amsterdam, 1834.

(*d.*) Maritime law, rights of neutrals, capture, etc.

R. J. Valin. Nouveau commentaire sur l'ordonnance de la marine du mois d'Avril, 1681, etc. Rochelle, 1762, 2 vols., 4to. Third ed., Paris and Marseilles, 1780. Also traité des prises, ou principes de la jurisprudence françoise concernant les prises qui se font sur la mer. Rochelle et Paris, 1782, 2 vols., 8vo.

G. M. Lampredi. Del commercio dei popoli neutrali in tempo di guerra. Florence, 1788, 2 vols.

Domenico A. Azuni. Sistema universale dei principii del diritto maritimo dell 'Europa. Florence, 1795, 2 vols. A French translation by the author appeared at Paris, 1805, in 2 vols., 8vo, under the title Droit maritime de l'Europe, and another by J. M. Digéon, at Paris, in the year VI. under the title Système universel des principes du droit maritime de l'Europe. The work has had also a Spanish and an English translation.

Fred. J. Jacobsen. Handbuch über das praktische Seerecht der Engländer und Franzosen, etc. Altona, 1804, 1805, 2 vols. Also Seerecht des Friedens und des Krieges, in Bezug auf die Kauffahrteischiffahrt. Altona, 1815.

Lucchesi-Palli (Count Ferdinand). Principii di diritto publico, etc. Naples, 1840. Also translated into French by A. de Galiani. Paris, 1842.

Theodore Ortolan. Régles internationales et diplomatie de la mer. Paris, 1845, third ed. ibid. 1856.

Massé, M. G. Le Droit commercial dans ses rapports avec les Droits des gens. 6 vols, Paris, 1844 and onward. The first vol. treats of the rights of trade. Comp. Mohl, I. 423.

J. Reddie. Researches, historical and critical, in maritime international law. Edinb. 1844, 2 vols.

C. von Kaltenborn. Grundsätze des praktischen europäischen Seerechts. Berlin, 1851, 2 vols.

L. B. Hautefeuille. Des droits et des devoirs des nations neutres en temps de guerre maritime. Paris, 1848. The second edition in 3 vols., revised and modified according to the treaty of Paris of 1856, appeared in 1858. An important work.

W. Hazlitt and R. Roche. A manual of maritime warfare, embodying the decisions of Lord Stowell. London, 1854.

H. Byerly Thomson. The laws of war affecting commerce and shipping. Lond. 1854.

Lock, W. A. A practical legal guide for sailors and merchants during war. Same place and year.

Hosack. The rights of British and neutral commerce, as affected by recent royal declarations. Same place and year. For an estimate of these four English works, see Mohl, I. 424.

C. F. Wurm. Von der Neutralität des deutschen Seehandels in Kriegszeiten. Hamburg, 1841.

C. W. Ascher. Beiträge zu einigen Fragen über die Verhältnisse der neutralen Schiffahrt. Hamburg, 1854.

H. Marquardsen, professor at Erlangen in Bavaria. Der Trent-Fall, zur Lehre von der Kriegs contrebande, und dem Transportdienst der neutralen. Erlangen, 1862.

Of works on the subjects of capture and search, we mention—

G. F. de Martens. Essai concernant les armateurs, les prises et surtout les reprises, etc. Göttingen, 1795.

J. G. F. Schlegel. Sur la visite des vaisseaux neutres sous convoi, etc.

Originally written in Danish, and translated into French by De Juge. Copenhagen, 1800.

Robt. Ward, the historian of the law of nations. A treatise of the relative rights and duties of belligerent and neutral powers in maritime affairs, in which the principles of armed neutralities, and the opinions of Hübner and Schlegel are fully discussed. Lond., 1801. Also an essay on contraband, being a continuation of the relative rights and duties, etc. Lond., 1801.

War in disguise of the neutral flags. Lond., 1806. Reviewed in No. 15 of the Edinburgh Review.

Answer to war in disguise, etc. New York, 1806.

H. Wheaton. Inquiry into the validity of the British claim to a right of visitation and search of American vessels. Lond., 1842.

J. de Neufville. De iis quæ ad tollendum servorum Afrorum commercium inde a Congressu Viennensi inter populos gesta sunt. Amsterd., 1840.

St. Pierre. Abrégé du projet de paix perpetuelle. Rotterdam, 1729. For this and other similar works comp. § 206.

Kamptz. Völkerrechtliche Erörterung des Rechtes der Mächte in die Verfassung eines einzelnes Staats Sich einzumischen. Berl., 1821.

H. C. von Gagern. Kritik von Völkerrechts. Leipzig, 1840.

H. von Rotteck. Das Recht der Einmischung in die inneren Angelegenheiten eines fremden Staates. Freiburg, 1845.

Villefort. De la propriété littéraire et artistique au point de vue international. Paris, 1851. For O. Wächters Verlagsrecht, comp. § 80, note.

G. F. de Martens. Erzählungen merkwurdiger Fälle des neueren europäischen Völkerrechts. Göttingen, 1800–1802, 2 vols.

Ch. de Martens. Causes célèbres du droit des gens (Leipz., 1827, 2 vols.), and nouvelles causes célèbres. Leipz., 1844, 2 vols.

R. von. Mohl. Die Pflege der internationalen Gemeinschaft, als Aufgabe des Völkerrechts, and Die Völkerrechtliche Lehre von Asyl, monographies in his Staatsrecht, Völkerrecht und Politik. Vol. 1. Tübingen, 1860.

Many discussions of important points in international law are to be found in the periodicals, especially in the Edinburgh, British Quarterly, and North American Reviews, in the speeches of distinguished statesmen, and in state papers. Some of these state papers, issued by our government, are republished in the collected works of their authors, as those of Webster; but the greater part of them must be searched for in the public documents. The expense of time in making such search, is often so great, that it were desirable if a collection could be made of all the more important discussions on the law of nations, to which the government has been a party, since the year 1775, or since the framing of the present Constitution, accompanied by the notes or introductions of a competent editor.

APPENDIX II.

LIST OF THE MOST IMPORTANT TREATIES SINCE THE REFORMATION, WITH A BRIEF STATEMENT OF THEIR PROVISIONS.

[In this list the dates of the treaties are intended to represent the day of their signature, and always in new style. For the modern ones we cite the collection of Martens and his continuators thus: Martens rec. or r. for the *recueil*, Martens nov. rec., or n. r. for the *nouveau recueil*, and Murhard, or Murhard-Samwer, by the volume, for the *nouveau recueil général*.]

TREATIES OF THE AGE OF RELIGIOUS ANTAGONISM.

1526, Jan. 14. (Dumont, IV. 1, 399.) Treaty of Madrid, by which Francis I. of France, then a prisoner, covenanted to give up his claims to Milan, Genoa, and Naples, Flanders and Artois, and to transfer to the Emperor Charles V. the duchy of Burgundy—with its dependencies the county of Charolais and the seigniories of Noyers and of Chateau Chinon,—together with the viscounty of Auxonne and the 'ressort' or jurisdiction of Saint-Laurent, as being dependencies of Franche-Comté. These and other onerous and humiliating conditions upon which he obtained his liberty he neither fulfilled nor intended to fulfil. Indeed a 'protestation' (Dumont, u. s. 412) of the day before declares that the treaty is null, being made by constraint. (Comp. § 100.) Having by such fraud obtained his liberty, he refused, when the estates of Burgundy would not separate themselves from France, to return to prison, as he had stipulated. Then followed the Holy League (at Cognac, May 22, 1526, between Pope Clement VII., Francis I., Venice, Florence and the Duke of Milan against Charles V.), and a new Italian war, and in

1529, Aug. 5. (Dumont, IV. 2, 7.) the treaty of Cambray, or paix des dames, so called from Margaret of Austria, the Emperor's sister, and Louisa of Savoy, mother of Francis I., who negotiated it. By this treaty, which was in form a renewal of the treaty of Madrid with certain important exceptions, Francis was secured in the possession of Burgundy and its dependencies, renounced Flanders, Artois, etc., gave up his claims in Italy, abandoned his allies, and in fact annihilated French influence in that peninsula. His two sons, hostages at Madrid, were freed on an engagement to pay two million crowns of gold or ducats. The adherents and heirs of the Constable de Bourbon were to be restored to their estates and civil standing. This treaty, which was humiliating enough in itself, was made more so by the solemn formalities of its ratification, as if to show that the word of Francis could not be trusted. (Comp. § 106.)

On the 29th of June, just before this, at Barcelona, a peace was concluded between the Pope and the Emperor, in which the former agreed to give the latter the Imperial crown, and the investiture of Naples as a fief without payment of vassals' dues except that of a palfrey, with the right of nomination to 24 Episcopal sees in that kingdom. Charles in turn agreed to restore the Pope's relatives, the banished Medici, and to stop the growth of heresy in Germany. (Dumont, IV. 2, 1–7.) A secret article, it is said, stipulated that the Pope should not give his consent to the divorce of the King of England from the Emperor's aunt.

1530, Dec. 31. Recess or convention made at Schmalkalden, preliminary to the league concluded at the same place Feb. 6, 1531, between a part of the Protestant princes and towns for mutual protection in case of attack on account of their religion. (Dumont, IV. 2, pp. 75, 78.) It was renewed for ten years, and enlarged in 1536, Sept. 29. (Dumont, u. s. 141.) For the Catholic counter-league of June 10, 1538, comp. Dumont, u. s. 164.

1544, Sept. 18. The peace of Crespy was chiefly a ratification of previous treaties, as that of Cambray, and that of Nice (June 18, 1538), which latter was a ten years' truce.

1547, May 19. The Protestants of the Schmalkalden League, having taken up arms against the Emperor Charles V. without success, and John Frederick, Elector of Saxony, being made prisoner at the battle of Mühlberg, he submits in the capitulation of Wittenberg of this date to the loss of his Electoral office and Principality, and to imprisonment during the Emperor's pleasure. The Electorate is transferred from the Ernestine to the Albertine line of Saxony, which is still the leading house; and to the captive Elector's children were granted a number of towns and districts, as Eisenach, Weimar, Jena, Gotha, Saalfeld, and Coburg,—the latter to be used first for the benefit of his brother. (Dumont, u. s. 332.) Out of these grew the Saxon duchies.

1552, Aug. 2. Treaty of Passau, by which the Landgrave of Hesse was set free, other Protestant princes were restored to their honors and estates, and religious freedom was promised to the adherents of the Augsburg Confession, etc. (Dumont, IV. 3, 42.) This was preliminary to the religious peace, concluded between the estates of Germany in the year

1555, Sept. 25, at Augsburg. By this the Lutheran religion acquired a legal status by the side of the Catholic, but the Reformed religion gained no privileges. The peace embraced knights holding immediately of the empire, and both imperial and free towns, as well as higher members of the confederation. Subjects professing another religion from that of their lord might have the liberty of emigrating without loss of goods. The church property already in the hands of Protestant estates, and not immediately related to the empire, was confirmed to them. All ecclesiastics who should renounce the Catholic religion for that of the Augsburg Confession, "whether archbishop, bishop, prelate or any other of the spiritual order," should lose the church goods and rights which they had before enjoyed. This goes by the name of the *reservatum ecclesiasticum*, and proved to be a source of countless troubles. (Dumont, u. s. IV. 3, 88.)

1579, Jan. 23. The union of Utrecht, out of which grew the Dutch republic. (Dumont, V. 1, 322.)

1631, April 6. Treaty of Cherasco (Querasque), between the Emperor Ferdinand II. and Louis XIII. of France (Dumont, VI. 1, 9), carrying out the treaty of Ratisbon (Regensburg), of Oct. 13, 1630, by virtue of which the Emperor was to acknowledge Charles Duke of Nevers as Duke of Mantua and Montferrat. (Dumont, V. 2, 615.) But Trino (Train) and certain other places in Montferrat were to go to the Duke of Savoy. The French also renounced their conquests in Italy. In a secret treaty however between France and Savoy, the best parts of Montferrat, the town of Alba and its environs, were to be handed over to the Duke of Savoy, who in turn was to give back Pignerol, and a road from France leading to it, to the French king, thus opening the way into Italy. By this secret treaty the Pope was deceived, and the interests of the French pretendant to Mantua were sacrificed. (Comp. Schlosser's Weltgesch. XIV. 398.)

1648, Oct. 24. PEACE of Westphalia, consisting of the two treaties of Münster where the French, and of Osnabrück where the Swedes negotiated with the Emperor—the smaller German powers being also represented. This peace put an end to the thirty years' war, and adjusted the relations of a large part of Europe. In the same year, on the 30th of January, Spain and Holland made a treaty of peace at Münster.

Some of the more important diplomatic transactions, before this war or during its course, and relating to the quarrels in the German empire, were the Protestant *Union*, May, 1608; the Catholic *Liga*, 1610 (Dumont, V. 2, 118); the *treaty of Ulm*, July 3, 1620, by which the Protestant princes virtually abandoned the Elector Palatine, as far as Bohemia was concerned (Dumont, u. s. 369); *the peace of Lübeck*, May 22, 1629, in which the King of Denmark withdrew from the war in Germany (Dumont, u. s. 584); *the edict of restitution*, March 6, 1629 (Dumont, u. s. 564); and *the peace of Prague*, May 30, 1635 (Dumont, VI. 1, 88), between the Emperor and the Elector of Saxony, to which last nearly all the German estates ere long acceded, thus abandoning the war and the cause of the Swedes. *The edict of restitution* was an interpretation, given by the Emperor's arbitrary act, to the treaties of Passau and of Augsburg, to the effect that all ecclesiastical property, seized by the Protestant estates since the year 1552, should be restored; that Catholic princes had the right of requiring their Protestant subjects to conform to their religion or of sending them out of their territories; and that the peace did not include any Protestants, except those who adhered to the Confession of Augsburg *non variata*, thus excluding the Reformed or Calvinists. *The peace of Prague*, on the other hand, virtually gave into the hands of the Protestant estates all immediate property which they had appropriated *before*, and all mediate or immediate which they had appropriated *since* the religious peace, by conceding to them the control and use of it for forty years, etc.

The principal provisions of the peace of Westphalia (Dumont VI. 1, 450, 469 in French,—for the original Latin see Ghillany, manual diplom. I. 1–100) were in brief these:

1. Sweden, as a satisfaction for restoring places occupied in the war, received hither Pomerania, the isle of Rügen, parts of further Pomerania, viz.: Stettin, Garz, Damm, Golnow and the isle of Wollin, the course of the Oder between these places, the 'frische Haff' and its mouths, etc., with the expectancy of the rest of further Pomerania, should the males of the house of Brandenburg become extinct; further, the archbishopric of Bremen (the city retaining its rights and immediate relation to the empire), the bishopric of Werden, the town and port of Wismar with various appurtenances. These were to continue parts of the Empire, of which the King of Sweden, as Duke of Bremen, Werden and Pomerania, Prince of Rügen, and Lord of Wismar, was to become a member with three votes in the Diet; with the privilege of supreme jurisdiction on condition of erecting a court of highest instance within the territory,—which was established at Wismar;—with the power of choosing between the Aulic Council and the Imperial Chamber, in case suits should be brought against Sweden touching these German territories; and with the right of founding a University, for which Greifswald was afterward selected (peace of Osnabrück, Art. X).—To the Swedish troops five million rix dollars were to be paid by the Empire (Art. XVI), and a secret article bound the Emperor to pay to Sweden 600,000 rix dollars, and determined the mode of payment.

2. To France were ceded the bishoprics of Metz, Toul and Verdun, the town of Pignerol (see treaty of Cherasco), Breisach, the landgravate of Upper and Lower Alsace, the Sundgau, the prefecture or "landvogtei" of ten imperial towns in Alsace, and the right to occupy the fortress of Philippsburg. The ceded places in Alsace, the Sundgau and the prefecture were to *pertain to the Crown of France forever and to be incorporated with its dominions* (peace of Münst. § 70–§ 76). Yet a later article of this peace, (§ 87) binds the King of France to leave the bishops of Basel and of Strasburg, with all estates in either Alsace holding immediately of the Empire, the ten imperial towns before mentioned, etc., "in that liberty and possession of immediacy toward the Empire which they had before enjoyed." For the questions which grew out of these articles, see De Garden, I. 213–223.

3. A general amnesty running back to the beginning of the war, and a restitution of the state of things in 1624 among the estates of the Empire were agreed upon. But in express terms a number of the German States had territory confirmed to them, or granted by way of compensation. Thus to the Elector of Brandenburg, for his territory ceded to Sweden, were assigned the bishoprics of Minden, Halberstadt and Camin, and archbishopric of Magdeburg or rather the greater part of its territory, after the rights of its present administrator, the Duke of Saxony, should cease. It came into the hands of the Prussian House not until 1680. Whatever power of collation within the bishopric of Camin the Dukes of hither Pomerania formerly had was to go to Sweden, but the patronage held by the former dukes of further Pomerania, the episcopal territory, and the part of further Pomerania not secured to Sweden, were to go to Brandenburg. Again, to Mecklenburg, in lieu of Wismar, were given the episcopal territories of Schwerin and Ratzeburg with two commanderies, or benefices of the Knights of St. John, within the Duchy, Mirau and Nemerau, the latter being put into the hands of the line of Gustrow, the rest into those of Schwerin. Further, to Brunswick-Lüneburg, as a compensation for rights renounced to Sweden, Brandenburg and Mecklenburg, was given, together with the monastic foundations of Walkenried and Gröningen, etc., the perpetual alternate succession in the bishopric of Osnabrück. After the decease of the present bishop, a Protestant one was to be elected from the houses of Brunswick, during whose office the archbishop of Cologne was to exercise episcopal rights, as metropolitan, but over Catholics only. The house of Hesse-Cassel received the abbey of Hersfeld or Hirschfeld, as a secular principality with the sovereignty over Schaumburg and other territory formerly claimed by the bishop of Minden, an indemnity in money of 600,000 thalers, and an acknowledgment of its claims to a share in the inheritance of Marburg (treaty of Osnab., Art. XI–XV).

4. The exiled and despoiled house of the Electors Palatine recovered the lower Palatinate, with the right of reversion to the upper; and an eighth electorate was erected in its favor, the old dignity of Elector Palatine and the upper Palatinate remaining with Bavaria until the expiration of its ducal line. So also the outlawed or expelled princes of Würtemberg, Baden, Nassau, etc., were restored to their pristine state (Art. IV).

5. Switzerland, long independent and disconnected from the Empire in fact, was acknowledged to be such in right.

6. The Emperor was to be governed by the votes of the diet,—which was thus conceded to be more than an advisory body,—in all matters pertaining to war, peace, legislation, etc. The members of the diet obtained the right not only of contracting alliances among themselves but with

foreign princes also, provided no prejudice came thereby to the Emperor and the Empire,—an unmeaning clause, which could not prevent the effect of this vast concession to weaken the power of the Emperor and the unity of the Empire very greatly. The imperial court was to have members of both religions in nearly equal numbers; that is, two Catholic presidents and twenty-six assessors, two presidents of the Augsburg Confession, appointed by the Emperor, and twenty-four assessors. If the opinions of the court were divided according to the religious faith of the members, a case was to go up to the Diet (Art. VIII., Art. V., §53).

7. Among the provisions affecting Religion, the most important are the following:—1. The religious freedom, guaranteed in the treaty of Passau and in the religious peace of Augsburg, was confirmed to the Lutherans, and extended to the Reformed or Calvinists. But no other form of religion besides these and the Catholic was to be tolerated in the Empire (Art. V., § 1, Art. VII). 2. The *reservatum ecclesiasticum* of the earlier treaties was replaced by a rule making the year 1624 the normal year for the purpose of deciding which confession should have the control over ecclesiastical properties: that is, a benefice, held by a Catholic or Protestant in January, 1624, should remain in perpetuity attached to the same religion (Art. V., §2). But in the Palatinate, Baden, Würtemberg, etc., by the act of amnesty (Art. IV., §§ 6, 24, 26) all things were to be restored to the condition which existed before the 'Bohemian movements,' *i. e.*, the year 1618 was the normal year for the Elector Palatine and his allies, the old religious constitution of whose territories would otherwise have been wholly altered. The Protestants long insisted on 1618 as the normal year, but as most of the counterreforms in the Emperor's hereditary dominions took place between this year and 1624, he would not yield, and the Swedes gave way. This suppressed the Reformation in Bohemia and a large part of Southern Germany. Moreover, as the amnesty (Art. IV. §§ 52, 53), conceded to subjects of Austria, included no restoration of their confiscated estates, their condition was a very hard one. An exception however was made in favor of certain of the higher Silesian nobility, and of the town of Breslau: though subjects of Austria, these were allowed to retain such rights of Protestant worship as they enjoyed before the war. Other nobles of Silesia and of lower Austria with their subjects, adherents of the Augsburg confession, had the right of private worship and could not be compelled to emigrate. Three Lutheran churches were to be allowed in Silesia (Art. V., §§ 38, 39, 40). 3. If a holder of an ecclesiastical benefice should change his religion, he was to vacate his benefice without restoring the former fruits of it, or losing his honor or good name. 4. If any territorial sovereign should change his religion (as from the Lutheran to the Reformed), or acquire sovereignty over a land where another *cultus* was established, he could there only enjoy his own domestic worship, without

having the power of altering the existing church, or filling the offices with persons of his own faith. If a community should go over to the religion of the new sovereign, it might do so unhindered, but the old state of things in school and church must continue (Art. VII., §§ 1, 2). 5. The jus reformandi of the old treaties was renewed to all the immediate estates of the Empire, but the following limitations were imposed on its exercise: Subjects differing in religion from their sovereign, and holding ecclesiastical goods in any part of 1624, were secured in possession of the same. Those who had enjoyed the right of public or of house worship, in any part of 1624, were to retain the right, and were secured in all things incidental to it. Those subjects of sovereigns of a different religion, who had neither the public nor the domestic exercise of their religion at the time aforesaid, or who should change their religion after the peace, had liberty of conscience and the civil advantages of other citizens guaranteed to them. This toleration consisted in the free exercise of private devotions, the public exercise of their religion in the vicinity, if they were near places of worship, and in the right of sending their children to schools abroad, or of employing instructors at home, of their own faith. They might however be compelled to emigrate, or might emigrate of their own accord. In this case they should be free to dispose of their own estates, and if required to leave their homes, a term of several years was to be granted to them for this purpose (Art. V., §§ 36, 37, 39, 40).

The peace of Westphalia, says Wheaton (Hist., part 1, at the beginning), "established the equality of the three religious communities of Catholics, Lutherans, and Calvinists, in Germany, and sought to oppose a perpetual barrier to further religious innovations and secularizations of ecclesiastical property. At the same time, it rendered the states of the Empire almost independent of the Emperor, its federal head. It arrested the progress of Germany toward national unity under the Catholic banner, and prepared the way for the subsequent development of the power of Prussia,—the child of the Reformation,—which thus became the natural head of the Protestant party, and the political rival of the house of Austria, which last still maintained its ancient position as the temporal chief of the Catholic body. It introduced two foreign elements into the internal constitution of the Empire,—France and Sweden, as guarantees of the peace, and Sweden as a member of the federal body,—thus giving to these two powers a perpetual right of interference in the internal affairs of Germany. It reserved to the individual states the liberty of forming alliances among themselves, as well as with foreign powers, for their preservation and security, provided these alliances were not directed against the Emperor and the Empire, nor contrary to the public peace and that of Westphalia. This liberty contributed to render the federative system of Germany a new security for the general balance of European power. The Germanic body thus placed in the centre of Europe, served, by its composition, in which so many political and religious interests were combined, to maintain the independence and tranquillity of all the neighboring states."

1648, Jan. 30. While the peace of Westphalia was still in agitation, Spain and Holland made a separate peace at Münster. By this treaty, (1.) the freedom and sovereignty of the United Provinces were recognized. (2.) Each party retained the places in its possession. Thus Holland gained Bois-le-Duc or Hertogenbusch, Bergen-op-Zoom with Breda in Brabant, Hulst, Axel, etc., in Flanders, certain joint rights in Limburg, etc. (3.) The Scheldt and certain water-courses connected with it were closed, by which Antwerp declined. (4.) Places won by the Dutch from Portugal were renounced by Spain. Important commercial concessions were made to Holland in the East and West Indies. (Dumont, VI. 1, 429, in French.)

1659, Nov. 7. Peace of the Pyrenees, which ended a twenty years' war between France and Spain connected with the long war in Germany. This peace was negotiated in an island of the Bidassoa, by the ministers of the two kingdoms in person, Louis de Haro and Cardinal Mazarin. By this peace the Prince of Condé was reëstablished in his estates and honors,—receiving however the government of Burgundy instead of that of Guienne; the Duke of Lorraine received his duchy again, giving up Moyenvic, the duchy of Bar and the county of Clermont, and allowing free transit for the troops of France; the dukes of Modena and Savoy, allies of France, were restored to the state they had been in before the war; and the Prince of Monaco was to be put in possession of his estates under the jurisdiction of the Spanish king, with the liberty of alienating them, etc. France received by this treaty Artois, except St. Omer and Aire, with places in Flanders, Hainault and Luxemburg; and on the borders of Spain the counties of Roussillon and Conflans, except the parts lying in the Pyrenees, and a portion of Cerdagne in those mountains looking toward France. It was stipulated that no aid should be given by France to Portugal, which Spain hoped to resubjugate. Finally the marriage of Louis XIV. and the Infanta of Spain, Maria Theresa, was agreed upon in this treaty, and in a special contract of the same date; and it was stipulated that the Infanta, for herself and the issue she might have by the French king, in consideration of a dowry of 500.000 gold crowns, should renounce before marriage for herself, and conjointly with him after marriage, all right of succession to the crown of Spain. (Dumont, VI. 2, 264–292.) This treaty added to the advantages gained by France in the treaty of Münster, and her ascendency in Europe was now secured.

1660, May 3 and June 6. Treaty of Oliva near Dantzig between the King of Poland of the house of Wasa in the elder branch with his allies, and the King of Sweden; and treaty of Copenhagen between the kings of Denmark and Sweden. By the first the Polish king renounced for himself and his line all claim to Sweden, Finland, etc., recovered supremacy over Courland and certain towns, Marienburg, Elbing, etc., and gave up to Sweden Esthonia and Livonia in great part. The duchy of Prussia was entirely severed from Poland's suzerainty in favor of the Elector of Brandenburg. The treaty of Copenhagen confirmed in part that of Roetskild (or Rotschild, March 8, 1558. Dumont, VI. 2, 205). The provinces of Halland, Schonen, Bleckingen, the islet of Hween, Bahus and its precinct were secured to Sweden, which restored to Denmark the island of Bornholm, and Drontheim in Norway, conquered in the war, and renounced its claims to the county of Delmenhorst and Ditmarsch in Germany. Arrangements were made also with regard to the right of passage through the Sound and the Belt. Of the treaty of Oliva, France was a guarantee; of the treaty of Copenhagen, France, England, Holland.

Treaties of the Age of Louis XIV.

1667, July 31. Treaties of Breda between England and France, England and Holland, England and Denmark. England restored to France Acadia (Nova Scotia), and recovered Antigua, Montserrat, and the English part of St. Christopher's in the West Indies. Between England and Holland the *status quo* of May 20, 1667, determined in regard to the acquisitions they might have made from one another in the war. By this rule England retained New Netherlands (New York), and Holland, Surinam. Another article of great importance for Holland modified the English navigation act of 1651, in such sort that merchandise coming down the Rhine could be imported into England in Dutch vessels. (Dumont, VII. 1, 40–56.)

1668, Jan. 23. Triple alliance between England, Holland and Sweden in order to promote a peace between France and Spain. (Dumont, u. s. 68–70.) In May of the same year peace was concluded between France and Spain, at Aix-la-Chapelle, by which places, taken by the French in the Spanish Netherlands, were retained,—Charleroi, Binche, Ath, Douay, Tournay, Oudenarde, Lille, Armentières, Courtray, Bruges, Furnes, the fort of Scarpe;—and Franche Comté was restored to Spain.

1668, Feb. 23. Treaty of Lisbon between Spain and Portugal, England acting as mediator and guarantee. The independence of Portugal is virtually acknowledged by Spain's making a treaty; and all territory, except Ceuta in Africa, is restored. (Dumont, VII. 1, 70.)

1678–9. Peace of Nymwegen (Nimeguen), ending the Dutch war, the parties in which had been France, England, Sweden, some of the smaller states of the Empire on the one hand, and Holland, the Elector of Brandenburg, Spain, the Emperor, Denmark, and some of the smaller German states on the other. The English king (Charles II.) was forced by the

Parliament to make peace with the Dutch in 1674, and a close alliance between the two powers was arranged at Westminster (March 3, 1678). The treaties made at Nimeguen were those of Holland with France, Aug. 10, 1678, of Spain with France, Sept. 17 of the same year, of the Emperor with France, and also with Sweden, Feb. 5, 1679, and of Holland with Sweden, Oct. 12, 1679. Denmark treated with France at Fontainebleau, Sept. 2, 1679, and with Sweden at Lund, Sept. 26, 1679. The Elector of Brandenburg made a treaty with France and Sweden at St. Germain-en-Laye, June 29, 1679,—not to mention other less important transactions. (Dumont, VII. 1, 351, etc.) In this general pacification, (1.) Holland had restored to her all the places taken by the French in the war; and by a separate article restitution was to be made to the Prince of Orange, of Orange and other estates in the dominions of the French king. (2.) Spain got back in the Netherlands, Charleroi, Binche, Oudenarde, Ath, Courtray (see treaty of Aix-la-Chapelle, 1668), the land beyond the Meuse, Ghent, the fort of Rodenhus, the district of Waes; also the town and duchy of Limburg, the towns of Leuve and St. Ghilain, and in Catalonia the town of Puycerda. Spain ceded to France all Franche Comté, Valenciennes, Cambray and the Cambrésis, Aire, Poperingen, St. Omer, Ypern (Ypres), etc. (3.) The Emperor ceded to France Freiburg in the Breisgau, with right of road from Breisach, recovered Philippsburg for the Empire (see treaty of Westphalia), procured the restoration of the Duke of Lorraine to his duchy and estates, yet only on the most onerous conditions, and engaged to put the Fürstenburg princes in the state in which they were before the war. As regards its eastern borders, France had a very great advantage by these treaties, especially at the cost of Spain. (4.) Sweden recovered what Denmark had conquered, Wismar, the isle of Rügen, etc., and the Danes engaged to restore the Duke of Holstein-Gottorp to his state before the war. Sweden moreover recovered what the Elector of Brandenburg had conquered from her in hither Pomerania, but gave up the lands beyond the Oder, except the towns of Dam and Golnow. (See peace of Westphalia.)

1697, Sept. 20, and Oct. 30. Peace of Ryswick, made at a palace near the Hague, and closing a war of almost ten years' duration, often called the war of Orleans, between France and the principal powers of Europe. Soon after the peace of Nimeguen, Louis XIV., by means of courts erected for the purpose 'reunited,' as it was called, to his kingdom parts of the adjoining foreign territory, seized Strasburg in 1681, and committed other flagitious acts of aggression. Leagues were formed against him, but amounted to nothing, until in 1686, at Augsburg, many of the German powers concluded one for mutual protection, which was signed at Vienna in 1687. The next year Louis began open war by invading the Empire, urging as his pretexts besides this league the claim of his sister-in-law, the Duchess of Orleans, to the allodial property of her brother who was the last male of the Simmern branch of Electors Palatine, as also the indignities offered to him in the disputed election of the archbishop at Cologne. To oppose him an alliance was concluded between Holland and the Emperor and Empire at Vienna, May 12, 1689, to which England under William III. and Spain afterward acceded, with whom the Duke of Savoy and the King of Denmark acted in concert. The parties engaged to treat with Louis only on the basis of the treaties of Westphalia and of the Pyrenees, to procure the restoration of the Duke of Lorraine to his rights in full, and,—in a separate article,—to secure to the Emperor and his heirs the succession in Spain, if Charles II. should die childless. (Dumont, VII. 2, 229–230, 241, 267.)

The peace of Ryswick consisted of treaties of France with England, Spain, Holland and the Emperor and Empire, with which last peace was not effected until Oct. 30, 1697. (Dumont, VII. 2, 399, 408, 381, 421.) (1.) England and France mutually restored what had been taken in the war, William of Orange was acknowledged to be lawful king of Great Britain, and Louis promised not to help his enemies, *i. e.*, James II. (2.) To Spain France restored all the 'reunions' made since the peace of Nimeguen, 82 places excepted, together with the conquests of the war. (3.) Holland returned Pondichery in India to the French East India company and received valuable commercial privileges from France. (4.) The French king gave up all his 'reunions' made from the Empire, *except in Alsace*, which lost henceforth all connection with the Empire, and became an integral part of France. Another article gave up Strasburg expressly to France; others still ceded Breisach and Freiburg to the Emperor, Philippsburg to the Empire (see peace of Westphalia), restored the duchy of Zweibrücken (Deuxponts) to the King of Sweden, as Count Palatine of the Rhine, and Mumpelgard (Montbeliard) to Würtemberg, etc., provided for the Duke of Lorraine on the terms granted to his father by France in 1670, reinstated the Cardinal Fürstenburg in his bishopric of Strasburg and other rights, rased a number of forts, declared the navigation of the Rhine free, etc.—An earlier treaty of Aug. 29, 1696, between France and Savoy, was confirmed in the peace of Ryswick, in which Louis agreed to give back Pignerol (see peace of Westphalia, peace of Cherasco), with its fortifications demolished, and to restore the conquests of the war. (Dumont, VII. 2, 368, 383, art. 16 of treaty with Holland.)

In the fourth article of the treaty with the Emperor restoring the conquests and reunions outside of Alsace (Dumont, VII. 2, 422), occurs this clause: "religione tamen Catholica Romana in locis sic restitutis in statu quo nunc est remanente." During the French occupation of these districts, Protestantism had been suppressed by force. The Protestants protested against this peace on this account, and claimed that it violated the peace of Westphalia on the basis of which it was made. The Diet, however, ratified it, Nov. 26, 1697, but added in a postscript that the Catholics would make no use of this clause against the Protestants. The clause, moreover, was said to relate only to certain churches endowed by Louis XIV. The Emperor confirmed the vote of the Diet in ratification of the peace, but passed over the postscript in silence. Soon afterward the French minister claimed that the clause related to churches in 1,922 places, where the chaplains of regiments passing through had said mass.

1698. First partition treaty, concluded at the Hague, Oct. 11, between William III. of England, Holland, and Louis XIV. In expectation of the death of Charles II. of Spain—the last Hapsburger—without heirs, William, doubting his ability to prevent Spain from coming under the control of France, consents to a partition of the Spanish monarchy. In general, Naples and Sicily were assigned to the Dauphin of France, the duchy of Milan to the Archduke Charles of Austria, second son of the Emperor, and Spain, with the Spanish Netherlands and the foreign dependencies, to the eldest son of the Duke of Bavaria. (Dumont, VII. 2, 442.)

The young Bavarian prince died Feb. 8, 1699, at the age of six. A new treaty of partition between the same powers (London, March 13, the Hague, March 25, 1700) provided in general that Naples, Sicily, the duchies of Lorraine and Bar, should go to the Dauphin; the Duke of Lorraine should be transferred to the duchy of Milan; the crown of Spain, the Netherlands and Indies should fall to the Archduke Charles. (Dumont, u. s. 477.) For the claims or want of claims of the parties obtruded upon Spain by these treaties, comp. Garden, II. 220 ff.; Smyth, mod. hist., lecture xxiii. No grosser instance of intervention is to be found in history, unless it be the partition of Poland.

1699, Jan. 26. Peace of Carlowitz, consisting of a treaty of the Sultan for a twenty-five years' truce with the Emperor, of a treaty of the same with the King of Poland, and of one with Venice negotiated by the ambassadors of the two other Christian powers. Prince Eugene having annihilated the Turkish army at Zentha, Sept. 11, 1697, the Sultan acknowledged Transylvania to be an Austrian province, and agreed that the southern bank of the Danube should separate his dominions from Hungary, etc. Venice retained possession of what it held in Greece except Lepanto, and in Dalmatia,—where the limits were fixed by a series of forts ceded to the Republic,—Castel Novo and Risano, near Cattaro, remained Venetian. (Dumont, VII. 2, 448–458.)

1713 and 1714. Treaties of UTRECHT and of RASTADT, ending the war of succession to the crown of Spain, which began in 1701. Charles II. of Spain had made a testament in favor of the electoral prince of Bavaria as his successor, before the death of that boy in 1699. Afterward he inclined to the Archduke Charles of Austria, and made a will to that effect, but as Austria delayed consenting to fulfil the conditions, he was persuaded by the French party at his court to burn the will, and to bestow the crown upon Philip, duke of Anjou, second son of the Dauphin of France, or in case of his death without heirs or his elevation to the throne in his own country, upon his next brother, the Duke of Berry, and so in succession on the Archduke Charles, and on the Duke of Savoy and his children who were descended from the sister of Philip II. of Spain. At all events, the Spanish monarchy was to be kept entire.

The King of Spain died Nov. 1, 1700, and Louis XIV. decided, a few weeks afterward, to accept the testament for his grandson, although in the spring of the same year he had been a party to the treaty of partition, not to speak of the renunciations made in the treaty of the Pyrenees. (See that treaty.) England and other states at first recognized the Bourbon in the way of ceremony as king of Spain; but Louis having avoided giving a guaranty that the crowns of France and Spain should be kept apart, having also on the death of James II. of England (Sept. 16, 1701), in violation of the peace of Ryswick, acknowledged his son as king of England, a war was inevitable, which the death of William III. (March 8, 1702) could not prevent. An understanding between William, who was the centre of the opposition to France, and the Emperor, led to the *grand alliance*, formed Sept. 7, 1701, to which Great Britain, Holland, and the Emperor were the original parties; and to which, afterward, Denmark, the Elector of Brandenburg (or king of Prussia), Portugal, Sweden, the Empire, Savoy, etc., acceded. The main points of the alliance were, to compensate the Emperor for the loss of the Spanish monarchy, and so to seize on the Spanish Netherlands, the duchy of Milan, the two Sicilies, and the ports of Tuscany; to secure to England and Holland all the conquests they might make in Spanish America; and to make peace with France only on condition that the two crowns of France and Spain should never be united. The principal allies of France were the Elector of Bavaria and his brother the Archbishop of Cologne. The Emperor invaded Italy in 1701. War was declared by England, May 4, 1702.

The peace of Utrecht consists of separate treaties made by France with Great Britain, Portugal, Prussia, Savoy, and Holland (April 11, 1713), and by Spain with Great Britain (July 13), and with Savoy (Aug. 13), which were followed by treaties of Spain with Holland (June 26, 1714), and with Portugal (Feb. 6, 1715), signed at the same place. The treaty of Rastadt (March 6, 1714), made by the Emperor, for himself and the Empire, with France, was modified slightly and finished at Baden in Switzerland, Sept. 7, 1714.

The most important features of these treaties were the following:

1. In her treaty with Great Britain (Dumont, VIII. 1, 339), France ceded or restored to that kingdom Hudson's bay and strait, St. Kitts, Nova Scotia (Acadia), Newfoundland with the adjacent islands—reserving, however, Cape Breton and the islands in the mouth of the St. Lawrence, with the right to catch and dry fish on a considerable part of the Newfound-

land coast. Dunkirk is to be dismantled and its harbor filled up. The Hanoverian succession, as settled by Parliament, is acknowledged. The reciprocal renunciations, by Philip V. of Spain, of the French crown, and by the dukes of Berry and Orleans of the Spanish, are inserted in the treaty, and it is declared to be an inviolable law that the two crowns shall remain separate and disunited.—In a commercial treaty of the same date between the same powers (Dumont, u. s. 345), it is stipulated, that between the parties the ships of each shall be free to carry goods not contraband and persons not military pertaining to the enemies of the other. The same principle is sanctioned in the commercial treaty between France and Holland of the same date.

In the treaty between Spain and Great Britain (Dumont, u. s. 393), Gibraltar and Minorca with Port Mahon are ceded to the latter power; the perpetual separation of the French and Spanish crowns is solemnly pledged; Spain engages not to transfer, to France or any other nation, any land or lordship in America; and Great Britain promises, in case the line of Savoy shall die out, to do her best in order to reunite Sicily with Spain. (See treaties with Savoy.) The 12th article has had an unhappy celebrity; it gives to a British company, for the space of thirty years from the date of the treaty, a contract (*el pacto de el assiento de negros*) for exclusively supplying Spanish America with negroes, on the same terms under which the French, *i. e.*, the French Guinea company, founded in 1701, had acted.

2. In the treaty of France with Holland (Dumont, u. s. 366), France engages to put into the hands of Holland for the purpose of being transferred to the house of Austria, the Spanish Netherlands, as they were after the treaty of Ryswick, except a part of Guelders ceded to Prussia, and a tract in Luxemburg or Limburg to be formed into a principality for the Princess Orsini,—which last arrangement, however, through the opposition of Austria, never took effect. Of the French Netherlands, Tournay, Furnes, and their districts, Ypres, Poperingen, etc., were ceded on like terms to Holland. France engaged to make the Elector of Bavaria abandon any claim he had to the Low Countries from an earlier Spanish cession of 1702 and 1712; but the town and duchy of Luxemburg, Namur and its county, and Charleroi, were to be under his sovereignty until he should be restored to his estates and dignities in Germany. The separation of the crowns of Spain and France was pledged both in this treaty and in the later one of Spain with Holland (Dumont, u. s. 427), which was delayed by the scheme of the Princess Orsini, who ruled Philip V., to get for herself a sovereignty in the Netherlands. In this treaty Spain engaged to keep all other nations, except the Dutch, from trading with the Spanish East Indies.

3. The treaties with Portugal are of less importance. (Dumont, u. s. 353, 444.) France renounces in favor of Portugal all right to the tract called the Cap du Nord, between the Amazon and the Vincent Pinson or

Japoc, and admits that the two shores of the Amazon and the right to navigate it belong to that state. Spain cedes to Portugal the territory and colony of S. Sacramento on the north shore of the La Plata.

4. France cedes to the king of Prussia, in virtue of power received from Spain, Upper or Spanish Guelders, and admits his right to the principality of Neufchatel (or Neuenburg) and Valengin in Switzerland. He, on the other hand, renounces all his pretensions to the principality of Orange and its dependent lands in France, but may bear the arms and title. (Dumont, u. s. 356.)

5. Spain (Dumont, u. s. 401) confirms to the Duke of Savoy the island of Sicily—already ceded by a special instrument made at Madrid, June 10, 1713. (Dumont, u. s. 389.) The sovereignty is to follow the line of the duke and his male descendants, and—this being extinct—the male line of the Prince of Carignan and his brother. If the Savoy line die out, the island is to revert to Spain, and if the Spanish line die out in Spain, the house of Savoy shall succeed in that kingdom. France recognizes the cession of Sicily and restores to Savoy the territory conquered in the war: the boundary of France toward the county of Nice and Piedmont is determined by the summits of the Alps; and the cessions made to the duke by the Emperor in 1703,—viz.: the Mantuan part of Montferrat, the provinces of Alessandria and Valentia, the land between the Po and the Tanaro, the Lomellina, etc.—are confirmed in both treaties. (Dumont, u. s. 362.) The Duke of Savoy was crowned king of Sicily at Palermo in 1713, but was not acknowledged either by the Pope or the Emperor.

By the treaties of Rastadt and Baden (Dumont, u. s. pp. 415, 436), France engages to leave the Emperor master of the places and states which he occupies in Italy,—viz.: the kingdom of Naples, the duchy of Milan, the island of Sardinia, the ports of Tuscany,—consents that he shall take possession of the Spanish Netherlands according to the treaty with Holland, gives up Alt-Breisach, Freiburg, the fortress of Kehl, according to the stipulations of the treaty of Ryswick, which is made the basis of arrangements touching Germany. The Emperor engages to restore the Duke of Bavaria and the Archbishop of Cologne to their state before the war. By the treaty of Baden, the Emperor is allowed to retain possession of the duchies of Mantua and Mirandola, and the town of Commachio.—No treaty arrangements were made between the Emperor and Spain, the former delaying to acknowledge the Bourbon king, and Philip V. not consenting to the dismemberment of the Spanish monarchy by which the Emperor was a gainer.

The *barrier treaties*, three in number, deserve a brief notice in this place. An article of the grand alliance having promised to the Dutch a barrier against France, the two first barrier treaties, made Oct. 29, 1709, and Jan. 30, 1713, that is, before the peace of Utrecht, between Great

25

Britain and the States General, contemplated giving to the latter a number of fortified places in the Spanish Netherlands, with revenues for the payment of the garrisons, to be drawn from the country itself; and the first treaty, by a separate article, gave them the hope of acquiring Upper Guelders and some other places. The second treaty diminished the number of forts they were to hold, and said nothing of Guelderland, which had, since the first treaty, been promised to Prussia. Both treaties pledge the States General to the maintenance and defence of the Protestant succession in England, as by law established.

Both these treaties come to nothing. The third, signed at Antwerp by Austria, Great Britain and the Dutch, Nov. 15, 1715, provides that the latter shall transfer to Austria the Spanish Netherlands, both the territory held by Charles II. of Spain and that ceded by France,—Austria engaging that they shall remain under Austrian sway and never pass over to France or any other power. An army of about 30,000 men shall be maintained there by the Emperor and the Dutch; the former to furnish two thirds of the force, and the latter, one third. The Dutch shall garrison exclusively Namur, Tournai, Menin, Furnes, Ypres, Warneton and the fort of Knock, and in common with Austria Dendermonde. They may repair and fortify the towns of the barrier, but not build any new forts without the Emperor's consent. He agrees to let them occupy such forts and territory, and to make such intrenchments and inundations, beyond their frontiers in the Austrian Netherlands, as may be necessary in case of the invasion of those provinces. He also cedes to them Venlo and some other places in Guelders, and engages to pay for the support of their troops 1,250,000 Dutch florins, hypothecated on the revenues of the Netherlands. It is also agreed (article 26) that ships and cargoes, going between Great Britain or Holland and the Austrian Netherlands, shall pay the same duties of entry and exit as at present, until the three powers shall enter into other arrangements by a commercial treaty, to be made as soon as possible,—which treaty, however, was never effected. Great Britain confirmed and guaranteed this treaty. From the failure to make the commercial arrangement above spoken of Austria drew a pretext for regarding the barrier treaty as annulled. (Dumont, VIII. 1, 243, 322, 458.)

1717, Jan. 4. The triple alliance between France, Great Britain and Holland, to maintain the treaty of Utrecht and defend one another in case of attack. France also engaged to render no succor to the Pretender and to induce him to go beyond the Alps. (Dumont, VIII. 1, 484.)

1718, Aug. 2. The quadruple alliance, concluded at London by France and Great Britain, and so called as intended to include Holland, which acceded, Feb. 16, 1719, and the Emperor, who accepted the terms of the alliance, Sept. 16, 1718. (Dumont, u. s. 531.) As yet no peace had been made between the Emperor and Spain. The former was dissatisfied with the arrangements made in Italy, especially with the giving of Sicily to the Duke of Savoy. Spain, now under the influence of the intriguing and ambitious Cardinal Alberoni, aimed to recover what she had lost by the peace of Utrecht, and for this purpose sought to disturb the politics of France and England. Sicily and Sardinia are invaded by Spanish troops, but the fleet of that kingdom having been almost destroyed by the English, and the forces of both France and England having entered Spain, the king, finding his projects too great for his resources, gives way, dismisses Alberoni, and accedes to the alliance in 1720 (Jan. 26). The Duke of Savoy had done the same in 1718. Defensive treaties in 1721 made by Spain with France and Great Britain complete the arrangements with those powers. In conformity with the quadruple alliance, and with other treaties made in the same spirit, Spain renounced the Low Countries and the Spanish part of Italy; the Emperor renounced the monarchy of Spain, ceded to Philip V. by the peace of Utrecht, and acknowledged him as lawful sovereign of that country; Savoy and the Emperor exchanged Sardinia and Sicily with one another; and Spain renounced its right of reversion to Sicily in exchange for a similar right to Sardinia. Leghorn should be a free port in perpetuity, and the Italian duchies of Tuscany, Parma, and Piacenza, where the male lines of the Medici and Farnese family were likely to become extinct, were to be regarded as male fiefs of the Empire, the investiture of which should be given to Don Carlos of Spain, etc., and in no case pertain to the crown of Spain.

Thus by the peace of Utrecht and these auxiliary treaties, (1.) a barrier was erected in favor of Holland against France by giving the Spanish Netherlands to Austria, (2.) France and Spain could never be united under one monarch by the public law of Europe, (3.) the Emperor recovered some of the old Germanic influence in the affairs of Italy, (4.) the Duke of Savoy, with an accession of power as king of Sardinia, became a stronger check against any designs of France upon Italy, and against Austrian predominance in that peninsula.—The remaining minor differences between the Emperor and Spain were discussed at the Congress of Cambray (from 1722, onward).

Treaties of the Age of England's Maritime Preponderance and of the Growth of Prussia.

1718, July 21. Peace of Passarowitz, between the Emperor and the Sultan, after Prince Eugene's victory at Peterwardein and capture of Belgrade. (Dumont, u. s. 520.) Austria came by this peace into possession of the Bannat of Temeswar, of Belgrade, and of a portion of Servia, Wallachia, etc.

1721, Aug. 30. Peace of Nystadt in Finland between Sweden and the Czar,—one of several treaties, in which Sweden, now controlled by the estates of the realm, made terms with its neighbors, after the fall of Görtz, the intriguing ally of Alberoni, and after the death of Charles XII. Sweden in 1719 yielded to the king of England, as elector of Hanover, the duchies of Bremen and Werden (see peace of Westphalia) for a million rix dollars (Dumont, VIII. 2, 15); in 1720, Feb. 1, to Prussia, Stettin and the lands in Pomerania between the Oder and the Pehne, etc. for twice that sum (Dumont, u. s. 21); in the same year to Denmark the right of toll over Swedes in the Sound and Belts with a payment of 600,000 rix dollars, promising also not to interfere as to Schleswig and the duke of Holstein, in consideration of Denmark's abandonment of its Swedish conquests. (Dumont, u. s. 29.) To this peace France and England were guarantees. In the peace of Nystadt (Dumont, u. s. 36), Sweden ceded to Russia Livonia, Esthonia, Ingermannland, part of Carelia, Wiborg, the isle of Oesel, etc., and received back Finland which Russia had conquered, with two million rix-dollars. Sweden enjoyed peace for some time, but fell henceforth in political importance below Prussia and Russia.

1735, Oct. 3. Preliminary treaty of Vienna, definitively signed Nov. 18, 1738, between the king of France and the Emperor, to which the kings of Sardinia and of Spain, and the actual occupant of Naples and Sicily, Don Carlos, acceded. By this treaty the duke of Lorraine, upon the impending extinction of the Medici family in the male line, was to be constituted grand duke of Tuscany, with right of succession in his family; and the exiled king of Poland, Stanislaus Lescinsky, father-in-law of Louis XV., having abdicated his royal office, was to be put in possession of the duchy of Bar, and of that of Lorraine also when the above-mentioned transfer of its duke should take effect. On the death of the Polish king these duchies were to be united to the kingdom of France. Naples and Sicily, with the ports of Tuscany possessed by the Emperor, were ceded to Don Carlos, eldest son of Philip V. of Spain by his second marriage with Elizabeth Farnese, who thus founded the second or Neapolitan line of Spanish Bourbons. The king of Sardinia gained the territory of Novara and Tortona as fiefs of the empire, with the territorial superiority in the district of Langhes, and the Emperor acquired Parma and Piacenza in full property. France guaranteed the *pragmatic sanction* of the Emperor Charles VI., and most of the powers of Europe at different times did the same thing. By this sanction, having no male heirs, he constituted his eldest daughter the inheritor of the entire mass of the Austrian monarchy, and for the sake of it consented to the abandonment of a large portion of his dominions in Italy, as well as to the incorporation of Lorraine in France. (Wenck's Codex Juris Gent. I. pp. 1, 88.)

1742, June 11. Preliminary peace of Breslau, and July 28, definitive peace of Berlin between Frederick II. of Prussia and Maria Theresa. Austria ceded all Silesia, lower and upper (not including the principality of

Teschen, the town of Troppau, the tract beyond the Oppa, and the Moravian districts enclosed in Upper Silesia), together with the county of Glatz: Frederick to pay the interest on the late Emperor's Silesian debt. Religion to remain as it is.—The peace of Dresden (Dec. 25, 1745) confirmed that of Breslau, and Frederick acknowledged Maria Theresa's husband, the grand duke of Tuscany, as Emperor. An act of the king of England guaranteeing Silesia to Prussia, accompanies the treaty. A treaty between Saxony and Prussia, made at the same time and place, secured the payment of a million rix dollars from the former to the latter, with other advantages. (Wenck, I. 734 et seq., II. 191 et seq.)

1748, April 30. Preliminary, and, Oct. 18, definitive peace of Aix-la-Chapelle, between France, Great Britain, and Holland—Spain, Austria, Sardinia, Genoa, Modena being accessaries. (Wenck, II. 310 et seq.) This peace ended the war, which grew originally out of the Austrian succession, by a mutual restitution of conquests, and general renewal of former important treaties. The duchies of Parma, Piacenza, and Guastalla were assigned to the Spanish infante Don Philip, and were ceded by their present possessors, the Empress and the King of Sardinia, (the latter as holding by the treaty of Worms in 1743 the city and part of the duchy of Piacenza), with the right of reversion to the said present possessors in case Don Philip should die without male children, or in case the King of the Two Sicilies should inherit the throne of Spain. Among the renewals of former stipulations, that of the assiento contract (see treaty of Utrecht) was expressly named, a misunderstanding concerning which had been one of the causes of the war with Spain on the part of England in 1739. "Never perhaps," says Lord Mahon, speaking of this peace, "did any war, after so many great events, and so large a loss of blood and treasure, end in replacing the nations engaged in it so nearly in the same situation as they held at first."

1759, Oct. 3. Treaty of Naples between Austria and Charles III. of Spain and the Two Sicilies. The Two Sicilies can never be united to the crown of Spain, except in case the line of Spanish kings of the present house shall be reduced to one person, and shall then be separated again, as soon as a prince shall be born who is not king of Spain nor heir presumptive. (Wenck, III. 206.)

1761, Aug. 15. Treaty, at first secret, between France and Spain, known as the family compact, to which the accession of the king of the Sicilies, and the duke of Parma, the Spanish king's two sons, were to be procured, but no one except a Bourbon should be invited to join in it. This treaty bound the parties to a very close offensive and defensive alliance, with the furnishing of a definite number of troops on demand of either party, and contemplated a guarantee of the dominions of each and of the two other Bourbon sovereigns. (Wenck, III. 278 et seq.; Martens, Rec.

I. 16–28.) In a secret convention of the same date it is said to have been stipulated, that if France should still be at war with England on the 1st of May, 1762, Spain should declare war against the latter, and that France should at the same time restore Minorca to Spain.

1763, Feb. 10. Peace of Paris, between France, Spain, England, and Portugal, and

1763, Feb. 15. Peace of Hubertsburg (a hunting château near Meissen in Saxony). By the first, the great contest between France and England, all over the world, to which Spain and Portugal became parties, was closed greatly to the advantage of England; and by the second, the seven years' war of Austria and its powerful allies against Frederick the Great. Of these allies, France, against its immemorial policy, had, in May, 1756, become one.

By the peace of Hubertsburg, Prussia ended the war with no loss of territory, standing where she stood after the treaties of Dresden, Berlin, and Breslau.

By the peace of Paris, England, which had stripped France of a considerable part of her colonial possessions, retained many of them, and received a large accession of power, especially on the western continent. In North America, France renounced her pretensions to Acadia, ceded Canada, Cape Breton, and the islands and coasts of the St. Lawrence, retaining the right of fishery on part of the coast of Newfoundland according to a stipulation of the treaty of Utrecht, and also the same right in the Gulf of St. Lawrence, three leagues away from British coasts, and at a distance of fifteen leagues from Cape Breton. The islands of St. Pierre and Miquelon also were to be retained by France, as shelters for her fishermen, but might not be fortified. The Canadian Catholics were to be left free to enjoy their religion. (Articles 4–6.) The middle of the Mississippi, from its source to the Iberville, and a line thence, through Lakes Maurepas and Pontchartrain to the Gulf of Mexico, were to bound the territory of the two nations. Only New Orleans on the western bank of the Mississippi was to remain French. (Art. 7.) By a secret treaty with Spain, of Nov. 3, 1762, France had already ceded Louisiana and New Orleans to that kingdom, but possession of them was not taken until 1769. This was a set-off for Spain's cession of Florida to Great Britain, which had been already decided upon and which this peace concluded. (Art. 20.) Great Britain agreed to restore to France Guadeloupe, Mariegalante, Desirade, Martinique, Belleisle, St. Lucia, and received, by way of cession, Granada, St. Vincent, Dominique and Tobago (Art. 8, 9), in the West Indies. In Africa, Goree was restored to France, and Senegal retained. (Art. 10.) In the East Indies, the forts and factories owned by France in 1749 on the coasts of Coromandel, Orissa, and Malabar, and in Bengal, were restored, and France engaged not to build forts nor keep troops in Bengal, and renounced all acquisitions made in Coromandel and Orissa since 1749. (Art. 11.) Dunkirk was to be put in the condition stipulated in the treaty of Aix-la-Chapelle and earlier treaties; Minorca to be restored to the English; the places occupied in Germany by the French to be evacuated and restored; Cuba, as far as conquered by England, to be ceded back to Spain; the forts erected by the English, in the Bay of Honduras and other places of Spanish America, to be demolished; but their workmen were to be unobstructed in cutting and transporting dye or cam wood, and no right of fishery near Newfoundland was to be allowed to Spanish subjects. (Art. 12–19. Wenck, III. 329, Martens, Rec. I. 104–166.

1768, May 15. A treaty of this date, between Genoa and France, yielded up Corsica to the sovereignty of the latter until the republic should demand its restitution and pay all expenses. The oppressive Genoese government of the island led to prolonged resistance, which was subdued by French troops, and the islanders preferred to be freed from the Genoese yoke. (Wenck, III. 714; Martens, I. 591).

1772, July 15. First partition of Poland, arranged in treaties between Russia and Austria, and Russia and Prussia, of this date, made at St. Petersburg. The treaties, alleging as the reasons for such a step the security of the neighboring states against the discords and intestine war of Poland, declare, 1. That Russia will take possession of the remainder of Polish Livonia, of the part of the palatinate of Polock which is east of the Dwina, of the palatinate of Witepsk, the two extremities of that of Minsk, and the whole of that of Mscislaw (or Mohilev). The Dwina to the point where the provinces of Polock, Witepsk, and Minsk meet, thence a straight line drawn nearly to the source of the Drujac (or Druets), the course of that stream and of the Dnieper, are to be the boundaries of the part cut off toward Poland. 2. Russia guarantees to Austria a territory consisting of East Galicia and Lodomiria. 3. Russia guarantees to Prussia Pomerellia except Dantzic, a part of Great Poland lying westward of the Netze, the remainder of Polish Prussia, to wit, the palatinate of Marienburg with the town of Elbing, the bishopric of Warmia (or Ermeland), and the palatinate of Culm, except Thorn, which is to remain a part of Poland. Poland, by this flagitious transaction, lost five million inhabitants and a third of its territory. The diet of Poland was brought by threats to give its rights to a committee, which in August, 1773, obeyed the will of the great powers, and consented to this dismemberment. (Martens, II. 89 onw.)

1774, July 21. Peace of Kutschuk-Kainardsché (a village of Silistria), between Russia and Turkey. Bessarabia, Wallachia, and Moldavia were restored to Turkey, which engaged to protect the inhabitants of the principalities in their religion, etc., to receive a *chargé d'affaires* from the governor or hospodar of each of them, and to allow the ministers of Russia resident at Constantinople to speak in their favor. Russia obtained free navigation for ships of commerce in the Black Sea, in the Propontis or Sea of Marmora, in the Danube, and in the Turkish waters generally. The forts of Jenicale and Kertsch in the Crimea, the town of Azow with its district, the castle of Kinburn at the mouth of the Dnieper were ceded to the same power. The two powers acknowledged the Tatars of the Crimea, Budjack, Kuban, etc., to be independent. Arrangements were made for a minister resident of Russia at Constantinople, and for consuls with their interpreters in places of commerce. (Martens, II. 286. The original is in Italian.)

1779, May 13. Peace of Teschen in Austrian Silesia, between Frederick the Great of Prussia and Maria Theresa, Queen of Austria. (Martens, II. 661.) The electoral Bavarian line of the Wittelsbach house being near extinction, the next heir was the elector palatine, who had no legitimate children, and the next to him the duke of Zweibrücken or Deux-Ponts. The Emperor Joseph, by making brilliant provision for the illegitimate children of the elector palatine, induced him to cede beforehand all Lower Bavaria and other territory to the house of Austria. Frederick the Great, having won over the duke of Deux-Ponts, in connection with the elector of Saxony and the duke of Mecklenburg, who had claims to the Bavarian inheritance, prepared to resist this aggrandizement of Austria by armed force. The war of "the Bavarian succession" was a show of arms rather than a war, and led to the peace of Teschen, of which the terms were dictated by Frederick. They were, in brief, (1.) That Austria, instead of a territory of 250 German square miles, acquired a district of 34, between the Danube, the Inn, and the Salza. (2.) That Prussia was confirmed in the right of succession to the principalities of Baireuth and Anspach, if the existing families should fail. (3.) That Saxony received a compensation of six million guilders for its claims, and Mecklenburg acquired the right of having a supreme court of appeal of its own. The Emperor and Empire were required to accede to the treaty, to which also the Empress of Russia and the king of France were mediating and guaranteeing parties. (Comp. § 105.)

1780, Feb. 28. Declaration of Russia introducing the first armed neutrality. (Martens, III. 158 et seq. Comp. § 174.)

1782, Nov. 30. Preliminary, and, Sept. 3, 1783, definitive peace signed at Paris, in which Great Britain acknowledged the independence of the United States, and conceded certain rights of fishery. (§ 55.) Boundaries were fixed, debts incurred before the war could be collected, etc. (Martens, III. 495, 553.)

1783, Jan. 20. Preliminary treaties of the peace of Versailles, between Great Britain on the one part, and France, Spain, and (Sept. 2, 1783) Holland on the other. Definitive treaties of Versailles, Sept. 3, 1783, between Great Britain, France, and Spain. To France, Great Britain restored the islands of St. Pierre and Miquelon in full property, reaffirmed the French rights of fishery near and on Newfoundland as mentioned in the treaty of Utrecht, restored St. Lucia and ceded Tobago in the West Indies, and recovered Grenada, St. Vincent, St. Dominique, St. Kitts, Nevis, and Montserrat. In Africa, Senegal (see peace of Paris, 1763) was ceded back to France, and Goree restored. In the East Indies there was a general restitution of conquests made from France in the war. The articles of the treaty of Utrecht and of other subsequent treaties relative to Dunkirk were abrogated. To Spain, Great Britain ceded Minorca and Florida; Spain restored Providence Island and the Bahama, and reaffirmed the right of the English to cut logwood (see peace of Paris, 1763), settling the limits within which it could be exercised.—The Dutch did not make a final peace with England until May 20, 1784. The *status quo ante bellum* was its basis, excepting that Holland ceded Negapatam on the coast of Coromandel. (Martens, III. 503 onward).

TREATIES OF THE AGE OF THE FRENCH REVOLUTION AND OF NAPOLEON.

1791, Aug. 27. Declaration of Pilnitz, signed by the sovereigns of Austria and Prussia, relative to interference in the affairs of France. (§ 46. Martens, V. 260.)

1792, Jan. 9. Peace of Jassy, between Russia and Turkey. The left bank of the Dniester is to serve as the boundary between the two sovereignties. Thus the tract between the river and the Bug with Oczakow became Russian. (Martens, V. 291.)

1793. Second partition of Poland, which appears in the shape of treaties between Russia and the king and republic of Poland (Grodno, July 13 and Oct. 16, the latter a treaty of alliance), and of a treaty between Prussia and Poland (Grodno, Sept. 25, 1793). Although, in the treaty of cession and limits, Russia renounces for ever all right or claim, under pretext of any events or circumstances whatever, to any province or the least part of the territory now comprised in Poland, and guarantees to maintain Poland in its actual state; yet the *third partition* took place in 1795, after the insurrection in 1794 had ended in the taking of Warsaw by the troops of Suwarrow. To this Russia, Austria, and Prussia were parties, and by a convention dated Petersburg, Jan. 3 and Oct. 24, 1795, they settled the boundaries between their respective acquisitions, which included the whole of Poland yet remaining. Austria now held all Galicia and Lodomiria, or in general the territory between the Vistula and the Bug; Russia, Curland, Samogitia, Little Poland, Lithuania, Volhynia, all the territory east of the Bug and Niemen; Prussia that west of the Niemen and of the Vistula, including Dantzig, Thorn, and Warsaw, the old capital. (Martens, V. 531 onward; VI. 168 onward.)

1792 and onward. Coalition against France, into which all the states of Europe successively entered, except Sweden, Denmark, Switzerland, Tuscany, Venice, and Genoa. A particular grievance on the part of the German empire was the disregard shown by the Constituent Assembly for the rights of princes of the empire holding lordships in Alsace, besides which the fear and dislike of French revolutionary principles, especially after the death of Louis XVI., Jan. 21, 1793, acted on all. In the course of the war republican France conquers the Austrian low countries, Holland (which is revolutionized and becomes an ally), Savoy, and other territory on the frontiers, Lombardy, Modena and the legations of the Papal state; constitutes the Cisalpine republic; forces a number of its foes to a suspension of arms or to peace and alliance; and is stripped, together with its confederate, Holland, of foreign possessions by the naval power of England, which also annihilates the fleets of Holland and of Spain. Spain made peace with France in 1795, and became an ally by the treaty of St. Ildefonso, August 19, 1796. The most noticeable treaties, by which this grand coalition was weakened or broken, were those of France with Prussia and with Austria. Those with Sardinia and with the Pope also deserve mention.

1795, April 5. Peace of Basel between France and Prussia. Prussia promises to furnish no aid to the enemies of the French republic, nor to allow them a passage through her territories. French troops may continue to occupy territory on the left bank of the Rhine belonging to the Prussian king, until a general pacification shall take place between the Empire and France. The two contracting parties will unite their efforts to remove the theatre of war from the north of Germany. The republic will accept of the good offices of the king of Prussia in favor of princes of the Empire who seek his intervention, in the desire of making peace with France, and will regard as neutrals those princes and estates west of the Rhine, in favor of whom the king shall intercede. By a treaty of May 17, made by the same powers, at the same place, a line of demarcation was drawn through the middle of Germany, and the French engaged to regard as neutrals those states lying to the north of this line who should observe a strict neutrality, as well as those on the right bank of the Main situated within the line. Four routes were left open for French and German troops along the Rhine by way of Frankfort, and along the right bank of the Main.—This treaty gave up the left bank of the Rhine to France, separated the North from the South of Germany, and placed Prussia in a position to profit by any changes which might be effected in the Empire in consequence of French conquests. (Martens, VI. 45–52.)

1795, July 22. Peace between France and Spain, made at the same place. The French restore the places beyond the Pyrenees occupied by French troops, and Spain cedes to France the Spanish part of St. Domingo. The French republic is thus acknowledged by the Bourbon house of Spain. (Martens, VI. 124.)

1796, May 15. Treaty of peace signed at Paris between the king of Sardinia and the French republic (Martens, VI. 211), by which the former renounces the coalition; cedes to France Savoy, with the counties of Nice, Tende, and Beuil; agrees upon the boundary line between the two states; engages to exclude French émigrés from his territories; gives the right of transit to French troops through his lands to and from Italy; and suffers a number of important fortresses to be occupied, until treaties of commerce and of general peace shall be completed. The Batavian republic is comprised in this and other treaties, in accordance with a provision in the treaty of alliance between the two republics, signed at the Hague, May 16, 1795 (Martens, VI. 88), that no peace can be made by France with any of the coalitionists, in which the republic of the United Provinces shall not be included.

1797, Feb. 19. Treaty of peace between France and the Pope, signed at Tolentino (in the Papal state, and in the delegation of Macerata). The terms had been adjusted in part in the suspension of arms made at Bologna, June 23, 1796. (Martens, VI. 239, 241.) The Pope agreed to renounce the coalition, to cede Avignon and the Venaissin (§ 54), as well as the legations of Bologna, Ferrara, and Romagna, to France, to allow Ancona and its territory to be occupied by French troops until the event of a continental peace, to pay thirty-one millions of livres besides five already paid since the armistice, to hand over a hundred works of art and five hundred manuscripts, etc.

1797, April 17. Preliminaries of a peace between the French republic and the Emperor, agreed to at Leoben, a small town in Styria. The definitive peace followed, made and signed near Campo Formio in Friule, Oct. 17, 1797. (Martens, VI. 385, 420.) In this important treaty (1.) the Austrian Netherlands are ceded to France. (2.) Venice having been lately extinguished by Bonaparte, its territory is divided between the contracting parties and the Cisalpine republic, established June 29, 1697. The French take the Venetian islands in the Levant—Corfu, Zante, Cephalonia, Santa Maura, Cerigo, etc., and in general all the Venetian establishments in Albania situated below the Gulf of Lodrino, and the Austrians take Istria, Dalmatia, the Venetian islands of the Adriatic, the mouths of the Cattaro, the city of Venice with the lagoons, and its territory on the Italian mainland east and north of the Adige and the lago di Garda. (3.) The Emperor acknowledges the Cisalpine republic, and renounces all claims which he may have had before the war to territory incorporated into it. This republic includes Austrian Lombardy, the districts of Bergamo, of Brescia (both Venetian) and of Cremona, Mantua with its fortress and district, Peschiera, the part of the Venetian possessions in Italy lying to the east and south of the lands newly ceded to Austria, Modena, Massa, Carrara, the legations of Bologna, Ferrara, and Romagna. Bonaparte had already severed Chiavenna, the Vatteline, and Bormio from the Grisons, and invited them to join the Cisalpine republic. (4.) The Emperor binds himself to cede to the duke of Modena the Breisgau, as an indemnity for his former possessions in Italy. (5.) There shall be a congress held at Rastadt, to be composed of plenipotentiaries of France and the Empire, in order to make peace between these powers. (6.) In secret articles agreed upon at the same time, the Emperor consents that the left bank of the Rhine from Switzerland to the Nette above Andernach, comprising the *tête de pont* of Mannheim, and the town and fortress of Mainz, shall belong to France, and engages to try to induce the empire, in the congress to be assembled, to agree to this line of boundary. The Emperor also promises, when a peace with the empire shall be made, to cede to France the Frickthal (in the canton of Argau, Switzerland), and other contiguous possessions of Austria, in order to be united to the Helvetian republic. He also cedes to France the county of Falkenstein. France, on the other hand, will endeavor to procure for the Emperor the bishopric of Salzburg, and the part of Bavaria lying between that bishopric, the Inn, the Salza, and Tyrol. In case the territory of Prussia beyond the Rhine shall be restored to her, which the French are willing to do, she shall have no claim to new acquisitions. Indemnifications are to be made to estates of the empire, who shall have lost territory by this peace or by the contemplated peace with the empire.

The Congress of Rastadt was opened Dec. 9, 1797, and closed with no definite result in April, 1799. For the atrocious murder of two of the French negotiators on their way home, comp. § 92, *e*. Between these dates Switzerland, Rome, and Naples had been transformed respectively into the Helvetic, Roman, and Parthenopæan republics, the two last of which were almost as short-lived as Jonah's gourd; the king of Sardinia, worried out by French aggressions, had renounced his authority in Piedmont, in favor of a provisory government, and gone over to the island of Sardinia; an expedition under Bonaparte had been sent to Egypt; and Austria had decided to join a second coalition to which Russia, England, Naples, and Turkey were parties. The French were almost driven out of Upper Italy by Suwarrow, Rome and Naples were rescued from their sway, but the withdrawal of the Emperor of Russia from the alliance, and the great victories of Bonaparte, now first consul, at Marengo (June 14, 1800), and of Moreau at Hohenlinden (Dec. 2, 1800), disposed Austria to peace.

1800, Dec. 16. Conventions of Russia with Sweden and Denmark, and on the 18th of Dec. with Prussia, constituting *the second armed neutrality*. The account of this transaction in § 191 is erroneous, the mistake of Heffter being copied. The parties to this league declared the same principles which are spoken of in § 174, as the basis of the first armed neutrality, and with them another—that the declaration of an officer commanding a public convoying vessel to the effect that there is no contraband on board of the ships under his protection shall be sufficient security against all search. Then follow agreements to arm, to defend one another, and to notify the belligerents of the league, etc.

Then followed the battle of Copenhagen, etc., as mentioned in § 191, and then, in 1801, June 17, a convention was concluded between England and Russia, Denmark and Sweden acceding, the leading features of which are given in § 191, but are erroneously confounded with the agreements of the armed neutrals themselves respecting convoy. (Martens, Rec. VII. 172–196, 260–280.)

1801, Feb. 9. Treaty of Luneville between France and the German Emperor, acting also, without previous authority of the diet, for the Empire, which ratified the peace soon afterward. (Martens, VII. 296. In this treaty several of the important stipulations of the treaty of Campo Formio are repeated. The Emperor cedes the Austrian Netherlands, the Frickthal, and the county of Falkenstein; the division of Northern Italy is the same, except that the Adige from the point where it leaves Tyrol to the sea is to be the western limit of Austrian territory; the duke of Modena is to have the Breisgau as before; indemnifications are again mentioned as to be made by the empire for princes whose territories had been ceded to France. The left bank of the Rhine, 'from the place where it leaves the Helvetic territory to where it enters the Batavian,' is to be French. The grand duke of Tuscany, the Emperor's brother, it is agreed, shall renounce his duchy, and the parts of Elba dependent upon it, in favor of the duke of Parma, and shall be paid off by an indemnity in Germany. The treaty is declared to embrace the Batavian, Cisalpine, Helvetic, and Ligurian republics, the independence of which is guaranteed by the contracting parties. Fiefs of the empire had already been given by the treaty of Campo Formio to the Ligurian republic. These fiefs are now renounced by the Emperor for himself and the empire.

The arrangements respecting the duke of Parma had already been a subject of negotiation between France and the king of Spain, whose son-in-law the duke was. It was agreed by the treaty of St. Ildefonso, of Oct. 1, 1800, that Parma and Louisiana should be ceded to France, and by the treaty of Madrid (March 21, 1801, Martens, VII. 336), it was agreed, as in the peace of Luneville, that the dukes of Parma and Tuscany should resign their duchies, that the former should take possession of Tuscany with the title of king (afterward called king of Etruria), and that he should cede to France the part of the island of Elba belonging to Tuscany, and be compensated for this by Piombino, then pertaining to the king of Naples.

1802, March 27. Definitive treaty of peace of Amiens, between Great Britain on the one part, and the French and Batavian republics and Spain on the other. The preliminaries had been signed at London, Oct. 1, 1801. England renounces her conquests won from the three powers, except

Trinidad and Ceylon, which are ceded to her by Spain and the Batavian republic respectively; Malta is restored to the order of St. John of Jerusalem; the territories of Portugal and Turkey are maintained in their entireness as they were before the war; the boundaries of French and Portuguese Guiana are rectified; the republic of the seven Ionian islands (taken from France by the fleets of Russia and Turkey, in 1798 and the next year) is recognized; a fair compensation is promised by France to the house of Orange for its losses in the Netherlands; and the troops of France are to be withdrawn from Rome and Naples.—The peace of Amiens was a mere truce. War was again declared between England and France in a little less than a year. (Martens, VII. 377, 404.)

1803, Feb. 25. Recés or report of an extraordinary committee of the Empire (Reichsdeputationshauptschluss), ratified by the diet, March 24, and by the Emperor, April 27. (Martens, VII. 435, onward.) Several treaties, that of Luneville last of all, had contemplated the giving of indemnifications to dispossessed German princes, and several foreign princes were to be provided for in Germany who had lost their own lands. At the Congress of Rastadt this was a leading subject of negotiation, and it was agreed to make the indemnities by means of secularized ecclesiastical territory, but the congress broke up without anything being accomplished. To bring this matter to a conclusion, the diet appointed (Oct. 2, 1801) a deputation or committee of eight members, four of them electors and four not, before whom came the first plan of indemnity, offered by France and Russia as mediating powers, and who, after several sets of changes in the project, presented the report which the diet adopted. It was in truth little else than a formality, for the whole scheme depended on the will of Napoleon, with whom Russia now acted; and while the committee was sitting, the leading powers, or those who were in his good graces, got by special treaties better terms of indemnity in many cases than they had a right to demand. This transaction was in effect a change in the Constitution of Germany, but it loses its interest and importance from the fact that the old Empire tumbled to the ground a little afterward. By this measure, (1.) all immediate church territory was secularized except a little part of that of Mayence, and, this not sufficing, all but six of the fifty-one imperial towns and the villages of the same class lost their immediacy and were put into the hands of princes who received compensation. The archbishops of Cologne and Triers thus lost with their territories their electoral dignities. The see of Mayence was transferred to Ratisbon, the archbishop of which was always to be arch-chancellor, primate of Germany, and one of the electors, and to be the metropolitan over the former provinces of Mayence, Cologne, Triers, and Salzburg. The six towns remaining as estates of the empire were Augsburg, Nuremberg, Frankfort, Hamburg, Lübeck, and Bremen. (2.) Of the great number of princes for whom indemnification was thus found, we can name only a few. To the duke of Tuscany (see treaty of Luneville) was assigned the archbishopric of Salzburg, Berchtesgaden enclosed in Salzburg, a territory under a prince-provost, part of the bishopric of Passau, and most of that of Eichstadt. To the duke of Modena (see treaty of Campo Formio) the Breisgau and the Ortenau. To the prince of Nassau-Dillenburg, former stadtholder of Holland (see treaty of Amiens), through the intervention of Prussia, the bishopric of Corvey, Dortmund, and various abbeys. To Austria, in lieu of the Ortenau, conveyed to the duke of Modena, the bishoprics of Trent and Brixen. To the king of Prussia, in lieu of Guelders and Cleves, lying west of the Rhine, the bishoprics of Hildesheim, Paderborn, and in part Münster, with several towns and abbeys. To the king of England, as elector of Hanover, for his claims on territory awarded to Nassau and Prussia, the bishopric of Osnaburg. To the elector palatine of Bavaria, in lieu of Deux-Ponts, Juliers, etc., the bishoprics of Bamberg, Freisingen, Augsburg, and in part Passau, the properties of ecclesiastical foundations in the city of Augsburg, various abbeys, and as many as seventeen towns or villages of the Empire. To the duke of Würtemberg, the provostship of Ellwangen, nine imperial towns, and seven abbeys. To the margrave of Baden, the bishopric of Constance, lands east of the Rhine pertaining to the bishoprics of Basel, Strasburg, and Spires, a part of the palatinate of the Rhine, with Heidelberg and Mannheim, ten abbeys, seven towns, etc., by which his territory was nearly doubled.' To Hesse-Darmstadt, the duchy of Westphalia, with some districts of Mayence and of the palatinate. To Hesse-Cassel, a small part of the territory of Mayence. To the duke of Holstein-Oldenburg the bishopric of Lübeck (a Protestant territory) and some lands in Hanover and Münster. (3.) A number of new votes in the college of princes were created. The electoral dignity was given to the duke of Tuscany, to Baden, Würtemberg, and Hesse-Cassel (with reversion to Hesse-Darmstadt), while the electoral office of the archbishops of Cologne and Triers fell with the secularization of their territories.

1803, April 30. Treaty signed at Paris between the French republic and the United States of America, touching the cession of Louisiana. By a secret treaty of Nov. 3, 1762, signed at Fontainebleau and first published in 1836, France ceded to Spain, Louisiana and New Orleans. By the treaty of St. Ildefonso (Oct. 1, 1800), Louisiana was retroceded by Spain to France (see treaty of Madrid under peace of Luneville, 1801), as part of an equivalent for the establishment of the duke of Parma in Tuscany. Napoleon now, in the apprehension, it would seem, that England might take possession of this territory, conveys it to the United States, "as fully and in the same manner as it had been acquired by the French republic." The third article of the treaty of St. Ildefonso had conveyed it to France, "with the same extent that it now has in the hands of Spain, and that it had when France possessed it, and such as it should be, after the treaties subsequently entered into between Spain and other states"—which treaties would relate to the recognition of the duke of Parma as king of Etruria. Thus the limits of the territory conveyed to the United States are not defined by a single word. The inhabitants were to be admitted, as soon as possible, to the enjoyment of all the rights, advantages, and immunities of citizens of the United States, and in the mean time to be protected in the enjoyment of their liberty, property, and religion. The treaties made by Spain with the Indians were to be executed by the United States. Ships of France and of Spain coming from those respective countries or their colonies, and laden with their products or those of their colonies respectively, and the vessels of no other nations, should be admitted for twelve years into the ports of entry of the ceded territory. By two conventions of the same date it is agreed that the United States shall pay France, by the first, a sum of sixty millions of francs (11,250,000 dollars, at the rate of $5\frac{1}{3}$ francs to the dollar), and by the other a sum which cannot exceed 20,000,000 francs, and which is intended to cover the debts due "to citizens of the United States who are yet creditors of France for supplies, for embargoes, and for prizes made at sea, in which the appeal has been properly lodged, within the time mentioned" in the convention of Sept. 30, 1800, etc. The treaty is signed in English and French, but the original is declared to be in French. It was ratified at Washington, Oct. 21, 1803. De Garden (VIII. 50) informs us that Spain, in the treaty of cession to France, reserved the preference or refusal to herself, in case France should allow the territory to pass out of her hands. All claim from this source was cut off by the consent of Spain to the alienation, which was given early in 1804. (Martens, VII. end.) The treaties of 1762 and of St. Ildefonso are given by De Garden, u. s. The latter at least is not in De Martens.

1805, Dec. 26. Peace of Presburg, between Austria and France. (Martens, VIII. 388.) In 1802 (Sept. 21) Piedmont was united to France—all that part of it at least which had not been incorporated in the Cisalpine republic. In 1803 war was again declared by England against France, and in revenge, the electorate of Hanover, although a German state, was occupied by French troops. In 1804 (March 21) the Duke d'Enghien was seized on German territory—in Baden—and murdered after a pretended sentence. The delay of Napoleon to provide compensation for the king of Sardinia, together with the criminal violations of German territory above mentioned, facilitated a new coalition between England, Sweden and Russia, to which Austria gave her adhesion in 1805. Meanwhile Napoleon had become Emperor of the French in 1804, and in March, 1805, king of Italy—which title of kingdom of Italy the Cisalpine republic had now taken. Lucca had been made a hereditary principality; the Ligurian republic had been united to France; Parma, Piacenza, and Guastalla had been declared French territory by a simple decree of the Emperor;

and two of his creatures, the dukes of Würtemberg and of Bavaria, had of their own movement taken the title of king. The war with England, which did not end until the peace of Europe in 1814, put a stop to the disastrous attempts of Bonaparte to recover St. Domingo, annihilated the fleets of France and Spain at the battle of Trafalgar, and gave the possession of a number of French colonies to the English. The war with Austria was decided, in a short campaign, by the capitulation of Ulm and the battle of Austerlitz. In the peace of Presburg, which soon followed, Austria (1.) recognized the arrangements made by France in Italy, including the union of territory to France—as in the case of Piedmont, Genoa (the Ligurian republic), Parma, and Piacenza—and the new government organized in Lucca and Piombino. (2.) Austria renounced the part of the republic of Venice ceded to her by the treaties of Campo Formio and Luneville, which was to be united to the kingdom of Italy. The French Emperor was also recognized as king of Italy; but as the crowns of France and Italy were eventually to be separated, the Emperor of Germany engaged to recognize the successor whom Napoleon should name king of Italy. (3.) The electors of Bavaria and Würtemberg having taken the title of king without leaving the German confederation, they are recognized by Austria in that quality. (4.) Austria cedes and gives up to the king of Bavaria the margravate of Burgau, the principality of Eichstadt, part of Passau, Tyrol, including Brixen and Trent, Vorarlberg, and other territory. To the king of Würtemberg are ceded the five towns of the Danube so called, the upper and lower county of Hohenberg, and other territory. To the elector of Baden the Brisgau and the Ortenau, the city of Constance, and the commandery of Meinau. These three powers shall enjoy, it is agreed, the same full sovereignty which the Emperor and the king of Prussia have in their estates. (5.) Salzburg and Berchtesgaden, which had been given by the peace of Luneville and the report of the deputation of the empire, to the duke of Tuscany, are now taken from the archduke Ferdinand and incorporated in the Austrian empire. As an equivalent, he is to have the principality of Würzburg, which the French Emperor engages to obtain for him from the king of Bavaria, and the electoral dignity attached to Salzburg is to be transferred to this new territory. (6.) The contracting powers dispose of two German estates in a very summary way. The city of Augsburg is put into the hands of the Bavarian king; and the office of grand master of the Teutonic order, with its rights and domains, is transferred to some prince of the house of Austria, whom the Emperor shall designate, and in whose male line it shall descend.

This humiliating peace of Presburg, by which Austria lost 23,000 square miles of territory and almost 3,000,000 of inhabitants, was a prelude to the complete overthrow of the German empire. *In* 1806, *July* 12, *was signed at Paris the Confederation of the Rhine* (Rheinbund), consisting originally of the kings of Bavaria and Würtemberg, the grand dukes of Baden and Hesse-Darmstadt, the prince primate of Germany (see report of deputation of empire), the duke of Berg, the princes of Nassau-Usingen and Nassau-Weilburg, and many smaller princes. (Martens, VIII. 480 onw.) To these, in time, were added the elector of Würzburg—the Emperor's brother—(see peace of Presburg), the elector of Saxony (who had leave from Napoleon in Dec. 1806, to call himself king), the dukes of Oldenburg and Mecklenburg; so that Germany was now split up into three parts: Austrian, Prussian, and French Germany. The confederation of the Rhine was made known to the diet August 1, 1806, and the members renounced their connection with the German empire—as the league had provided; soon after which (Aug. 6) the Emperor published an act declaring the empire extinct, laying aside the crown and absolving all from their allegiance. He was henceforth Emperor of Austria only, a title which he had assumed two years before. The Rhenish league was to have its own diet at Frankfort; formed an alliance for all continental wars, offensive and defensive, with France; determined the contingents of the members, etc. Many estates of the old empire within the territory of the confederation were mediatized, or brought under the sovereignty of some one of its members: thus Frankfort and Nuremberg lost their independence, and the race of knights holding immediately of the empire (Reichsritter) was extinguished.

1807, July 7. Peace of Tilsit, made by Russia, and July 9, by Prussia, with Napoleon. (Martens, VIII. 637, 661.) After the peace of Presburg, Napoleon proceeded still more boldly in his aggressions and plans of aggrandizement. The Bourbons were declared to reign no longer in Naples, and his brother Joseph was made king there; Holland was converted into a kingdom for another brother, Louis; his sisters received principalities in Italy; Murat was made grand duke of Berg; and a plan of creating an imperial nobility out of his generals and courtiers, with estates provided from the conquered territory, was vigorously pursued. Toward Prussia and its vacillating king he pursued a course of mingled insult and craft. He took Anspach into his own hands before a treaty permitted it; he persuaded the king to give up Cleve and Wesel, which were given to Murat, on whom also Berg, ceded by Bavaria, was bestowed; he required him to occupy Hanover, thus leading the way to a collision between Prussia and England. The counsels of the patriotic party so far prevailed in Prussia, that war was inevitable; but the aristocracy was debased, the king was weak, the system of war was antiquated, and the result was the utter prostration of the country. The campaign of 1806, by the battles of Jena and Auerstadt, and by various capitulations, made Napoleon master of most of German Prussia: he entered Berlin, and there issued his decree called by the name of the city, in pursuance of his continental system. (§ 189.) In the autumn of 1806 his troops penetrated into Prussian Poland, where

French agents had stirred up an insurrection, and in 1807 the Russsians, Prussia's only hope, were defeated at Friedland. The whole kingdom was now overrun and conquered, and the king sued for peace. The conferences were attended in person by Napoleon, by the czar, and, after the first interview, by the king of Prussia; and the result was that Alexander, fascinated by the genius of Napoleon, and guided by him in his views of his interests, practically abandoned his ally, who was thus forced to accept of the most humiliating terms possible. By the peace of Tilsit, Prussia renounced all its territory on the west of the Elbe, including Hanover—which provinces, with others in Napoleon's hands, were to constitute a kingdom of Westphalia under Jerome Bonaparte—and renounced also the lands acquired by the second and third partitions of Poland, with the southern part of West Prussia. These Polish possessions constituted into a duchy of Warsaw—except the district around Bialystock, which passed over to Russia—together with the circle of Kotbus in Lower Lusatia, were ceded to the king of Saxony, who was to be made grand duke of Warsaw, and who was to have the use of a military road across Prussia between Saxony and Poland. Dantzig, it was agreed, with two leagues of territory around it, should be an independent district under the protection of Prussia and Saxony, with its ports closed to English commerce during the present maritime war with England. The rest of its former territory was restored to Prussia, which thus retained about half of its population of 10,500,000. It was obliged to recognize also Napoleon's new creations, the Rhenish confederation, the kings of Westphalia, Naples, and Holland. By conventions made in 1808 (Martens, nouv. rec. I. 102 onw.), Prussia was forced to pay 140 millions of francs "for extraordinary contributions and arrears of revenue"—which afterward were dropped to 120 millions—and to leave the forts of Glogau, Stettin, and Custrin in the hands of the French until payment, under engagement to provision the troops and to allow military roads between the places thus occupied, up to their evacuation.

The treaty with Russia contains little worthy of mention and not already contained in the treaty with Prussia, unless that Napoleon agreed that the dukes of Saxe-Coburg, Oldenburg, and Mecklenburg-Schwerin should be restored to their estates, with the provision that, as long as the war with England should last, the ports of the two latter districts should be occupied by French garrisons. Also the small lordship of Jever in East Friesland, which came down to the czar from his grandmother, Catharine II., was ceded to the king of Westphalia.

Secret articles annexed to these treaties contain the stipulations that the seven islands (Ionian) shall belong to Napoleon; that if Hanover shall form a part of the kingdom of Westphalia, a territory on the west bank of the Elbe, containing from three to four hundred thousand inhabitants, shall be restored to Prussia; and that Prussia should make common cause with France, in case England, by Dec. 1, 1807, should not have consented to a peace conformable to the true principles of maritime law. (De Garden, X. 234, not in Martens.)

A treaty of alliance between France and Russia, made on the same day with the treaty of peace, contains some noteworthy provisions: (1.) Russia was to make common cause with France, if, by Nov. 1, 1807, England should not have made peace on the basis of an equal and perfect independence of all flags upon the sea, and upon that of restoring to France and her allies conquests made since 1805. (2.) If England, by the first of December, should not have given a satisfactory answer upon these points, France and Russia should summon the courts of Copenhagen, Stockholm, and Lisbon to close their ports to the English, and to declare war against that nation. But if England should come to the terms of the allies, Hanover should be restored in lieu of colonies conquered from France, Holland, and Spain. It was the knowledge of this article which led England in September of the same year to bombard Copenhagen and take the Danish fleet. (3.) In a certain event, the two parties should agree to remove all the provinces of the Ottoman Empire in Europe, except Roumelia and the city of Constantinople, from under the Turkish yoke. (De Garden, X. 235, not in Martens.)

Secret and somewhat chimerical articles between the two Emperors, in addition to these, are spoken of, which rest on doubtful evidence. Russia was to take Turkey and to aid France by its fleet to take Gibraltar; the Bourbons in Spain and the house of Braganza in Portugal should give place to a prince of Napoleon's blood; the Pope should lose his temporal power, and his kingdom be united to the kingdom of Italy; the towns of Africa, as Tunis and Algiers, should be occupied by the French, and given, at a general peace, as a compensation to Sardinia; France should occupy Malta and Egypt; all flags but those of France, Spain, Italy, and Russia, should be excluded from the Mediterranean. Even an attack on the British power in India was talked of.

1807, Oct. 27. Secret treaties of Fontainebleau, between France and Spain. Portugal was to be divided into three parts specially defined: one was to be given to the king of Etruria, in lieu of Tuscany transferred to Napoleon as king of Italy, one to be bestowed on the vile Godoy, prince of Peace, and one unappropriated. The second convention fixes the number of Spanish and other troops to be employed, etc. (Martens, rec. VIII. 701.) Portugal was accordingly occupied by Marshal Junot in the same autumn, and French troops, moving down into the north of Spain also, treat it somewhat as a conquered country. Another secret treaty is said to have contemplated ceding the provinces north of the Ebro to France, and taking Portugal in exchange. The royal family of Spain is alarmed, and there is talk of fleeing to America. Tumults break out, Godoy is put down, and, after a series of intrigues, the king and his son, who were in deadly quarrel, meet Napoleon in Bayonne: the father is induced to abdicate the crown, and the son, with the two other infanti, signs an act of renunciation. A junta at Madrid is induced to ask that Joseph Bonaparte may be the king. He is appointed, and Murat takes his place as king of Naples. The spirit of the Spanish people is roused against the French. A long war ensues, in which Portugal is wrested from the French, and Spain finally recovered, through the skill of Wellington, the resources of England, and the obstinacy of the Spanish character. To maintain a great army in the peninsula, and be equal at the same time to his enemies on the east, was too much for Napoleon, and this, with the expedition into Russia, caused his overthrow.

1809, Sept. 17. Peace of Sweden with Russia, made at Friedrichshamm in which Finland and West Bothnia, with Aland and other islands, are ceded to the latter power. In 1810 Sweden made a peace with Napoleon, in which Swedish Pomerania and the isle of Rügen are restored to her, and she agrees to adopt the continental system. (Martens, nouv. rec. I. 19.)

1809, Oct. 14. Treaty of Vienna, between Austria and France, signed at Schönbrunn by Napoleon Oct. 15, and hence sometimes called the *peace of Schönbrunn*. (Martens, nouv. rec. I. 210.) The disasters of Prussia in the last war with Napoleon had roused the spirit of the people, led to a better military system, brought men more upright into power, and given rise to a set of patriotic clubs (Tugendbünde). The same revival of a German feeling spread on every side, into Austria and the lands of the Rhenish league. The aristocratic statesmen of Germany, stung by the haughtiness of Napoleon, encouraged by the war in Spain, and thinking that the people might be induced to rise against the oppressor, brought on by their intrigues the fourth war of Austria with revolutionary France, while as yet the German people was unprepared for it. In this war, Prussia was forced to remain neutral, and Austria had no aid; for the expedition, sent from England to Walcheren, was too late and too unsuccessful to be of any use. In a short campaign the Austrians, although little inferior to the French at Aspern and Wagram, became disheartened, and the armistice of Znaym prepared the way for the peace of Vienna or Schönbrunn, which Napoleon's situation would have made it desirable for him to accept, had the terms been less hard for the other party. In this peace—which was declared to be common to the confederation of the Rhine and the other vassals of Napoleon.—(1.) Austria placed at the disposition of Napoleon, for the benefit of the confederation of the Rhine, Salzburg, Berchtesgaden, and part of Upper Austria, consisting of the Inn-Viertel and the Hausruck-Viertel. This territory was bestowed upon Bavaria. (2.) To Napoleon, as king of Italy, were ceded the county of Görz (Gorizia) and principality of Falkenburg (Montefalcone), forming

Austrian Friule, the city and government of Trieste, Carniola, the Villach circle in Carinthia, and the country on the right of the Save, from where it leaves Carniola to the frontier of Bosnia, or half of Croatia, the Hungarian littoral, Fiume, Austrian Istria, etc. These became the Illyrian provinces with a separate French government. By this cession Austria was cut off from the sea, but was allowed, except for English commerce and products, to use the port of Fiume. (3.) To the king of Saxony were ceded some Bohemian villages enclosed in Saxony, and to the same king, as duke of Warsaw, Western or New Galicia, a district around Cracow, and a circle in East Galicia. Wieliczka and the salt mines were to be common to Austria and the Polish duchy. (4.) To Russia was ceded a territory in the most easterly part of old Galicia, which should contain 400,000 inhabitants, and not include the town of Brody. (5.) The Teutonic order having been suppressed within the confederation of the Rhine, the Emperor of Austria renounces on the part of the Archduke Antony, who was the grandmaster, this dignity conferred by the peace of Presburg, and consents to the disposition of the property beyond the limits of Austria which had been made. The employés of the order had pensions promised to them. —In separate and secret articles (De Garden, XII. 136), the Emperor of Austria submits to a military contribution of 85 millions of francs, and agrees to reduce his army to the number of 150,000 of all kinds of troops so long as the maritime war of France with England should continue. By this peace Austria lost over 43,000 square miles of territory, with 4,500,000 inhabitants. The Tyrolese, who were making a heroic resistance against France and Bavaria, were given up to their fate.

1812, May 18. Peace of Bucharest, between Russia and Turkey. The boundary was to follow the Pruth, from the point where it came out of Moldavia, to the Danube, and the Danube to the sea. In this way Bessarabia, and a small strip of Moldavia, with the fortresses of Choczim and Bender, became Russian. Other conquests were restored. Servia was to remain Turkish, but with the interior administration in the hands of the inhabitants. (Martens, n. r. III. 397.)

TREATIES OF 1814 AND 1815, CONTAINING THE GREAT SYSTEM OF PACIFICATION AND READJUSTMENT WHICH FOLLOWED THE DOWNFALL OF NAPOLEON.

The peace of Schönbrunn humbled the last enemy capable of offering serious resistance upon the land to the decrees of Napoleon; and the consent of the Emperor of Austria soon afterward to give his daughter in marriage to the French Emperor at once showed his weakness and seemed to bind him to the policy of the conqueror. Even before this fourth war with Austria, Napoleon had commenced the policy of uniting parts of

Europe to his empire, instead of controlling them, as he had done at first, by his vassals. A decree dated May 17, 1809, from his camp at Vienna, incorporated the Papal states into his dominions. Other portions of Italy were subjected to the same process. The Swiss district of Valais was absorbed in the autumn of 1810. In March of the same year (Martens, Nouv. rec. I. 327) he forced his brother Louis to cede to France all of the kingdom of Holland lying to the left of the Waal, or Dutch Brabant, Zeeland, and part of Guelders. Soon after the abdication and flight of Louis (July 9, 1810), the whole of Holland was made French territory. (Martens, u. s. 338.) A decree of the Senate of France subjected to the same fate all the north coast of Germany, as far as to the sea near Lübeck, comprising Oldenburg, the Hanse towns, Werden, parts of Hanover and Westphalia, Lauenburg, etc. (Martens, u. s. 346.) Against this high-handed proceeding in regard to the duke of Oldenburg, the Emperor Alexander, his near connection, protested, who had already taken offence at the enlargement of the grand duchy of Warsaw, effected at the peace of Schönbrunn. He now instituted a commercial policy hostile to the views of Napoleon, and in 1811 preparations were made on both sides for war. The only powers from which Russia could hope for concert of action were England and Sweden. Between England and Russia there was no difficulty in arranging an alliance. But Sweden was slow in incurring the resentment of Napoleon. At length, after Swedish Pomerania had been occupied by the French, Sweden made an alliance with the czar (March 12, 1812), agreeing, in the event of war, to put 30,000 men into Northern Germany, and receiving the promise of Alexander that he would aid her in the acquisition of Norway. England and Sweden came together in the peace of Oerebro on the 13th of July, 1812 (Martens, u. s. 431), and on the 13th of March, 1813, England made an engagement, similar to that of Russia respecting Norway, promising also a subsidy of a million sterling to Sweden, and ceding to her the island of Guadaloupe, taken from the French. (Martens, u. s. 558.) It was of great importance in the subsequent war that Sweden allowed the Russian army, which was in Finland, and was to aid in the conquest of Norway, to be employed in Poland, and that the peace of Bucharest left another army free to act against the French invader.

Napoleon, on his side, made new treaties of alliance with Prussia and Austria. (Feb. 24, March 14, 1812, Martens, u. s. 417–431.) In the open and secret articles of the Prussian treaty, it is agreed that Prussia shall make common cause with France, without being obliged to furnish troops for wars in Italy, Turkey, or beyond the Pyrenees; that the number of such troops in the field, in the event of war with Russia, shall be 20,000, besides a large garrison force; that these shall be kept in one body as much as possible, and be used in preference for the defence of the Prussian provinces, but shall be for all new movements under French control; that any part of Prussia included within the lines of operations shall be open to the French and their allies, except Upper Silesia and the city of Potsdam; and that provisions and munitions of war shall be furnished to the French troops, to be charged to the contributions yet due from Prussia according to the peace of Tilsit. A promise is held out of an indemnity, in the shape of new territory, for the expenses of Prussia in the war, should it come to a happy issue. The fortresses of Glogau, Custrin, and Stettin were still held by French garrisons, and the leading patriots had to quit the king's presence and service. Austria stipulated to furnish, as her contingent, 30,000 troops and 60 pieces of cannon, in four divisions, under an Austrian commander, subject to the immediate orders of their own sovereign. The integrity of Turkey is guaranteed. In case of the reconstruction of the kingdom of Poland, Austria is to hold Galicia, or, if that should be united to the Polish monarchy, the Illyrian provinces in exchange, besides being compensated for the costs of the war by the acquisition of new territory.

Secured thus in his rear, and strengthened by the forces of his allies, Napoleon crossed the Niemen, June 24, 1812, too late in the season for success, and returned the same autumn a fugitive, his vast army nearly destroyed by war, famine, and cold. The wrath of the German people, especially of humiliated Prussia, now began to burst forth against the tyrant. The first impulse was given by General York, commander of the Prussian contingent, who, on the 30th of December, 1812, without the privity of his sovereign, in a capitulation with the Russian general Diebitsch, agreed to keep his army neutral in a district of East Prussia, and if the king should not sanction the agreement, at least to observe the neutrality for two months. (Martens, u. s. 556.) The king was alarmed, but dragged forward by the boiling spirit of the people. A treaty made not long after this between Russia and Prussia, which has not seen the light, provided, it is said, that Prussia should recover the territory which she held before 1806, except Hanover, and should furnish 80,000 men for the war, against 150,000 to be furnished by Russia. Help was to be sought in the shape of an alliance with Austria, and of subsidies for Prussia from England. On the 19th of March, 1813 (Martens, u. s. 564), a convention was made between Russia and Prussia, in which a proclamation was agreed upon, inviting the princes and people of Germany to unite for the liberation of their country. Every German prince, who should not respond to this appeal within a given time, should be menaced with the loss of his estates. A council of administration also was provided for, fortified with unlimited powers for the carrying on of the war, especially for occupying and controlling the parts of Northern Germany yet under French influence. On the 27th of March war was declared against France, and the Prussians en masse formed an army of volunteers. The dukes of Mecklenburg, the duke of Anhalt-Dessau, the city of Hamburg soon followed the example of Prussia. The summer of 1813 was full of negotiations relating to the war, the principal of which were, (1.) Conventions at Reichenbach in the middle of June, between Great Britain on the one part and Russia and Prussia on the other. The parties agree to carry on the war with energy, the first engaging to furnish subsidies, and the others to have in the field 160,000 and 80,000 soldiers respectively. Prussia promises to aid the Brunswick houses in recovering their territory, and England is to have the use and coöperation of the Russian fleet. (Martens, u. s. 568.) (2.) An armistice was made, June 5, between the belligerents, Austria acting as mediator, which was to continue until Aug. 10: meanwhile a peace congress sat at Prague without effecting or being expected to effect anything. (Martens, u. s. 582.) (3.) Austria at length forsook Napoleon decisively, and joined the alliance of the three great powers by treaties signed at Töplitz, Sept. 9, agreeing to furnish a quota of 60,000 troops, and to make no peace unless in common with the allies. (Martens, u. s. 596.) (4.) Bavaria, by a treaty with Austria, dated Oct. 8, and, in the course of the autumn, but not until the battle of Leipzig had decided the campaign against Napoleon, the other members of the Rhenish confederation, joined the allies, and this creation of the French Emperor was dissolved. (5.) In the winter, Jan. 11, 1814, Murat, king of Naples, separated his cause from that of Napoleon in a treaty with Austria, for the purpose of retaining possession of his kingdom. (Martens, u. s. 660.) (6.) The treaties of Kiel, made by Denmark with Sweden and with Great Britain, Jan. 14, 1814, and one with Russia, signed at Hanover, Feb. 8, 1814, separated from Napoleon his last and most honorable ally. Denmark engaged to place 10,000 men for the war under the control of Bernadotte, prince royal of Sweden, and renounced possession of Norway in favor of Sweden, who in return ceded to Denmark Pomerania and the isle of Rügen, promising her good offices for some further indemnification. Great Britain pledged its efforts for the same purpose, and restored all territory gained by conquest from Denmark, excepting the isle of Heligoland. (Martens, u. s. I. 667–683.)—Denmark afterward, in a treaty, signed at Vienna, June 4, 1815, ceded Swedish Pomerania and Rügen to Prussia, receiving in return the duchy of Lauenburg, except the *amt* or bailiwick of Neuhaus, together with a payment of two million thalers and of a considerable sum of money due from Sweden. (Martens, u. s. II. 349.)

As the allied armies reached the Rhine and entered France, various negotiations were set on foot, looking toward peace and the readjustment of the political state of Europe. The most important were, (1.) the congress of Chatillon, from Feb. 5 to March 19, 1814, in which Napoleon, hoping still for success in the war, made too high terms, so that nothing was effected. (Comp. Martens, u. s. I. 668.) (2.) While this congress was in session, a new treaty was made between the four great powers at Chaumont, March 1, 1814. England was to furnish to the other powers a subsidy of five millions sterling for the year 1814, and the parties were to keep in the field an army of 150,000 men each; to aid one another in case of attack, etc. (Martens, u. s. 683.) Secret articles are said to have settled the relations of Europe on the basis afterward adopted. (3.) The capitulation of Paris, March 31, 1814. (4.) The abdication of Napoleon, in a treaty made by him with Austria, Russia, and Prussia, April 11, to which England acceded, as to the main points, April 27. Napoleon renounces all right of sovereignty in France and everywhere else for himself, his family, and his descendants. His domains in France are to go to the crown. He and the Empress are to preserve their titles during life, and his near connections are to be styled princes of his family. The isle of Elba is given him as his principality, with an annual revenue of two million francs, chargeable to France, one half reversible to the Empress, and the duchies of Parma, Piacenza, and Guastalla are assigned to the Empress Maria Louisa. From these duchies their son is to derive his title. Two and a half millions of francs are granted as an annual revenue to members of his family; Josephine also, and Eugene Beauharnois, are provided for. Napoleon is to have an armed corvette and a guard of 400 men at his disposal. The allied powers promise that France shall adopt and guarantee this treaty. (Martens, u. s. I. 696.)

The immediate arrangements consequent upon the downfall of Napoleon were made

1814, May 30, at the first peace of Paris, consisting of treaties, nearly identical, between France, now under Louis XVIII., and each of the four great powers. (Martens, nouv. rec. II. 1–18.) The limits of France are by this treaty to be what they were in 1792, with some augmentations on the eastern frontier, which are particularly specified. France renounces all sovereignty over districts in Europe outside of these limits: Monaco is to be as it was before 1792, and Avignon, the Venaissin, Montbelliard, and all other *enclaves* within these limits are to be French territory. Great Britain retains Malta, Tobago, and St. Lucia, the isle of France with its dependencies, and the part of St. Domingo which Spain ceded to France in the treaty of Basel in 1795, and which Great Britain engages to cede back to his Catholic Majesty. All other places gained by conquest from France, rights of fishery, etc., she places on the footing of 1792. Sweden restores Guadaloupe to France, and Portugal restores French Guiana, as it was at that date. (For other arrangements see the next article.)

By a separate and secret article of this treaty, which appears in Murhard's Nouv. suppl. I. 329, the disposal of the territories renounced by France in the open treaty, and the relations tending to produce a system of real and durable equilibrium in Europe, were to be decided upon by the allied powers *among themselves*. Thus France was to have no voice in the leading measures of the coming Congress. But in fact, at the Congress of

Vienna, the adroit audacity of Talleyrand and the disagreement of the allies between themselves secured for France a considerable amount of influence.

1815, June 9. Final act of the CONGRESS OF VIENNA, the most important document, in an international respect, of modern times. The peace of 1814, just spoken of, provided for the meeting of such a congress within two months, in order to complete the arrangements there begun, but it was not opened until Nov. 1, 1814. It closed June 11, 1815. Eight powers composed the congress, Great Britain, Russia, Austria, Prussia, France, Spain, Portugal, and Sweden; but the Spanish representative refused his signature, on account of the dispositions touching the three Italian duchies of Parma, Piacenza, and Guastalla, as well as for other reasons affecting the pride of Spain. The congress was for some time seriously disturbed by the claim of Russia to appropriate the entire grand duchy of Warsaw, and of Prussia to swallow up Saxony. What should be done with Belgium was also a problem of some difficulty. In March the alarming news reached the congress that Napoleon had left Elba, that he had landed in France, that he had recovered his throne without a struggle. He was put under the ban of Europe, a new compact was made by the four great powers with many accessories, on the 25th of March, for the maintenance of the peace of Paris, and in June the field of Waterloo baffled this attempt of the wonderful man to regain his lost power.

The Congress of Vienna was a meeting of dictators for arranging the affairs of Europe according to their arbitrary views, and in effect required the smaller powers to submit to their decrees, without a share in their deliberations. To perfect the arrangements which appear in the final act, a multitude of special compacts had to be made, some of which were annexed to that instrument, and declared to be a part of it. For the final act see Martens, u. s. II. 379; Martens and Cussy, III. 61; Wheaton's Int. Law, Appendix; Klüber's Acten des Wiener-Congress; and comp. Flassan, Hist. du Cong. de Vienne, 3 vols. Paris, 1829.

The leading points of this instrument are the following:

1. The grand duchy of Warsaw was united, as a kingdom of Poland, under a distinct administration, to the Russian empire, with the exception (1.) of the territory restored to Prussia, under the name of the grand duchy of Posen; (2.) of the districts in Eastern Galicia taken from Austria by the treaty of Schönbrunn and now restored; (3.) of Cracow and a territory around it, which was constituted into a free neutral republic, the privileges of which are defined in a treaty annexed to the final act. "The Poles," it is stipulated, "subjects of Russia, Austria, and Prussia, respectively, shall have a representation and institutions of a national character, regulated by the mode of political existence, which each of the governments, to which they appertain, shall judge it useful and suitable to grant to them."

2. Prussia, having thus lost a considerable part of its Polish spoils, was anxious to get the whole of Saxony into its hands, whose king, as the vassal of Napoleon, in the new adjustments of Germany found no favor; but Austria was jealous and prevented this, so that only a part of Saxony, seven thirteenths of the territory and two fifths of the population, became Prussian. The former territory of Prussia, such as it was before the peace of Tilsit, was in general restored. New acquisitions on the east side of the Rhine, besides the part of Saxony just spoken of, were a portion of Fulda and of Hanau, the city of Wetzlar with its territory, the duchy of Berg with lands formerly belonging to the bishopric of Cologne and more lately incorporated in this duchy, the duchy of Westphalia, such as it was under the grand duke of Hesse, the county of Dortmund, Corvey, the lands of sundry mediatized princes, and the possessions of the house of Nassau-Dietz, ceded by the king of the Netherlands, or their equivalents received in exchange for them from other members of the house of Nassau. On the west bank of the Rhine, Prussia acquired a territory which was formerly in the main the duchy of Juliers, and part of Cleves and Guelders and of the two archbishoprics of Cologne and Treves.

3. The king of Great Britain, as king of Hanover, received from Prussia, Hildeshiem, Goslar, East Friesland, the lower county of Lingen, and part of Prussian Münster; and ceded to Prussia the parts of the duchy of Lauenburg lying east of the Elbe, with other smaller districts. Lauenburg was soon transferred to Denmark. (See peace of Kiel, p. 409.) The commerce on the Ems, and at Embden, which now became a Hanoverian port, was to be open to Prussian merchants without restriction, and Hanover engaged to keep the river in a navigable condition within its own territory.

4. Austria recovered nearly all that she lost in 1797 by the treaty of Campo Formio or afterward, whether in or out of Germany, except the Austrian Netherlands, and acquired that part of the Venetian lands in the peninsula which Napoleon appropriated, and all other territory between the Tessin, the Po, and the Adriatic, together with the Valtelline, Bormio, and Chiavanna, formerly pertaining to the Grisons, as well as the former republic of Ragusa.

5. The duchy of Würzburg, as the peace of Presburg made it in 1805, and the principality of Aschaffenburg, which formed a part of Napoleon's grand duchy of Frankfort, were given to Bavaria.

6. The city of Frankfort was restored to its condition in 1803.

7. In lieu of the duchy of Westphalia, the grand duke of Hesse acquired a territory on the left bank of the Rhine, in the late department of Mt. Tonnerre, containing 140,000 inhabitants. The landgrave of Hesse-Homburg was restored to his estates, from which he had been ejected in consequence of the formation of the confederation of the Rhine. Several princes—the last named, the dukes of Oldenburg, Mecklenburg-Strelitz, Saxe-Coburg—

received grants of territory on the Prussian frontier beyond the Rhine, in the late French department of the Sarre, which was to be placed under Prussian protection, and to serve as small change in future adjustments. All German lands not before disposed of, on the left bank of the Rhine, were given to Austria.

8. The Germanic body, including the king of Denmark as duke of Holstein, and the king of the Netherlands as grand duke of Luxemburg, was constituted into a confederation of equal members, thirty-eight in number, having seventeen votes in an ordinary assembly, and sixty-nine votes in a general assembly, in which latter organic laws and other affairs of great importance were to be brought forward. The diet was to be permanent, under the presidency of Austria, to meet at Frankfort, and to adjourn for not more than four months. In a general assembly a vote of two thirds was required for the passage of any measure. The confederation being intended for the protection of all Germany and of each member against foreign powers, no member was allowed to negotiate or make truce or peace with any state with which the confederation should be at war. Differences between the confederates were to be pursued without force of arms, and submitted to the diet, which should intervene between the parties in the first instance by a mediating committee, and, if a judicial sentence should be necessary, by an "Austrägalinstanz" or court of high arbitration. In the "act concerning the federative constitution of Germany" (Martens, u. s. 353), which accompanies the final act, it is declared that in the states of the confederation there shall be assemblies of estates or of deputies ("eine landesständliche verfassung"); that all Christian confessions shall enjoy equality of civil and political rights; and that the civil disabilities of the Jews ought to be removed as far as practicable. To the mediatized nobility, who had before 1806 an immediate connection with the empire, privileges were allowed in respect to rank, taxation, privileged courts, exemption from military duty, the exercise of civil and criminal jurisdiction over the settlers on their estates in the first instance, and, when their estates were great enough, in the last instance. The act of confederation was amended in 1820, 1832, and 1834; overthrown in 1848–'49, and restored in 1851.

9. The Dutch United Provinces, with the larger part of the Austrian Netherlands, were constituted, as the peace of Paris had determined, into a kingdom of the Netherlands, under the prince of Orange-Nassau, to which territories the grand duchy of Luxemburg, including a part of the duchy of Bouillon not ceded to France, was added, by way of compensation for German possessions parted with by the Orange family. Luxemburg remained a German state and made the king a member of the diet. The town of Luxemburg was to be a fortress of the confederation.—In a convention signed at London, Aug. 13, 1814 (Martens, u. s. 57), England en-

gaged to restore to Holland all the colonies, factories, and establishments she had gained by conquest since 1803, except the Cape of Good Hope, Demarara, Essequibo, and Berbice.

10. The relations of Switzerland are determined by a declaration of the powers forming the congress, dated March 20, 1815 (Martens, u. s. 157), by the act of accession of the cantons of the same date (ibid. 173), and by the final act. Switzerland is to take the relation of perpetual neutrality (§ 155), and, in order to secure this end the better, a treaty with the king of Sardinia of May 26, 1815, provides that the provinces of Chablais and Faucigny, south of Lake Leman, and all of Savoy north of Ugine shall assume the same neutral attitude. To the old nineteen cantons, Geneva, Valais, and Neufchatel are added—the latter under Prussian sovereignty, which continued from the peace of Utrecht until 1848. The territory of Geneva is enlarged by a cession of a small district in Savoy. The routes from Geneva along the lake in both directions—by Versoix in France toward the canton of Vaud, and by the route of the Simplon through Savoy toward Valais—are to be exempt from transit dues and examination of merchandise. The former bishopric of Basel and most of the territory of Bienne are united to the canton of Berne.

11. Sardinia gained the tracts called the imperial fiefs, which had been attached to the Ligurian republic of Napoleon, and the territory of the former republic of Genoa, including the island of Capraja. The limits of this kingdom are nearly the same as in 1792, but the boundary of France, as determined by the first treaty of Paris, is made to take in a portion of Savoy then contained in the French department of Mont Blanc, viz., most of the sub-prefectures of Chambery and Annecy.

12. The Archduke Francis of Este, his heirs and successors, were to hold the duchies of Modena, Reggio, and Mirandola, according to the limits which they had by the treaty of Campo Formio. The Archduchess Maria-Beatrix of Este, her heirs and successors, were to hold the principalities of Massa and Carrara, with the imperial fiefs in Lunigiana, which last might be exchanged for other properties between Modena and Tuscany at the will of the parties.—Tuscany, as it was before the treaty of Luneville, was restored to the duke of the Austrian line, Ferdinand, his heirs and successors, and to this territory were added the part of Elba formerly under the suzerainty of the king of the Two Sicilies, Piombino, certain imperial fiefs formerly enclosed in Tuscany and "l'état des Presides."—The duchies of Parma, Piacenza, and Guastalla were granted, as was provided by the treaty of abdication of Napoleon (see p. 410), to the Empress Maria Louisa, and the reversibility of these territories—saving the old rights of reversion of Austria and Sardinia—was to be determined by common agreement between the five leading powers and Spain. Such an agreement was made at Paris, June 10, 1817. (Martens, n. r. IV. 416 onw.) It related espe-

cially to the Spanish ducal house of Lucca.—The Congress of Vienna establlished the Infanta Maria Louisa and her male heirs in Lucca as a duchy; added to the revenues of the duchy a rent of 150,000 francs, to be paid by Austria and Tuscany; and gave the reversion, in case of failure of the line or their *removal to another establishment*, to Tuscany. The duke of Tuscany engaged to cede certain districts to the duke of Modena, whenever the reversion of Lucca should fall to him, viz.: Fivizzano, Pietra Santa, Barga, and others. By the treaty above mentioned, of June 10, 1817, it was agreed that, after the decease of the Empress Maria Louisa, her duchies of Parma, Piacenza, and Guastalla—with the exception of certain districts on the left bank of the Po, enclosed in the dominions of Austria, which should belong to that power—should go to the Lucchese house. The reversion of these duchies, in case of the extinction of the branch of the Infant Don Charles Louis, was to follow the provisions of the treaty of Aix-la-Chapelle (1748), and of a separate article of the treaty of 1815 between Austria and Sardinia. (See Martens, n. r. II. 298, and for that article Murhard, XV. 41.) This separate article confirms the rights of reversion of Sardinia to the duchy of Piacenza, but adds that the city of Piacenza with a radius of 2,000 toises from the crest of the glacis shall appertain, in case of such reversion, to Austria, for which she shall give to Sardinia contiguous territory equivalent in population and revenue.—The Holy See was restored to the possession of its former territory, viz.: the Marches with Camerino and their dependencies, Ponte-Corvo, the legations of Bologna, Ravenna, and Ferrara, except that part of the latter situated on the left bank of the Po. Austria was to have the right of garrison in Ferrara and Comacchio.—The king of Naples, Ferdinand IV., was reëstablished on the throne of the Two Sicilies.

13. The allies engage to use their best endeavors to induce Spain to yield up Olivenza and other places gained by the treaty of Badajos in 1801 to Portugal. The restitution of French Guiana to Portugal has been already mentioned.

14. For the arrangements of the congress in regard to river navigation, comp. § 58, and Martens, u. s. 434. For its rule touching the rank of ambassadors, comp. § 94, and Martens, u. s. 449. For the declaration concerning the slave trade, see Martens, u. s. 432.

1814, Dec. 24. Treaty of peace made at Ghent, between Great Britain and the United States. (Martens, u. s. II. 76, in a French translation.) Its leading features are general restitution, provision for the arrangement of boundaries, silence on the subject of maritime rights and the impressment of seamen, and an engagement of the parties to endeavor to put an end to the slave trade. (Comp. § 55, 198.)

1815, Nov. 20. Second treaty of Paris, after Napoleon's final downfall, consisting of four separate instruments, of the same tenor, between France and each of the four great powers. By this treaty, (1.) the limits of France toward Belgium, Germany, and Savoy, were somewhat narrower than the peace of 1814 had made them, being brought back nearly to the line of 1790. In this way the fortresses of Philippeville and Marienburg, with the whole of the duchy of Bouillon, instead of a part of it, were transferred to the kingdom of the Netherlands; Saarlouis, Saarbrück, and the course of the Saar became Prussian; the fort of Landau, and a French tract on the right of the Lauter went ultimately to Bavaria; half the bridge between Strasburg and Kehl pertained to Baden; a portion of the district of Gex on Lake Leman, between the cantons of Vaud and Geneva, was added to the latter; and the districts of Chambery and Annecy were restored to Sardinia. The neutrality of Switzerland and of a part of Savoy was extended to a district defined by a line drawn from Ugine (see act of the Congress of Vienna) through the lakes of Annecy and Bourget to the Rhone. The French fortress of Huningue (Hünningen), near Basel, was to be demolished. (2.) An indemnity of seven hundred million francs was to be paid to the allies. Their troops, not exceeding 150,000 in number, were to have military occupation of France, at the expense of the country, in certain specified places, for not more than five years, but might be withdrawn at the end of three years, if the security of Europe should permit. (Martens, u. s. II. 682.)—By a convention between the four allied powers, made at Paris, Nov. 5, 1815, the seven Ionian islands were to constitute a free state under the protectorate of Great Britain, with a resident lord high commissioner appointed by that power, a legislative assembly, etc.; the military force of the islands to be commanded and their forts to be garrisoned by Great Britain—the British garrisons being paid by the republic. [These islands, long Venetian, then the prey of France (treaty of Campo Formio, 1797), then, after being for a short time left to themselves, first under Turkish and afterward under Russian protection, then restored to France (peace of Tilsit, 1807), and conquered by England, have recently passed from under the protectorate of England into union with the kingdom of Greece, 1863.] (Martens, u. s. 663.)—The works of art which Napoleon had gathered from various countries of Europe were restored by another special instrument to their former owners. (Martens, u. s. 632 onw.)

TREATIES OF THE AGE OF REACTION AND INTERVENTION. PROMINENCE OF QUESTIONS RELATING TO TURKEY AND TO ITALY.

1815, Sept. 26. The Holy Alliance. Comp. § 46.

1818, Autumn. Congress at Aix-la-Chapelle, of the four allies and France. Comp. § 46. (Martens, nouv. rec. IV. 549–566.) By an agreement dated Oct. 9, the troops of the allies are to evacuate France on or before the last day of November, and to give up the forts, as they were when the occupation began. Some of the indemnity, agreed to in 1815 and still due, is remitted. France joins the holy alliance. For the protocol of Nov. 21, comp. § 94.

1820, Oct. 28 and onward. Congress of Troppau, afterward removed to Laybach, § 46.

1822, October. Congress of Verona, § 46.

1826, Oct. 7. Convention of Ackerman, between Russia and Turkey. In general a restatement of the peace of Bucharest (1812), confirming the privileges of Servia, and restoring the mode of electing the hospodars of Moldavia and Wallachia. A certain control over the power of the sultan to dismiss them from office is acquired by Russia. (Martens, n. r. VI. 1053 onw., esp. the separate acts.)

1827, July 6. Treaty of London between Great Britain and Russia, to which France afterward acceded. (Martens, u. s. VII. 282 and 463.) These powers offer their mediation to Turkey on behalf of Greece, which shall be, they propose, a vassal state under the sultan, like the Danubian principalities. On the 20th of October the Turkish fleet was annihilated at Navarino, and in 1828 the Morea was cleared of the troops of Ibraham Pacha. The boundaries of liberated Greece were thus enlarged.

1828, Feb. 22. Treaty between Russia and Persia signed at Tourkmantchaï, by which Persia ceded the khanats of Erivan and Nakhitshévan, promised an indemnity of twenty millions silver roubles, and agreed, as in the treaty ratified at Tiflis, Sept. 15, 1814, that no ships of war, except Russian, should navigate the Caspian. (Martens, u. s. VII. 564.) By this treaty of Tiflis, Persia gave up to Russia seven khanats south of the Caucasus, of which the Russians were actual masters, and renounced all claim to Daghestan, Georgia, Imeritia, Mingrelia, Abchasia, etc. (Martens, u. s. IV. 89.)

1829, Sept. 14. Treaty of Adrianople between Russia and Turkey. (Martens, u. s. VIII. 143.) Russia restores her conquests. The Pruth to bound the two countries as heretofore to the Danube, and the Danube to the Black Sea, but in such sort that the islands in the river shall be Russian territory. The boundaries in the east are so drawn that a part of Turkish Armenia, with the city of Akhalzik and the fortress of Akhalkalaki, passes under Russian sovereignty. Turkey also concedes that the sovereignty of Russia extends over Georgia, Imeritia, Mingrelia, Gouriel, and other Caucasian countries. Passage is allowed through the Dardanelles and Bosporus, or, in other words, the Black Sea is opened to vessels of nations at peace with Turkey, and Russia has the right of navigating the Danube. The prior agreements with regard to the Danubian principalities are confirmed, and the hospodars are to be appointed for life, being removable for crime only.

1831, Nov. 15. Treaty for the definitive separation of Belgium from Holland, signed at London between the five powers on the one part and Belgium on the other. Comp. § 49, § 155. (Martens, u. s. XI. 390.)

1832, May 7. Convention of London between France, England, and Russia on the one part, and Bavaria on the other. (Martens, u. s. X. 550.) The crown of Greece, now made a kingdom, is offered, with the authorization of the Greek nation, to the king of Bavaria, to be worn by his second son, Frederic Otho, and accepted. The limits of the kingdom are to be fixed by treaty with Turkey, according to a protocol of Sept. 26, 1831. A loan to the king of Greece is guaranteed by Russia, and, if the consent of the chambers and the parliament can be obtained, by France and England.

1833, July 8. Convention of Unkiar-Skelessi, between Russia and Turkey, after the victories of Ibrahim Pacha in Syria and Asia Minor, and the peace of Kutaiah between him and Turkey, May 6, 1832. The two parties form an alliance, agreeing to aid one another in case of attack, when such aid is invoked. In a secret article it is added that Russia exempts Turkey from rendering such aid on condition that she closes the Dardanelles against foreign vessels of war. (Martens, u. s. XI. 655.) In a protest of France against this treaty, as likely to give rise to an armed intervention of Russia in the internal affairs of Turkey, it is said that, if circumstances demand, France shall act as if no such treaty existed. (Martens, u. s. 659.) Comp. what Dr. Wheaton says in his history, part 4, §§ 29, 30, of this treaty and those of Ackerman and Adrianople.

1842, Aug. 9. Treaty of Washington, for adjustment of the boundary between the United States and the British possessions on the northeast. For the rules of extradition then made, comp. § 79. For the discussions on the right of search, comp. § 202. For the arrangements to suppress the slave trade, comp. §§ 199, 200.. (Murhard, nouv. rec., gen., continuing Martens, III. 456.)

1844, Nov. 28. Treaty between the dukes of Tuscany, Lucca, and Modena, in view of the death of the Empress Maria Louisa, duchess of Parma. This event took place Dec. 18, 1847, when the duke of Lucca would become duke of Parma, Piacenza, and Guastalla, and Lucca would become Tuscan. (See Congress of Vienna, No. 12.) The duke of Lucca (future duke of Parma) agreed to cede to Modena, Guastalla, and the Parmesan territory on the right bank of the Enza. Modena renounces to Tuscany the vicariats of Barga and Pietra Santa (Act of Cong. of Vienna, art. CII.)—which were to become Modenese when Lucca should become Tuscan—and to Parma the districts of Bazzano and Scurano on the left bank of the Enza. Tuscany cedes to Parma its possessions in the Lunigiana, Pontremole, Bagnone, and their dependencies. These arrangements rounded off the duchies, and did away with *enclaves*. Austria and Sardinia—whose rights of reversion were affected, that of Austria to Parma and Guastalla, that of Sardinia to

Piacenza, both derived from the treaty of Aix-la-Chapelle—concurred, and modified their rights in such sort that the reversion of Austria was made to apply to the new Parmesan territory in the Lunigiana, and was passed over to Sardinia by way of indemnity for the loss of the town of Piacenza, which, by a special article of May 20, 1815, concluded at Vienna, was to become Austrian whenever the duchy of the same name should revert to Sardinia. (Murhard, XV. 1–42.)—In the spring of 1861 these duchies, with Romagna, by a revolutionary action and the consent of the people, were annexed to the kingdom of Sardinia.

1848, Feb. 2. Treaty of Guadalupe-Hidalgo, by which Texas, New Mexico, and Upper California were ceded to the United States, which agreed to surrender all other conquests, to pay Mexico fifteen millions of dollars, and to assume all claims of its citizens against Mexico, decided or undecided, arising before the signature of the treaty. (Murhard, XIV. 7.) For article XXII. of this treaty, comp. § 152.

1852. Arrangements between Denmark and the German confederation, in settlement of the difficulties relative to Holstein and Schleswig (Murhard, XV. 319–414), after the armistice of Berlin, July 10, 1849 (Murhard, XIV. 544, 699), and when the two great German powers, early in 1851, had required the revolutionary authorities in those duchies to lay down their arms, promising to maintain the rights of Holstein and its old relations to Schleswig on the basis of the *status quo ante bellum*. The principal documents are a despatch of the Danish minister of foreign affairs to the Danish legations at Vienna and Berlin, with an annexed project, dated Dec. 6, 1851; a despatch of the president minister of Austria in reply, addressed to the Austrian legation in Denmark, dated Dec. 26, 1851; a proclamation of the king of Denmark, announcing to his subjects what had been done (Jan. 28, 1852); and the confirmation by the German diet of the arrangements between Austria and Prussia, acting on their behalf, and Denmark (July 27, 1852). The arrangements, not being in the usual diplomatic form, fail in precision. The leading engagements on Denmark's part are: (1.) not to incorporate Schleswig into the kingdom of Denmark; (2.) to preserve the relations other than political between the Danish duchy and the German duchy of Holstein; (3.) so to organize the Danish monarchy that no one of the separate parts shall be subordinate to the rest; (4.) to make such organization or new constitution in concurrence with the estates of Schleswig, of Holstein, and of Lauenburg; (5.) to let the estates of Schleswig and Holstein have a decisive voice in laws touching the imposts, and rights of person and property; (6.) to grant these duchies separate ministries of justice, worship, public instruction, internal administration, commerce, and industry; while foreign affairs, the forces, the finances, and council of state shall be common to Denmark and the duchies.

Not long after this, the five principal powers of Europe with Sweden, in a convention at London, engaged to acknowledge the right of the prince of Holstein-Sonderburg-Glücksburg to succeed to the Danish crown, in the event of the extinction of the reigning house—which event has recently happened. This prince was a near agnate, and was married to one of the nearest cognates, and the law authorized the succession of females; but the family of dukes of Holstein-Sonderburg-Augustenburg were nearer agnates, and as such, had some claim to succeed in Schleswig and Holstein, where the law of succession is said to be different. This, with other irritations, is, while we write, again involving Denmark in a new war with the German confederation. Comp. an article in the *London Quarterly* for Jan. 1864, written by a partisan of Denmark.

1856, March 30. Treaty of Paris after the Crimean war, between France, Austria, Great Britain, Sardinia, and the Ottoman Porte on the one part, and Russia on the other. (Murhard-Samwer, XV. 770.) By this treaty (1.) the Black Sea is neutralized and opened to the commerce of all nations, but interdicted to flags of war, excepting that a certain force can be kept on foot for revenue purposes by Turkey and Russia, who pledge themselves to maintain no naval arsenals on its coasts, § 57. In accordance with this, the old Turkish principle is to be maintained, of admitting no vessels of war into the Dardanelles and the Bosporus, the only exceptions being those of light vessels in the service of the legations of friendly powers, and of the powers who have a right under the treaty to station certain vessels at the mouths of the Danube. (Articles XI–XIV.) (2.) The Danube is thrown open to commerce, § 58. (Art. XV–XIX.) (3.) The limits of Bessarabia are somewhat altered, with the intention of taking away from Russia the command of the mouths of the Danube, and the tract thus ceded by Russia is added to Moldavia. (Art. XX–XXVI.) The places taken in the war from Russia are restored. (Art. IV.) (4.) Moldavia and Wallachia, as states under the suzerainty of Turkey, are confirmed in their privileges by the Sublime Porte, and guaranteed in them by the contracting powers; but no exclusive protection over them can be exercised by any of the guaranteeing states, nor any separate right admitted of interfering in their internal affairs. They are to have an independent national administration, liberty of worship, legislation, and commerce, an armed national force, and a revision of their laws, made under a joint commission of all the contracting parties. A new organization of these principalities shall be arranged by a convention at Paris of the treaty-making powers, and a hatti scheriff, conformed to the decisions of that convention, shall be the instrument under which their organization is to proceed. They are allowed, in concert with the Porte, to adopt measures against foreign aggression. If internal disorders should break out in them, the Porte shall have an understanding, with the other parties to the treaty, concerning measures to be taken for the purpose of maintaining or establishing legal order, but no armed intervention can take place without the previous accord of the aforesaid powers. (Art. XXI–XXVII.) For the convention, organizing the principalities, which was signed at Paris, Aug. 19, 1858, see Murhard-Samwer XVI. 2. 50. (5.) Servia, with its privileges, is placed under the same guaranty. The Sultan's right of having garrisons there is to remain as it had been. (6.) The Sultan is invited to participate in the European advantages of public law and concerted action, and is secured in the independence and integrity of his empire. The firman of Feb. 18, 1856, placing all Christian sects in Turkey on a level with Mohammedans, in respect to life, property, religion, etc., is acknowledged by the other powers, who, however, disclaim all right to interfere between the Sultan and his subjects, or in the internal administration of his kingdom. (Art. VII–IX.)

By a declaration of April 16 certain important rules of maritime law are adopted by the parties to this peace. See §§ 175, 122. (Murhard-Samwer XV. 791.)—Three powers, Austria, France and Great Britain, unite in a special guaranty of the independence and integrity of the Ottoman empire. All infractions of the treaty in that direction will be considered as *casús belli.* (Ibid. 790.)

1858. The treaties of this year, opening China to several of the Christian powers, are remarkable, as bringing that country in a degree within the sphere of the law of nations. In the French treaty of June 27, it is said that the diplomatic agents shall enjoy, where they reside, the privileges and immunities granted to them by the *law of nations*, that is to say, their persons, family, house, and correspondence shall be inviolable, etc. Consuls or consular agents may be appointed for certain sea and river ports. The right of building houses, churches, schools, etc. in the open ports is admitted. Frenchmen may resort to places in the interior and ports not open to foreign commerce, when armed with passports given by French diplomatic agents and consuls. Members of all Christian communions shall have freedom of person and worship, and missionaries passing into the interior, provided with passports as above, shall be protected. No obstacle shall be put in the way of any Chinese embracing Christianity. (Ibid. XVII. I. 1.) *

1859, July 11. Preliminaries of peace concluded at Villafranca between Austria, France and Sardinia, followed by a definitive peace signed at Zurich Nov. 10, of the same year. (Ibid. XVI. 2, 516.) The treaties are three in number, two between Austria and each of the other parties, and one in which all three are concerned. Austria cedes to France, and France transfers to Sardinia nearly all of Lombardy. The boundary line of the ceded territory runs from the southern limit of Tyrol on the Lago di Garda, through the middle of that lake, to the vicinity of the fortress of Peschiera,

* Quite recently we learn that a Chinese translation of Dr. Wheaton's Elements is in preparation. (1864.)

until it strikes the circumference of a zone made by a radius of 3,500 metres plus the distance from the centre of the fort to the outermost part of the glacis; thence along that circumference to where it strikes the Mincio; thence along the main channel of the Mincio to Le Grazie, and thence in a direct line to the Po; thence along the main channel of the Po to Luzzara, where the former boundary line of Austrian and Sardinian territory comes to the river. It is also agreed that Austria shall receive from France a payment of 40 millions of florins, being a portion of the national loan of 1854, in return for which Sardinia shall pay France 100 million francs, in five per cent. stock, besides 60 millions toward the cost of the war. The new government shall assume three fifths of the debt of the Lombardo-Venetian Monte, or bank for loans. In the treaty between France and Austria the two parties promise to favor an Italian confederation under the Pope, of which, when established, the Venetian part of the Austrian dominions in Italy shall be a member, although still remaining subject to the Austrian crown. In the same treaty it is said that the rights of the dukes of Tuscany, Modena and Parma, to their dominions, are reserved as being outside of the authority of the contracting parties, and not capable of being changed except with the concurrence of the powers which made the treaty of Vienna of 1815.

As a sequel to this cession of Lombardy, by a treaty signed at Turin, March 24, 1860, Sardinia cedes Savoy and the arrondissement of Nice to France, the parts of Savoy near Switzerland being transferred subject to the condition of neutrality imposed on them in 1815. § 155. (Murhard-Samwer XVI. 2, 539.)—By these two last treaties and the subsequent events in Italy the arrangements of the Congress of Vienna are effectually set aside, as it regards one important part of Europe, and the control then given to Austria over Italian affairs is lost.

INDEX.

THE END.

ADDITIONS AND CORRECTIONS.

§ 47, end of second paragraph. But this is not inconsistent with *independent action* on the part of the United States for carrying out the principles here spoken of.

§ 59, near the end. With regard to the navigation of the Amazon Mr. Charles Sumner informs me that Brazil is ready to open the navigation of this river to all riparian countries which concede the same privilege to the Brazilian flag. Conventions for this purpose have been made with Venezuela and Peru, limited to ten years, but as yet there is no convention with Equador or Bolivia.

§ 89, end. Diplomatic agents are now allowed to reside in Japan. Comp. treaty of the United States with Japan, July 29, 1856, in Murhard-Samwer, xviii. 1, 50. For resident ambassadors, now allowed by the Chinese, comp. Append. II., year 1856.

§ 92, *c.* A reason for the privilege of the Russian ambassador is that the emperor of Russia, being head of the Greek Church in that country, does not recognize the authority of the Patriarch of Constantinople.

§ 92, *e.* By employing merchants as foreign ministers is intended those merchants whose business lies in the country where they are ambassadors.

§ 114, end. Here it may be added that a sufficient time—say four months, as in several treaties—before reprisals are granted, may now be considered as the common law of nations. Phillimore iii. 161, quoting Valin.

§ 122, end. It has been said that the British Government would have accepted Mr. Marcy's proposition, but for the necessity of acting in concert with the other powers, but that, before any answer was received from England, President Buchanan withdrew Mr. Marcy's offer, unless England would abandon the right of blockade. (?) So much, at least, is true, that one of Buchanan's earliest acts, after coming into office, was to direct our ministers abroad not to press the Marcy propositions.

§ 131, second paragraph. What is here said of the requisition on Paris refers to Blücher's demands, which were reduced by the king of Prussia and the emperor of Russia. Comp. v. Rochau, "Geschichte Frankreichs, von 1814 bis 1852," i. 58. At the same time the allies made requisitions on the provinces where the invading armies were quartered for their support. After a little time an arrangement was made to use the intervention of certain specified French authorities in feeding, clothing, equipping, and paying the foreign troops.

§ 140, end. It may be added that in the war of 1812 our privateers, and even our men-of-war, burned their prizes, and sometimes in a summary way. In this they conformed to English practice and English rule. (Comp.

the cases of the Actæon and Felicity, in 2 Dodson's Admiralty Reports.) The French, while the Berlin and Milan Decrees were in force, burned a number of *neutral* American cruisers, having merchandise of British origin on board, while our cruisers seem to have destroyed enemy's vessels only. The same practice was followed by our cruisers during the Revolutionary war, and, probably, has been long, more or less, in vogue.

§141, beginning. At present, and by statutes 6 and 7 Vict., c. 38, all appeals may be referred to the judicial committee of the privy council, which is now the great court of appeal, as well in all maritime as ecclesiastical matters. Stewart's Note on Blackstone, iii. 70.

§159, end. The English Government has prohibited, in our present war, since June 1, 1861, the bringing of prizes by vessels of war and privateers of both parties into the waters of the British kingdom and its colonies. France, by a declaration of June 10, 1861, made the same prohibition, excepting that such vessels with prizes are allowed to remain twenty-four hours in her ports, and to remain in case of necessity (*relâche forcée*) as long as the necessity lasts. M. Hautefeuille, in his "Quelques questions du droit intern. marit.," 1861, discusses the question whether these prohibitions are compatible with previous treaties with the United States.

§180, end of No. 1. In conformity with this principle, an order in council of Great Britain, dated February 18, 1854, prohibits the exportation from the kingdom, or conveyance coastwise, of the parts of machinery used in steam vessels. See Phillimore, iii. 361, who adds that *coal* under the particular circumstances of the case, regard being had to its quality and destination, may become liable to seizure.

§181, last paragraph. It may be added that the French National Convention led the way, in seizing neutral ships laden with provisions, and bound to an enemy's port, by a decree of May 9, 1793, which provoked a retaliatory measure of Great Britain in June of the same year. Phillimore iii., 335. The decree, which may be found in Martens rec. v. 382, and in the reprint of the old *Moniteur*, vol. xvi., 351, provides that the provisions shall be paid for at their value, in the port to which they were destined, and that the freight stipulated by the shipper shall be allowed, together with compensation for detention, as fixed by a prize court.

The same decree contains the article referred to in §174 (last paragraph but two), relating to enemy's goods on board of neutral vessels.

§191, second paragraph. For a more correct account of the second armed neutrality, see Appendix ii., under the year 1800.

For a number of corrections, and other valuable hints, I am indebted to the kindness of Professor Torrey, of Harvard University.

www.ingramcontent.com/pod-product-compliance
Lightning Source LLC
LaVergne TN
LVHW021138110826
845150LV00005B/1059

* 9 7 8 1 4 2 5 5 4 9 0 3 9 *